The NEW COLOR WORK

26 Knitted Blankets *with* Modern Colors and Geometric Shaping

MARGARET HOLZMANN

STACKPOLE
BOOKS
Essex, Connecticut

STACKPOLE BOOKS
An imprint of The Globe Pequot Publishing Group, Inc.
64 South Main Street
Essex, CT 06426
www.globepequot.com

Illustrations by Margaret Holzmann
Photography by Gerard Holzmann

British Library Cataloguing in Publication Information available

Library of Congress Cataloging-in-Publication Data available

ISBN 9780811776615 (paperback)
ISBN 9780811776622 (electronic)

Printed in India

Contents

Resources

General Notes

1. See page 198 for Abbreviations.
2. See page 199 for a Glossary of techniques with written explanations. The icon is appended to entries with associated videos.
3. See page 214 for access to videos and other supplemental materials.
4. Use a 40"/100 cm circular needle (longer is fine) to work Borders. Smaller pieces may be knitted on straight needles, if desired.
5. When markers (m) are used, slip them when they are encountered unless directions say otherwise. Directions may not say when to slip markers.
6. Use a knitted cast-on (see the Glossary on page 199). If a CO edge will later have stitches picked up on it, a provisional CO may be substituted.
7. In written instructions, stitch generation, such as pu&k or casting on, counts as Row 1.
8. Instructions may refer to a "garter st ridge," which is created by working a RS knit row and then a WS knit row. One ridge equals two rows.
9. On blankets that use wrap & turn (short rows), when knitting a wrapped stitch, knit only the stitch on the needle. Do not knit wraps and wrapped stitches together. When instructions say, "Knit to <N> sts before end, w&t," the stitch wrapped is N. For instance, "Knit to 3 sts before end, w&t" means to knit to the 3rd stitch from the end of the row, wrap the 3rd stitch from the end, and then turn.
10. A gauge is specified for all patterns. Check gauge before starting, changing needle size if needed to obtain gauge. Block gauge swatch if using a natural fiber yarn. Yarn requirements are based on the given gauge. If gauge is different, more or less yarn may be required. Gauge may differ from yarn label because it is calculated over garter stitch, whereas yarn labels use stockinette stitch.
11. Using a different yarn weight and needle size will result in a larger or smaller blanket. Knit a garter stitch swatch in the substitute yarn, measure to get the 4"/10 cm gauge, and divide by 4 for the 1 inch gauge. If it is a heavier yarn than called for, add 5% to yarn requirements for each 0.5 stitch per inch (2.5 cm) decrease between pattern gauge and gauge of substitute yarn. If using a lighter weight yarn, decrease yarn requirements by 5% for each 0.5 stitch per inch (2.5 cm) increase between pattern gauge and gauge of substitute yarn.

    For example, if 400 yards of a color are required when the pattern says it is worked in worsted at a gauge of 4.5 sts per inch, changing to an aran weight with a gauge of 4 sts per inch requires adding 5%:

    400 yds + (400 yds × 0.05) = 400 yds + 20 yds = 420 yds

    Or, when changing to a DK with a gauge of 5.5 sts per inch, subtract 10%, because 5% less yarn is needed for every 0.5"/1.25 cm increase in the 1"/2.5 cm gauge:

    400 yds − (400 yds x 0.10) = 400 yds − 40 yds = 360 yds
12. If a pattern says to "leave a long tail" when cutting yarn but does not specify a length, leave a tail 3 to 4 times the length of the seam to be sewn in that yarn color. To manage these tails, wind them up and pin them to the edge of the piece with a safety pin or locking stitch marker. As soon as two adjacent pieces are complete, do a practice join, evaluate how much yarn is needed for the seam and weaving in, and adjust the tail length accordingly on future pieces.
13. When sewing seams, always use a yarn color that matches one of the pieces being sewn.
14. To organize yarn while knitting: (1) Place each color in a clear plastic bag and label with the assigned letter for the color, and/or (2) With a hole-puncher, make holes in an index card or cardboard. Label each hole with assigned letter for color, and then, through each hole, tie on a short strand of matching color yarn.
15. When working wrong-side rows with a small number of stitches, purl backward so that work does not need to be frequently turned.
16. For better control when working with a small number of stitches, work on wooden needles.
17. Instructions that are used more than once in a pattern are put into pattern stitch boxes, which are light green boxes. Pattern stitches are worked back and forth unless otherwise noted.
18. The Borders of all blankets are started by picking up and knitting stitches on Blanket edges.
19. If stitch counts are a little off after a pu&k, adjust stitch counts on the first WS row by using kf&b to add sts and k2tog to decrease sts. As a reminder, place a locking stitch marker through any two sts that are to be knit together, as well as a marker through any stitch that is to be worked as a kf&b. Remove markers when encountered.

20. When cutting yarn and fastening off, the preferred method of weaving in the resulting tail is to use duplicate stitch on the WS of the work. If using this method, it is not strictly necessary to tie off or otherwise secure yarns. See "Weaving in Ends" on page 212.
21. All knitting is performed flat (back and forth) unless specifically stated that it is in the round.
22. Symbols used in figures are defined as follows:

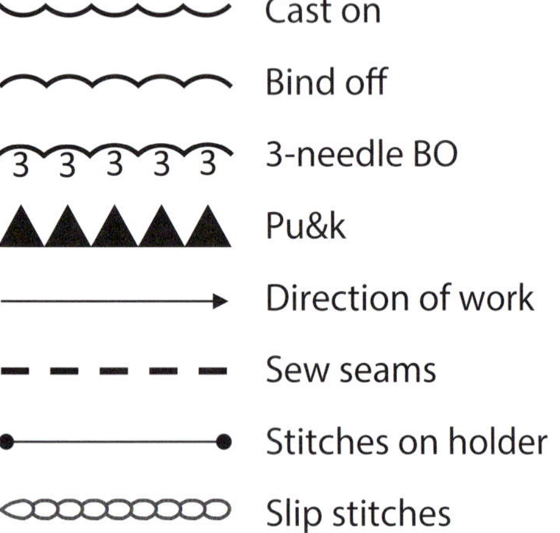

23. Keep one of the yarn labels for instructions on how best to launder your blanket. To avoid laundering mistakes, make and place a label on the back of your finished blanket at a corner. Cut out a 5" by 5"/13 x 13 cm piece of woven cotton fabric. Use a permanent felt-tip pen or fabric marker for writing (you may place some sandpaper underneath the fabric to avoid shifting), and then press with an iron to make it permanent. Trim the label; then either fray the edges or turn them under and press, and then hand sew on using matching thread color. Consider adding your name and date to the label like quilters do. A key to successful laundering is getting the maximum amount of water out after washing. Even 100% wool blankets that require hand washing can handle a spin cycle in the washer, which will remove an incredible amount of moisture and speed up drying. Place your blanket in a plastic laundry basket when moving it from the tub to the washer, to catch drips. If you have a ceiling fan, lay out the blanket underneath it and arrange the blanket neatly in the original size and shape, and turn the fan on high. If you wash in the morning, your blanket should be dry and usable by nighttime.
24. Due to space considerations, charts are included only for more complex pattern stitches. A complete set of charts is available at theknitwit.org. For access, see the link on page 214.
25. Since blankets are composed of a hierarchy of shapes, there are up to five levels of organization of each pattern. Being able to identify the levels of hierarchy is helpful in comprehending the pattern. The font sizes and colors used are:

LEVEL 1

Blanket instructions, Assembly, Borders, and Finishing

Level 2

Units of the blanket such as Blocks or Strips

Level 3

Pieces that make up a Block or Strip

Level 4

Smaller parts of the Pieces of a Block or Strip

Level 5

Smallest bits

Introduction

I am so pleased to bring you 26 more geometric knitted blankets. These designs combine my great loves: knitting, color, geometry, and repeating patterns. The reception of my first book, *Geometric Knit Blankets*, was so inspiring that as soon as I put down my pen and knitting needles, I started exploring additional designs, which have come together in this book.

Geometric Knit Blankets used quilts and tile designs for inspiration. There are a couple traditional quilt designs in this book, but the inspirations are more *opportunistic*. These ideas popped into my head while thinking about what I could create by combining pick up and knit, short rows, a little intarsia, shaping, 3-needle bind-off, and, occasionally, some sewing. As a result, these designs range from traditional to modern.

Many of the blankets are knit modularly, meaning that new sections of the blanket grow from the edges of previously completed sections. Some blankets are worked in strips that are joined with a 3-needle bind-off. A few are assembled by sewing and make excellent take-along projects.

The photographed samples were worked in superwash wool yarns, acrylics, and acrylic/wool blends. Yarn weights range from DK to chunky, with most blankets worked in worsted. Each design has a carefully chosen yarn line and color scheme, but these designs invite fiber and color experimentation.

Gauge is important only as it affects yarn amounts and the resulting size of the blanket. As with all yarn substitution, make a good-sized gauge swatch in garter stitch to compare the gauge with the pattern and to evaluate the "hand" of the knitted fabric. Avoid slick yarns such as linen, cotton, and silk. They do not contain enough surface fuzz to hide small holes between stitches and stitch maneuvers.

The most frequent request I receive is for tutorials for my patterns, so I have created additional technique videos to support the patterns in this book (access on page 214 or look up my Youtube channel @Knitwitme), and there are photo tutorials of the techniques starting on page 200. The video tutorials are an ongoing project and will not all be complete when this book is published. I will also be adding videos upon request, so *subscribe* to my channel and you will be notified when I publish something new that you may find helpful.

I often see comments on my Facebook group or receive emails from knitters who read over the instructions without trying them and don't believe they will work. I tell them to follow the instructions, trust them temporarily, suspend disbelief, and knit the first Block or Strip. Usually I don't hear from them again.

If you have already paged through this book, you probably have noticed that each blanket has a motif, which is repeated in the same or different colors to create the whole design. In fact, all of knitting relies on repetition. To learn, you practice the knit stitch and then the purl stitch. Knitting patterns tell you how to do something in detail once, and then you repeat it.

Without repetition in knitting, there would have to be a separate instruction for every row of knitting. This would not be fun and would be practical only if our brains were computers! It is the repetitive nature of knitting that we find so calming. If variety is the spice of life, repetition is its balm.

The patterns in this book rely on repetition to an even greater extent than normal for knitting. A group of instructions that create a certain shape are placed in a green box that is referred to, when needed, from the main instructions. Instructions for a Strip or Block are described in detail once, and then that Strip or Block is worked multiple times, possibly in different color combinations. Watching the blanket grow and seeing new colors incorporated keeps us interested and motivated to finish.

Choose a blanket to start with, and get down to some serious knitting. Because of repetition, you'll be able to knit while listening to a podcast, watching TV, or waiting for the slowpokes in your family.

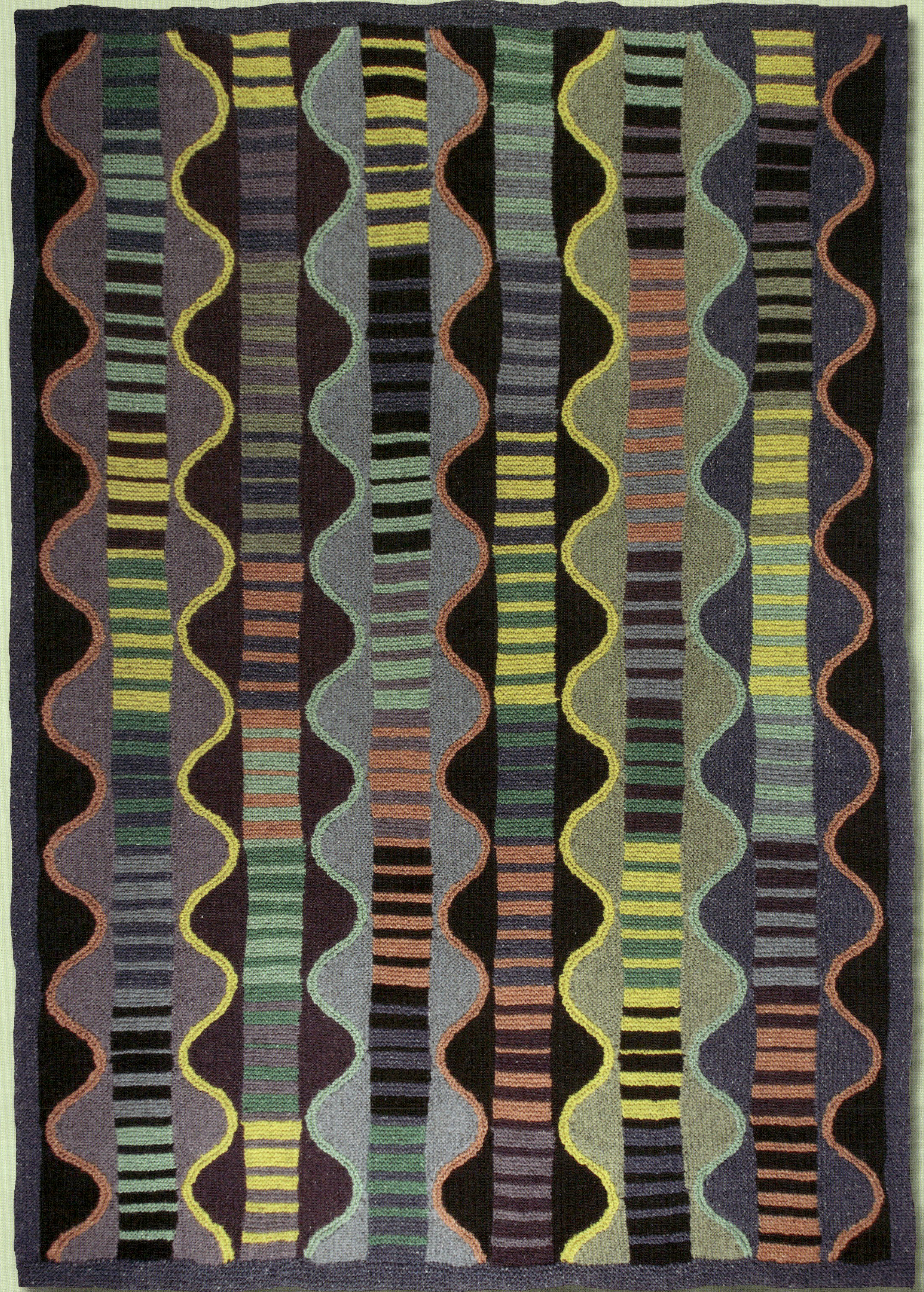

ANCESTRY

This blanket of DNA-like shapes is worked in contrasting colors for maximum impact.

SIZE 60 x 74.5"/152 x 189 cm

TECHNIQUES 3-needle BO, pu&k

YARN Rowan Felted Tweed, DK (50% wool, 25% alpaca, 25% viscose; 191 yds/175 m; 1.75 oz/50 g):

Pattern Color ID	Color Swatch	Color ID	Color Name	Color Description	# Balls
A		220	Sulfur	light yellow-gold	3
B		184	Celadon	light olive green	3
C		204	Vaseline Green	muted mint green	2
D		203	Electric Green	green	1
E		173	Duck Egg	light blue-gray	4
F		178	Seasalter	medium blue-gray	9
G		192	Amethyst	lavender	4
H		151	Bilberry	dark plum	4
I		212	Peach	dusty pink	4
J		211	Black	black	7

NEEDLES (2) US Size 10/6 mm 40"/100 cm circular needles or size needed to obtain gauge, (1) US Size 11/8 mm needle for 3-needle BO

NOTIONS Tapestry needle, stitch markers, needle protectors, stitch holders

GAUGE 14 sts x 28 rows = 4"/10 cm in garter stitch with yarn held double

NOTES

- Yarn is held double throughout.
- Each vertical piece, or Strip, has a striped Column, to which curved Hills are added. Stitches for the Hills are picked up and knit (pu&k) on the side edges of Columns. When Strips are complete, they are joined together with a 3-needle BO, referred to as a Snake. Stitches for joining are picked up and knit on edges of Hills. Right and Left Borders are worked separately from the blanket. Hills are then added to the Border, and they are joined to the adjacent Strip using a 3-needle BO. Top and Bottom Borders are picked up and knit from blanket edges.
- When working the horizontal striping for a Column, drape yarn slightly loosely between uses along the right edge of the piece, and cut only after the last stripe in the sequence is complete. Yarn is also draped between the bind-off of a Hill and the start of the next Hill. Draped yarns are woven in during the subsequent pu&k that is worked along the edge. When draping yarn, leave about 0.5"/1.25 cm extra yarn, or stretch the edge and leave the same length as the length of the stretched edge. (The latter method is preferred for drapes between Hills.) See also "Tacking Draped Yarn" on page 210.

BLANKET INSTRUCTIONS

Left Edge (LE)

Left Border

With F, CO 255.

Rows 1-11: Knit. *Note:* After the first few rows, pm on RS of work (facing when working odd-numbered rows).
Row 12 (WS): Knit to end, and simultaneously pm after 15th st then every 30th st thereafter (8 m's total). Cut F.

Beg on RS, attach J, and knit 1 row.

Hills for LE

Beg on WS, work [HH1, on page 4] between end of Border and next m. Rm. Do not cut yarn.

(Drape yarn slightly loosely, and work [Hill, page 4] over next 30 sts to next m, rm) 8 times, working the last rep to end of row. Cut yarn and fasten off.

Right Edge (RE)

Work as for Left Edge (LE).

Strip – Make 6

A Strip is composed of a Column, Hills, and part-Hills (HH1 and HH2) that are attached to the edges of the Column, as illustrated in Figure 1.

Column

- See Figure 2 for the Strip Sequence for Columns and the number of rows to work in Color 1 (C1) and Color 2 (C2) for each repeat of the Strip's striping.
- See Figure 3 for colors C1 and C2 to use for Columns.

For each Strip, numbered 1-6, CO 15 sts using first C2 for Strip. Knit 510 rows, alternating between Color 1 (C1) and Color 2 (C2) as shown in Figure 2, changing colors at "Δ C1" and "Δ C2," respectively. Drape yarn slightly loosely between uses until instructed to cut yarn.

For example, for Strip 1, CO with C2 (J), and use C for C1 until reaching "Δ C1" in Figure 2. Cut C1 (C) and attach the next C1 (E). Continue working through Figure 2 to complete the first repeat. At the beginning of the 2nd repeat, at the red arrow labeled "Δ C2," cut C2 (J), and attach the next C2 (F).

Repeat the striping sequence in Figure 2 [5] times, ending the 5th repeat after completion of the 3rd C2 stripe, at the blue arrow.

Place sts on holder.

Use the tracking chart (Figure 7 on page 6) to mark completed colors. Plus signs (+) denote addition of a color and minus signs (-) the end/cutting of a color.

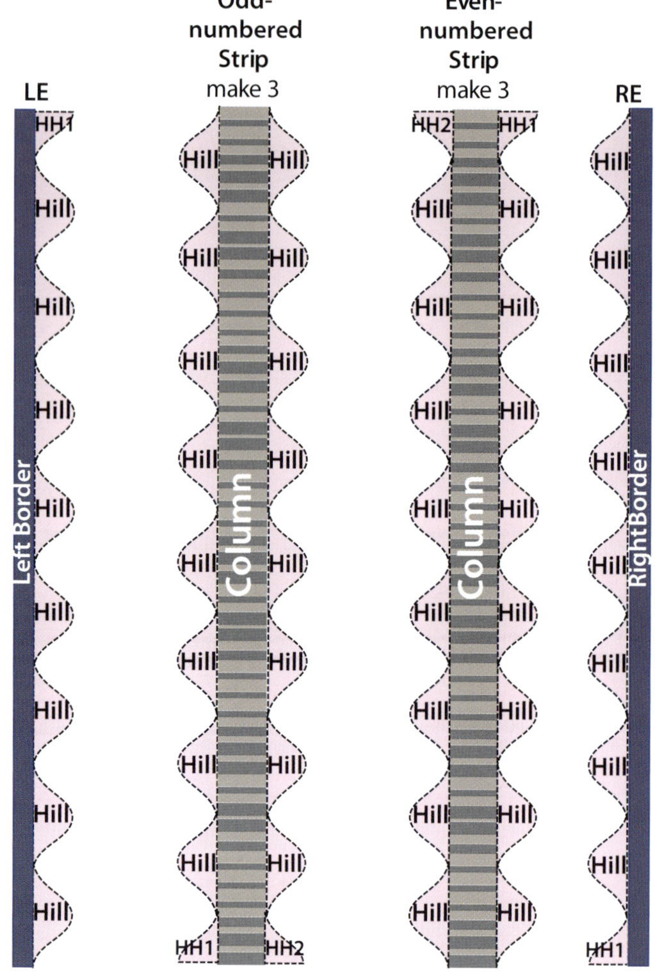

Figure 1: Identification of Blanket Parts

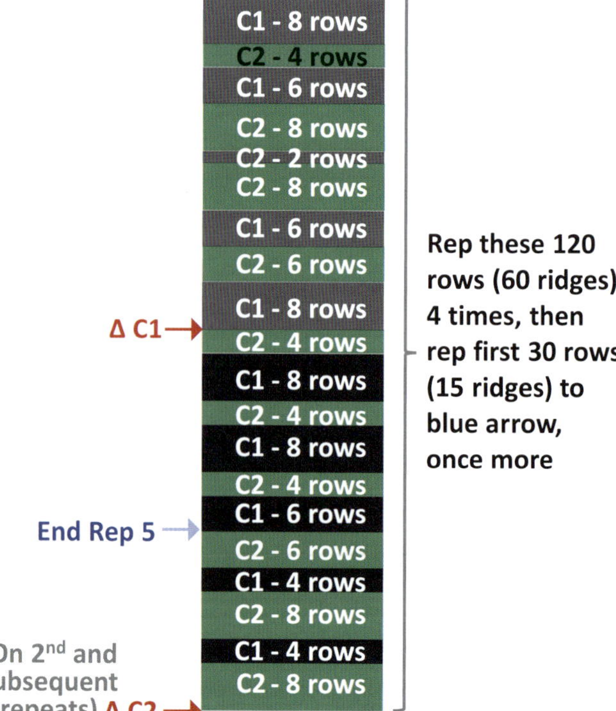

Figure 2: Stripe Sequence for Columns

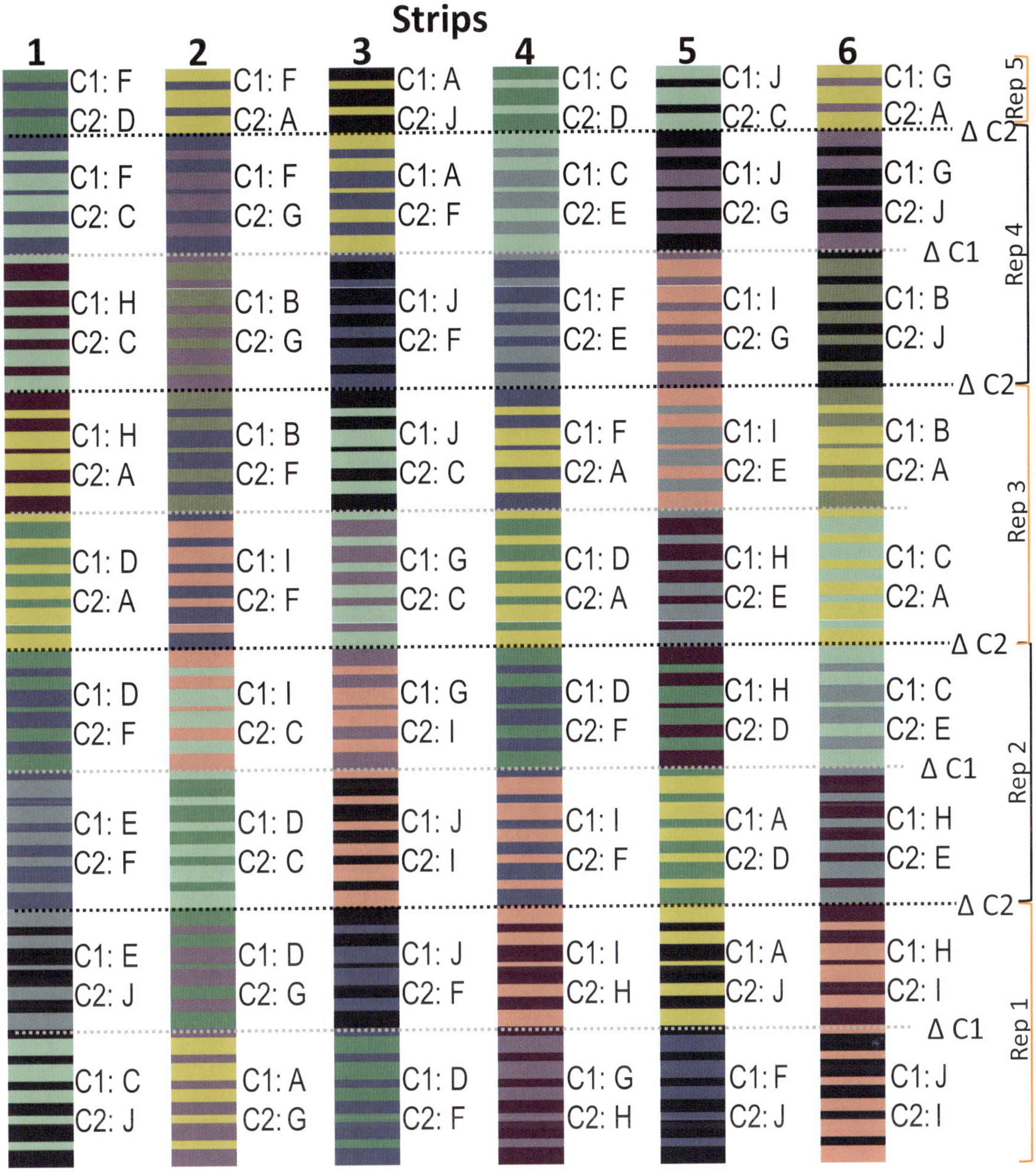

Strips

Rep	1	2	3	4	5	6	
Rep 5	C1: F C2: D	C1: F C2: A	C1: A C2: J	C1: C C2: D	C1: J C2: C	C1: G C2: A	Δ C2
Rep 4	C1: F C2: C	C1: F C2: G	C1: A C2: F	C1: C C2: E	C1: J C2: G	C1: G C2: J	Δ C1
	C1: H C2: C	C1: B C2: G	C1: J C2: F	C1: F C2: E	C1: I C2: G	C1: B C2: J	Δ C2
Rep 3	C1: H C2: A	C1: B C2: F	C1: J C2: C	C1: F C2: A	C1: I C2: E	C1: B C2: A	
	C1: D C2: A	C1: I C2: F	C1: G C2: C	C1: D C2: A	C1: H C2: E	C1: C C2: A	Δ C2
Rep 2	C1: D C2: F	C1: I C2: C	C1: G C2: I	C1: D C2: F	C1: H C2: D	C1: C C2: E	Δ C1
	C1: E C2: F	C1: D C2: C	C1: J C2: I	C1: I C2: F	C1: A C2: D	C1: H C2: E	Δ C2
Rep 1	C1: E C2: J	C1: D C2: G	C1: J C2: F	C1: I C2: H	C1: A C2: J	C1: H C2: I	Δ C1
	C1: C C2: J	C1: A C2: G	C1: D C2: F	C1: G C2: H	C1: F C2: J	C1: J C2: I	

Figure 3: C1 and C2 colors used in Striping

Hill – 30 sts dec'ing to 4 sts

Row 2 (WS): BO2, knit to end – 2 sts dec'd; 28 sts.
Rows 3-5: Rep [Row 2] 3 times – 6 sts dec'd; 22 sts.
Row 6 and all even-numbered (WS) rows to 20: Knit.
Row 7: K2tog, knit to last 2 sts, ssk – 2 sts dec'd; 20 sts.
Row 9: Rep [Row 7] – 2 sts dec'd; 18 sts.
Rows 11 & 13: Knit.
Rows 15, 17, and 19: Rep [Row 7] 3 times – 6 sts dec'd; 12 sts.
Rows 21-23: Rep [Row 2] 3 times – 6 sts dec'd; 6 sts.
Row 24: BO 2 sts, knit to end. Place rem 4 sts on holder. Pm for "peak" on holder bet the center sts.

After adding Hills to a Column, label the Strip and set it aside for Joining in a later step.

Note: Adding Hills to a Column starts with pu&k of stitches along the entire edge of a Column. These pu&k sts count as Row 1 (RS).

Hills for left edges of 1, 3, and 5

Attach yarn color for Hills (located below the Strip in Figure 4) at red triangle at top left corner of Column. *Pu&k 255 sts to end of Column (1 st per garter stitch ridge), placing a marker every 30 stitches (8 m's total). *Note:* There will be 15 sts bet 8th m and end of row.

Work as for "Hills for LE" on page 2.

Hills for right edges of 1, 3, and 5

Attach yarn color for Hills (Figure 4), at orange triangle at bottom right corner of Column. Pu&k 255 sts to end of Column (1 st per garter stitch ridge), placing a marker after the 15th st, then every 30 stitches thereafter (8 m's total). Tack draped yarns while performing the pu&k. See "Tacking Draped Yarn" on page 210.

Beg on WS, (attach yarn, work [Hill] over 30 sts to next m, do not cut yarn, and drape to next use, rm) 8 times, then work [HH2] over last 15 sts. Cut yarn and fasten off.

Hills for right edges of 2, 4, and 6

Work "Hills for left edges of 1, 3, and 5" from * attaching yarn at bottom right corner of Column at orange triangle. Tack draped yarns while performing pu&k.

Hills for left edges of 2, 4, and 6

Work from * of "Hills for right edges of 1, 3, and 5," attaching yarn at red triangle at top left corner of Column.

Half Hill 1 (HH1) – 15 sts dec'ing to 2 sts

Row 2 (WS) and all even-numbered rows to 24: Knit.
Row 3: BO2, knit to end – 2 sts dec'd; 13 sts.
Row 5: Rep [Row 3] – 2 sts dec'd; 11 sts.
Row 7: K2tog, knit to end – 1 st dec'd; 10 sts.
Row 9: Rep [Row 7] – 1 st dec'd; 9 sts.
Rows 11 & 13: Knit.
Rows 15, 17, and 19: Rep [Row 7] 3 times – 3 sts dec'd; 6 sts.
Rows 21 & 23: Rep [Row 3] 2 times – 4 sts dec'd; 2 sts.
After completing Row 24, place rem 2 sts on holder.

Half Hill 2 (HH2) – 15 sts dec'ing to 2 sts

Row 2 (WS): BO2, knit to end – 2 sts dec'd; 13 sts.
Row 3 (RS): Knit.
Rows 4 & 5: Rep [Rows 2 & 3] – 2 sts dec'd; 11 sts.
Rows 6 and all even-numbered (WS) rows to 20: Knit.
Row 7: Knit to last 2 sts, ssk – 1 st dec'd; 10 sts.
Row 9: Rep [Row 7] – 1 st dec'd; 9 sts.
Rows 11 & 13: Knit.
Rows 15, 17, and 19: Rep [Row 7] 3 times – 3 sts dec'd; 6 sts.
Rows 21 & 23: Knit.
Rows 22 & 24 (WS): Rep [Row 2] 2 times – 4 sts dec'd; 2 sts. Place rem 2 sts on holder.

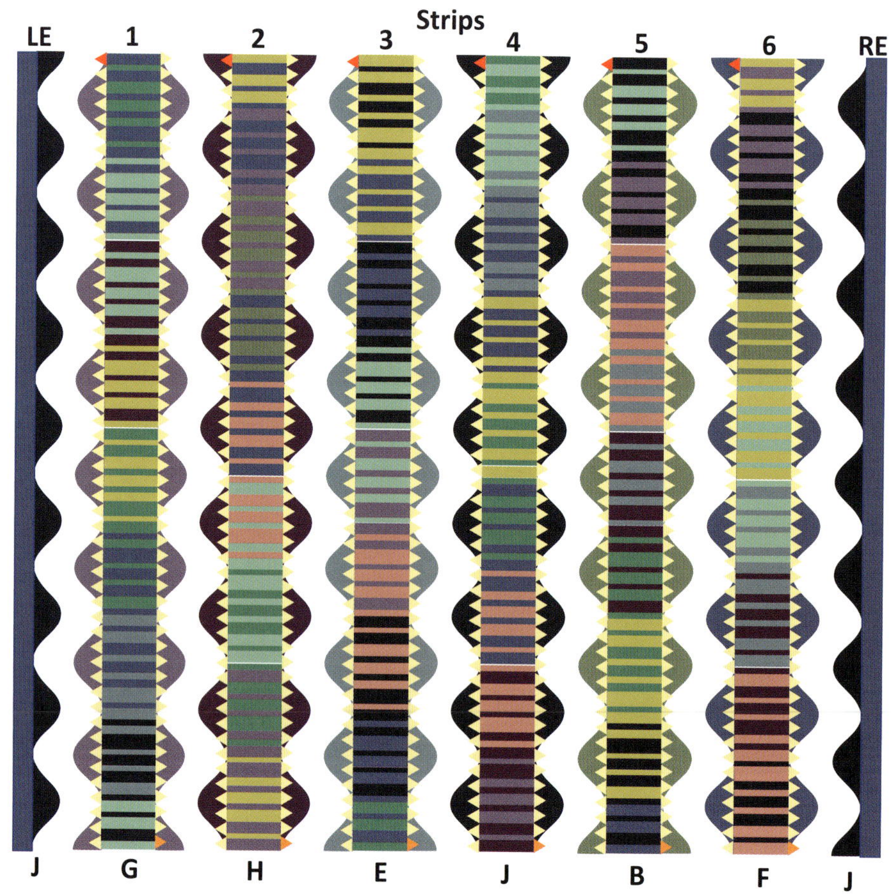

Figure 4: Yarn Colors for Hills

Table 1: Strip Joining Order, Pairings, and Yarn Color

	Join		
Order	**Left Strip**	**Right Strip**	**Snake Color**
1	LE	Strip 1	I
2	Strip 1	Strip 2	A
3	Strip 2	Strip 3	C
4	Strip 3	Strip 4	I
5	Strip 4	Strip 5	A
6	Strip 5	Strip 6	C
7	Strip 6	RE	I

Join Strips

Arrange LE, Strips, and RE as shown in Figure 4, RS facing and orienting CO ends of Strips at the bottom. Join these Strips, pairwise, in the order specified in Table 1.

A Snake refers to the curved band of knitting that is created while joining a pair of Strips. For each Join of a pair of Strips, work the 4 steps below:

1) Place Markers, 2) Prep Left Strip, 3) Prep Right Strip, and 4) 3-needle BO of Left and Right Strips.

1) Place Markers

Pm's at valley of each Hill, HH1, and HH2 on right edge Hills of the Left Strip and left edge of Right Strip, as shown by green dots in Figure 5. Add intermediate markers of a different color or shape bet every 3 ridges counting from the top of the Hill, at locations of red dots in Figure 5.

2) Prep Left Strip

With a circular needle and yarn for Snake (Table 1), attach yarn at bottom right of Strip at the red triangle in Figure 6. Using Figure 5 as a guide for rate of sts to pu&k on the edge of the Hills, pu&k 20 sts bet adjacent valley (green) and peak (blue) m's, transferring blue and green m's (only) to needle while simultaneously tacking any draped yarns (see "Tacking Draped Yarn" on page 210) – 340 sts.

Knit 1 row.*

Cut yarn and fasten off. Leave sts on needle and place needle protectors on needle points.

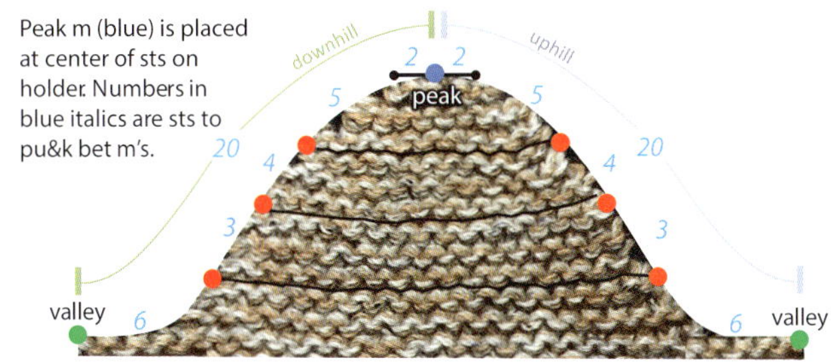

Figure 5: Marker Placement for Pu&k of Sts for Snake

Tip: Uphill cadence for pu&k starting at valley m is 1 st in each of 4 BO sts, next 6 bumps, (leg, bump) twice, 1 st in each of 4 BO sts bef holder, knit 2 sts off holder to peak m. Downhill cadence is reverse of uphill cadence.

3) Prep Right Strip

Working on a 2nd circular needle, with a second strand of yarn for Snake, attach yarn at the green triangle at the top left of the Strip, and work as for 2) Prep Left Strip.

Do not cut yarn.

4) 3-needle BO of Left and Right Strips

Turn Left Strip and Right Strip with RS together and needle tips parallel. Rotate work so that Strip with working yarn attached is behind. With 3rd needle and working yarn, perform 3-needle BO loosely over all 340 sts – 1 st rem. Cut yarn and fasten off.

Note: Align sts using m's on needles. If too many sts, decrease while binding off by inserting needle knitwise through 2 sts.

Figure 6: Snakes

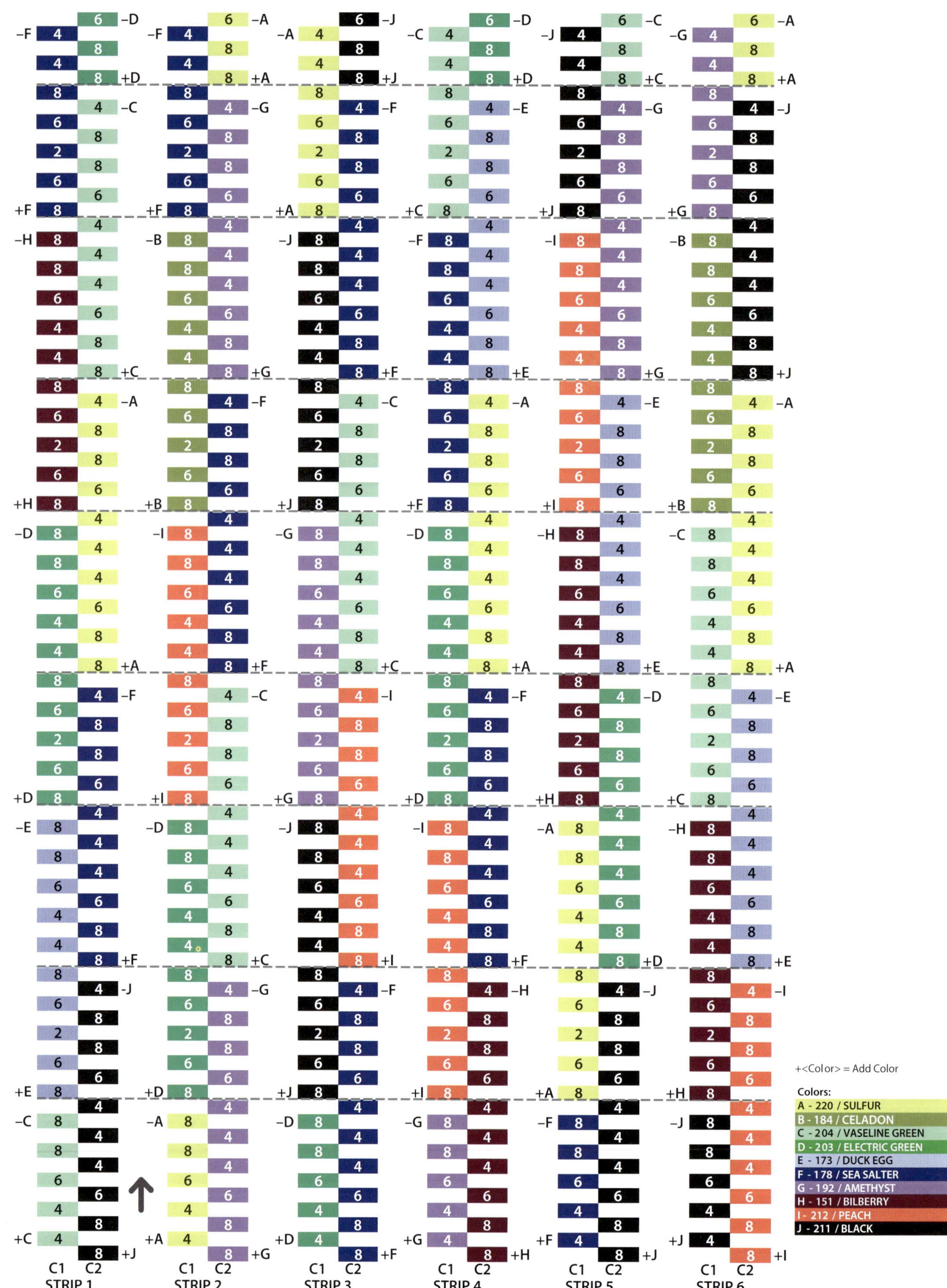

Figure 7: Column Tracking Chart

BORDERS

Top Border

Attach F at top right corner of RE. Pu&k 7 sts (1 per garter st ridge) on Right Border, then 15 sts on each Join (Hill + Snake), knit 15 sts from each holder for Strip and then 7 sts on Left Border – 209 sts. Knit 15 rows. BO loosely. Cut yarn and fasten off.

Bottom Border

Work as for Top Border, attaching yarn at bottom left corner of blanket, and pu&k 15 sts on each Strip instead of knitting from holders.

FINISHING

Weave in ends.

CAROUSEL

The twirling discs on this blanket give the impression of continuous motion.

SIZE 60 x 75"/152 x 191 cm

TECHNIQUES Crochet, pu&k, sewing

YARN Cascade 220 Superwash and Cascade 220 Superwash Wave worsted (100% superwash wool; 220 yds/200 m; 3.5 oz/100 g):

Pattern Color ID	Cascade 220 Yarn Line	Color Swatch	Color ID	Color Name	Color Description	# Balls
A	220 Superwash Wave		115	Dusk	brown, blue, and dark gray	10
B	220 Superwash		817	Aran	off-white	8

NEEDLES US Size 7/4.5 mm 40"/100 cm circular needles and dpns, or size needed to obtain gauge

NOTIONS US Size G-6/4 mm crochet hook, tapestry needle, stitch markers

GAUGE 19 sts x 29 rows = 4"/10 cm in stockinette st

16 sts x 32 rows = 4"/10 cm in garter st

Note: Follow washing instructions on yarn label before measuring swatches.

NOTES

- The blanket is worked in stockinette stitch. Hexagons and part-hexagons are worked and then finished with a single crochet edge and sewn together. A garter stitch border is picked up and knit around the blanket edge. Because stockinette stitch has a tendency to curl, the assembled blanket will not lie completely flat until it is laundered.
- See Figure 1 for shape key.
- Cut yarn only when instructed. Carry non-working yarn along right edge and twist together with working yarn at beginning of right-side rows, or drape and weave into subsequent pick up and knit (pu&k) on the edge (see "Tacking Draped Yarn" on page 210).

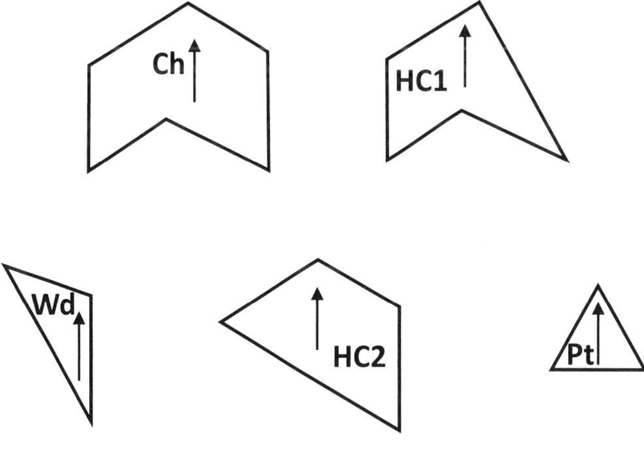

Figure 1: Shapes

BLANKET INSTRUCTIONS

HEXAGONS – Make 7

See Figure 2 for construction. Each Hexagon is composed of 6 Chevrons (Ch1-Ch6).

Ch1

With A, CO 40 sts, leaving 36"/91 cm tail.

Note: Wind up CO tail and secure to WS of work after completing Rows 1 & 2.

Work [Ch] – 16 sts rem. Cut B.

Chevron (Ch) – 40 sts dec'ing to 16 sts

Row 1 (RS): With A, k2tog, k21, kyok, knit to last 2 sts, ssk.
Row 2 (WS): Purl.
Rows 3 & 4: Rep [Rows 1 & 2].
Attach B.
Rows 5-8: With B, rep [Rows 1-4] once.
Rows 9-16: Rep [Rows 1-8] once.
Rows 17-19: With A, rep [Rows 1-3] once.
Row 20: Bind off first 16 sts purlwise, then purl to end – 16 sts dec'd; 24 sts.
Cut A.
Row 21: With B, k2tog, knit to last 2 sts, ssk – 2 sts dec'd; 22 sts.
Row 22: Purl.
Rows 23-28: Rep [Rows 21 & 22] 3 times – 6 sts dec'd; 16 sts.

Ch2

*On RS, attach A at red triangle; pu&k 24 sts (6 sts every 7 rows) on right edge of Ch1, and then knit rem 16 sts from needle – 40 sts.

Work [Ch, Rows 2-28] – 16 sts rem. Cut B.*

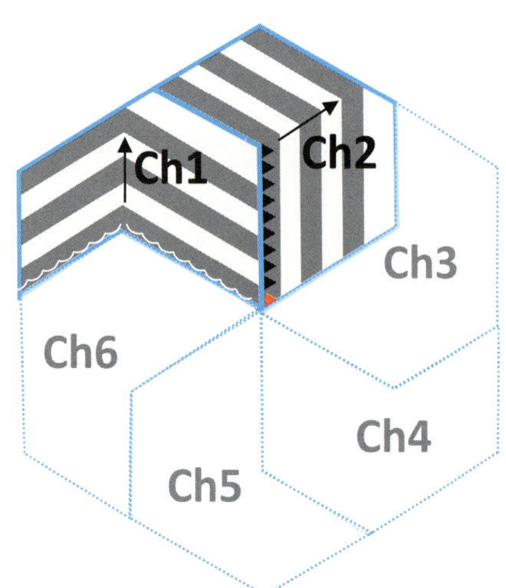

Figure 2: Hexagon Construction

Ch3 – Ch6

Rep bet * and * 4 times. On the final rep (Ch6), do not cut A after Row 20. BO rem sts loosely with B. Cut B.

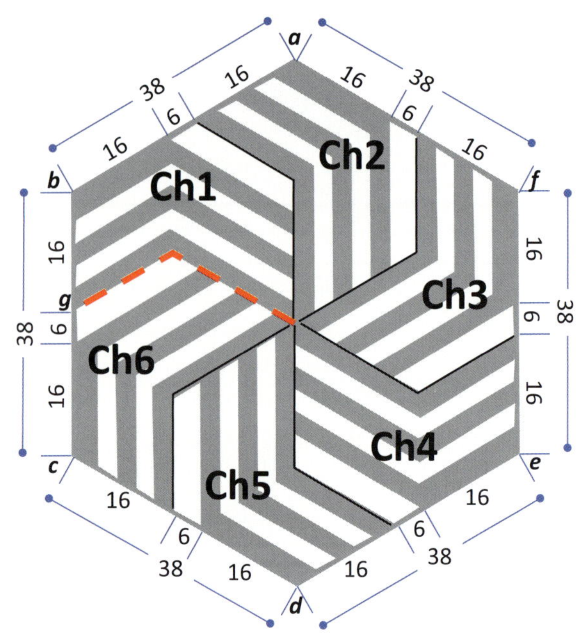

Figure 3: Hexagon Seam and Crochet St Counts

Working on RS, with mattress st and long CO tail of A from Ch1, sew seam between CO edge of Ch1 and BO edge of Ch6, as shown by red-dashed line in Figure 3, matching corners. At the center where the Chevrons meet, take a few sts to close the hole.

Crochet Trim

Using A from Ch6 (still attached), single crochet the number of sts shown in Figure 3 starting bet ***b*** and ***c***, working counterclockwise, and ending with a slip stitch in the 1st single crochet; then cut yarn, leaving 20"/50 cm tail. Wind up tail and secure to edge with a locking stitch marker. Pm's at each of the 6 points, ***a-f***.

HALF HEXAGONS 1 (HH1) – Make 6

See Figure 4 for construction.

Wd

With A, CO 1 st. Work [Wd] – 16 sts rem. Cut yarns.

Ch1

On RS, attach A at lower right corner of prev shape at red triangle in Figure 4, and pu&k 24 sts to corner, pm, knit 16 sts from needle – 40 sts. Work [Ch, Rows 2-28]. Cut yarns.

Ch2

Rep bet * and * once.

HC1

On RS, with A, and starting at red triangle at lower right corner of Ch2, pu&k 24 sts to corner, pm in the 24th st (this is the "center" stitch), knit 16 sts from needle – 40 sts. Work [HC1] – 1 st rem. Cut B. Do not cut A.

Crochet Trim

Working on RS, using A from HC1 (still attached), sc the number of sts shown in Figure 4 from ***a*** counterclockwise back to ***a***, taking a sl st in the 1st sc to complete round. With A from CO, and a tapestry needle, take a few sts at the red triangles in Figure 4 to join the tips of the shapes together. Cut yarn, leaving 20"/50 cm tail. Pm's at each of points ***a-e***.

Wedge (Wd) – 1 st inc'ing to 16 sts

Row 2 (WS): CO 1, purl to end – 1 st inc'd; 2 sts.
Row 3 (RS): K1, kf&b – 1 st inc'd; 3 sts.
Row 4: Purl.
Row 5: K2tog, knit to end – 1 st dec'd; 2 sts.
Row 6: CO 2, purl to end – 2 sts inc'd; 4 sts.
Attach B.
Row 7: With B, rep [Row 5] – 1 st dec'd; 3 sts.
Row 8: Rep [Row 6] – 2 sts inc'd; 5 sts.
Rows 9 & 10: Rep [Rows 5 & 6] – 1 st inc'd; 6 sts.
Rows 11-14: With A, rep [Rows 5 & 6] twice – 2 sts inc'd; 8 sts.
Rows 15-18: Rep [Rows 7-10] - 2 sts inc'd; 10 sts.
Rows 19-22: Rep [Rows 11-14] – 2 sts inc'd; 12 sts.
Rows 23-30: With B, rep [Rows 7-10] twice – 4 sts inc'd; 16 sts.

Figure 4: Half Hexagon 1 (HH1)

Half Chevron 1 (HC1) – 40 sts dec'ing to 1 st

Row 2 (WS): Purl to last 2 sts, p2tog – 1 st dec'd; 39 sts.
Row 3 (RS): With A, k2tog, knit to 1 st bef center st, kyok in center st, knit to last 2 sts, ssk. Rm.
Note: The yarn over of the kyok is now the "center" stitch.
Row 4: Purl to last 3 sts, p3tog – 2 sts dec'd; 37 sts.
Attach B.
Rows 5-8: With B, work [Rows 1-4] – 3 sts dec'd; 34 sts.
Rows 9-16: Rep [Rows 1-8] – 6 sts dec'd; 28 sts.
Rows 17-19: Rep [Rows 1-3] – 1 st dec'd; 27 sts.
Row 20: BO 17 purlwise, p6, p3tog – 19 sts dec'd; 8 sts.
Note: BO until 9 unworked sts rem on L needle.
Row 21: With B, k2tog, knit to last 2 sts, ssk – 2 sts dec'd; 6 sts.
Row 22: Purl to last 2 sts, p2tog – 1 st dec'd; 5 sts.
Row 23: Rep [Row 21] – 2 sts dec'd; 3 sts.
Row 24: P3tog – 2 sts dec'd; 1 st.

Half Hexagons 2 (HH2) – Make 4

See Figure 5 for construction.

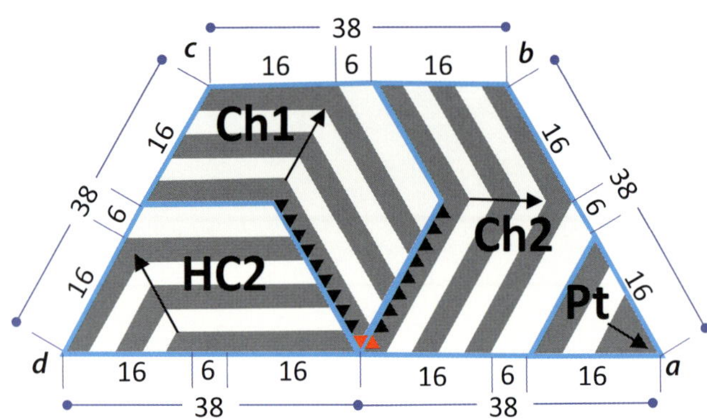

Figure 5: Half Hexagon 2 (HH2) Construction and Crochet Stitch Counts

HC2

With A, CO 25 sts.

Work [HC2] – 16 sts rem. Cut yarns.

Half Chevron 2 (HC2) – 25 sts inc'ing to 40 sts dec'ing to 16 sts

Row 1 (RS): With A, k2tog, k21, kyok, knit to last st, kf&b – 2 sts inc'd; 27 sts.
Row 2 (WS): Purl.
Row 3: K2tog, k21, kyok, knit to end – 1 st inc'd; 28 sts.
Row 4: Knit.
Attach B.
Rows 5-8: With B, rep [Rows 1-4] – 3 sts inc'd; 31 sts.
Rows 9-16: Rep [Rows 1-8] – 6 sts inc'd; 37 sts.
Rows 17-19: Rep [Rows 1-3] – 3 sts inc'd; 40 sts.
Row 20: BO 16 sts, purl to end – 16 sts dec'd; 24 sts.
Cut A.
Row 21: With B, k2tog, knit to last 2 sts, ssk – 2 sts dec'd; 22 sts.
Row 22: Purl.
Rows 23-28: Rep [Rows 21 & 22] 3 times – 6 sts dec'd; 16 sts.

Ch1

On RS, attach A at lower right corner of prev completed shape at red triangle in Figure 5, and pu&k 24 sts to corner, knit 16 sts from needle – 40 sts. Work [Ch, Rows 2-28]. Cut yarns.

Ch2

Rep bet * and * once – 16 sts rem. Do not cut yarns.

Point (Pt)

Work [Pt] – 1 st rem. Cut B. Do not cut A.

With A from CO, and tapestry needle, take a few sts at red triangles in Figure 5 to join tips of shapes.

Point (Pt) – 16 sts dec'ing to 1 st

Row 1 (RS): With A, k2tog, knit to last 2 sts, ssk – 2 sts dec'd; 14 sts.
Row 2 (WS): Purl.
Rows 3 & 4: Rep [Rows 1 & 2] – 2 sts dec'd; 12 sts.
Attach B.
Rows 5-8: With B, rep [Rows 1-4] – 4 sts dec'd; 8 sts.
Rows 9-12: With B, rep [Rows 1-4] – 4 sts dec'd; 4 sts.
Row 13: With A, k2tog, ssk – 2 sts dec'd; 2 sts.
Row 14: P2tog – 1 st dec'd; 1 st.

Crochet Trim

With A (still attached), single crochet the number of sts shown in Figure 5 from ***a*** counterclockwise back to point ***a***, taking a slip stitch in the 1st single crochet to complete round. Cut yarn, leaving 20"/50 cm tail. Wind up tail and secure to edge with a locking stitch marker. Pm's at ***a***, ***b***, ***c***, and ***d***.

Corners (Cr) – Make 2

See Figure 6 for construction.

Work Wd and Ch1 as for HH1. Do not cut yarns. Work [Pt]. Cut B. Do not cut A. Using A from Pt, single crochet the number of sts shown from ***a*** in counterclockwise back to ***a***, taking a slip stitch in the 1st single crochet to complete the round. Pm's at ***a***, ***b***, ***c***, and ***d***.

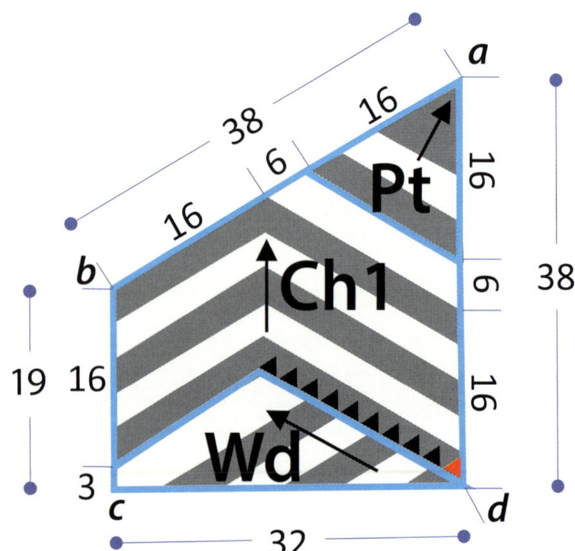

Figure 6: Corner (Cr) Construction and Crochet Stitch Counts

ASSEMBLY

Arrange completed pieces as shown in Figure 7 on page 14. With long tails of A from crochet trims and mattress st, sew red seams to create horizontal strips; then sew blue seams, matching marked corners, to join Strips. Rm corner markers.

Borders

When performing pu&k to generate sts for Borders, pu&k 1 st in back leg of each single crochet stitch. Refer to Figure 7 for the number of stitches to pu&k on the edge of each shape. Place a marker between each set of stitches at the blue dots in Figure 7 to assist with counting. If counts are a little off between markers, adjust stitch counts between markers on Row 1 by using kf&b to add sts and k2tog to decrease sts. Rm's after completing Row 1.

Right Border

Attach A at bottom right corner of blanket and pu&k 284 sts to next corner. Knit 13 rows. BO loosely, leaving last st on needle. Do not cut yarn.

Top Border

Pu&k 7 sts on edge of Right Border, 224 sts on top edge of blanket – 232 sts. Knit 13 rows. BO loosely, leaving last st on needle.

Left Border

Pu&k 7 sts on left edge of Top Border, 284 sts on Left Border – 292 sts. Knit 13 rows. BO loosely, leaving last st on needle.

Bottom Border

Pu&k 7 sts on bottom edge of Left Border, 224 sts on bottom edge of blanket, and 8 sts on bottom edge of Right Border – 240 sts. Knit 13 rows. BO loosely. Cut yarn and fasten off.

FINISHING

Weave in ends. Follow yarn manufacturer's instructions for washing and drying.

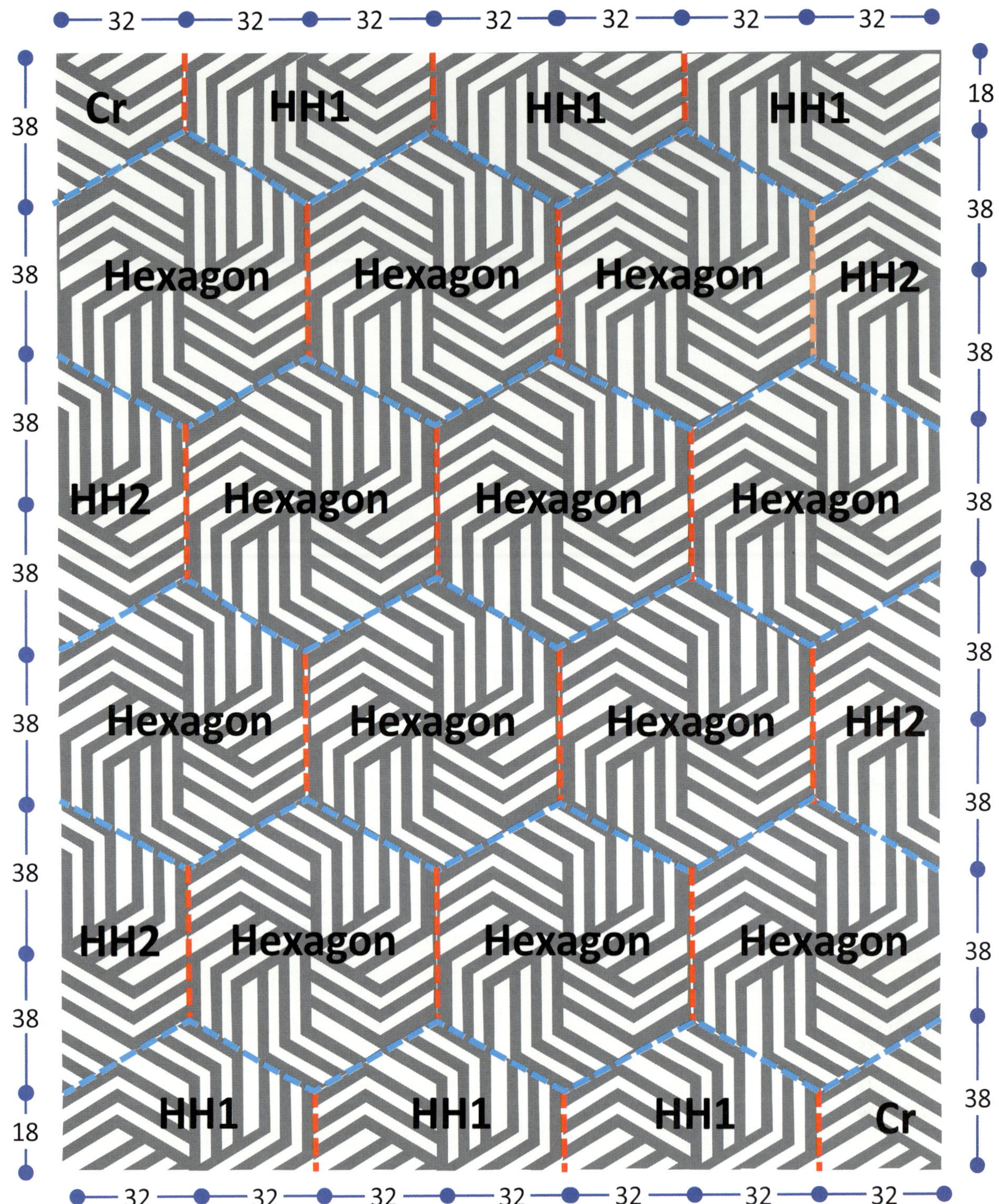

Figure 7: Assembly and Stitch Counts for Border

CHROMATIC

One glorious color blends into the next in this dramatic blanket of 4-point stars on a dark background.

SIZE 61.5 x 77.5"/156 x 197 cm

TECHNIQUES Method A: Pinhole CO, pu&k, sewing
Method B: Pinhole CO, pu&k, working in the round

YARN Noro Silk Garden and Noro Silk Garden Solo, heavy worsted (45% silk, 45% mohair, 10% wool; 110 yds/100 m; 1.8 oz/50 g):

Pattern Color ID	Noro Yarn Line	Color Swatch	Color ID	Color Name	Color Description	# Skeins
A	Silk Garden		483	Rumoi	self-striping	11
B	Silk Garden Solo		09	Hanabatake	charcoal gray	23

NEEDLES US Size 7/4.5 mm 40"/100 cm circular needles and dpns, or size needed to obtain gauge

NOTIONS Tapestry needle, stitch markers, stitch holders

GAUGE 15 sts x 30 rows = 4"/10 cm in garter st

NOTES

- See Figure 1 on page 18 for an overview of construction options.
- Twelve 4-Point Stars are worked first. Each star starts with a square worked from center out, followed by the Arms worked from the stitches on each edge of the square.
- For Method A, 4-Point Stars are turned into square Blocks by working a Wedge between each pair of Arms; then the Blocks are sewn together.
- For Method B, 4-Point Stars are joined by working a Diamond in the round between each set of 4 Arms, and Wedges are worked around outer edges.
- The Border is picked up and knit (pu&k) on the edges of the completed blanket.

BLANKET INSTRUCTIONS

4-Point Stars (PS) – Make 12

A 4-Point Star has an inside-out square (IS) in the center surrounded by 4 Arms. See Figure 2 for construction.

Inside-Out Square (IS) – 8 sts inc'ing to 80 sts

With B, CO 8 sts using pinhole cast-on (see Glossary on page 199), divided evenly over 4 dpns.

Work [IS].

(Transfer next 20 sts to separate holder) 3 times – 60 sts on 3 holders. Continue with rem 20 sts.

Note: For those preferring to knit the Square shape flat (aka "back and forth"), CO 20 sts and knit 39 rows. Using the 20 sts still on the needle, work [Arm]. To generate stitches for the other 3 Arms, working on the RS, pu&k 20 sts on each edge.

Inside-Out Square (IS) – 8 sts inc'ing to 80 sts

Worked in the round.

Rnd 1: *Kf&b, knit to 1 st bef end of dpn, kf&b; rep from * 3 more times – 8 sts inc'd; 16 sts.
Rnd 2: *Pf&b, purl to 1 st bef end of dpn, pf&b; rep from * 3 more times – 8 sts inc'd; 24 sts.
Rnd 3: Rep [Rnd 1] – 8 sts inc'd; 32 sts.
Rnd 4: Purl.
Rnds 5-16: Rep [Rnds 3 & 4] 6 times – 48 sts inc'd; 80 sts. Cut yarn.

Arms 1-4

Arm 1

With 20 rem sts and starting on RS, attach A. Work [Arm].

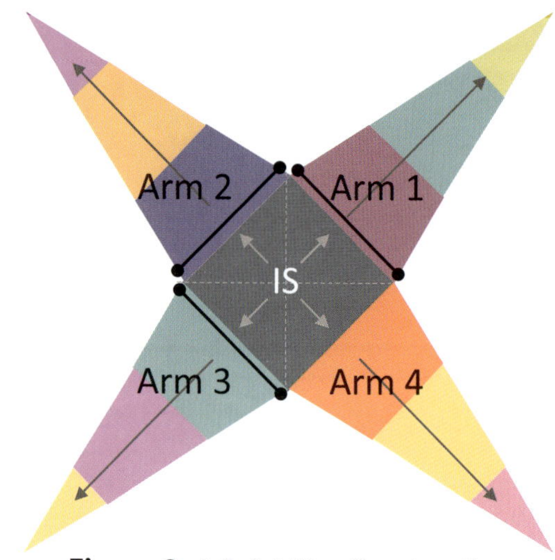

Figure 2: 4-Point Star Construction

Arms 2-4

*Working counterclockwise, transfer next 20 sts from holder to needle, and starting on RS, attach A, work [Arm]; rep from * 2 more times on rem 2 sets of sts on holders.

Arm – 20 sts inc'ing to 21 sts, dec'ing to 1 st

Row 1 (RS): K10, bli, knit to end – 1 st inc'd; 21 sts.
Rows 2 (WS)-6: Knit.
Row 7: K1, k2tog, knit to last 3 sts, ssk, k1 – 2 sts dec'd; 19 sts.
Rows 8-14: Knit.
Rows 15-70: Rep [Rows 7-14] 7 times – 14 sts dec'd; 5 sts.
Row 71: K2tog, k1, ssk – 2 sts dec'd; 3 sts.
Rows 72-78: Knit.
Row 79: Cdd – 2 sts dec'd; 1 st.
Cut yarn and fasten off.

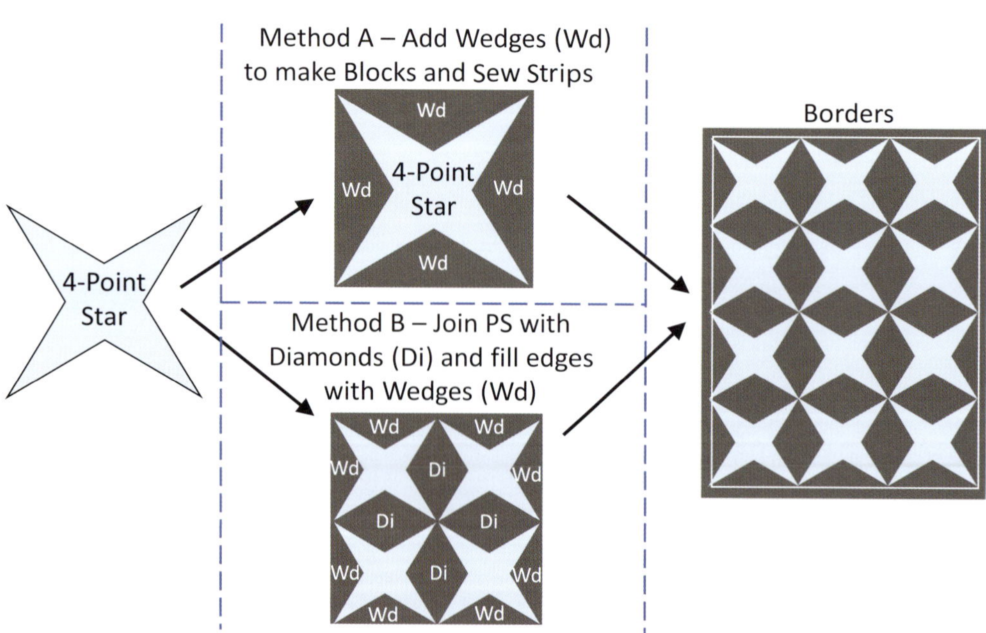

Figure 1: Overview of Construction Options

Method A – Wedges

Figure 3: Method A: Wedge Construction

For each completed 4-Point Star, between each of the four pairs of Arms (the space labeled "Wd"), attach B at the tip of the right Arm of the pair, at the red triangle in Figure 3, and pu&k 40 sts (1 st per garter st ridge) to corner bet Arms, pm, pu&k 40 sts to the tip of the left Arm – 80 sts.

Work [Wd].

Wedge (Wd) – 80 sts dec'ing to 1 st

Row 2 (WS): K2tog, knit to last 2 sts, ssk – 2 sts dec'd; 78 sts.
Rows 3 & 4: Rep [Row 2] twice – 4 sts dec'd; 74 sts.
Row 5: K2tog, knit to 2 sts bef m, ssk, k2tog, knit to last 2 sts, ssk – 4 sts dec'd; 70 sts.
Rows 6-29: Rep [Rows 2-5] 6 times – 60 sts dec'd; 10 sts.
Rows 30-32: Rep [Rows 2-4] – 6 sts dec'd; 4 sts.
Row 33: Sl2 knitwise, rm, k2tog, p2sso, ssk – 3 sts dec'd; 1 st.

Cut yarn and fasten off, leaving 30"/75 cm tail for sewing.

Method A – Assembly

Arrange 12 completed Blocks as shown in Figure 4. Orient Blocks as desired.

Using mattress st and long tails of B, where available, sew tog Blocks along dashed lines.

Note: Long tails on outer edges of blanket that are not used for sewing should be trimmed.

Figure 4: Method A: Assembly

Method B – Diamonds & Wedges

Diamonds

Arrange 12 completed 4-point stars as shown in Figure 6. In the 12 spaces labeled "Di," attach B at the tip of an Arm at the green triangle as shown in Figures 5 & 6, and, using a circular needle, *pu&k 40 sts to next corner, pm1; rep from * 3 more times, placing markers 2-4 as shown in Figure 5 – 160 sts. Work [Di].

Diamond (Di) – 160 sts dec'ing to 4 sts

Start on circular needle and rm's and change to dpns when needed to accommodate sts.
Rnd 2: P2tog, purl to 2 sts bef m2, p2tog tbl, p2tog, purl to 2 sts bef m4, p2tog tbl – 4 sts dec'd; 156 sts.
Rnd 3: K2tog, knit to 2 sts bef m2, ssk, k2tog, knit to 2 sts bef m4, ssk – 4 sts dec'd; 152 sts.
Rnd 4: Rep [Rnd 2] – 4 sts dec'd; 148 sts.
Rnd 5: *K2tog, knit to 2 sts bef next m, k2tog, ssk, knit to 2 sts bef next m, ssk; rep from * once more – 8 sts dec'd; 140 sts.
Rnds 6-29: Rep [Rnds 2-5] 6 times – 120 sts dec'd; 20 sts.
Rnds 30-32: Rep [Rnds 2-4] once – 12 sts dec'd; 8 sts.
Rnd 33: Rm's. K2tog 4 times – 4 sts dec'd; 4 sts.
Cut yarn, leaving 10"/25 cm tail. Thread tail onto tapestry needle and insert needle through rem 4 sts on needle. Pull tightly and fasten securely.

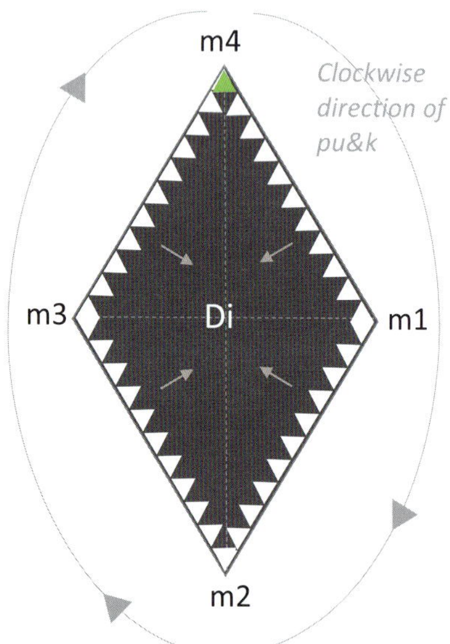

Figure 5: Method B: Detail of Diamond Construction

Wedges

In each of the 12 spaces labeled "Wd" in Figure 6, attach B at right Arm tip at the red triangle and pu&k 40 sts to corner, pm, pu&k 40 sts to left Arm tip – 80 sts. Work [Wd]. Cut yarn and fasten off.

Figure 6: Method B: Assembly

BORDERS

Note: Pu&k 70 sts on the edge of each Wedge.

Right Border

Attach B at lower right corner of blanket, pu&k 280 sts. Knit 17 rows. BO loosely, leaving last st on needle. Do not cut yarn.

Top Border

Pu&k 9 sts on left edge of Right Border and 210 sts on top of blanket – 220 sts. Knit 17 rows. BO loosely, leaving last st on needle. Do not cut yarn.

Left Border

Pu&k 9 sts on left edge of Top Border and 280 sts on left edge of blanket – 290 sts. Knit 17 rows. BO loosely, leaving last st on needle. Do not cut yarn.

Bottom Border

Pu&k 9 sts on bottom edge of left border, 210 sts on bottom edge of blanket, and 10 sts on bottom of Right Border – 230 sts. Knit 17 rows. BO loosely.

FINISHING

Weave in ends.

CORONADO

Hotel Del Coronado ("The Del") is a historic hotel in southern California.

SIZE 53 x 64.5"/135 x 164 cm

TECHNIQUES Pu&k, sewing

YARN Tahki Yarns Coronado, DK (90% cotton, 10% silk; 121 yds/111 m; 1.76 oz/50 g):

Pattern Color ID	Color Swatch	Color ID	Color Name	Color Description	# Balls
A		01	White	white	20
B		08	Hunter	forest green	9
C		07	Leaf	moss green	3
D		12	Teal	teal	3
E		14	Persimmon	pink-red	2
F		06	Straw	yellow	2
G		05	Plum	purple	2
H		15	Burgundy	maroon	3

NEEDLES US Size 5/3.75 mm or 6/4 mm 40"/100 cm circular needles or size needed to obtain gauge

NOTIONS Tapestry needle, 3 stitch markers, stitch holders or scrap yarn

GAUGE 21 sts x 42 rows = 4"/10 cm in garter st

NOTES

- The blanket is worked in Blocks that are sewn together.
- The Border is picked up and knit along the edges of the blanket.
- Long tails may be wound up and secured to the back of work until needed for seaming.

INSTRUCTIONS

Blocks - Make 80 [20 of each CS in Figure 3]

A Block consists of a diagonally striped Square with a 2-sided border, called a Frame.

Figure 1 specifies the color abbreviations for the diagonal stripes in a Square, and Figure 3 specifies yarn colors for Color Schemes (CS).

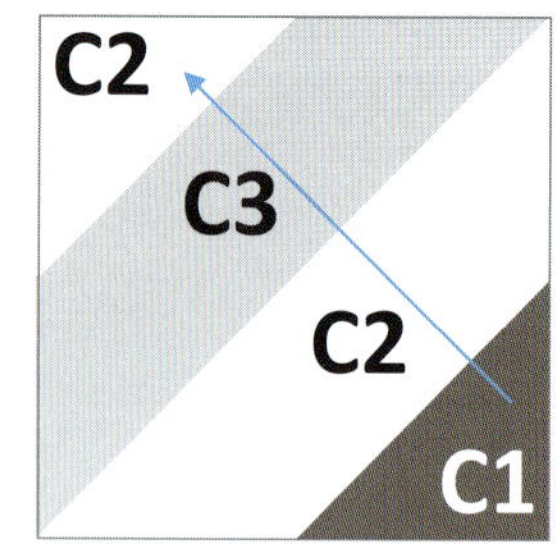

Figure 1: Color Abbreviations for Square

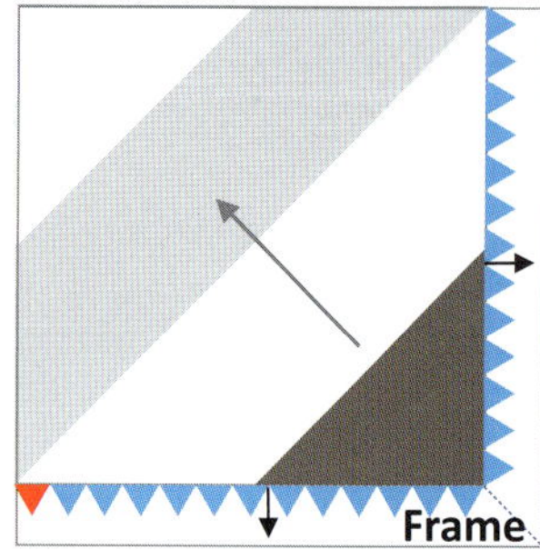

Figure 2: Frame for Block

Square

In C1 for Square, CO 1 st.

Work [Square].

Note: Cut yarns after completing each stripe.

Square – 1 st inc'ing to 41 sts dec'ing to 1 st

Note: Place m to identify RS after Row 2.
Row 1 (RS): (K1, yo, k1) in same st – 2 sts inc'd; 3 sts.
Row 2 (WS): Knit.
Row 3: Kf&b, knit to last st, kf&b – 2 sts inc'd; 5 sts.
Row 4: Knit.
Rows 5-20: Rep [Rows 3 & 4] 8 more times – 16 sts inc'd; 21 sts.
Cut C1. Attach C2.
Rows 21-40: Rep [Rows 3 & 4] 10 more times – 20 sts inc'd; 41 sts.
Cut C2. Attach C3.
Row 41: K2tog, knit to last 2 sts, ssk – 2 sts dec'd; 39 sts.
Row 42: Knit.
Rows 43-60: Rep [Rows 41 & 42] 9 more times – 18 sts dec'd; 21 sts.
Cut C3, leaving long tail of 15"/40 cm. Attach C2.
Rows 61-78: Rep [Rows 41 & 42] 9 more times – 18 sts dec'd; 3 sts.
Row 79: Cdd – 2 sts dec'd; 1 st.
Cut C2, leaving long tail of 15"/40 cm.

Frame

Attach A at bottom left corner of Square at the red triangle in Figure 2. Pu&k 29 sts to corner, pm, pu&k 29 sts to next corner – 58 sts.

Work [Frame]. BO loosely.

Frame (Fr) – 58 sts inc'ing to 62 sts

Row 2 (WS): Knit.
Row 3 (RS): Knit to 1 st bef m, kf&b, sm, kf&b, knit to end – 2 sts inc'd; 60 sts.
Row 4: Knit.
Row 5: Rep [Row 3] – 2 st inc'd; 62 sts.
Row 6: Knit.
BO loosely. Cut yarn, leaving 20"/50 cm tail.

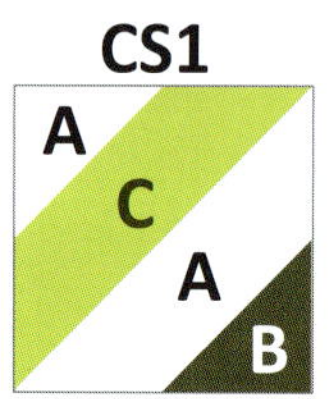

Figure 3: Color Schemes (CS) for Squares (make 20 in each of CS1-CS4)

Units - Make 20

Select 4 Blocks: One in each of CS1, CS2, CS3, and CS4. Orient Blocks as shown in Figure 4, with RS facing up. Using long tails of matching color, starting at the black dot and using mattress st, sew Blocks together along dashed red lines shown in Figure 4 to form horizontal strips, and then sew strips together along green dashed lines.

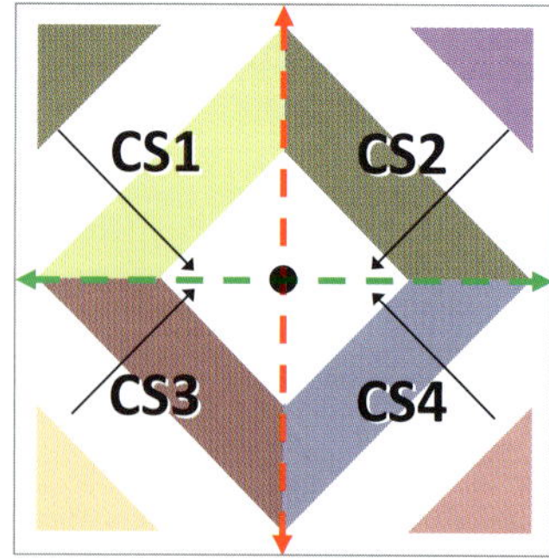

Figure 4: Assembly of Unit

Assembly of Units

Arrange Units as shown in Figure 5, with RS up, orienting top of each Unit toward the top of the blanket. Using tails of matching color and mattress st, sew tog Units into horizontal strips along red dashed lines, aligning corners and color changes, and then sew horizontal Strips together, aligning corners and color changes.

Figure 5: Assembly of Units

BORDERS

Inner Border

See Figure 7 on page 26 for construction.

Triangles

In each of the 18 spaces labeled "Tr," attach A to edge of blanket at location of blue triangle (11 sts to right of Block's vertical seam). Pu&k 11 sts (1 st per BO edge st) to seam, then 11 more sts (1 st per BO edge st) across BO sts to left of seam – 22 sts. See Figure 6 for details of construction. Work [Tr].

Triangle (Tr) – 22 sts dec'ing to 1 st

Row 2 (WS): K10, k2tog, knit to end – 1 st dec'd; 21 sts.
Row 3 (RS): K2tog, knit to last 2 sts, ssk – 2 sts dec'd; 19 sts.
Rows 4-19: Rep [Rows 2 & 3] 8 more times – 16 sts dec'd; 3 sts.
Row 20: Cdd – 2 sts dec'd; 1 st. Cut yarn and fasten off.

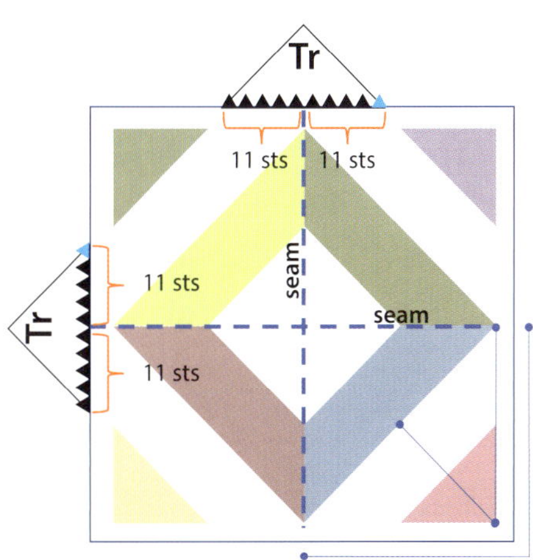

Figure 6: Details of Inner Border Construction

Wedges

At each space labeled "Wd," attach B at red triangle at tip of Tr. Pu&k 14 sts to corner, pm, pu&k 42 sts to next corner (1st per BO st), pm, pu&k 14 sts to next corner – 70 sts.

Work [Wedge]. Place rem 30 sts on holder.

Wedge – 70 sts dec'ing to 30 sts

Numbers in parentheses are st counts bet: (beg of row & 1st m – 1st & 2nd m – 2nd m and end).
Row 1 (WS): Knit (14–42–14).
Row 2 (RS): K2tog, knit to last 2 sts, ssk – 2 sts dec'd; 68 sts (13–42–13).
Row 3: Knit.
Row 4 (RS): *K2tog, knit to 2 sts bef m, ssk, sm; rep from * once more, k2tog, knit to last 2 sts, ssk – 6 sts dec'd; 62 sts (11–40–11).
Rows 5-16: Rep [Rows 1-4] 3 more times – 24 sts dec'd; 38 sts (2–34–2).
Row 17: Knit.
Row 18: Rm's. Cdd twice, knit to last 6 sts cdd twice – 8 sts dec'd; 30 sts.
Row 19: Knit.

Corners

At each of the 4 spaces labeled "Cr," attach B at red triangle at tip of Tr. Pu&k 14 sts to corner, pm (1st m), 22 sts to next corner, pm (2nd m), 22 sts to next corner, pm (3rd m), and 14 sts to next corner – 72 sts.

Work [Corner]. Place first 28 sts on a holder. Place rem 28 sts on second holder.

Corner (Cr) – 72 sts dec'ing to 56 sts

Numbers in parentheses are st counts bet: (beg of row & 1st m – 1st & 2nd m – 2nd & 3rd m – 3rd m & end).
Row 1 (WS): Knit (14–22–22–14).
Row 2 (RS): K2tog, knit to 1 st bef 2nd m, kf&b, sm, kf&b, knit to last 2 sts, ssk (13–23–23–13).
Row 3: Knit.
Row 4: K2tog, knit to 2 sts bef 1st m, ssk, sm, k2tog, knit to 1 st bef 2nd m, kf&b, sm, kf&b, knit to 2 sts bef 3rd m, ssk, sm, k2tog, knit to last 2 sts, ssk – 4 sts dec'd; 68 sts (11–23–23–11).
Rows 5-16: Rep [Rows 1-4] 3 more times – 12 sts dec'd; 56 sts (2–26–26–2). Rm's.
Rows 17-18: Rep [Rows 1 & 2] once more – 56 sts (1–27–27–1).
Row 19: Knit.

Outer Border

Right Border – 331 sts inc'ing to 341 sts

See Figure 8. Beg at bottom right corner. With A, knit 28 sts off bottom right holder.

*Pu&k 31 sts on edge to next holder, knit 30 sts off holder. *

Rep bet * and * 3 more times, pu&k 31 sts on edge to last holder, knit 28 sts from last holder – 331 sts.

Row 2 (WS): Knit.
Row 3 (RS): Kf&b, knit to last st, kf&b – 2 sts inc'd.
Row 4: Knit.
Rows 5-12: Rep [Rows 3 & 4] 4 more times – 8 sts inc'd.
BO loosely. Cut yarn, leaving 12"/30 cm tail.

Left Border – 331 sts inc'ing to 341 sts

Attach A at top left corner of blanket and work as for Right Border.

Top Border – 270 sts inc'ing to 280 sts

Attach A at top-right corner of blanket and work as for Right Border, making 3 total reps bet * and *.

Bottom Border – 270 sts inc'ing to 280 sts

Attach A at bottom left corner of blanket and work as for Top Border.

Corner Seams

Using long BO tail from Border, and mattress st, sew together diagonal seams at blanket corners.

FINISHING

Weave in ends.

Figure 7: Inner Border Construction

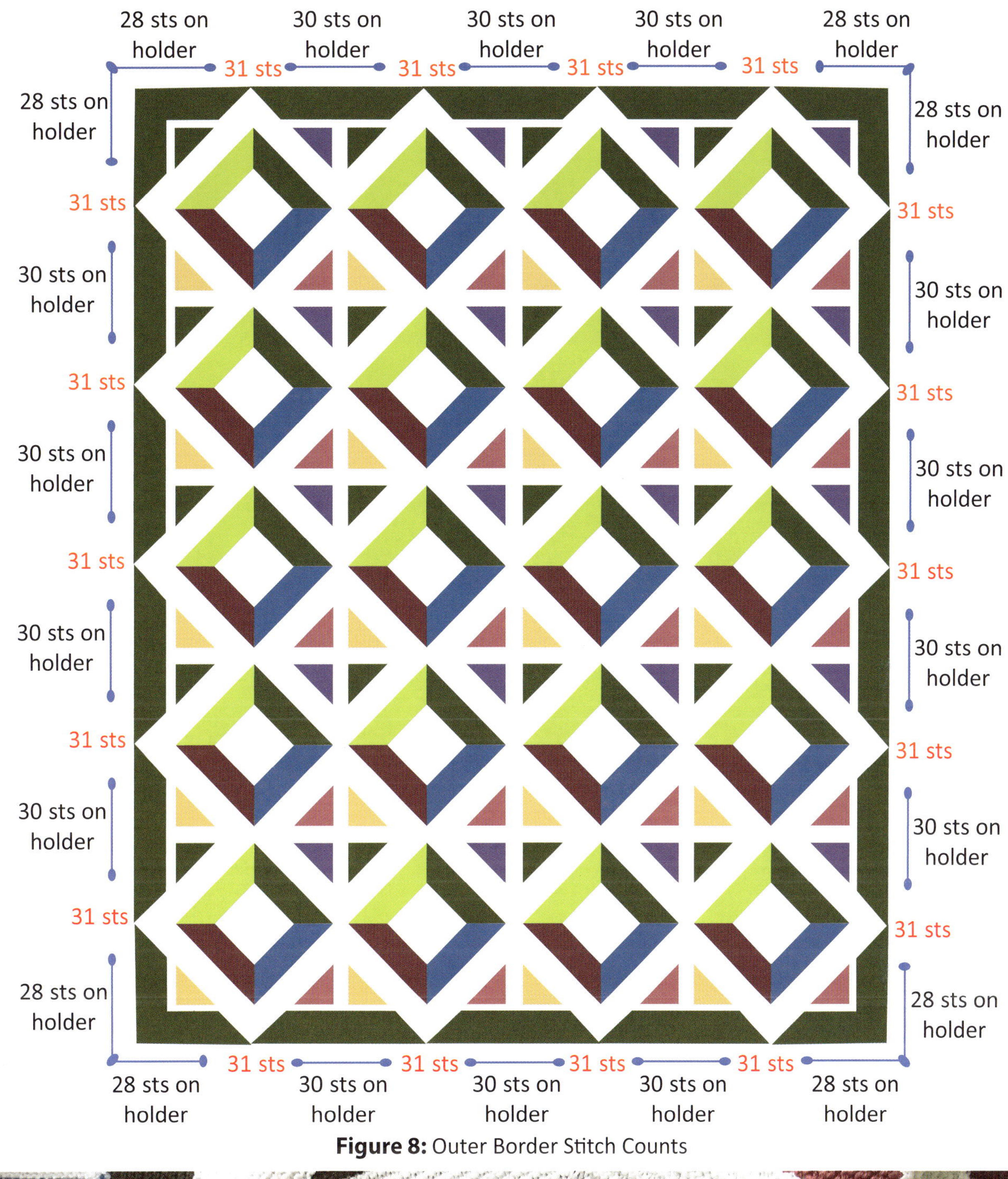

Figure 8: Outer Border Stitch Counts

CURRENTS

Swirling eddies of color flow through this blanket of blues, aquas, and a touch of green.

SIZE 51 x 63"/130 x 160 cm

TECHNIQUES Intarsia, pu&k, sewing

YARN Valley Yarns Valley Superwash, worsted (100% extrafine superwash merino wool; 97 yds/89 m; 1.75 oz/50 g):

Pattern Color ID	Color Swatch	Color ID	Color Name	Color Description	# Balls
A		260	White	white	13
B		502	Blue	medium blue	5
C		305	Blue Mood	dark blue	7
D		694	Spring Leaf	yellow-green	5
E		303	Daquiri Ice	mint green	5
F		522	Teal	medium teal	5
G		600	Forest	dark green	5

NEEDLES US Size 7/4.5 mm 40"/100 cm circular needles or size needed to obtain gauge

NOTIONS Tapestry needle, yarn bobbins (optional), stitch markers or safety pins (optional)

GAUGE 20 sts and 40 rows = 4"/10 cm in garter st

NOTES

The blanket is worked in vertical Strips of garter stitch intarsia that are then sewn together. The Borders are picked up and knit (pu&k) on the edges of the completed blanket.

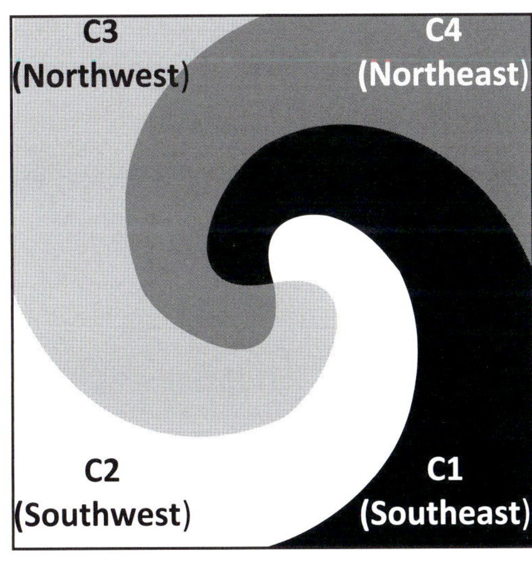

Figure 1: Color Areas and Abbreviations

Figure 2: Color Schemes for Blocks

BLANKET INSTRUCTIONS

Strips 1-8

Vertical Strips are composed of 10 Blocks each, worked continuously. Blocks are named by their Color Scheme (CS) in Figure 2 on page 29, specified as a sequence of four colors, C1-C4, as defined in the "Yarn" table.

For areas A2, A4, and A6 (Table to the right), if desired, cut lengths of yarn specified in Table and wind onto bobbins. Yarn amounts are estimates and should be adjusted after working the first Block. The other areas, which require more yarn, should be worked from the skein. Untangle yarns as needed or at the beginning of each row. Colors A1-A8 refer to the areas of the chart in Figure 3.

Using colors specified for Block 1 of the Strip in Figure 4 on page 32, with C2, CO 15 sts, with C1, CO 15 sts. Work [Rows 1-60] of Color Chart (Figure 3) 10 times, following Block CS sequence in Figure 4. Do not BO or cut yarn between reps. After final repeat, BO all sts.

Table Yardage and Colors for Block Areas

Color	C1		C2		C3		C4	
Area from Figure 3	A1	A2	A3	A4*	A5	A6**	A7	A8**
Yards	12	1	11	3	12	1	5	8
Meters	11	1	10	3	11	1	4.5	7.5

Note: As the Strip gets longer, it may be rolled up and secured with stitch markers or safety pins to keep the Strip from being unwieldy.

**Note:* When dropping A4 after Row 30, do not cut excess yarn; wind it up and secure to the edge of the Strip using a safety pin or stitch marker for later use sewing seams.

***Note:* To minimize ends to weave in, do not cut yarn after A6 and A8 because they are used as A3 and A1, respectively, on the next Block.

To open the digital version of this Color Chart, use the password: Iksndsnthhrglss2

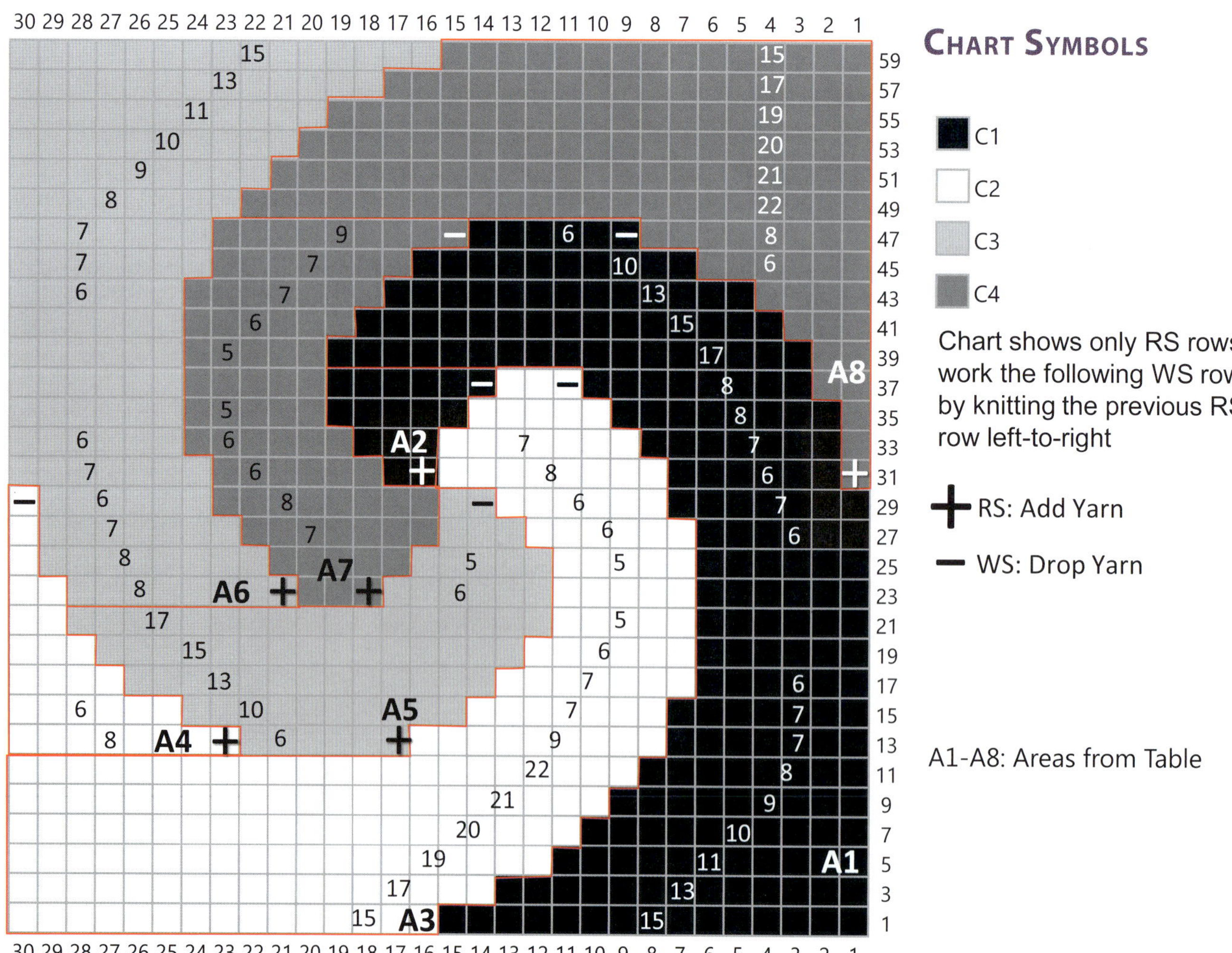

Figure 3: Color Chart for Block

Figure 4: Color Schemes (CS) and Strip Layout

ASSEMBLY

Arrange Strips as shown in Figure 4. Using mattress st and long tails of A4's, sew Strips together, aligning start and end of Blocks and color changes at the middle of each Block.

BORDERS

Right Border

On RS, attach C at bottom right corner of blanket. Pu&k 30 sts per Block (1 st per garter st ridge) on right edge of blanket – 300 sts.

Row 2 (WS): Knit.

Row 3 (RS): Kf&b, knit to last st, kf&b – 2 sts inc'd; 302 sts.

Row 4: Knit.

Rows 5 & 6: Rep [Rows 3 & 4] – 2 sts inc'd; 304 sts.

Cut C, leaving 8"/20 cm tail. Attach A.

Rows 7-16: Rep [Rows 3 & 4] 5 times – 10 sts inc'd; 314 sts.

BO loosely. Cut yarn, leaving 10"/25 cm tail.

Left Border

Rep as for Right Border, attaching yarn at top left corner of blanket.

Top Border

On RS, attach C at top right corner of blanket. Pu&k 30 sts per Block (one per BO st) on top edge of blanket – 240 sts.

Work as for Right Border, ending with 254 sts.

Bottom Border

Rep as for Top Border, attaching yarn at bottom left corner of blanket.

Using long tails of matching color and whip st, sew border corners.

FINISHING

Weave in ends. Block if desired.

FELICITY

Surround yourself with color with this easy blanket of squares.

Size 58 x 58"/147 x 147 cm

Techniques Pu&k, sewing

Yarn Cascade Yarns 220 Superwash, worsted (100% superwash wool; 220 yds/200 m; 3.5 oz/100 g):

Pattern Color ID	Color Swatch	Color ID	Color Name	Color Description	# Balls
A		817	Ecru	off-white	2
B		820	Lemon	light yellow	3
C		263	Gold Fusion	bright gold	3
D		826	Tangerine	yellow-orange	2
E		907	Tangerine Heather	orange	3
F		290	Chrysanthemum	pink-red	4
G		879	Very Berry	deep magenta	4
H		1944	Westpoint Blue Heather	faded denim blue	1
I		811	Como Blue	deep turquoise	1
J		849	Dark Aqua	aqua	3
K		250	Laurel Green	pale yellow-green	3

Needles US Size 7/4.5 mm 40"/100 cm circular needles or size needed to obtain gauge

Notions Tapestry needle, stitch markers

Gauge 18 sts x 36 rows = 4"/10 cm in garter st

Notes

- The blanket is worked in Blocks, Edge Blocks, and Corners that are sewn together. Borders are added by picking up and knitting on the edge of the blanket.
- Pattern instructions use pick up and knit (pu&k) to generate stitches for Squares and Triangles. However, on shapes where pu&k will occur later on the edge, a provisional CO may be used.
- All pu&k is performed on the RS.
- When cutting yarn at color changes, leave a 12"/30 cm tail for sewing seams.
- Assemble the blanket before weaving in any yarn ends.

BLANKET INSTRUCTIONS

Blocks

A Block consists of 4 Squares (S1-S4) worked in C1, C2, and C3 as shown in Figure 1.

Make Blocks in Color Schemes and Quantities specified in Figure 2.

Square 1 (S1)

In C1, CO 16 sts, pm, CO 15 sts – 31 sts. Work [MS], described below.

Square 2 (S2)

On RS, with C1, starting at green triangle between S1 and S2 in Figure 2, pu&k 15 sts (one per CO st of S1) to next corner, pu&k 1 st corner, pm, CO 15 sts – 31 sts. Work [MS].

Square 3 (S3)

Work as for Square 2, starting the pu&k at green triangle between S2 and S3 in Figure 2.

Square 4 (S4)

On RS, with C1, starting at green triangle between S3 and S4 in Figure 2, pu&k 15 sts to corner, 1 st in corner of S2, pm, and 15 sts on edge of S1 to next corner – 31 sts. Work [MS].

Mitered Square (MS) – 31 sts dec'ing to 1 st

Row 2 (WS): With C1, knit.
Row 3: Knit to 2 sts bef m, rm, cdd, pm, knit to end – 2 sts dec'd; 29 sts.
Row 4: Knit.
Rows 5-10: Rep [Rows 3 & 4] 3 times – 6 sts dec'd; 23 sts.
Cut C1. Attach C2.
Rows 11-20: Rep [Rows 3 & 4] 5 times – 10 sts dec'd; 13 sts.
Cut C2. Attach C3.
Rows 21-30: Rep [Rows 3 & 4] 5 times – 10 sts dec'd; 3 sts.
Row 31: Cdd – 2 sts dec'd; 1 st. Cut C3.

Edge Blocks

An Edge Block consists of a Square (S1) and two triangles (T1 and T2). Triangles are worked in C1, C2, and C3 as shown in Figure 3. Make 20 Edge Blocks in colors and quantities shown in Figure 4.

Square 1 (S1)

In C1, CO 16 sts, pm, CO 15 sts – 31 sts. Work [MS].

Triangle 1 (T1)

On RS, with C1, pu&k 16 sts from green triangle on edge of S1 in Figure 4 to end of edge. Work [T1].

Triangle 1 (T1) – 16 sts dec'ing to 1 st

Row 2 (WS): With C1, knit.
Row 3: K2tog, knit to end – 1 st dec'd; 15 sts.
Row 4: Knit.
Rows 5-10: Rep [Rows 2 & 3] 3 times – 3 sts dec'd; 12 sts.
Cut C1. Attach C2.
Rows 11-20: Rep [Rows 2 & 3] 5 times – 5 sts dec'd; 7 sts.
Cut C2. Attach C3.
Rows 21-30: Rep [Rows 2 & 3] 5 times – 5 sts dec'd; 2 sts.
Row 31: K2tog – 1 st dec'd; 1 st. Cut C3.

Triangle 2 (T2)

On RS, with C1, pu&k 16 sts from purple triangle on edge of S1 in Figure 4 to next corner. Work [T2].

Triangle 2 (T2) – 16 sts dec'ing to 1 st

Work as for T1, replacing Row 3 with:
Row 3: Knit to last 2 sts, ssk – 1 st dec'd.

Corners

A Corner consists of a Triangle 1 and a Triangle 2 (T1 & T2). Make 4 Corners in colors shown in Figure 5.

Triangle 1 (T1)

With C1, CO 16 sts. Work [T1].

Triangle 2 (T2)

On RS, with C1, pu&k 16 sts from green triangle on edge of T1 in Figure 5 to next corner. Work [T2].

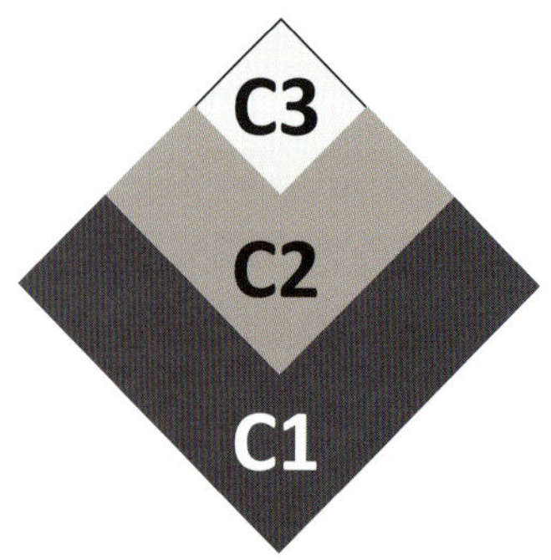

Figure 1: Color Identification for Square

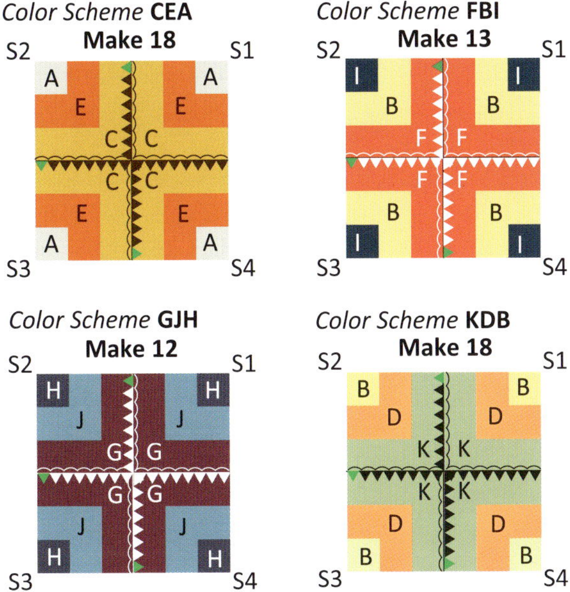

Figure 2: Block: Color Schemes, Quantities, and Construction

Triangle 1 (T1)

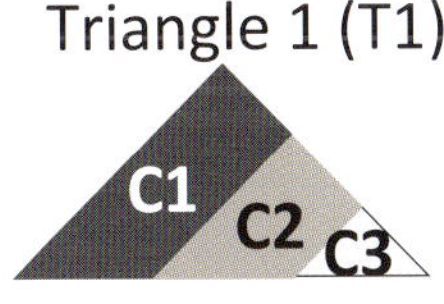

Triangle 2 (T2)

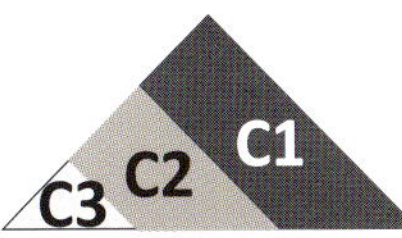

Figure 3: Triangles, T1 and T2: Color Identification

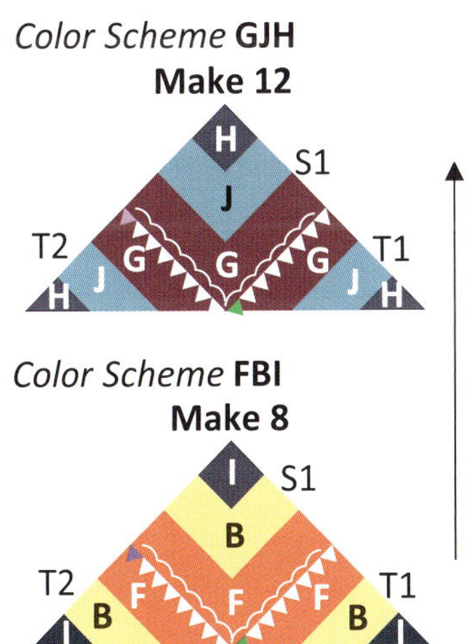

Figure 4: Edge Block: Color Schemes, Quantities, and Construction

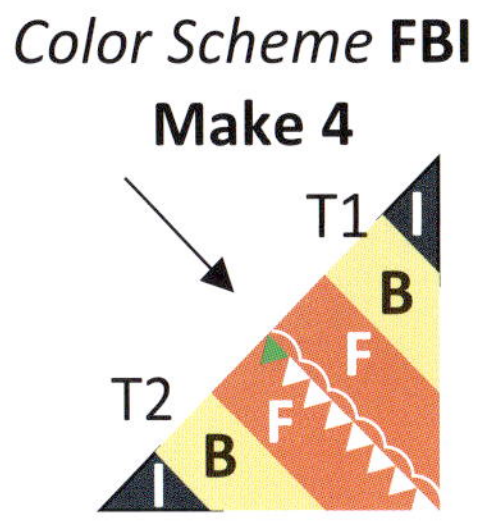

Figure 5: Corner: Color Schemes, Quantities, and Construction

ASSEMBLY

Lay out completed Blocks, Edge Blocks, and Corners as shown in Figure 6 on page 38, orienting Edge Blocks and Corners according to directional arrows. With long tails and mattress st, sew adjacent shapes tog along red dashed lines to form diagonal strips, aligning color transitions and corners, and then sew strips tog along green dashed lines.

BORDERS

When cutting yarn colors off, leave 12"/30 cm tail.

Right Border

Starting at bottom right corner of blanket, with A, pu&k 252 sts (7 per stripe, 21 per Triangle).

Row 2 (WS): Knit.
Row 3 (RS): Kf&b, knit to last st, kf&b – 2 sts inc'd; 254 sts.
Row 4: Knit.
Cut A. Attach J.
Rows 5-8: With J, rep [Rows 3 & 4] twice – 4 sts inc'd; 258 sts.
Cut J. Attach E.
Rows 9-12: With E, rep [Rows 3 & 4] twice – 4 sts inc'd; 262 sts.
Cut E. Attach G.
Rows 13-16: With G, rep [Rows 3 & 4] twice – 4 sts inc'd; 266 sts. BO loosely.
Cut E.

Top, Left, and Bottom Borders

Rep as for Right Border, attaching yarn at top right, top left, and bottom left corners, respectively.

With long tails of matching color and mattress st, sew tog the 4 corner diagonal corner seams.

FINISHING

Weave in ends.

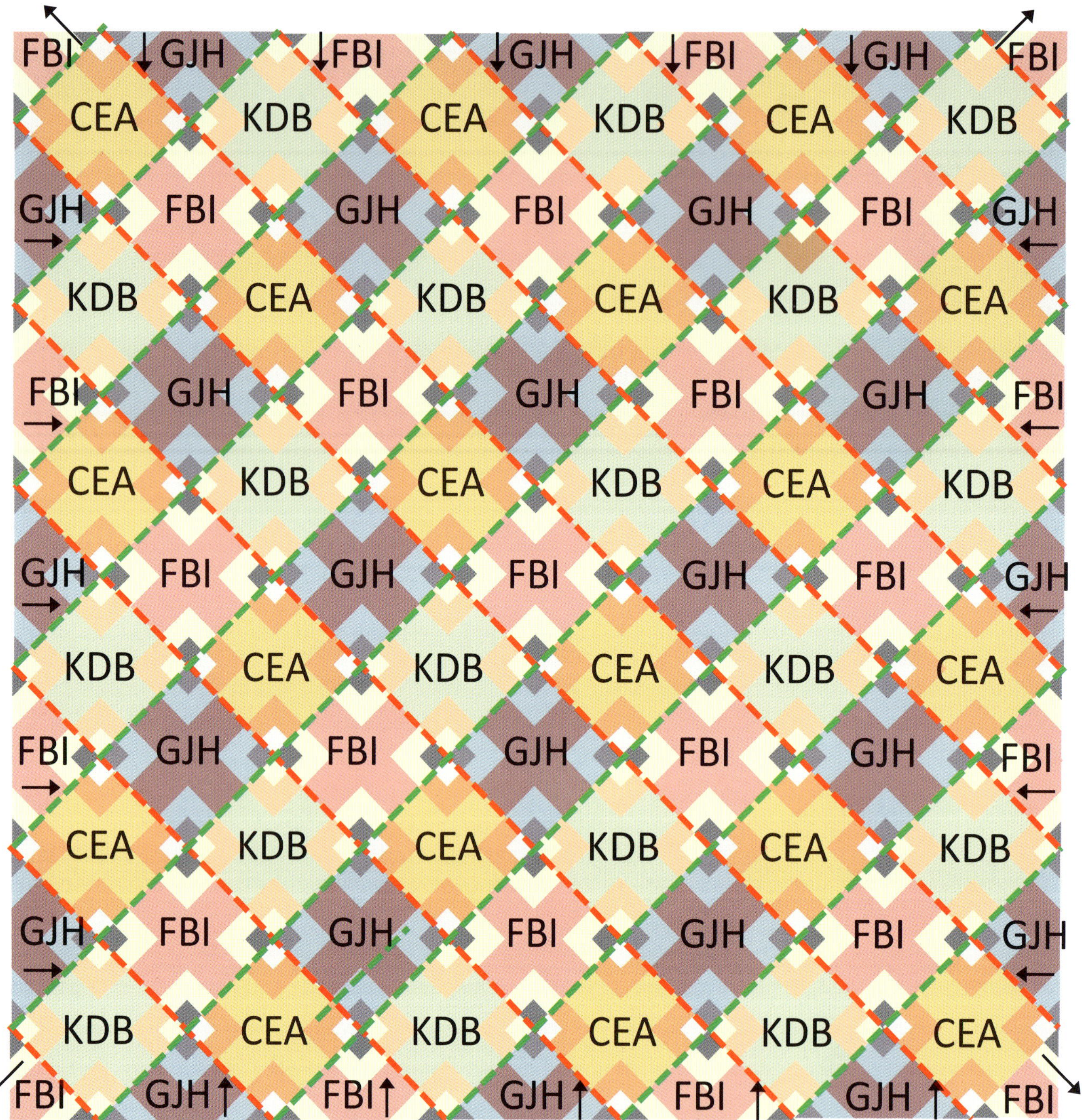

Figure 6: Assembly

HEARTSTRINGS

Nothing says "I love you" like this warm blanket of hearts.

SIZE 53.5 x 63"/136 x 160 cm

TECHNIQUES Pu&k

YARN Rowan Pure Wool Superwash Worsted, worsted (100% superwash wool; 219 yds/200 m; 3.5 oz/100 g):

Pattern Color ID	Color Swatch	Color ID	Color Name	Color Description	# Skeins
A		102	Soft Cream	off-white	4
B		149	Navy	dark blue	5
C		189	Windsor	dark red	2
D		197	Teal	dark teal	1
E		188	Toffee	dark brown	1
F		198	Eggplant	dark purple	1
G		200	Verdant	dark green	1
H		194	Sky	light blue	2
I		191	Mauve Mist	light mauve	2
J		192	Mineral	medium blue	1
K		133	Gold	gold	2
L		125	Olive	yellow-green	1
M		195	Rose	pink	2

NEEDLES US Size 7/4.5 mm 40"/100 cm circular needles or size needed to obtain gauge

NOTIONS Tapestry needle, stitch markers, stitch holders

GAUGE 20 sts and 40 rows = 4"/10 cm in garter st

NOTES

- The blanket is constructed modularly (no sewing). A Foundation is created from Twin Peaks and Corner shapes. When each Foundation shape is complete, its stitches are placed on holders.
- Starting from the Foundation and using a combination of pick up and knit (pu&k), knitting stitches from holders, and CO, 33 layers of hearts—alternating between 5 and 4 hearts per layer—are added in a color scheme that repeats over 6 layers. Edge shapes are picked up and knitted from the completed blanket face, and then the Borders are picked up from the edge pieces.
- For pu&k, pick up and knit 1 st per CO/BO stitch, or 1 st per garter stitch "bump" (per 2 rows of knitting).

BLANKET INSTRUCTIONS

Foundation

Twin Peaks (TP) – Make 4

With B, CO 1 st.

Row 1 (RS): Kf&b – 1 st inc'd; 2 sts. Pm between sts.
Row 2 (WS): Kf&b twice – 2 sts inc'd; 4 sts.
Row 3: Kf&b, knit to 1 st bef m, kf&b, sm, kf&b, knit to last st, kf&b – 4 sts inc'd; 8 sts.
Row 4: Knit.
Rows 5-12: Rep [Rows 3 & 4] 4 times – 16 sts inc'd; 24 sts.
Row 13: Kf&b, knit to m – 13 sts. Rm. Place rem 12 unworked sts on holder.
Note: Sts on this holder are bet ***a*** and ***b*** in Figure 1.
Row 14: Knit.
Row 15: Kf&b, knit to end – 1 st inc'd; 14 sts.
Row 16: Knit.
Rows 17-36: Rep [Rows 15 & 16] 10 times – 10 sts inc'd; 24 sts. Cut yarn. Place sts on holder.
Note: Sts on this holder are bet ***c*** and ***d*** in Figure 1.
Transfer 12 sts from holder bet ***a*** and ***b*** to needle. Turn to RS, attach B.
Row 13 (RS): Knit to last st, kf&b – 1 st inc'd; 13 sts.
Row 14: Knit.
Rows 15-36: Rep [Rows 13 & 14] 11 times – 11 sts inc'd; 24 sts. Place sts on holder.
Note: Sts on this holder are bet ***e*** and ***f*** in Figure 1.

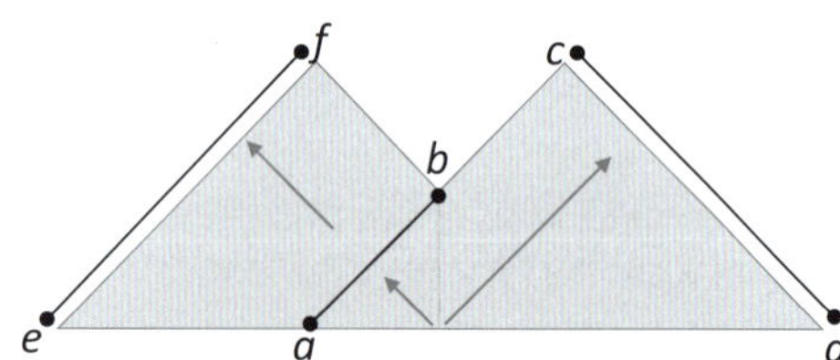

Figure 1: Twin Peaks Construction

Corners (CR) – Make 2

With B, CO 1 st.

Row 1 (RS): Kf&b – 1 st inc'd; 2 sts.
Row 2 (WS): Knit.
Row 3: Kf&b, knit to last st, kf&b – 2 sts inc'd; 4 sts.
Row 4: Knit.
Rows 5-24: Rep [Rows 3 & 4] 10 times – 20 sts inc'd; 24 sts. Place sts on holder.

Figure 2: Corner Construction

Arrange Foundation pieces as shown at the top of Figure 4, orienting shapes according to arrows.

Heart Layers

There are 33 heart layers, as shown in Figure 7 on page 45. Odd-numbered layers have 5 Hearts and even-numbered layers have 4 Hearts. Hearts are worked using 3 colors, C1, C2, and color A.

In Figures 4 and 7, each Heart is labeled with 2 colors as follows: [C1-C2] where C1 is the outer color and C2 is the middle color. The center color is always color A and is therefore omitted.

Stitches for each Heart are generated by knitting stitches from holder, pu&k, CO, or a combination of these. Markers placed during stitch generation identify the location of decreases and to split the stitches into 4 "Stitch Generation" groups as shown in Figure 3. Each group of stitches may have a different stitch generation method. Symbols (defined on page vi) indicate the method to use for generating each group of stitches.

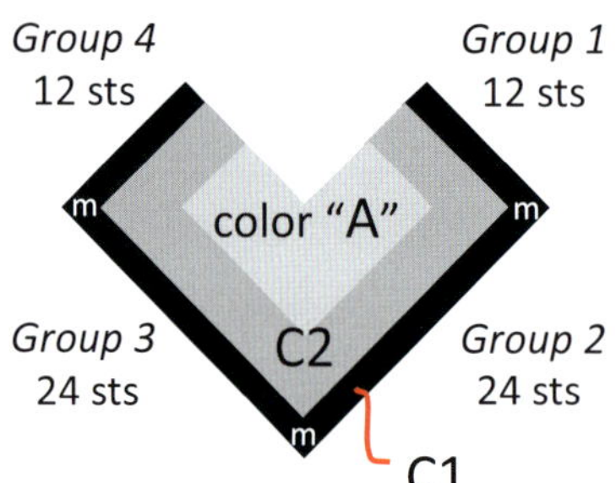

Figure 3: Stitch Generation Groups

Layer 1

See Figure 4, Layer 1, for colors and techniques for generating stitches.

In each of the 5 heart-shaped spaces shown for Layer 1, using the stitch generating method indicated in Figure 4, generate 12 sts (Group 1), pm, 24 sts (Group 2), pm, 24 sts (Group 3), pm, 12 sts (Group 4) – 72 sts.

Work [Ht].

Heart (Ht) – 72 sts dec'ing to 2 sts

Row 2 (WS): Knit.
Row 3 (RS): (Knit to 2 sts bef next m, ssk, k2tog) 3 times, knit to end – 6 sts dec'd; 66 sts.
Row 4 (WS): Knit.
Cut C1. Attach C2.
Rows 5-12: Rep [Rows 3 & 4] 4 times – 24 sts dec'd; 42 sts.
Cut C2. Attach color A.
Rows 13-24: Rep [Rows 3 & 4] 6 times – 36 sts dec'd; 6 sts. Rm's.
Row 25: Cdd, twice – 4 sts dec'd; 2 sts.
Slip right st over left st. Cut yarn and fasten off.

Layer 2

See Figure 4, Layer 2, for colors and techniques for generating stitches.

In each of the 4 heart-shaped spaces shown for Layer 2, using the stitch generating method indicated in Figure 4, generate 12 sts (Group 1), pm, 24 sts (Group 2), pm, 24 sts (Group 3), pm, 12 sts (Group 4) – 72 sts.

Work [Ht].

Figure 4: Foundation, and Layers 1 and 2

Layers 3-33

Notes:

- See Figures 5 and 6 for construction and techniques for generating stitches.
- When working these Layers, Group 2 and Group 3 sts are generated by picking up 12 stitches from the Layer directly below (labeled "-1" in Figure 5) and 12 stitches from the Layer that is two levels below (labeled "-2" in Figure 5).
- The colors used in Layers 1-6 are repeated over Layers 7-12, 13-18, 19-24, and 25-30. The colors used in Layers 1-3 are repeated over Layers 31-33.

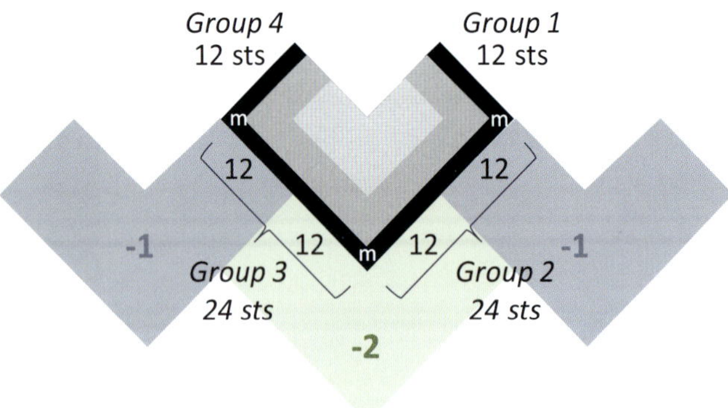

Figure 5: Groups and Stitch Counts for Hearts in Layers 3-33

Odd Layers 3-33

In each of the 5 heart-shaped spaces shown in Figure 6, Odd-Numbered Layers using the stitch generating method indicated by symbols, generate 12 sts (Group 1), pm, 24 sts (Group 2), pm, 24 sts (Group 3), pm, 12 sts (Group 4) – 72 sts.

Work [Ht] (page 42).

Even Layers 4-32

Work as for Layer 3, in each of the 4 heart-shaped spaces shown in Figure 6, Even-Numbered Layers.

Edge Shapes

Small Triangles (ST)

On edges of blanket, in each space labeled "ST" in Figure 7, attach B at red triangle and pu&k 12 sts to corner, pm, and 12 sts to next corner – 24 sts.

Work [MT].

Mitered Triangle (MT)

Row 2 (WS): Knit.
Row 3 (RS): K2tog, knit to 2 sts bef m, ssk, k2tog, knit to last 2 sts, ssk – 4 sts dec'd.
Row 4: Knit.
Rep [Rows 3 & 4] until 4 sts rem.
Next row (RS): Slip next 2 sts to R needle, rm, k2tog, p2sso – 3 sts dec'd; 1 st.
Cut yarn and fasten off.

Large Triangles (LT)

On RS, in each of the 4 spaces labeled "LT" in Figure 7, attach B at the yellow triangle, pu&k 24 sts to corner, pm, and 24 sts to next corner – 48 sts.

Work [MT].

Corners (CT)

On RS, in the two spaces labeled "CT" in Figure 7, at top right and top left corners, attach B at red triangle, and pu&k 12 sts to next corner.

Work [Tr].

Triangle (Tr) – 12 sts dec'ing to 1 st

Row 2 (WS): Knit.
Row 3 (RS): K2tog, knit to last 2 sts, ssk – 2 sts dec'd.
Rep [Rows 2 & 3] until 2 sts rem, ending after a RS row.
Next row (WS): K2tog – 1 st dec'd; 1 st.
Cut yarn and fasten off.

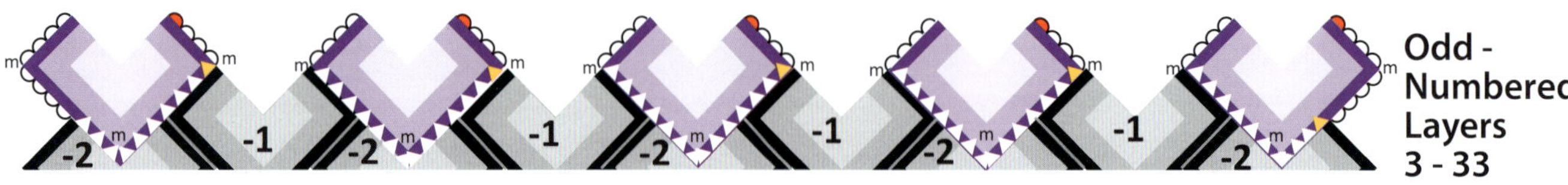

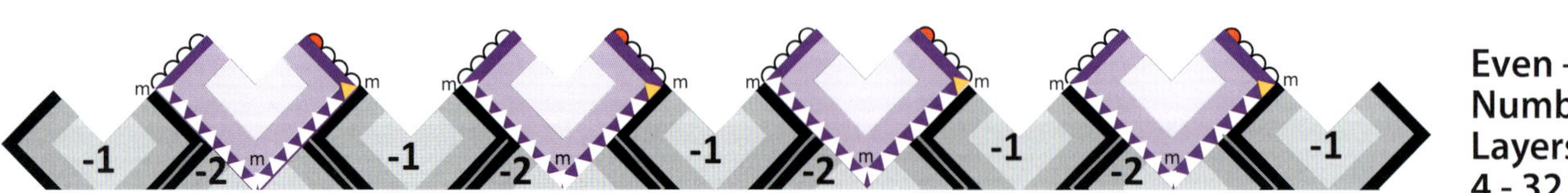

Figure 6: Odd and Even Layer Constructions

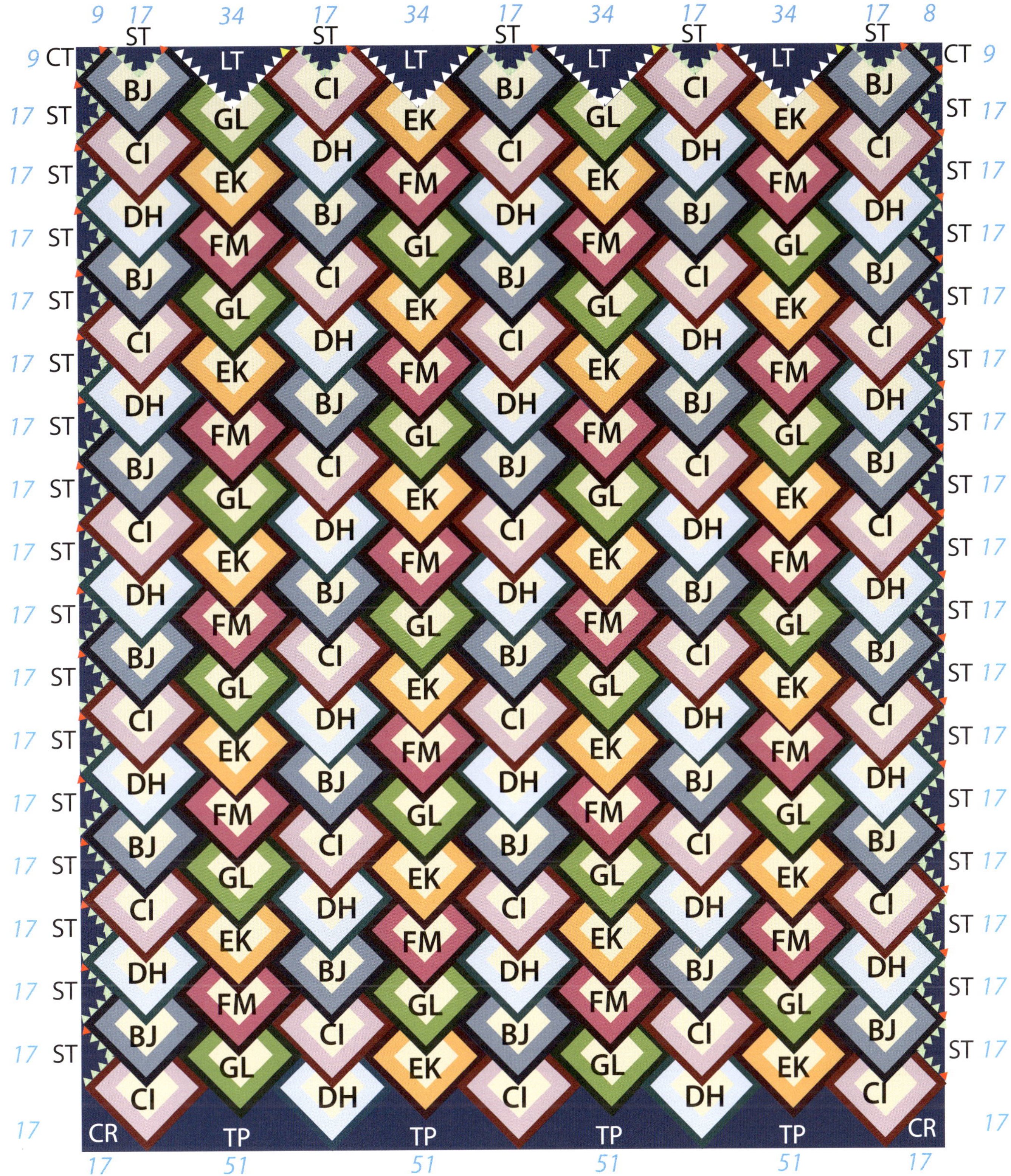

Figure 7: Colors for Hearts, Edge Shapes Construction, and St Counts for Edge Shapes

BORDERS

See Figure 7 on page 45 for pu&k stitch counts per edge shape.

Right Border

On RS, attach B at bottom right corner of blanket. Pu&k 298 on right edge of blanket.

Knit 15 rows. BO loosely, leaving last st on needle, and do not cut yarn.

Top Border

On RS, pu&k 8 sts on edge of Right Border and 238 sts on top edge of blanket – 247 sts.

Knit 15 rows. BO loosely, leaving last st on needle.

Left Border

On RS, pu&k 8 sts on left edge of Top Border and 298 sts on left edge of blanket – 307 sts.

Knit 15 rows. BO loosely, leaving last st on needle.

Bottom Border

On RS, pu&k 8 sts on bottom edge of Left Border, 238 sts on bottom edge of blanket, and 9 sts on bottom of Right Border – 256 sts.

Knit 15 rows. BO loosely. Cut yarn and fasten off.

FINISHING

Weave in ends.

Chart for Twin Peaks

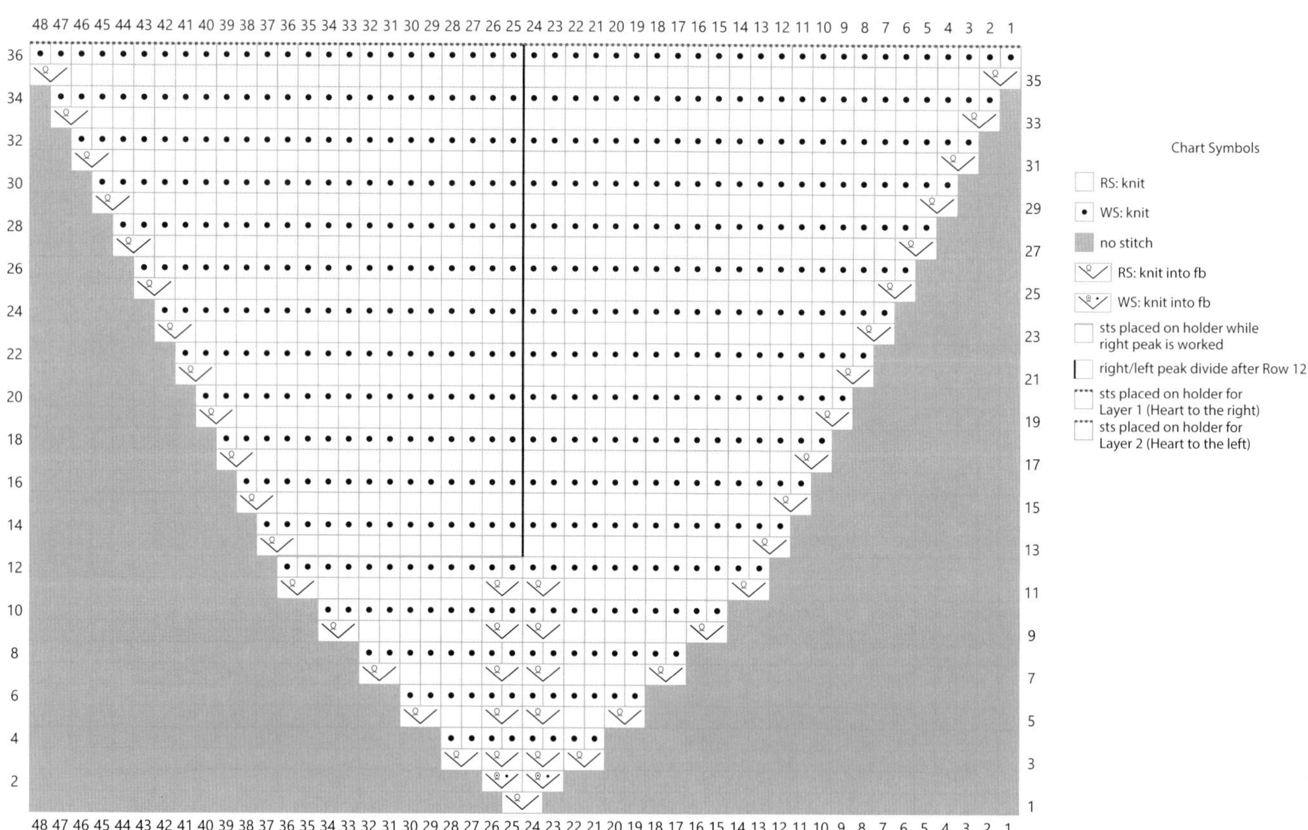

HIGH RISE

Abstract buildings arch into the sky in this blanket for our modern times.

SIZE 56.5 x 68"/144 x 173 cm

TECHNIQUES 3-needle BO, pu&k

YARN Knitpicks Wool of the Andes Tweed, worsted (100% wool, 110 yds/100 m; 1.75 oz/50 g):

Pattern Color ID	Color Swatch	Color ID	Color Name	Color Description	# Skeins
A		25970	Oyster Heather	ecru	17
B		25459	Farmhouse Heather	dark brown	6
C		28308	Sarsaparilla Heather	medium brown	5
D		28307	Olive Heather	gold-olive	5
E		25449	Marine Heather	teal	5
F		25964	North Pole Heather	light teal	4

NEEDLES [2] US Size 7/4.5 mm 40"/100 cm circular needles or size needed to obtain gauge, [1] US Size 10/6 mm straight needle for 3-needle BO

NOTIONS Stitch markers, tapestry needle

GAUGE 18 sts x 36 rows = 4"/10 cm in garter st

NOTES

- The blanket is worked in vertical Strips.
- A Strip starts with a checkerboard "Ric Rac."
- Mitered Squares and Triangles are added to a Ric Rac.
- Strips are widened by picking up and knitting (pu&k) on edges and working "Zigzags" in the background color.
- Adjacent Strips are joined with a 3-needle BO.
- Borders are worked by pu&k on edges of blanket.

BLANKET INSTRUCTIONS

Strip - Make 7 (4 odd, 3 even)

See Figure 1 for construction of Ric Racs.

Note : Do not cut MC or C1 between uses. Drape yarn to next use, and weave in during subsequent pu&k on edge (see "Tacking Draped Yarn" on page 210).

Odd Ric Racs (OR)

Make 4 ORs in these color combinations:

- For Strips 1 & 5: 2 ORs with color D for MC and color B for C1
- For Strips 3 & 7: 2 ORs with color B for MC and color E for C1

working a BT1, 5 Elbows, and a Half Elbow as follows:

BT1

With MC, CO 1. Work [BT1].

Elbow 1

Attach C1. *(With C1, knit 12 rows, with MC, knit 12 rows) twice, with C1, knit 12 rows*.
With MC, work [RT].
Rep bet * and * once more.
With MC, work [LT].

Elbows 2-5

Rep [Elbow 1] 4 more times.

Half Elbow

Rep bet * and *. With MC, work [TT]. Cut yarns.

Even Ric Racs (ER)

Make 3 ER in these color combinations:

- For Strips 2 & 6: 2 ERs with color E for MC and color D for C1
- For Strip 4: 1 ER with color E for MC and color C for C1

working a Quarter Elbow Right, 5 Elbows, and a Quarter Elbow Left as follows:

Quarter Elbow Right

With MC, CO 1. Work [BT2].
Attach C1; knit 12 rows.
With MC, knit 12 rows.
With C1, work [LT].

Elbow 1

(With MC, knit 12 rows, with C1, knit 12 rows) twice, with MC, knit 12 rows.
With C1, work [RT].
Rep bet * and * once more.
With C1, work [LT].

Elbows 2-5

Rep [Elbow 1] 4 more times.

Quarter Elbow Left

With MC, knit 12 rows; with C1, knit 12 rows. With MC, work [TT]. Cut yarns.

Bottom Triangle 1 (BT1) – 1 st inc'ing to 6 sts

Row 1 (RS): Knit to last st, kf&b – 1 st inc'd; 2 sts.
Row 2 and all even-numbered (WS) rows to 10: Knit.
Rows 3, 5, 7, and 9: Rep [Row 1] – 4 sts inc'd; 6 sts.

Right Turning square (RT) – 6 sts

Row 1 and all odd-numbered (RS) rows to 19: Knit.
Row 2 (WS): K5, w&t.
Row 4: K4, w&t.
Row 6: K3, w&t.
Row 8: K2, w&t.
Row 10: K1, w&t.
Rows 12, 14, 16, 18, and 20: Work even-numbered Rows 2-10 in reverse order, starting with Row 10.

Left Turning square (LT) – 6 sts

Row 1 (RS): K5, w&t.
Row 2 and all even-numbered (WS) rows to 20: Knit.
Row 3: K4, w&t.
Row 5: K3, w&t.
Row 7: K2, w&t.
Row 9: K1, w&t.
Rows 11, 13, 15, 17, and 19: Work odd-numbered Rows 1-9 in reverse order, starting with Row 9.

Top Triangle (TT) – 6 sts dec'ing to 1 st

Rows 1 (RS) & 2 (WS): Knit.
Row 3: K2tog, knit to end – 1 st dec'd; 5 sts.
Row 4 and all even-numbered (WS) rows to 10: Knit.
Rows 5, 7, 9, and 11: Rep [Row 3] – 4 sts dec'd; 1 st.

Bottom Triangle 2 (BT2) – 1 st inc'ing to 6 sts

Row 1 (RS): Kf&b, knit to end – 1 st inc'd; 2 sts.
Row 2 and all even-numbered (WS) rows to 10: Knit.
Rows 3, 5, 7, and 9: Rep [Row 1] – 4 sts inc'd; 6 sts.

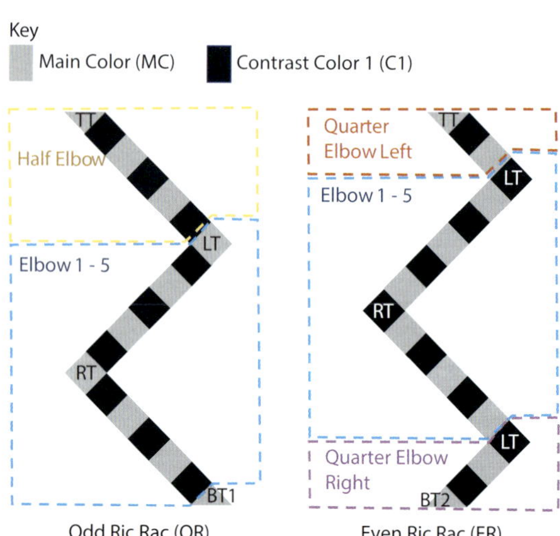

Figure 1: Construction of Ric Racs

Mitered Squares

In spaces labeled "MS" in Figure 2, with yarn color for the MS specified in square brackets, starting at the red triangle, pu&k 18 sts on edges of 3 squares to corner, 1 st in corner, pm, pu&k 18 sts on edges of next 3 squares – 37 sts. Work [MS]. Cut yarn.

Note: Weave in any draped yarns encountered while performing pu&k on the right edge of a Ric Rac (see "Weaving in Ends" on page 212).

Mitered Square (MS) – 37 sts dec'ing to 1 st

Row 2 (WS): Knit.
Row 3 (RS): Knit to 2 sts bef m, cdd, pm, knit to end – 2 sts dec'd; 35 sts.
Row 4: Knit.
Rows 5-36: Rep [Rows 3 & 4] 16 times – 32 sts dec'd; 3 sts.
Row 37: Cdd – 2 sts dec'd; 1 st.

Mitered Triangles on Top/Bottom Edges

In the spaces labeled "MT" in Figure 2, with yarn color specified in square brackets, CO 18 sts, and then, starting at red triangle, pu&k 19 sts to end of Ric Rac – 37 sts. On RS, pm after 19th st. Work [MT]. Cut yarn and fasten off.

Mitered Triangle (MT) – 37 sts dec'ing to 1 st

Row 2 (WS): Knit.
Row 3 (RS): K2tog, knit to 2 sts bef m, rm, cdd, pm, knit to last 2 sts, ssk – 4 sts dec'd; 33 sts.
Row 4: Knit.
Rows 5-18: Rep [Rows 3 & 4] 7 times – 28 sts dec'd; 5 sts.
Row 19 (RS): Cdd2 – 4 sts dec'd; 1 st.

Mitered Triangles on Left/Right Edges

In spaces labeled MT in Figure 2, attach A at red triangle. Pu&k 18 sts to corner, 1 st in corner, and 18 sts to next corner –37 sts. Work [MT]. Cut yarn and fasten off.

Figure 2: Mitered Squares (MS) and Mitered Triangles (MT)

Attaching Strips (See Figure 3)

Strips 1 & 2

On RS, attach A at red triangle at bottom right corner of Strip 1. *Pu&k 18 sts to next corner while simultaneously inserting needle above and below draped yarn, pm; rep from * 21 more times to end of Strip – 396 sts. *Note*: See "Tacking Draped Yarns" on page 210.

Work [Zigzag A]. Leave sts on needle. Cut yarn.

With second circular needle, attach A at red triangle at top left corner of Strip 2. *Pu&k 18 sts to next corner, pm; rep from * 21 more times to end of Strip – 396 sts.

Work [Zigzag B].

Turn Zigzag A and Zigzag B so that RSs are together, and with A and the 3rd, larger needle, 3-needle BO all sts. Rm's as encountered. Cut yarn and fasten off.

Strips 3 & 4 and 5 & 6

Work as for Strips 1 & 2.

Zigzag A

Row 2 (WS): Knit.
Row 3 (RS): Kf&b, *knit to 2 sts bef m, ssk, k2tog, knit to last st bef next m, kf&b; rep from *10 more times.
Row 4: Knit.
Rows 5-10: Rep [Rows 3 & 4] 3 more times.

Strips 2 & 3

On RS, attach A at red triangle at the top left corner of Strip 3. *Pu&k 18 sts to next corner while simultaneously inserting needle above and below draped yarn, pm; rep from * 21 more times to end of Strip – 396 sts.

Work [Zigzag B]. Cut yarn and fasten off.

With second circular needle, attach A at red triangle at bottom right corner of Strip 2. *Pu&k 18 sts to next corner, pm; rep from * 21 more times to end of Strip – 396 sts.

Work [Zigzag A]. Leave sts on needle.

Turn Zigzag A and Zigzag B so that RSs are together, and with A and the 3rd, larger needle, 3-needle BO all sts. Rm's as encountered.

Strips 4 & 5 and 6 & 7

Work as for Strips 2 & 3.

Zigzag B

Row 2 (WS): Knit.
Row 3 (RS): K2tog, *knit to 1 st bef m, kf&b twice, knit to 2 sts bef next m, ssk; rep from * 10 more times.
Row 4: Knit.
Rows 5-10: Rep [Rows 3 & 4] 3 more times.

Figure 3: Zigzags

BORDERS

Right Border

On RS, attach A at lower right corner of blanket, (pu&k 25 sts on MT edge, pu&k 26 sts on MT edge) 5 times, pu&k 25 sts on MT edge – 280 sts. Knit 17 rows. BO loosely, do not cut yarn and leave last st on needle.

Top Border

Pu&k 9 sts on top edge of Right Border, 234 sts across top of blanket, picking up sts per shape as specified in the Table (right) – 244 sts. Knit 17 rows. BO loosely, do not cut yarn, and leave last st on needle.

Left Border

Pu&k 9 sts on left edge of Top border, (Pu&k 25 sts on MT edge, pu&k 26 sts on MT edge) 5 times, pu&k 25 sts on MT edge – 290 sts. Knit 17 rows. BO loosely, do not cut yarn and leave last st on needle.

Bottom Border

Pu&k 9 sts on edge of Left Border, 234 sts across bottom of blanket as specified in the Table (below), and 10 sts on edge of Right Border – 254 sts. Knit 17 rows. BO loosely. Cut yarn and fasten off.

FINISHING

Weave in ends.

Table: Number of Stitches to Pu&k on Edge of Each Shape for Top/Bottom Borders

Shape	# Sts to Pu&k per Shape
Mitered Triangle (MT)	25
Zigzag A+B	13
Ric Rac	8

INTERLOCK

The pieces of this blanket fit together like a puzzle.

SIZE 64.5 x 64.5"/164 x 164 cm

TECHNIQUES Pu&k, sewing

YARN Rowan Felted Tweed, DK (50% wool, 25% alpaca, 25% viscose; 191 yds/175 m; 1.75 oz/50 g):

Pattern Color ID	Color Swatch	Color ID	Color Name	Color Description	#Skeins
A		211	Black	black	7
B		197	Alabaster	off-white	3
C		185	Frozen	light pink	2
D		221	Candy Floss	light mauve	2
E		183	Peony	dark mauve	1
F		186	Tawny	burgundy	1
G		204	Vaseline Green	medium green	2
H		203	Electric Green	green	1
I		152	Watery	turquoise	3
J		165	Scree	light gray-blue	2
K		194	Delft	medium gray-blue	3
L		167	Maritime	medium blue	2
M		178	Sea Salter	navy blue	2
N		214	Ultramarine	ultramarine blue	1

NEEDLES US Size 7/4.5 mm 40"/100 cm circular needles or size needed to obtain gauge

NOTIONS Tapestry needle, 3 stitch markers (mA, mB, mC), locking stitch markers or safety pins (optional; for securing long ends to edges of completed shapes)

GAUGE 18 sts x 36 rows = 4"/10 cm in garter st

NOTES

- The blanket is worked in Blocks, Edges, and Corners that are sewn into diagonal Strips. The Strips are then sewn together. The Border is picked up on the edges of the completed blanket.
- Charts for shapes are provided at the end of the pattern, starting on page 62.
- In figures for shapes P1, P2, P3, and Tr, yellow edges represent stitches generated by casting on or picking up and knitting (pu&k) to begin the shape.

BLANKET INSTRUCTIONS

- See Figure 2 or Table 1 for shape colors. Check off cells in Table 1 as shapes are completed to track progress.
- The order of instruction in this pattern is as follows: Blocks (41 of them), Edges (16 of them), then Corners (4 of them). However, the shapes for Strip 1 can be worked and then sewn together, and the same for successive Strips, with Strips being sewn together as soon as they are complete. This option may be more satisfying and will eliminate the need to label completed Shapes for future assembly.

Table 1: Colors for Shapes

	Starting Shape (Bottom of Strip)		Blocks***		Ending Shape (Top Left of Strip)	
	Ed*	**Cr****	**Colors**	**Block Qty**	**Ed***	**Cr****
Strip 1		GH				
Strip 2	JKM		JKMB	1	KMB	
Strip 3	FCB		FCBD	3	CBD	
Strip 4	LHG		LHGN	5	HGN	
Strip 5	BKI		BKIJ	7	KIJ	
Strip 6		DC	DCBE	9		BE
Strip 7	LMG		MGIL	7	ILM	
Strip 8	BJI		JIKB	5	KBJ	
Strip 9	DFC		FCBD	3	BDF	
Strip 10	KNG		NGHK	1	HKN	
Strip 11		BC				

- Shapes (Blocks, Edges, Corners) are composed of Points (P1, P2, or P3) and Triangles.
- Points start with color A and change to the Main Color (MC) [one of colors B-Q] after Row 2. Do not cut A until instructed to do so. When CO follows pu&k, turn work to WS to work the CO.

Notations for Table

* For Ed with color specification [1][2][3], work Tr in [1], P1 in [2], and P2 in [3].

** For Cr with color specification [1][2], work Tr in [1], and P3 in [2].

*** For Block with color specification [1][2][3][4], work P1A in [1], P1B in [2], P1C in [3], and P1D in [4].

Blocks - Make 41

Blocks are composed of four P1 shapes: P1A, P1B, P1C, and P1D, worked in that order. See Figure 3 for construction.

P1A

With A, CO 48 sts. On RS, pm after 6th st (mA), 24th st (mB), and 42nd st (mC). Work [P1].

Mark P1A to aid in orienting Block during assembly.

P1B-P1D

On RS, with A, and starting at red triangle on right corner of prev shape, pu&k 6 sts to green triangle, pm (mA), pu&k 18 sts to end of edge, pm (mB), turn and CO 18 sts, pm (mC), CO 6 sts – 48 sts. Work [P1].

After P1D, cut A, leaving 50"/125 cm tail. Thread tail onto tapestry needle, and, working on WS, make stitches at center of Block to close hole; then, using mattress st, sew seam bet P1A and P1D on blue dashed line shown in Figure 3. Wind up rem tail and secure to edge Block with stitch marker or safety pin.

Point 1 (P1) – 48 sts dec'ing to 1 st

Row 2 (WS): Knit.

Change to MC for Point. Do not cut A.

Row 3 (RS): Knit to 2 sts bef mA, ssk, k2tog, knit to 2 sts bef mC, ssk, k2tog – 4 sts dec'd; 44 sts.

Row 4: Knit.

Row 5: *Knit to 2 sts bef m, ssk, k2tog, rep from * 2 more times – 6 sts dec'd; 38 sts.

Row 6: Knit.

Rows 7-10: Rep [Rows 3-6] – 10 sts dec'd; 28 sts.

Rows 11-12: Rep [Rows 3-4] – 4 sts dec'd; 24 sts.

Row 13: RmA, cdd, knit to 2 sts bef mB, ssk, k2tog, knit to 2 sts bef mC, rmC, cdd – 6 sts dec'd; 18 sts.

Rows 14-16: Knit.

Row 17: Knit to 2 sts bef mB, ssk, k2tog, knit to end – 2 sts dec'd; 16 sts.

Rows 18-45: Rep [Rows 14-17] 7 times – 14 sts dec'd; 2 sts. RmB.

Row 46: Knit.

Row 47: Ssk – 1 st dec'd; 1 st.

Cut MC and fasten off.

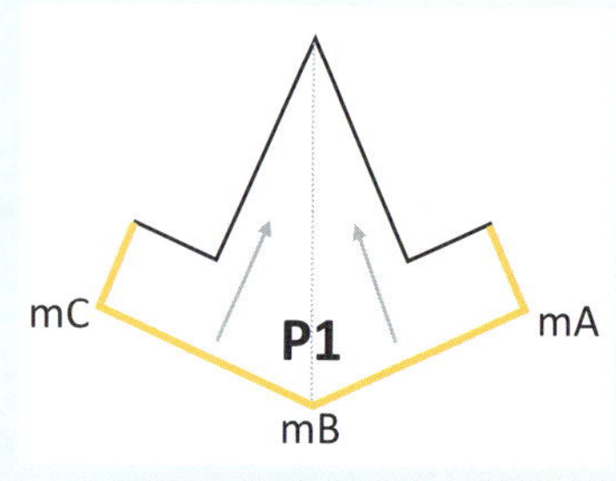

Figure 1: Point 1 (P1)

Figure 2: Colors

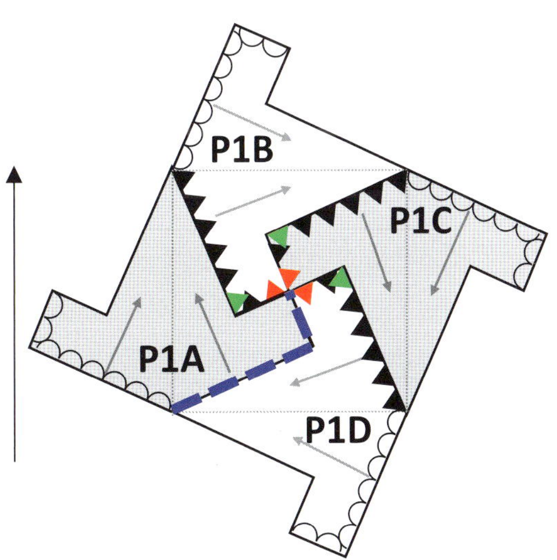

Figure 3: Construction of Block

EDGES (ED) – Make 16

An Edge consists of one each of the Tr, P1, and P2 shapes. See Figure 5 for construction.

Tr

With MC for Tr, CO 37 sts, leaving 20"/50 cm tail. On RS, pm after 19th st. Work [Tr].

Triangle (Tr) – 37 sts dec'ing to 1 st

Row 2 (WS): Knit to 2 sts bef m, rm, cdd, pm, knit to end – 2 sts dec'd; 35 sts.
Rows 3 & 4: Rep [Row 2] twice – 4 sts dec'd; 31 sts.
Row 5: K2tog, knit to 2 sts bef m, rm, cdd, pm, knit to last 2 sts, ssk – 4 sts dec'd; 27 sts.
Rows 6-13: Rep [Rows 2-5] twice – 20 sts dec'd; 7 sts.
Row 14: Rep [Row 2] – 2 sts dec'd; 5 sts. Rm.
Row 15: Cdd2 – 4 sts dec'd; 1 st. Cut yarn and fasten off.

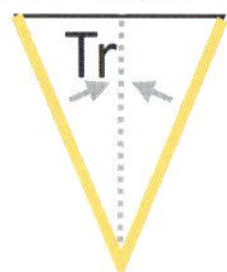

Figure 4: Triangle (Tr)

P1

With A, CO 6 sts, pm (mA), starting at red triangle, pu&k 18 sts to end of edge, pm (mB), turn to WS CO 18 sts, pm (mC), CO 6 sts – 48 sts. Work [P1]. Do not cut A.

P2

Working on RS and starting at red triangle on P1, with A still attached, pu&k 6 sts to corner, pm (mA), pu&k 18 sts on P1 edge, pm (mB), turn to WS and CO 18 sts, pm (mC), CO 6 sts – 48 sts. Work [P2].

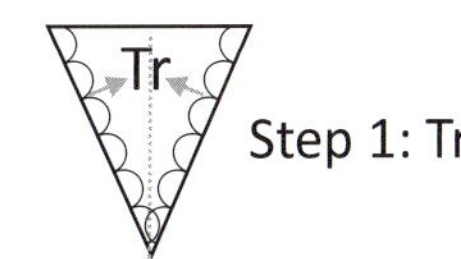

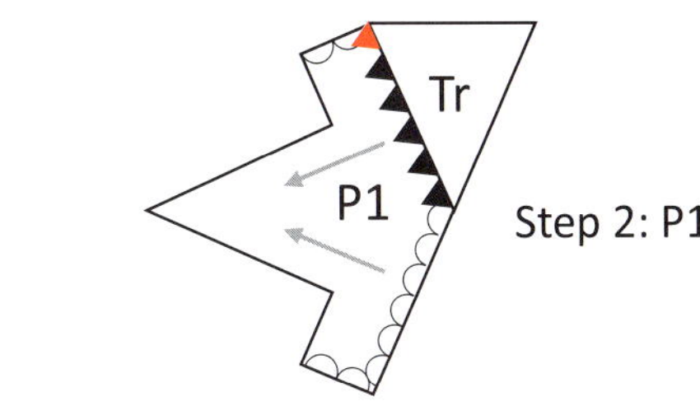

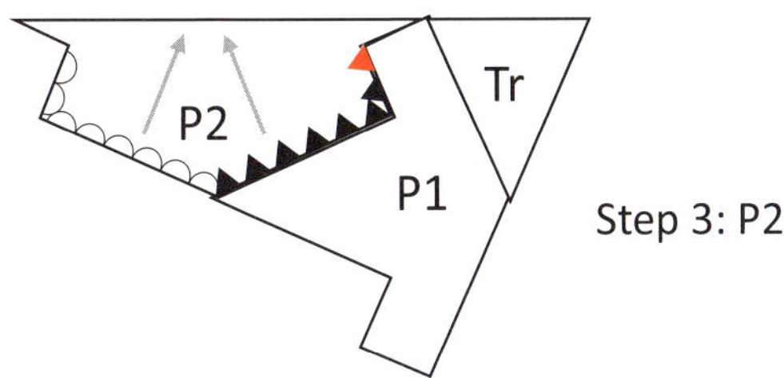

Figure 5: Construction of Edge (Ed)

Point 2 (P2) – 48 sts dec'ing to 1 st

Rows 2 (WS)-14: Work [Point 1, Rows 2-14; see page 56] – 30 sts dec'd; 18 sts. *Note:* Blue line in Figure 6 represents sts on needle after Rows 2-14.
Row 15: Drape yarn from point ***c*** to ***a*** in Figure 7, and, starting at the green triangle at point ***a***, pu&k 6 sts to red triangle at ***b***, and 6 sts from ***b*** to ***c***, while simultaneously weaving in draped yarn, knit all sts on needle, then pu&k 6 sts from blue triangle at point ***d*** to ***e***, and, finally, turn and CO 6 sts – 24 sts inc'd; 42 sts.
Row 16: Knit.
Row 17: K2tog, knit to 2 sts bef mB, ssk, k2tog, knit to last 2 sts, ssk – 4 sts dec'd; 38 sts.
Row 18: K2tog, knit to 2 sts bef end, ssk – 2 sts dec'd; 36 sts.
Rows 19 & 20: Rep [Row 18] 2 times – 4 sts dec'd; 32 sts.
Rows 21-32: Rep [Rows 17-20] 3 more times – 30 sts dec'd; 2 sts. RmB.
Row 33: Ssk – 1 st dec'd; 1 st.
Cut MC and fasten off.

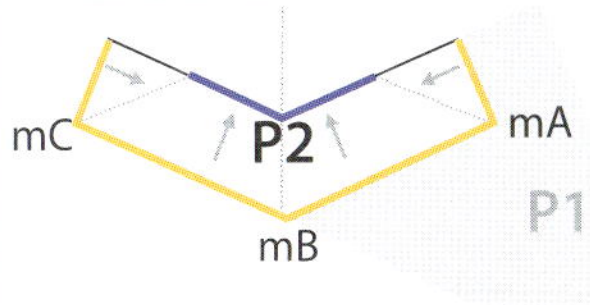

Figure 6: Step 1: Rows 1-14

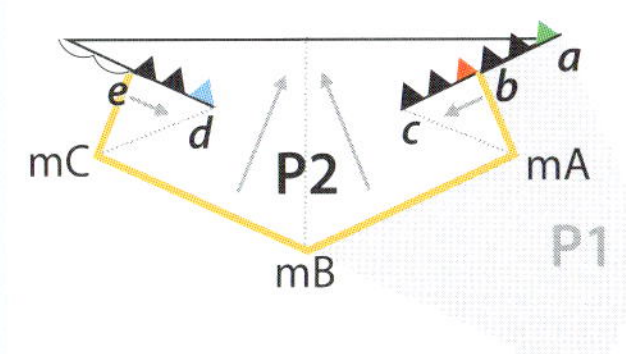

Figure 7: Step 2: Rows 15-33

Corners (Cr) – Make 4

A Corner consists of one each of the Tr and P3 shapes. See Figure 8 for construction.

Tr

With MC for Tr, CO 37 sts. On RS, pm after 19th st. Work [Tr].

P3

On RS, with A, and starting at the red triangle on Tr, pu&k 18 sts along edge, pm (mA), turn, and CO 18 sts, pm (mB), CO 6 sts – 42 sts. Work [P3]. Cut A and fasten off.

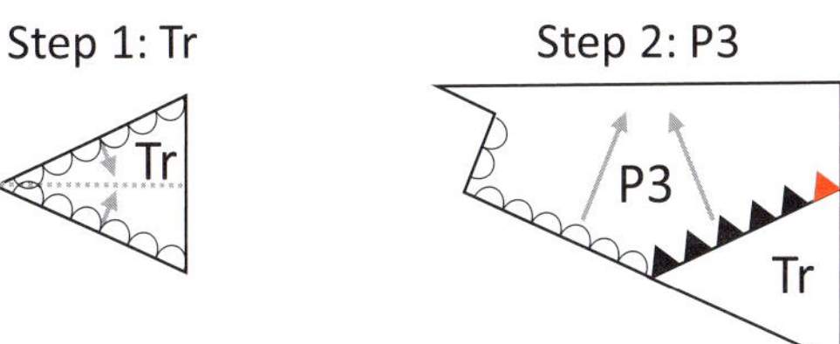

Figure 8: Construction of Corner (Cr)

Point 3 (P3) – 42 sts dec'ing to 1 st

Row 2 (WS): Knit. Cut A. Change to MC for P3.
Row 3 (RS): Knit to 2 sts bef mB, ssk, k2tog, knit to end – 2 sts dec'd; 40 sts.
Row 4: Knit.
Row 5 (RS): Kf&b, knit to 2 sts bef mA, ssk, k2tog, knit to 2 sts bef mB, ssk, k2tog, knit to end – 3 st dec'd; 37 sts.
Row 6: Knit.
Rows 7-10: Rep [Rows 3-6] – 5 sts dec'd; 32 sts.
Rows 11 & 12: Rep [Rows 3-4] – 2 sts dec'd; 30 sts.
Row 13: RmB. Kf&b, knit to 2 sts bef mA, ssk, k2tog, knit to last 3 sts, cdd – 3 sts dec'd; 27 sts.
Row 14: Knit.
Row 15: Knit to end, pu&k 6 sts beg at red triangle at point ***a*** to ***b***, turn, and CO 6 sts – 12 sts inc'd; 39 sts.
Row 16: Knit.
Row 17: Kf&b, knit to 2 sts bef mA, ssk, k2tog, knit to last 2 sts, ssk – 2 sts dec'd; 37 sts.
Row 18: K2tog, knit to end – 1 st dec'd; 36 sts.
Row 19: K2tog, knit to last 2 sts, ssk – 2 sts dec'd; 34 sts.
Row 20: Rep [Row 19] – 2 sts dec'd; 32 sts.
Row 21: K2tog, knit to 2 sts bef mA, ssk, k2tog, knit to last 2 sts, ssk – 4 sts dec'd; 28 sts.
Row 22: Rep [Row 19] – 2 sts dec'd; 26 sts.
Rows 23-30: Rep [Rows 19-22] 2 times – 20 sts dec'd; 6 sts.
Rows 31 & 32: Rep [Row 19] 2 times – 4 sts dec'd; 2 sts. RmA.
Row 33: K2tog – 1 st dec'd; 1 st.
Cut MC and fasten off.

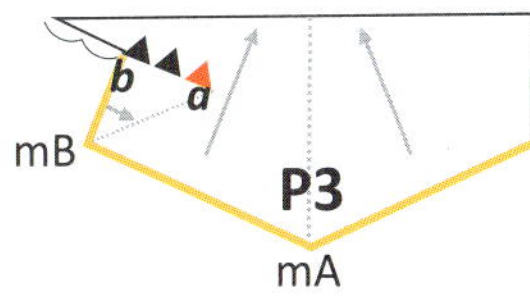

Figure 9: Point 3 (P3)

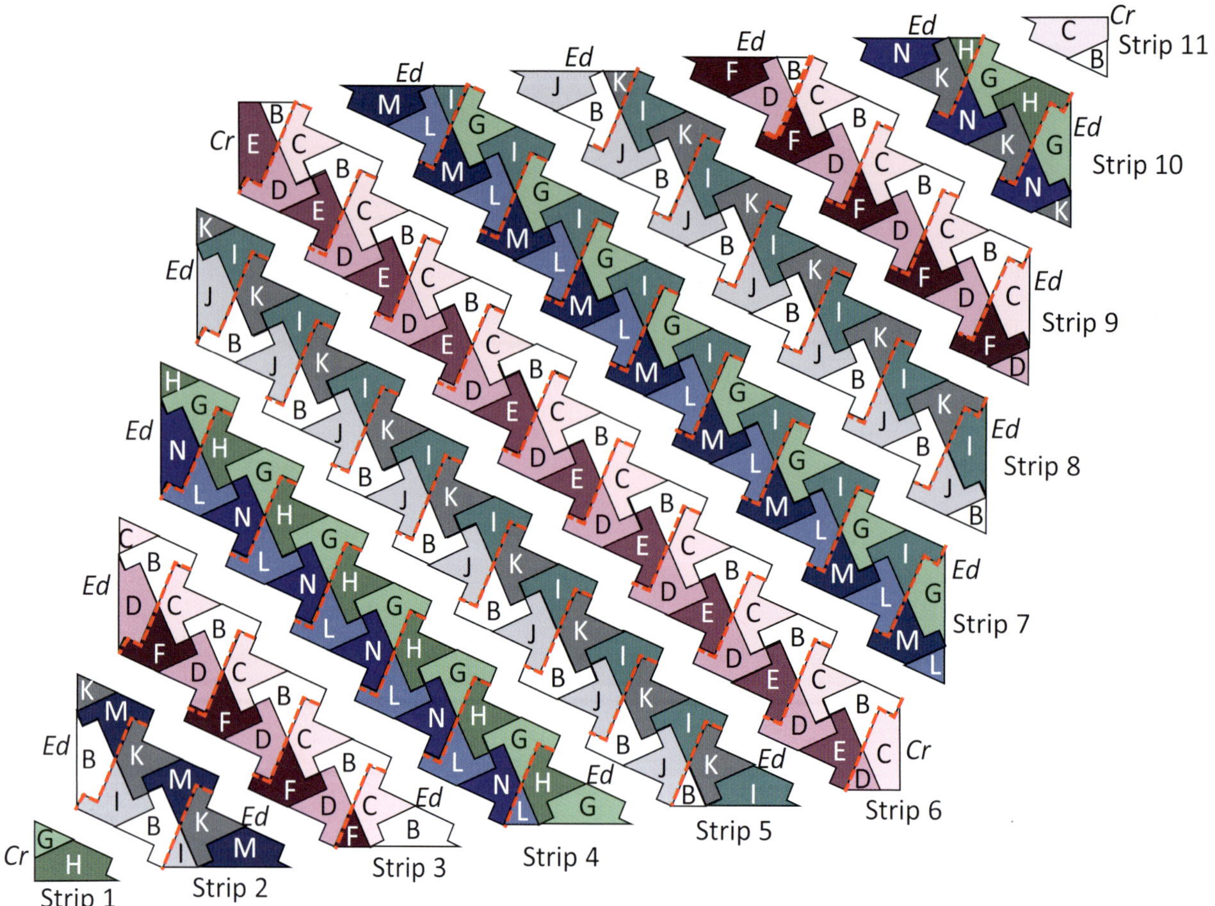

Figure 10: Assembly into Strips

Figure 11: Joining of Strips

ASSEMBLY

Arrange shapes as shown in Figure 10. Orient Blocks as in Figure 3 (P1A pointing up). Using long tails from P1s and mattress st, sew shapes tog along red dashed lines in Figure 10 to create Strips, and then sew Strips together along red dashed lines in Figure 11, matching corners.

BORDERS

Right Border

Table 2: Stitches to Pu&k on Edge of Shapes

	P2	Long edge of P3	Short edge of P3	Tr
Number of sts	39	35	10	18

On RS, attach A at lower right corner of blanket, pu&k 291 sts along edge of blanket, picking up the number of sts per shape specified in Table 2. Knit 17 rows. BO loosely.

Left Border

Work as for Right Border, attaching A at top left corner of blanket.

Top Border

On RS, attach A at top right corner of Right Border, pu&k 10 sts on edges of Right Border, 291 sts across top of blanket, picking up sts per shape as specified in Table 2, and 10 sts on edge of Left Border – 311 sts. Knit 17 rows. BO loosely.

Bottom Border

Work as for Top Border, attaching A at lower left corner of Left Border.

FINISHING

Weave in ends.

Scrappy version of Interlock made from leftover yarns from blankets in *Geometric Knit Blankets*

CHARTS

Point 1 (P1)

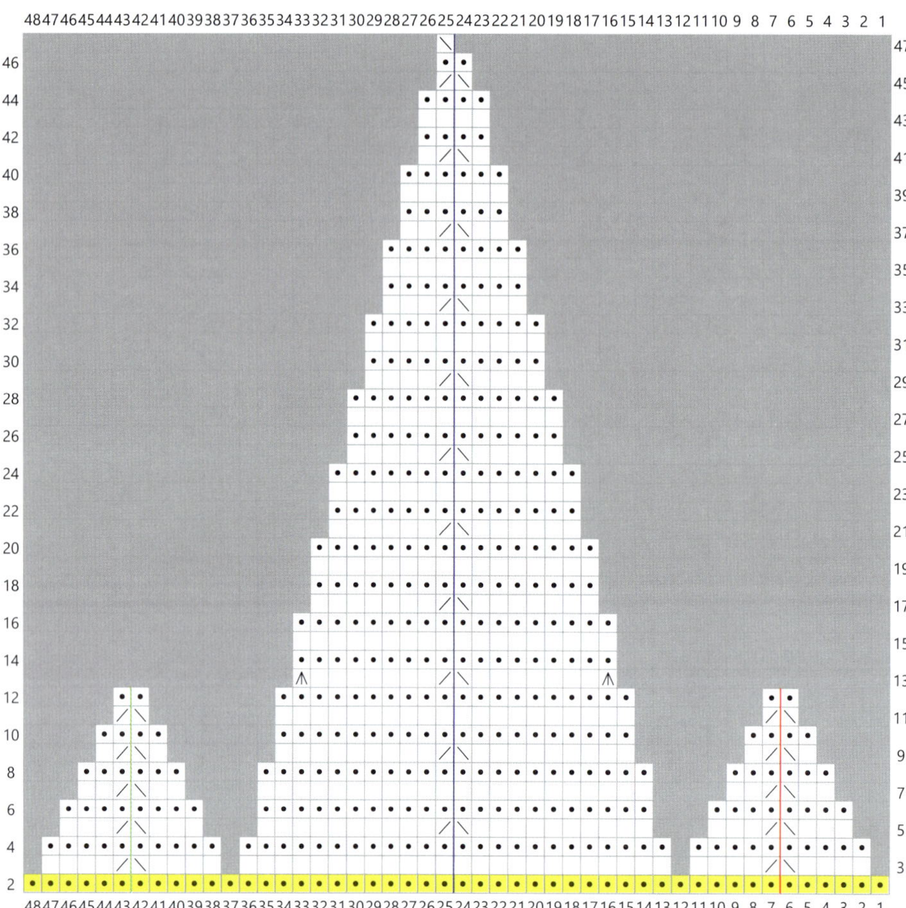

Point 2 (P2)

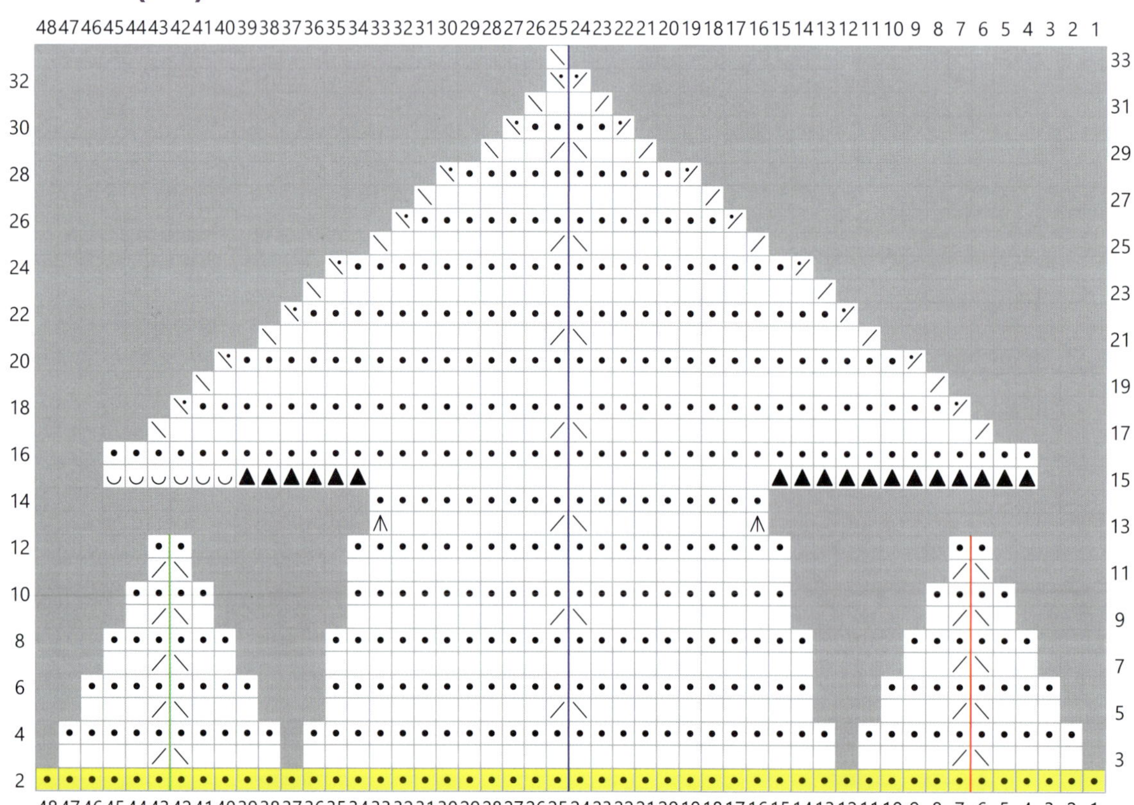

Point 3 (P3)

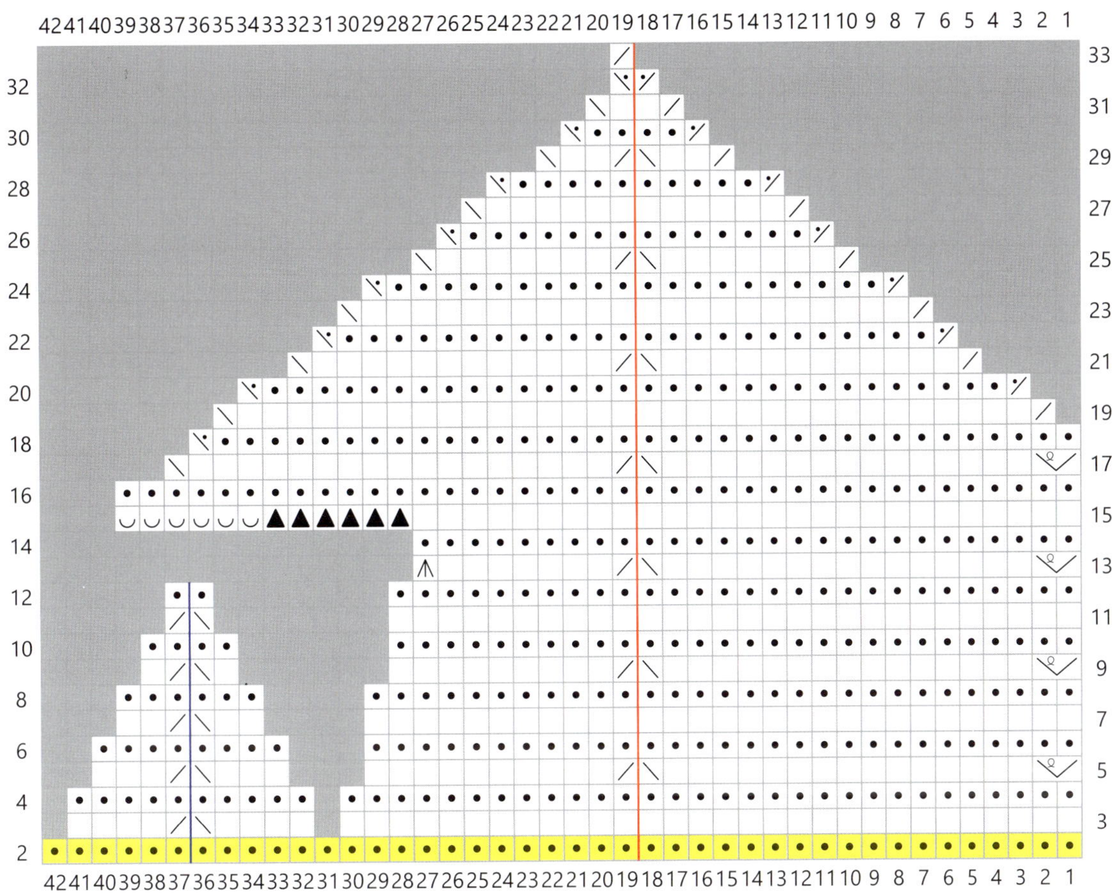

Triangle (Tr)

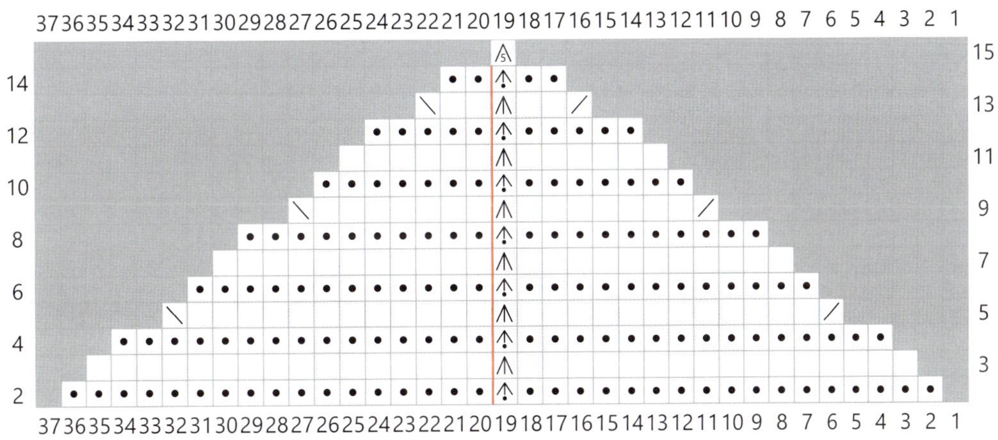

Chart Symbols

Main Color (MC)	A	RS: knit	WS: knit	RS: k2tog
RS: ssk	WS: ssk	WS: k2tog	RS: cdd	cdd2
RS: kf&b	CO	pu&k	no stitch	marker A (mA)
marker B (mB)	marker C (mC)	WS: cdd		

INTWINED

This blanket of twisting stripes in blues and greens reminds us of how much we depend on one another.

SIZE 57 x 69"/145 x 175 cm

TECHNIQUES 3-needle BO, join-as-you-go, pu&k

YARN Berroco Vintage Chunky, bulky (52% acrylic, 40% wool, 8% nylon; 136 yds/124 m; 3.5 oz/100 g):

Pattern Color ID	Color Swatch	Color ID	Color Name	Color Description	# Hanks
A		6101	Mochi	off-white	9
B		6172	Calico	light aqua	2
C		6108	Stone	tan	3
D		61173	Forest Floor	brown	4
E		6113	Misty	lightest blue	2
F		61191	Blue Moon	blue	2
G		6112	Minty	lightest green	2
H		6163	Caribbean Sea	teal green	2

NEEDLES (2) US Size 10/6 mm 40"/100 cm circular needles or size needed to obtain gauge, US Size 11/8 mm needle for 3-needle BO

NOTIONS Tapestry needle, stitch markers, stitch holders

GAUGE 13 sts and 26 rows = 4"/10 cm in garter st

NOTES

- When working Shapes S1-S5, do not cut yarn until instructed. Carry yarn between uses, making color changes at the beginning of each RS row.
- A special join for striping called S-Join is worked on Shapes S3-S5.

BLANKET INSTRUCTIONS

Twines – Make 5

Colors are for Twines 1, 3, & 5 with changes for Twines 2 & 4 in parentheses. See Figure 1 for construction.

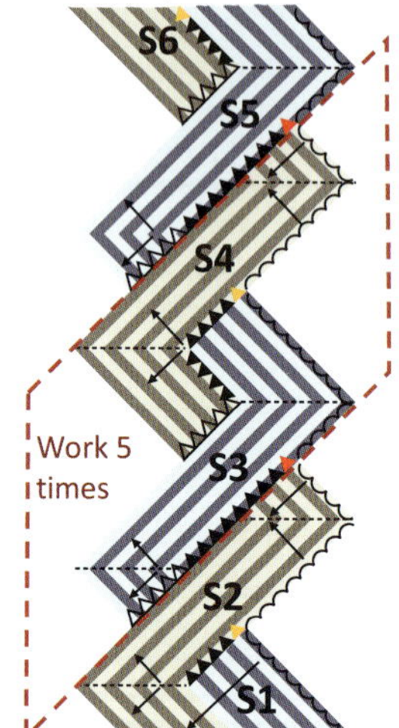

Figure 1: Twine Construction

Shape 1 (S1)

With F (H), CO 15 sts. Work [S1]. Transfer 8 sts to holder. Cut yarns and fasten off.

S1 – 15 sts dec'ing to 8 sts

Row 2 (WS): Knit.
Attach E (G).
Row 3 (RS): Knit to last 2 sts, ssk – 1 st dec'd; 14 sts.
Row 4: Knit.
Change to F (H).
Rows 5-16: Rep [Rows 3 & 4] 6 times, continuing established striping by changing colors at beg of RS rows – 6 sts dec'd; 8 sts.

Shape 2 (S2)

On the 2nd smaller needle, with C, CO 8 sts, pm, CO 16 sts. Turn needle, and, with RS of S1 facing and using C, starting at yellow triangle (at corner of S1), pu&k 8 sts (1 per garter st bump), to next corner of S1, pm, knit 8 sts off holder – 40 sts. Work [S2]. BO loosely. Cut yarns and fasten off.

S2 – 40 sts dec'ing to 33 sts

Row 2 (WS): Knit.
Attach D. Do not cut C.
Row 3 (RS): Knit to 2 sts bef m, ssk, k2tog, knit to 1 st bef m, rm, kyok, pm after center st of kyok, knit to last 2 sts, ssk – 1 st dec'd; 39 sts.
Row 4: Knit.
Change to C.
Rows 5-16: Rep [Rows 3 & 4] 6 times, continuing established striping by changing colors at beg of each RS row – 6 sts dec'd; 33 sts.

Shape 3 (S3)

With F (H) CO 16 sts, pm, CO 8 sts. Turn needle and, starting at red triangle at corner of S2, pu&k 16 sts (1 st in each of the 8 garter st bumps and 1 st each in the next 8 BO sts) – 40 sts. Work [S3]. BO loosely. Cut yarns and fasten off.

S3 – 40 sts

Row 2 (WS): Knit.
Attach E (G).
Row 3 (RS): Knit to 2 sts bef m, ssk, k2tog, knit to last st, kyok. Pm after center st of kyok. Work [S-Join] attaching to next BO st on edge of prev worked shape.
Row 4: Knit.
Change to F (H).
Row 5: Knit to 2 sts bef m, ssk, k2tog, knit to 1 st bef m, rm, kyok, pm after center st of kyok, knit to end. Work [S-Join] attaching to next BO st on edge of prev worked shape.
Row 6: Knit.
Rows 7-16: Rep [Rows 5 & 6] 5 times, continuing established striping by changing colors at beg of each RS row.

S-Join

After completing the current RS row, insert needle into the next "bump" on the adjacent edge and draw yarn loop to the front of the work.

Turn work. Slip the 2nd st on the needle over the 1st st. Slip this st to the R needle.

Work rem sts on WS row per pattern instructions.

Shape 4 (S4)

With C, CO 8 sts, pm, CO 16 sts. Turn needle and, starting at yellow triangle at the corner of S3, pu&k 8 (1 per garter st ridge) to next corner of S3, pm, and 8 sts to next corner – 40 sts. Work [S4]. BO loosely. Cut yarns and fasten off.

S4 – 40 sts

Row 2 (WS): Knit.
Attach D. Do not cut C.
Row 3 (RS): Knit to 2 sts bef m, ssk, k2tog, knit to 1 st bef m, rm, kyok, pm after center st of kyok, knit to end. Work [S-Join].
Row 4: Knit.
Change to C.
Rows 5-16: Rep [Rows 3 & 4] 6 times, continuing established striping by changing colors at beg of each RS row.

Four Additional Repeats of S3 and S4

Work Shape 3 and Shape 4 four more times, for a total of 5 reps.

Shape 5 (S5)

With F (H), CO 8 sts, pm, CO 8 sts. Turn needle and, starting at red triangle on corner of S4, pu&k 16 sts (1 st in each of the 8 garter st bumps and 1 st each in the first 8 BO sts) – 32 sts. Work S5 – 39 sts. BO loosely. Cut yarns and fasten off.

S5 – 32 sts inc'ing to 39 sts

Row 2 (WS): Knit.
Attach E (G).
Row 3 (RS): Kyok, knit to 2 sts bef m, ssk, k2tog, knit to last st, kyok. Pm after center st of kyok. Work [S-Join] attaching to next BO st on edge of prev worked shape – 1 st inc'd; 33 sts.
Row 4: Knit.
Change to F (H).
Row 5: Kf&b, knit to 2 sts bef m, ssk, k2tog, knit to 1 st bef m, rm, kyok, pm after center st of kyok, knit to end. Work [S-Join] attaching to next BO st on edge of prev worked shape – 1 st inc'd; 34 sts.
Row 6: Knit.
Rows 7-16: Rep [Rows 5 & 6] 5 times, continuing established striping by changing colors at beg of each RS row – 5 sts inc'd; 39 sts.

Shape 6 (S6)

With RS facing and C, and starting at yellow Triangle, at corner of S5, pu&k 8 sts to next corner. Work [S6]. BO loosely. Cut yarns and fasten off.

S6 – 8 sts inc'ing to 15 sts

Row 2 (WS): Knit.
Attach D.
Row 3 (RS): Kf&b, knit to end. Work [S-Join] – 1 st inc'd; 9 sts.
Row 4: Knit.
Change to C.
Row 5: Rep [Row 3] – 1 st inc'd; 10 sts.
Row 6: Knit.
Rows 7-16: Rep [Rows 5 & 6] 5 times, continuing established striping by changing colors at beg of each RS row – 5 sts inc'd; 15 sts.

Mitered Squares

Note: To accurately place the MS, begin pu&k in the 8th CO/BO st bef corner, and end pu&k in the 8th CO/BO st after corner.

On each Twine, in each of the 12 locations labeled "MS" in Figure 2, starting at red triangle, with A, pu&k 8 sts (1 st per CO/BO st), pm, then 8 sts in each of the 8 CO/BO sts after the corner – 16 sts. Work [MS]. Cut yarn and fasten off.

Mitered Square (MS) – 16 sts dec'ing to 1 st

Row 2 (WS): Knit.
Row 3 (RS): Knit to 2 sts bef m, ssk, k2tog, knit to end – 2 sts dec'd; 14 sts.
Row 4: Knit.
Rows 5-14: Rep [Rows 3 & 4] 5 times – 10 sts dec'd; 4 sts.
Row 15: Rm. K2tog, ssk. Pass 1st st over 2nd st – 3 sts dec'd; 1 st.

Triangle 1's

In each space labeled "T1" on Twines 1 & 5, in Figure 2, with A, and starting at the red triangle, pu&k 16 sts to next corner, pm, then 16 sts to next corner – 32 sts. Work [MT].

Triangle 2's

In each space labeled "T2" on Twines 1 & 5, in Figure 2, with A, and starting at the green triangle, pu&k 8 sts to next corner, pm, then 8 sts to next corner – 16 sts. Work [MT].

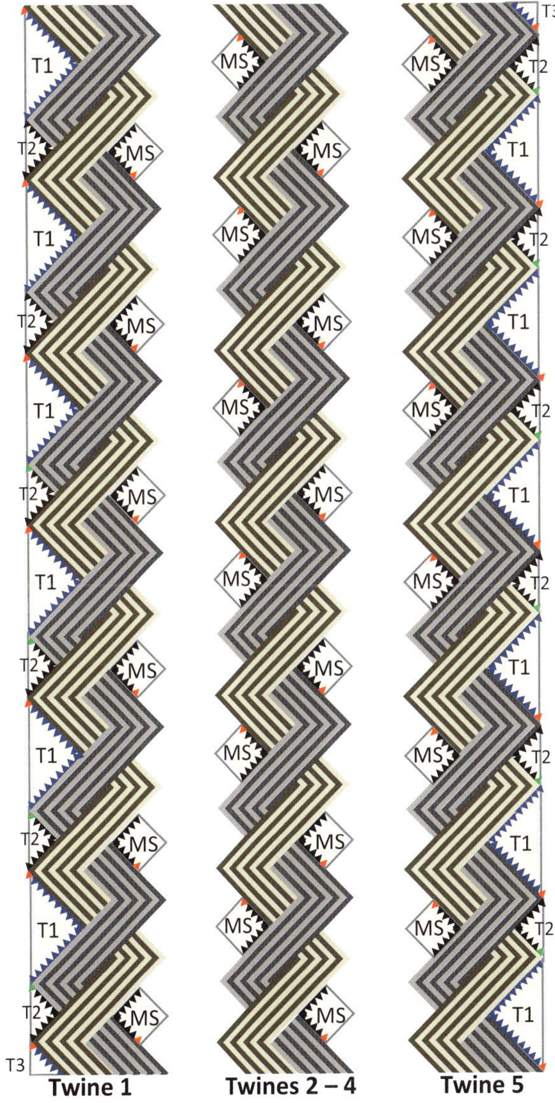

Figure 2: Mitered Squares and Triangles

Mitered Triangle (MT) – multiple of 4 sts dec'ing to 0 sts

Row 2 (WS): Knit.
Row 3 (RS): K2tog, knit to 2 sts bef m, ssk, k2tog, knit to last 2 sts, ssk – 4 sts dec'd.
Row 4: Knit.
Rep [Rows 3 & 4] until 4 sts rem. Rm.
Next row (RS): Slip 2 sts to R needle, k2tog, psso – 3 sts dec'd; 1 st.
Cut yarn and fasten off.

Triangle 3's

In spaces labeled "T3" on Twines 1 & 5 in Figure 2, pu&k 8 sts from red triangle to next corner. Work [T3].

Triangle 3 (T3) – 8 sts dec'ing to 0 sts

Row 2 (WS): Knit.
Row 3 (RS): K2tog, knit to last 2 sts, ssk – 2 sts dec'd; 6 sts.
Row 4: Knit.
Rows 5 & 6: Rep [Rows 3 & 4]– 2 sts dec'd; 4 sts.
Row 7: Rep [Row 3] – 2 sts dec'd; 2 sts.
Next row (WS): K2tog – 1 st dec'd; 1 st.
Cut yarn and fasten off.

Spacers and Left/Right Borders

Starting at the top left corner of Twine 1, at the green triangle, in Figure 3, with A, pu&k 210 sts (green numbers are number of sts to pu&k per shape). Knit 5 rows. Cut A. With D, work [Border, Rows 2-16], starting at Row 2.

Border

Row 2 (WS): Knit.
Row 3 (RS): With D, kf&b, knit to last st, kf&b – 2 sts inc'd.
Row 4: Knit.
Rows 5-8: Rep [Rows 3 & 4] 2 times – 4 sts inc'd.
Cut D, leaving 10"/25 cm tail.
Attach B.
Rows 9-16: Rep [Rows 3 & 4] 4 times – 8 sts inc'd.
BO loosely. Cut yarn, leaving 10"/25 cm tail.

Attach A at bottom right corner of Twine 5 and rep as for Twine 1.

Joining Twines (See Figure 3)

Twines are joined pairwise in this order: 1 & 2, 2 & 3, 4 & 5, then 3 & 4. This ordering reduces the bulk of the pieces. In each pair there is a Left (lower-numbered) Twine and a Right (higher-numbered) Twine.

Figure 3: Zigzags, Spacers, and Left/Right Borders

Zigzag for Left Twine

On RS of Left Twine, starting at bottom right corner at the orange triangle, *with A, pu&k 8 sts to next corner, pm; rep from * 35 more times, pu&k 8 sts to last corner – 296 sts. Work [Zigzag]. Leave sts on needle. Cut yarn.

Zigzag – 296 sts

Row 2 (WS): Knit.
Row 3 (RS): Kf&b, *knit to 2 sts bef next m, ssk, k2tog, knit to 1 st bef next m, kf&b twice; rep from * 17 more times, knit to last 2 sts, ssk.
Row 4: Knit.
Rows 5-10: Rep [Rows 3 & 4] 3 times.

Zigzag for Right Twine

With 2nd circular needle, on RS of Right Twine, starting at the top left corner at red triangle, *with A, pu&k 8 sts to next corner, pm; rep from * 35 more times, pu&k 8 sts to last corner – 296 sts. Work [Zigzag]. Leave sts on needle. Cut yarn.

Turn Twines RS tog, with Right Twine (with yarn still attached) at the back, and align needle tips. With larger needle, 3-needle BO all sts, removing m's when encountered. Cut yarn and fasten off.

TOP AND BOTTOM BORDERS

Top Border

On RS, starting at the top right corner of blanket, with D, pu&k 172 sts on top edge of blanket. See Figure 4 for stitch counts per shape. Work [Border].

Bottom Border

Attach D at bottom left corner of blanket and work as for Top Border.

Using long tails of matching colors and mattress st, sew diagonal edges of borders together, matching color changes.

FINISHING

Weave in ends.

Figure 4: Pu&k St Counts on Shapes for Top and Bottom Borders

MAGICAL

Create an explosion of color with overlapping medallions.

SIZE 57 x 57"/145 x 145 cm

TECHNIQUES Pu&k, a very small amount of sewing

YARN Berroco Vintage Baby, DK (52% acrylic, 40% wool, 8% nylon; 145 yds/133 m; 17.5 oz/50 g):

Pattern Color ID	Color Swatch	Color ID	Color Name	Color Description	# Skeins
A		10011	Buttercup	light yellow	2
B		10020	Sunflower	yellow	2
C		10006	Ballet Pink	light pink	2
D		10093	Guava	peach	2
E		10025	Fuchsia	bright pink	2
F		10033	Poppy	red	2
G		10010	Lavender	light purple	2
H		10076	Peony	light magenta	2
I		10022	Grape	purple	2
J		10008	Sky Blue	light blue	2
K		10021	Turquoise	blue-teal	2
L		10034	Royal Blue	royal blue	2
M		10035	Navy	navy blue	1
N		10024	New Leaf	green-yellow	2
O		10096	Jalapeno	green-blue	2

NEEDLES US Size 5/3.75 mm 40"/100 cm straight or circular needles or size needed to obtain gauge

NOTIONS Tapestry needle, stitch markers, safety pins

GAUGE 22 sts and 44 rows = 4"/10 cm in garter st

NOTES

- The blanket is worked in pieces that are joined into diagonal Strips by picking up and knitting (pu&k) on edges and working diamond shapes. Strips are joined by pu&k on edges and working Diamonds and Stars. Corners are worked separately and joined by pu&k and working a Star.
- All knitting is flat (back and forth). Small remaining seams are sewn closed with mattress stitch and a long tail left when cutting yarn.
- Charts are provided for Point (Pt), Triangle (Tr), Diamond (Di), Octagon (Oc), Mitered Square (MS), Joining Diamond (Jd), and Joining Star (Js) on pages 80 and 81.

BLANKET INSTRUCTIONS

Blanket construction begins by working the Composite Shapes shown in Figure 1, which are: Medallions and Edges. Each Composite Shape contains several Elemental Shapes (Triangles, Diamonds, Points, Mitered Squares, Stars, and Octagons), shown on the right side of the figure. Colors for shapes are in Figure 4. After completing each Composite Shape, write its identifier (from Figure 4) on a small piece of paper and attach it with a safety pin.

MEDALLIONS – Make 24 in colors specified in Figure 4.

8-Point Star (8PS)

Point 1 (Pt1)

With color for 8PS, CO 8 sts, work [Pt] – 1 st rem.

Point 2 (Pt2)

Starting at the red triangle on the corner of previous Point (P1), pu&k 7 sts to corner – 8 sts.

Work [Pt] – 1 st rem.

Points 3-8 (Pt3-Pt8)

Rep as for Point 2.

Fasten off, leaving 10"/25 cm tail.

Point (Pt) – 8 sts inc'ing to 14 sts dec'ing to 1 st

Row 2 (WS): Knit.
Row 3 (RS): Kf&b, knit to end – 1 st inc'd; 9 sts.
Row 4: Knit.
Row 5: Kf&b, knit to last st, kf&b – 2 sts inc'd; 11 sts.
Row 6: Knit.
Rows 7-10: Rep [Rows 3-6] – 3 sts inc'd; 14 sts.
Row 11: Kf&b, knit to last 2 sts, ssk.
Row 12: Knit.
Rows 13-20: Rep [Rows 11 & 12] 4 times.
BO all sts, leaving last st on needle.

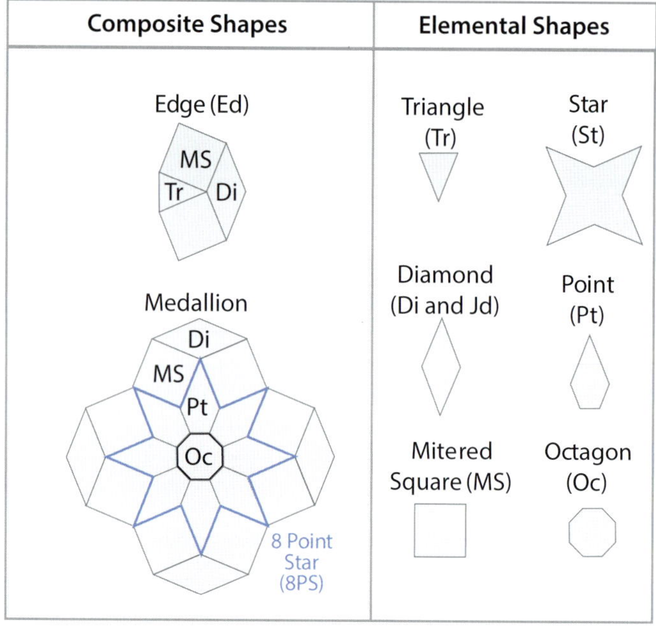

Figure 1: Overview of Shapes

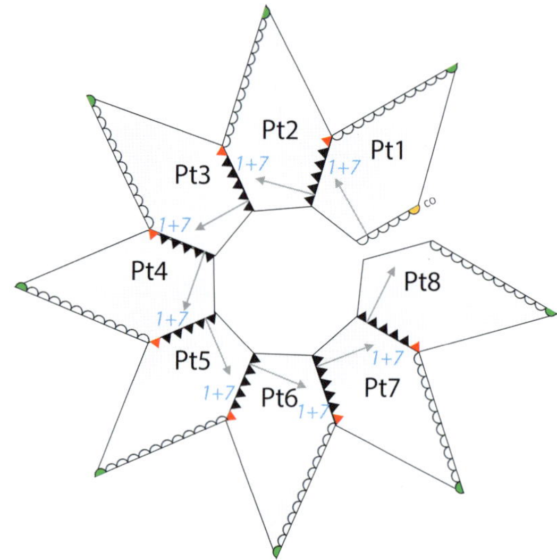

Figure 2: 8-Point Star (8PS) Construction

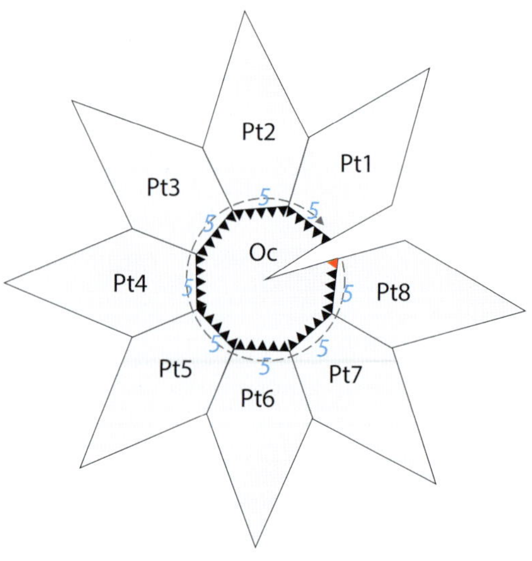

Figure 3: Octagon (Oc) Construction

Figure 4: Colors and Layout

Octagon (Oc)

Starting at the red triangle in Figure 3, and using the color for Octagon (from Figure 4), pu&k 40 sts (5 sts per Pt) along inner edge of 8PS.

Work [Oc].

Note: The completed Oc will look like more like a circle than an octagon.

Using mattress stitch and long tail of matching color, sew open seam, shown as red dashed line in Figure 5 on page 74.

Octagon (Oc) – 40 sts dec'ing to 0 sts

Row 2 and all even-numbered (WS) rows to 8: Knit.
Row 3: K2, k2tog, (k3, k2tog) 7 times, k1 – 8 sts dec'd; 32 sts.
Row 5: K1, k2tog, (k2, k2tog) 7 times, k1 – 8 sts dec'd; 24 sts.
Row 7: K2tog, (k1, k2tog) 7 times, k1 – 8 sts dec'd; 16 sts.
Row 9: (K2tog) 8 times – 8 sts dec'd; 8 sts.
Cut yarn, leaving 12"/30 cm tail. Thread onto tapestry needle and insert through 8 sts on needle, twice. Pull to tighten.

Mitered Squares (MS)

MS1

In the space labeled "MS1" in Figure 5, with color for MS, and starting at red triangle at the tip of Pt1, pu&k 14 sts to corner, pm, and 13 sts to next corner – 27 sts.

Work [MS]. Enlarge rem loop on needle, insert yarn ball through loop and tighten. Do not cut yarn.

Mitered Square (MS) – 27 sts dec'ing to 1 st

Row 2 (WS): Knit.
Row 3 (RS): Knit to 2 sts bef m, rm, cdd, pm, knit to end – 2 sts dec'd; 25 sts.
Row 4: Knit.
Rows 5-26: Rep [Rows 3 & 4] 11 times – 22 sts dec'd; 3 sts.
Row 27: Cdd – 2 sts dec'd; 1 st.

MS2-MS8

Work as for MS1, draping working yarn slightly loosely from the end of the previous MS to the starting point for the pu&k of the next MS as shown in Figure 5.

Cut yarn after completing MS8.

Diamonds (Di)

Di1

With color for Diamonds, and starting at red triangle in space labeled "Di1" in Figure 6, pu&k 14 sts to next corner while simultaneously tacking draped yarn (see "Tacking Draped Yarn" on page 210), 1 st in tip of Pt2, pm, pu&k 13 to next corner – 27 sts. Work [Di]. Cut yarn and fasten off.

Di2-Di4

Work as for Di1, in spaces labeled "Di2," "Di3," and "Di4."

Diamond (Di) – 27 sts dec'ing to 1 st

Row 2 (WS): Knit.
Row 3 (RS): K2tog, knit to 2 sts bef m, rm, cdd, pm, knit to last 2 sts, ssk – 4 sts dec'd; 23 sts.
Row 4: Knit.
Row 5: K2tog, knit to last 2 sts, ssk – 2 sts dec'd; 21 sts.
Rows 6-17: Rep [Rows 2-5] 3 more times – 18 sts dec'd; 3 sts. *Note:* 6 sts are dec'd per rep.
Row 18: Cdd – 2 sts dec'd; 1 st.

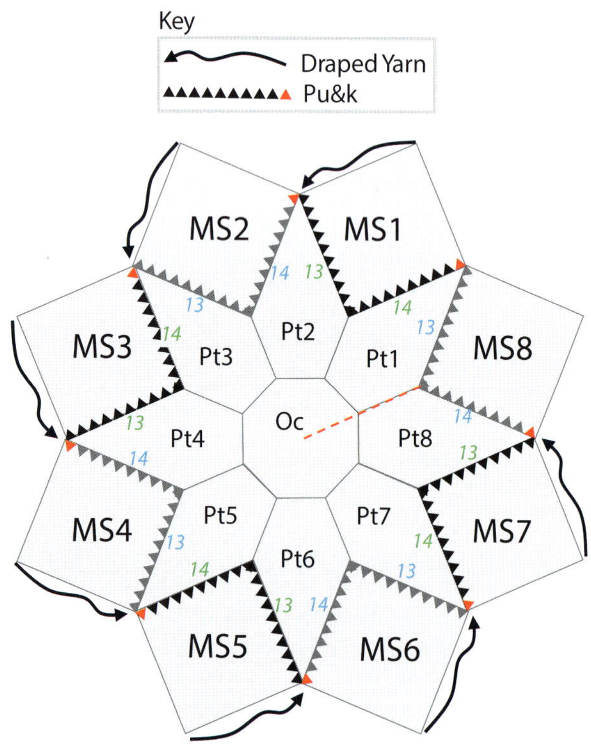

Figure 5: Mitered Square (MS) Construction

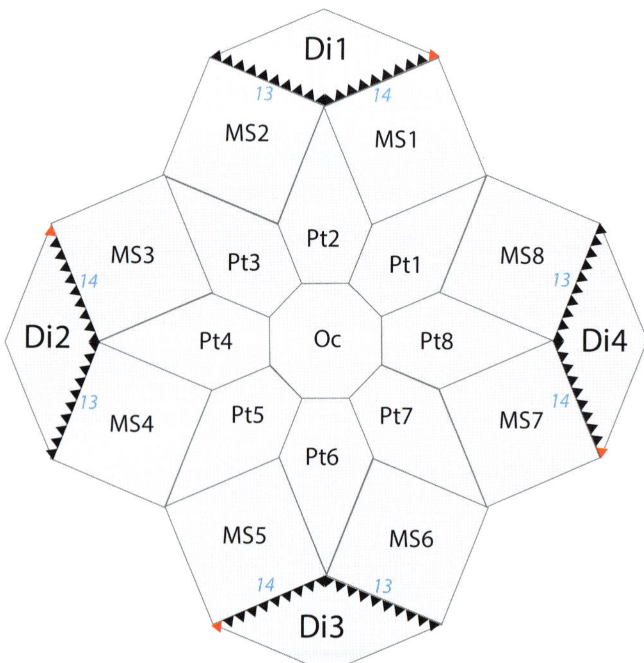

Figure 6: Diamond (Di) Construction

Edges (Ed) - Make 16

See Figure 7 for construction and Figure 8 on page 76 for colors. *Note*: Green-filled half-circles are the start of a CO.

Tr1

With color for Tr, CO 15 sts, pm, CO 14 sts – 29 sts. Work [Tr]. Cut yarn and fasten off.

Triangle (Tr) – 29 sts dec'ing to 1 st

Row 2 (WS): Knit to 1 st bef m, rm, cdd, pm bef cdd, knit to end – 2 sts dec'd; 27 sts.
Row 3 (RS): K2tog, knit to 4 sts bef m, rm, ssk, cdd, pm, k2tog, knit to last 2 sts, ssk – 6 sts dec'd; 21 sts.
Row 4: Rep Row 2 – 2 sts dec'd; 19 sts.
Row 5: Knit to 2 sts bef m, rm, cdd, pm, knit to end – 2 sts dec'd; 17 sts.
Row 6: Rep Row 2 – 2 sts dec'd; 15 sts.
Row 7: Rep [Row 3] – 6 sts dec'd; 9 sts.
Rows 8-10: Rep [Rows 4-6] – 6 sts dec'd; 3 sts.
Row 11: Cdd – 2 sts dec'd; 1 st.

MS1

With color for MS1, starting at red triangle in the space labeled "MS1" in Figure 7, pu&k 14 sts, pm, turn and CO 13 sts – 27 sts. Work [MS]. Cut yarn and fasten off.

MS2

With color for MS2, CO 14 sts, pm, and, starting at red triangle in space labeled "MS2" in Figure 7, pu&k 13 sts to corner – 27 sts. Work [MS]. Cut yarn and fasten off.

Di

With color for Di, starting at red triangle in space labeled "Di" on Figure 7, pu&k 14 sts to corner, pm, pu&k 13 sts to next corner – 27 sts. Work [Di]. Cut yarn and fasten off.

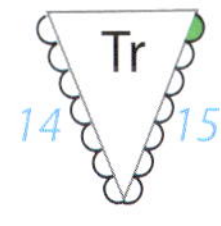

a. Triangle (Tr)

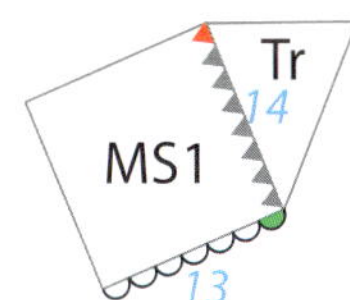

b. Mitered Square 1 (MS1)

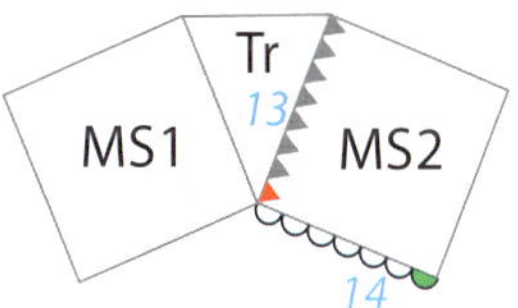

c. Mitered Square 2 (MS2)

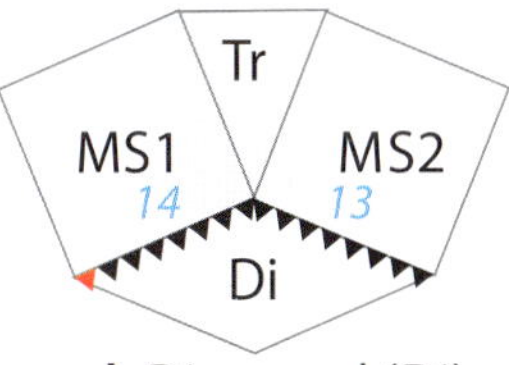

d. Diamond (Di)

Figure 7: Edge Construction

In this sample, diamonds are worked in a single dark color (yarn is Rowan Felted Tweed).

ASSEMBLY

Making Strips

Arrange the 24 completed Medallions and 16 Edges as in Figure 8, with Point of each Medallion oriented toward the top. Pin corners tog with locking stitch markers or safety pins.

Refer to Figure 9 for locations of pu&k for the Joining diamonds (Jd). Some shapes are omitted from the figure for simplification and to show details more effectively.

Joining diamonds (Jd) – **Make 30** in spaces labeled "Jd" in Figure 8.

Notes:

- Use pu&k for stitch generation on edges 2 and 3.
- For edges 1 and 4, use the method indicated by the symbols on the edge, specified in Figure 9. Pu&k is indicated by triangle symbols and CO indicated by half-circles.
- Tack draped yarns during the pu&k.

In each space labeled "Jd" in Figure 9, starting at the red-filled symbol (triangle or half-circle), and using method indicated by edge symbol, generate 14 sts, pm, (pu&k 14 sts, pm) twice, and then, using the method indicated by the edge symbol, generate 14 sts – 56 sts.

Work [Jd].

Using long tail and mattress st, sew rem seam.

Figure 8: Assembling into Strips

Joining diamond (Jd) – 56 sts dec'ing to 0 sts

Row 2 (WS): K2tog, knit to 1 st bef m2, rm and place on R needle, cdd, knit to last 2 sts, ssk – 4 sts dec'd; 52 sts.
Row 3 (RS): K3tog, knit to 2 sts bef m1, rm, cdd, pm, knit to 4 sts bef m2, rm, ssk, cdd, pm, k2tog, knit to 2 sts bef m3, rm, cdd, pm, knit to last 3 sts, sssk – 12 sts dec'd; 40 sts.
Row 4: Rep [Row 2] – 4 sts dec'd; 36 sts.
Row 5: K2tog, knit to 2 sts bef m2, rm, cdd, pm, knit to last 2 sts, ssk – 4 sts dec'd; 32 sts.
Row 6: Rep [Row 2] – 4 sts dec'd; 28 sts.
Row 7: Rep [Row 3] – 12 sts dec'd; 16 sts. Rm's.
Row 8: Rep [Row 2] – 4 sts dec'd; 12 sts.
Row 9: Rep [Row 5] – 4 sts dec'd; 8 sts.
Cut yarn, leaving 12"/30 cm tail. Thread tail onto tapestry needle and insert through rem sts on needle twice.

Triangles (Tr)

Using color for Tr specified in Figure 8, in spaces labeled "Tr" on Figure 9, starting at the red triangle on the edge of MS1 on one of the Ed's, pu&k 15 sts, pm, and 14 sts on the edge of MS2 of the other Ed – 29 sts.

Work [Tr]. Cut yarn and fasten off.

Technique for Sewing Open Seams

Use mattress st to sew seams on Jd and Js. Because these edges are on the diagonal, using only ridges will leave gaps. Therefore, between each ridge, insert the needle through the outer strands of yarn on each edge.

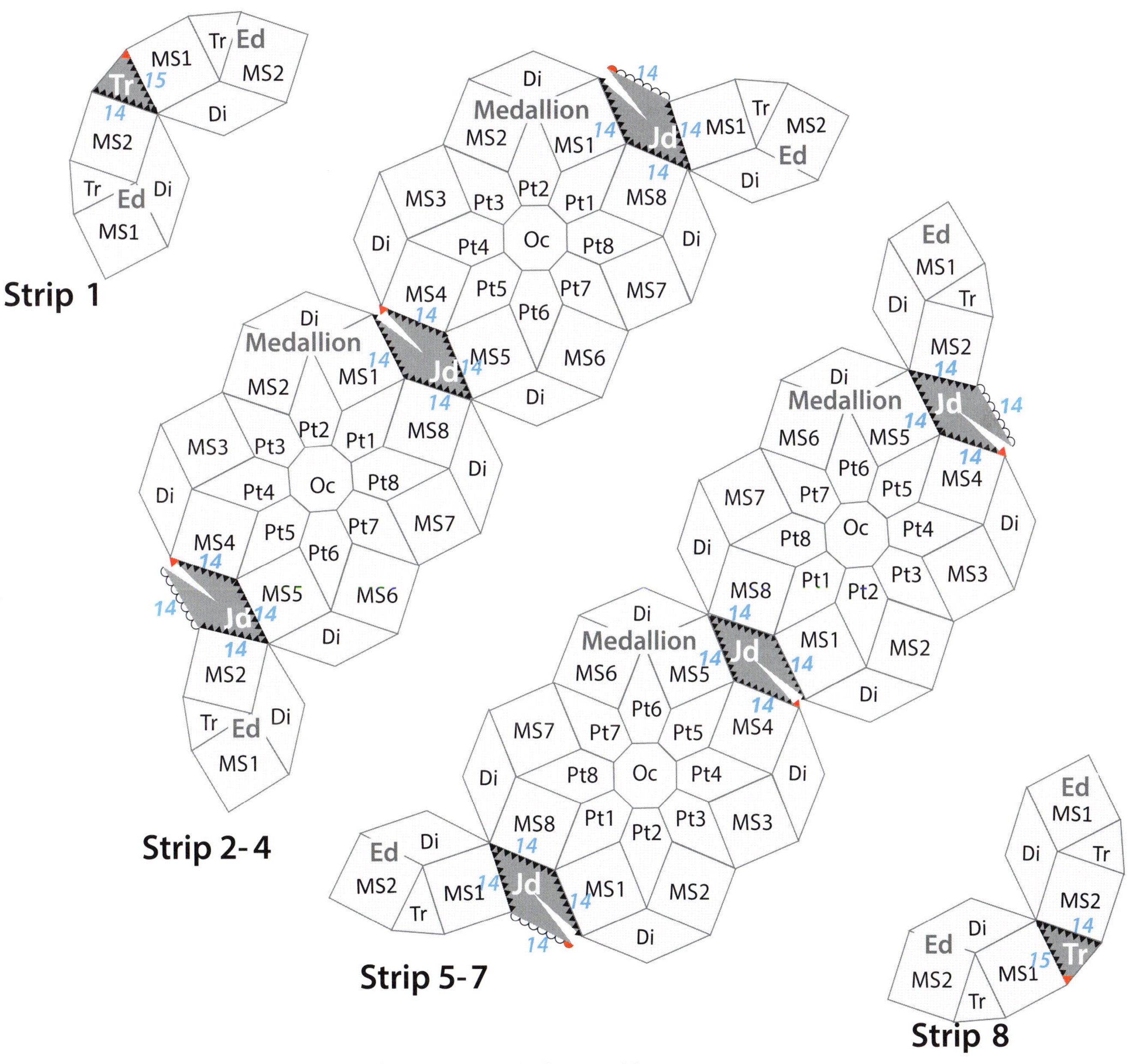

Figure 9: Detail of Assembling into Strips

Joining Strips Together

Lay out assembled Strips 1-8, as shown in Figure 12. Refer to this figure for yarn color for each Jd shape.

There are 3 Shapes used in the Joins: Joining diamond (Jd), Joining star (Js), and Triangle (Tr), as shown in Figure 10.

Note: When generating stitches for a shape, if using pu&k and a draped yarn is present on the edge, tack it while doing the pu&k.

Join A (Refer to Figure 10)

Work shapes in increasing order number, starting at shape 1 at the lower left of the Join. Order numbers are specified in the small circles at the bottom left corner of the shape. Use the symbols on shape edges to determine the method of generating stitches on that edge. Small triangles indicate pu&k, and half-circles indicate CO. Turn needle to start a CO, if needed.

For each shape in the Join:

When the shape label is "Jd," start at the red symbol at the top right corner of the shape, (generate 14 sts to corner, pm) 3 times, generate 14 sts along 4th edge back to red symbol – 56 sts. Work [Jd]. Using long tail and mattress st, sew rem seam.

When shape label is "Js," start at green symbol at the top right corner of the star-shaped opening, (pu&k 15 sts to next corner, pm) 7 times, pu&k 15 sts on last edge back to green triangle – 120 sts. Work [Js]. Using long tail and mattress st, sew rem seam.

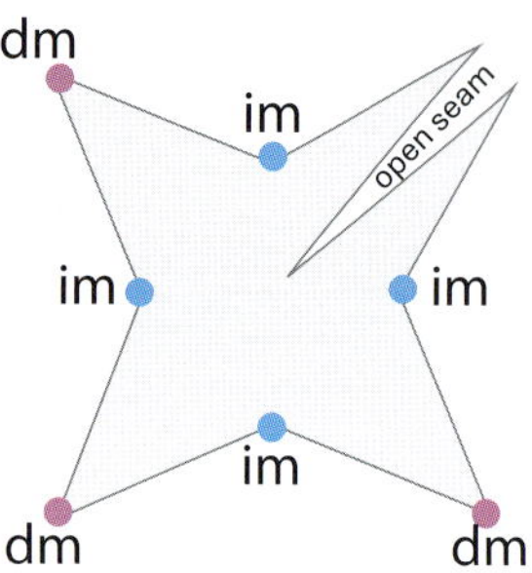

Figure 11: Markers for Js

Note: When placing markers, alternate bet 2 different colors or types. The 1st, 3rd, 5th, and 7th m's are increase markers (im), and the 2nd, 4th, and 6th m's are decrease markers (dm), as shown in Figure 11.

When shape label is "Tr," start at red triangle, pu&k 14 sts to next corner, pm, 13 sts to next corner – 27 sts. Work [Tr].

Joins B-G

Work as for Join A.

FINISHING

Weave in ends.

Note: There are no Borders for this blanket.

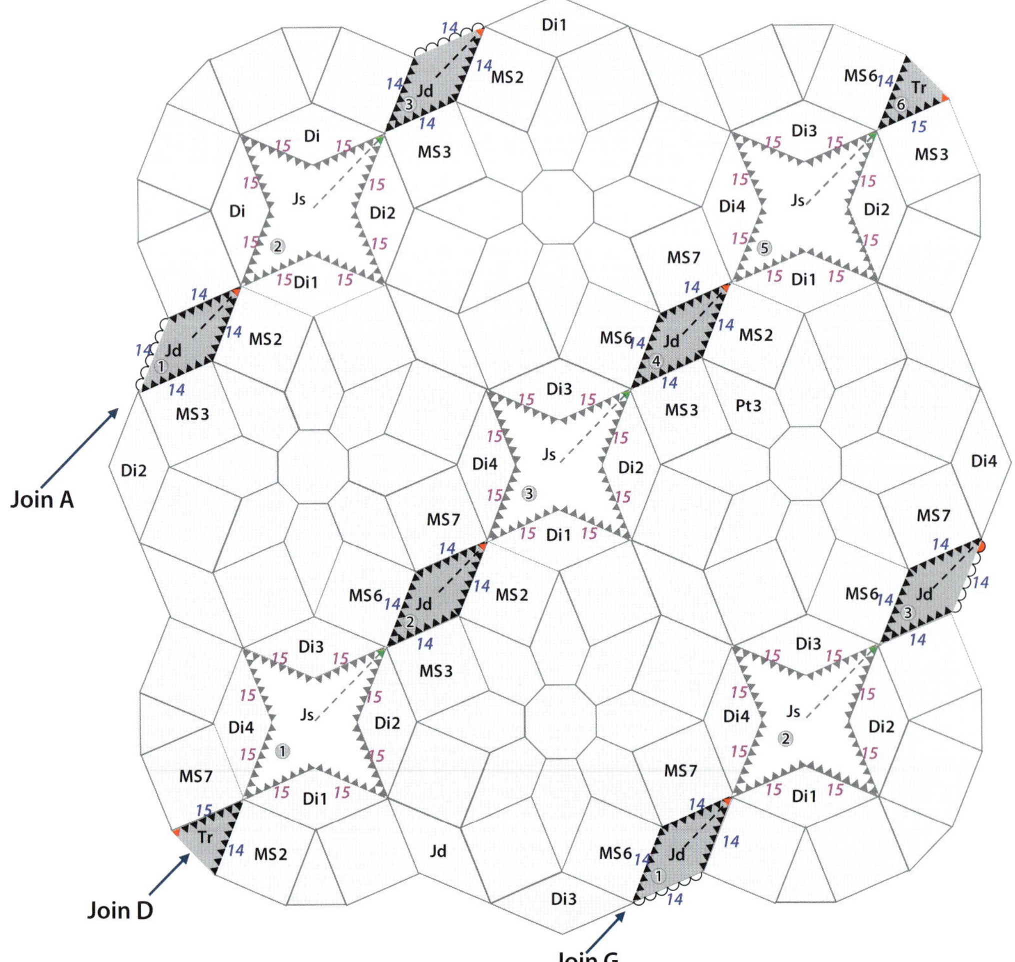

Figure 10: Detail of Joining Strips Together

This figure is a simplified version of the blanket that shows the details of the stitch generation for Joins. It shows Join A, D (with only some of the shapes), and G. Joins B and C are performed as for Join A but include the extra shapes shown in Figure 12. Joins E and F are performed as for Join G but include the extra shapes shown in Figure 12.

Figure 12: Joining Strips Together

Joining star (Js) – 120 sts dec'ing to 0 sts

Row 2 (WS): K2tog, *knit to 1 st bef next dm, rm and place on R needle, cdd; rep from * 2 more times, knit to last 2 sts, ssk – 8 sts dec'd; 112 sts.

Row 3 (RS): K3tog, *knit to 4 sts bef dm, rm, ssk, cdd, pm, k2tog; rep from * 2 more times, knit to last 3 sts, sssk – 16 sts dec'd; 96 sts.

Row 4: Rep [Row 2] – 8 sts dec'd; 88 sts.

Row 5: K2tog, *knit to 1 st bef next im, kyok, move m back 1 st, knit to 2 sts bef next dm, rm, cdd, pm; rep from * 2 more times, knit to 1 st bef last im, kyok, move m back 1 st, knit to last 2 sts, ssk – 0 sts dec'd; 88 sts.

Row 6: Rep [Row 2] – 8 sts dec'd; 80 sts.

Row 7: Rep [Row 3] – 16 sts dec'd; 64 sts.

Row 8: Rep [Row 2] – 8 sts dec'd; 56 sts.

Row 9: Rep [Row 5] – 0 sts dec'd; 56 sts.

Row 10: Rep [Row 2] – 8 sts dec'd; 48 sts.

Row 11: Rep [Row 3] – 16 sts dec'd; 32 sts.

Row 12: Rep [Row 2] – 8 sts dec'd; 24 sts.

Row 13: K2tog, *knit to 2 sts bef next dm, rm, cdd, pm; rep from * 2 more times, knit to last 2 sts, ssk – 8 sts dec'd; 16 sts. Rem all markers.

Row 14: K2tog, (cdd, k1) 3 times, ssk – 8 sts dec'd; 8 sts. Cut yarn, leaving 12"/30 cm tail. Thread tail onto tapestry needle and insert through rem sts on needle twice.

CHARTS

Point (Pt)

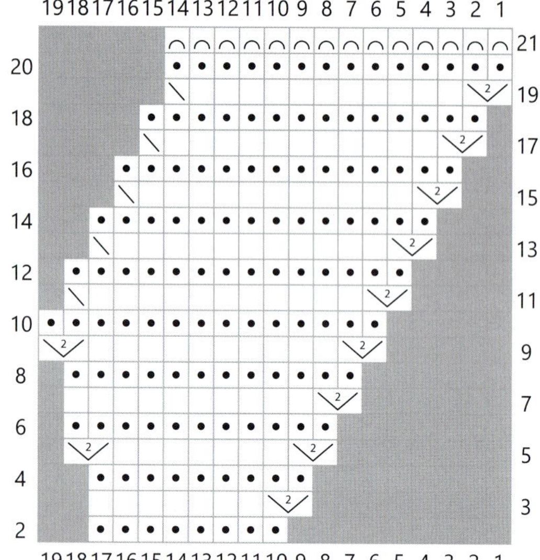

Triangle (Tr)

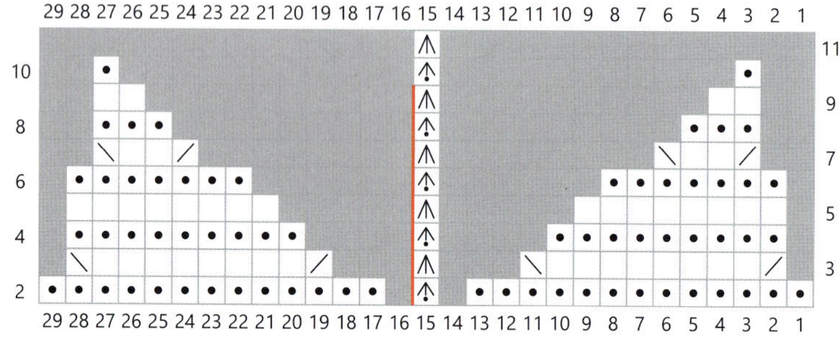

marker (m)

Diamond (Di)

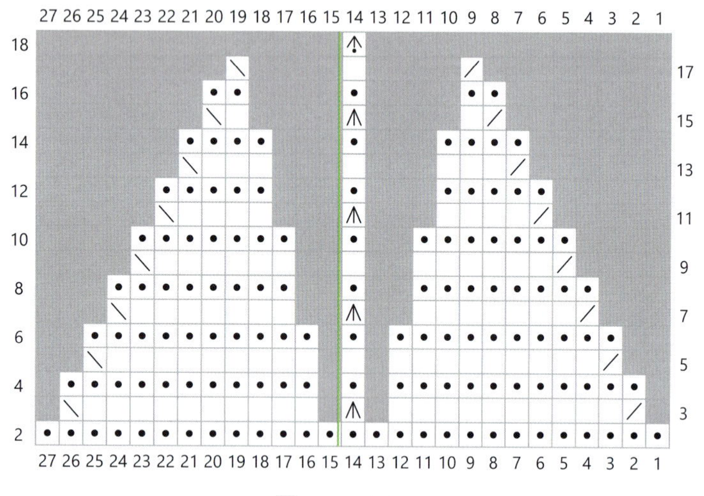

marker (m)

Octagon (Oc)

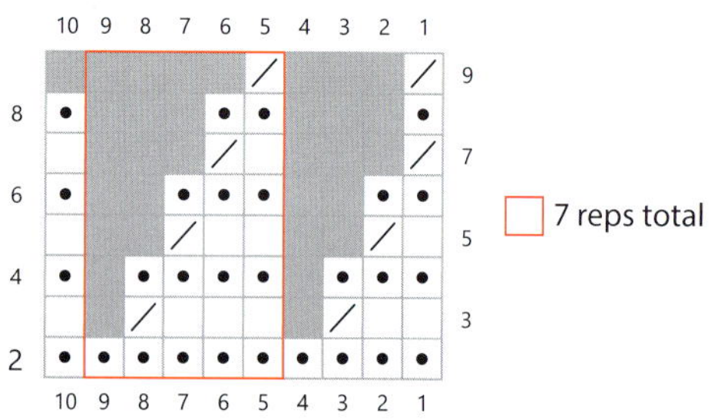

Mitered Square (MS)

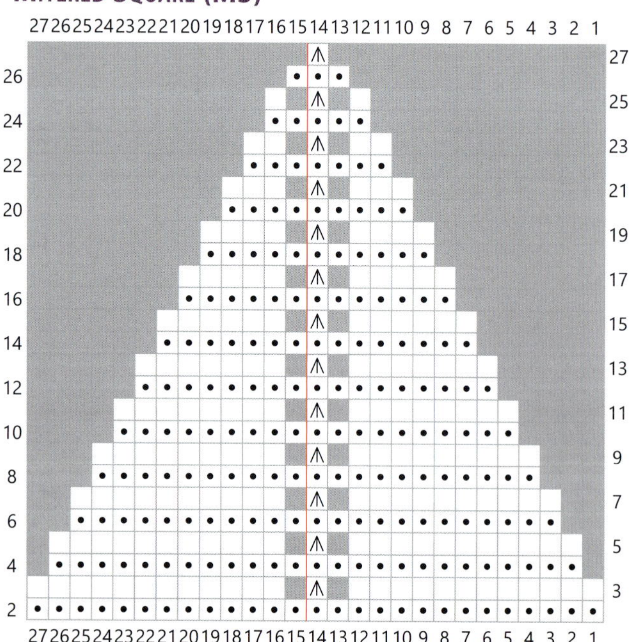

marker (m)

Chart Symbols

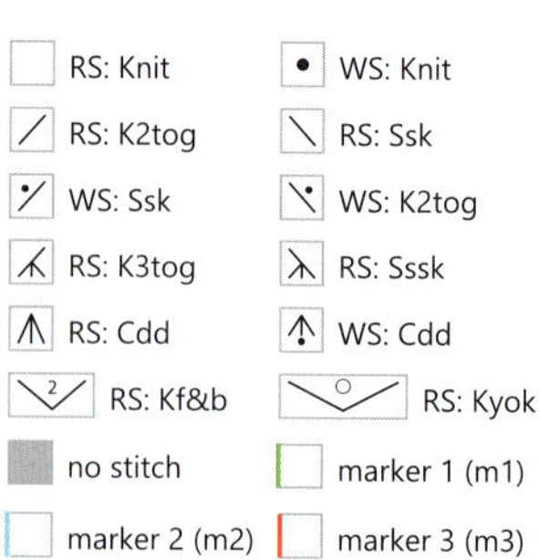

Joining diamond (Jd)

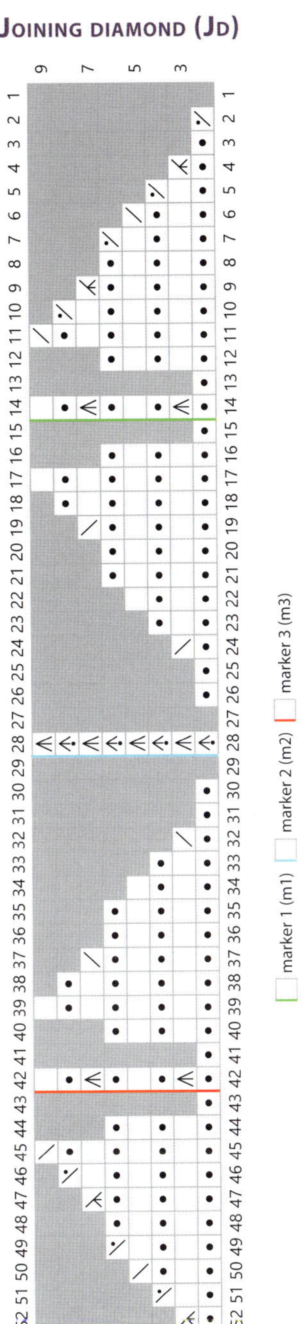

Joining star (Js)

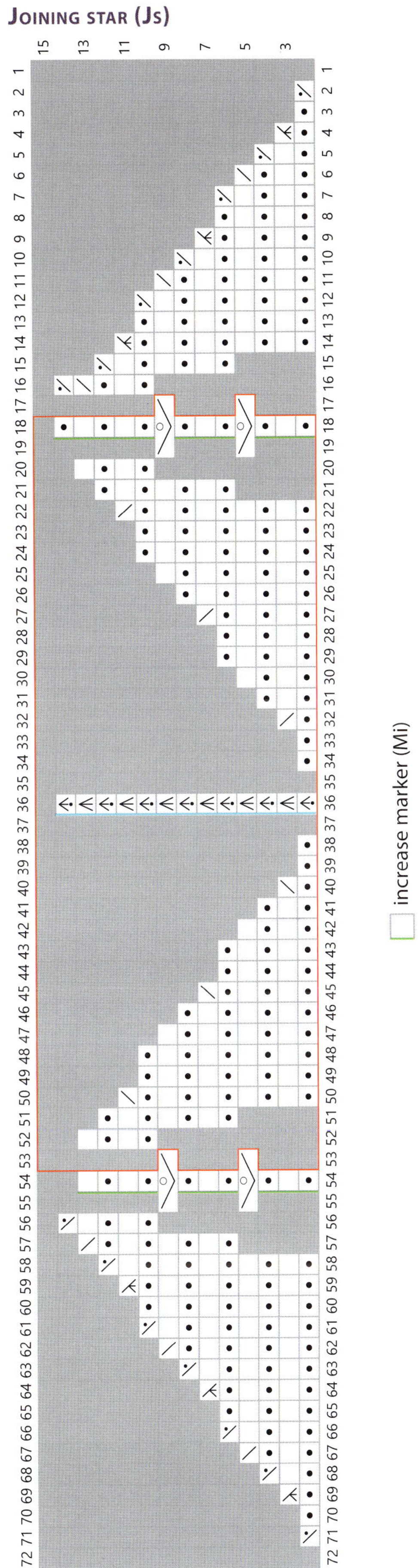

MODULATE

Charge up your decor with this visually exciting blanket in color-changing yarns.

SIZES Small (Large) 47 x 47" (62 x 62")/119 x 119 cm (157 x 157 cm)

TECHNIQUES Intarsia, pu&k, sewing

YARN Red Heart Yarns:
Gemstones, bulky (100% acrylic; 312 yds/285 m; 7 oz/200 g)
Dreamy, bulky (100% acrylic; 466 yds/426 m; 8.8 oz/250 g):

Pattern Color ID	Color Swatch	Red Heart Yarn Line	Color ID	Color Name	Color Description	# Skeins for Size	
						Small	Large
A		Gemstones	E871-2183	Ametrine	purple, mauve, & gray	3	6
B		Dreamy	E861-8341	Grey	light gray	3	5

Note: Color A is the darker color (shows as black on charts) and B is the lighter color (shown as white on charts).

NEEDLES US Size 9/5.5 mm 60"/150 cm and 32"/80 cm circular needles and dpns or size needed to obtain gauge

NOTIONS Tapestry needle

GAUGE 16 sts and 32 rows = 4"/10 cm in garter st

NOTES

- Instructions for size Small (shown in photos) are given, with changes for size Large in parentheses.
- The blanket is worked in garter stitch Blocks that are sewn together. Blocks use intarsia and are worked from charts. Charts show RS (odd-numbered) rows only. On WS rows, knit using same yarn colors as previous RS row. Blue arrows represent Yarn A, and red represents Yarn B.
- A garter stitch Border is worked on two sides, and then an I-cord border is worked around the blanket.
- Do not cut yarns until instructed to do so.

CHART SYMBOLS

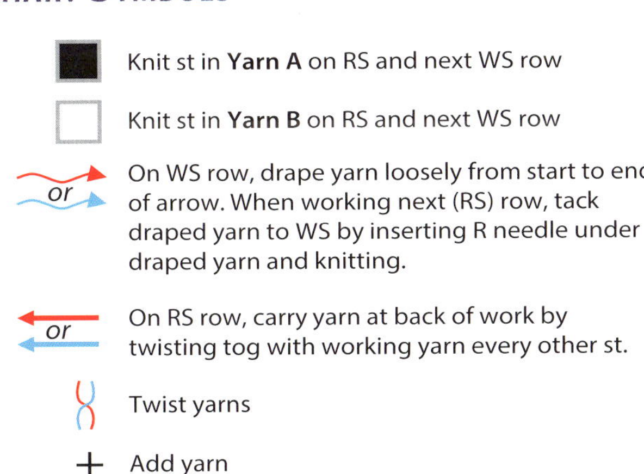

BLANKET INSTRUCTIONS

Blocks

There are two types of Blocks: B1 and B2.

B1 Blocks

See Figure 1 for construction of B1 Blocks.

B1 Blocks consist of a Rectangle (R1) and an extension (E1 or E1-Edge).

Rectangle 1 (R1) – Make 18 (32)

With A, CO 21 sts, leaving long tail of 30"/75 cm, and work [Chart R1, Rows 1-60]. BO loosely. Cut yarns.

Divide the 18 (32) R1's into two groups: 15 (28) for B1's and 3 (4) for B1E's.

B1 – Make 15 (28)

For the group of 15 (28) R1s, on RS, with A, and starting at red triangle, pu&k 27 sts (1 st per garter st ridge) along right edge to last 3 ridges; then, with B, pu&k 3 sts – 30 sts.

Work [Chart E1, Rows 2-18]. BO loosely. Cut yarns, leaving 30"/75 cm tails.

B1E – Make 3 (4)

For the group of 3 (4) R1s, on RS, with A, and starting at red triangle, pu&k 27 sts (1 st per garter st ridge) along edge to last 3 ridges; then, with B, pu&k 3 sts – 30 sts.

Work [Chart E1-Edge, Rows 2-18]. BO loosely. Cut yarns, leaving 30"/75 cm tails.

Chart Rectangle 1 (R1)

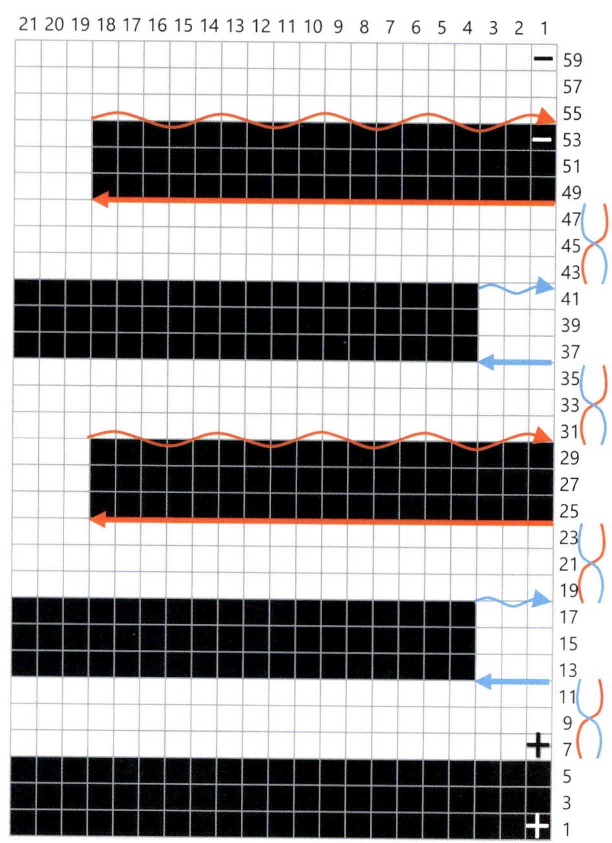

B1 – Make 15 (28)

R1 E1

B1E – Make 3 (4)

R1 E1E

Figure 1: B1 Block Constructions

Chart Extension 1 (E1)

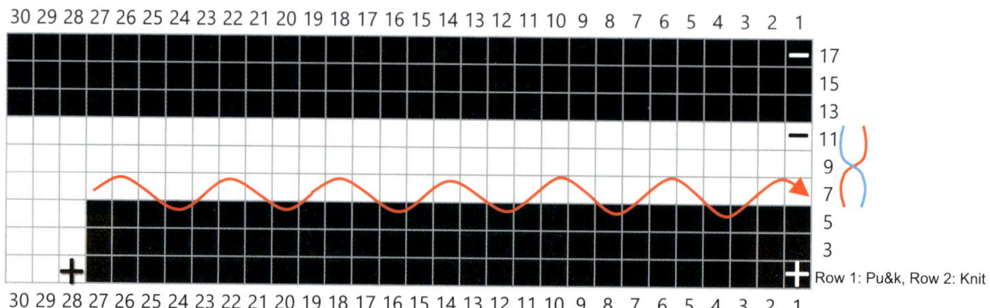

Chart Extension 1 Edge (E1-Edge)

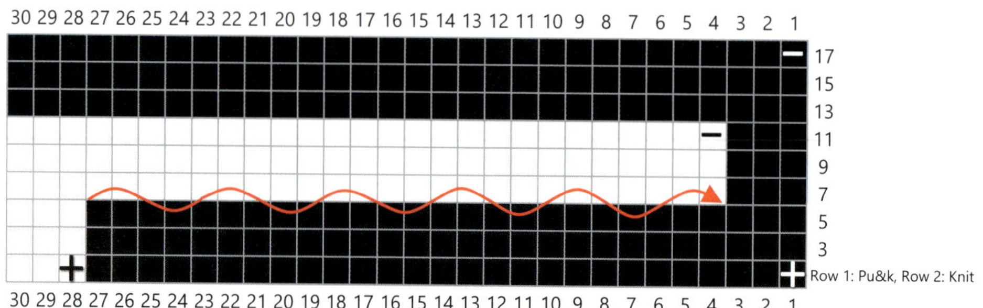

B2 Blocks

See Figure 2 for construction of B2 Blocks.

B2 Blocks consist of a Rectangle (R2) and an extension (E2 or E2-Edge).

Rectangle 2 (R2) – Make 18 (32)

With A, CO 21 sts, leaving long tail of 30"/75 cm.

Work [Chart R2, Rows 1-60]. BO loosely. Cut yarns.

Divide the 18 (32) R2's into two groups: 15 (28) for B2's and 3 (4) for B2E's.

B2 – Make 15 (28)

For the group of 15 (28) R2s, on RS, with B, and starting at red triangle, pu&k 3 sts (1 per garter ridge); then, with A, pu&k 27 sts along edge – 30 sts.

Work [Chart E2, Rows 2-18]. BO loosely. Cut yarns, leaving 30"/75 cm tails.

B2E – Make 3 (4)

For the group of 3 (4) R2s, on RS, with B, pu&k 3 sts (1 per garter ridge); then, with A, pu&k 27 sts along edge – 30 sts.

Work [Chart E2-Edge, Rows 2-18]. BO loosely. Cut yarns, leaving 30"/75 cm tails.

Chart Rectangle 2 (R2)

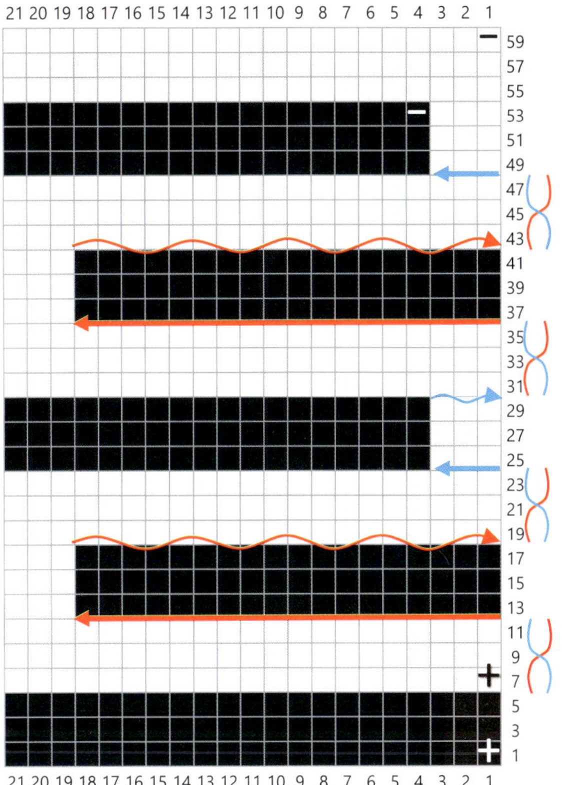

Chart Extension 2 (E2)

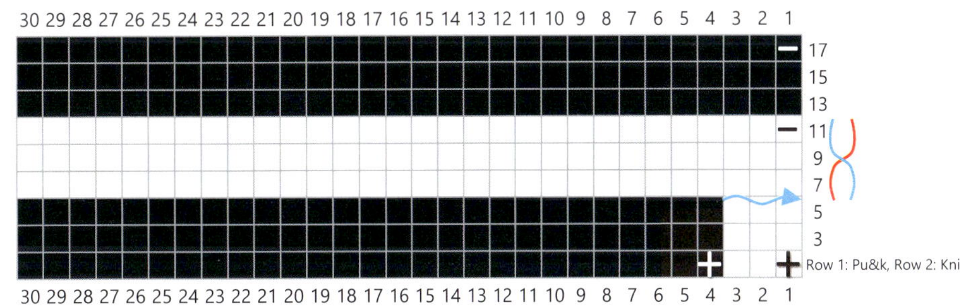

B2 – Make 15 (28)

E2

R2

B2E – Make 3 (4)

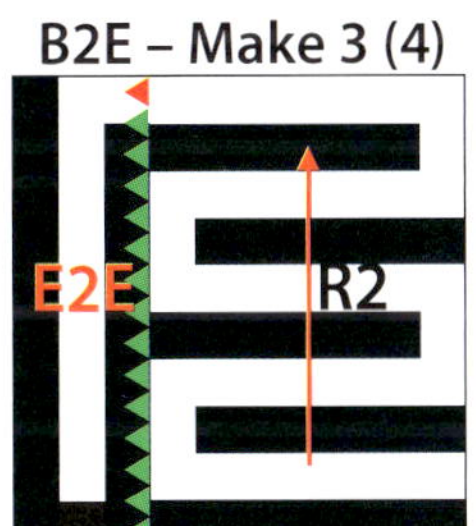

Figure 2: B2 Block Constructions

Chart Extension 2 Edge (E2-Edge)

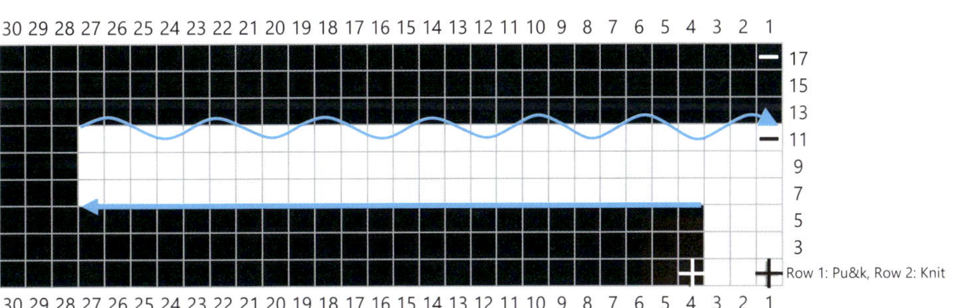

ASSEMBLY

Arrange 36 (64) completed Blocks as shown in Figure 3 (Figure 4), orienting according to the arrows indicating the direction of work for R1's and R2's and aligning corners and adjacent stripes. Using long tails of matching color, when available, and mattress st, sew Blocks into strips along blue lines, and then sew strips tog along red lines, aligning colors of Blocks.

Note: When an A edge is sewn to a B edge, use yarn A. When both edges are the same color, use that color.

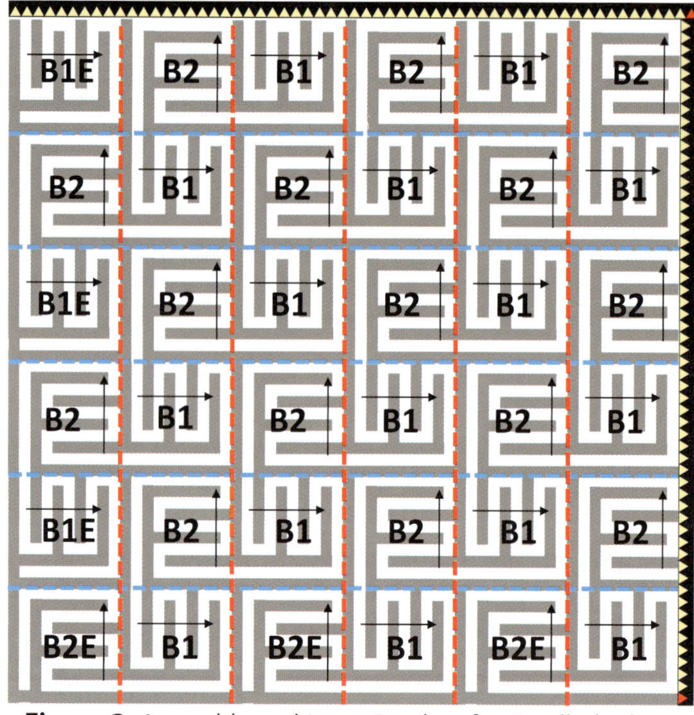

Figure 3: Assembly and Inner Borders for Small Blanket

INNER BORDER

Right Inner Border

On RS, attach A at red triangle at bottom right corner of blanket in Figure 3 (Figure 4), and pu&k 30 sts per Block to top right corner – 180 (240) sts. Knit 5 rows. BO loosely.

Top Inner Border

On RS, attach A at red triangle at top right corner of Right Inner Border and pu&k 7 sts on left edge of Right Inner Border and 30 sts per Block across top of blanket edge – 187 (247) sts. Knit 5 rows. BO loosely.

OUTER BORDER

On WS, attach A to bottom center of blanket and work I-cord Border (see Glossary on page 199) around entire blanket.

FINISHING

Weave in ends. Block if desired.

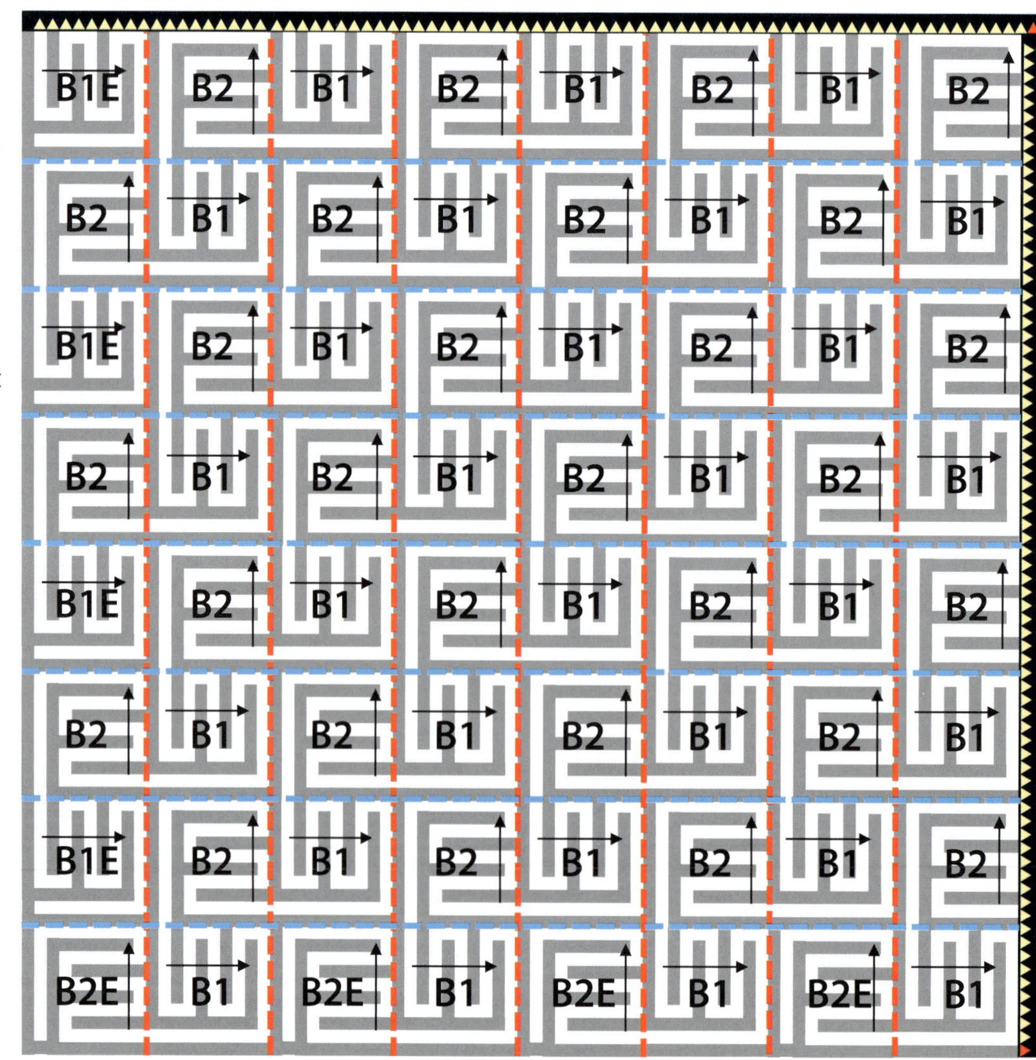

Figure 4: Assembly and Inner Borders for Large Blanket

Photograph is of size Small.

OURAY

This blanket evokes Native American woven blanket designs. Ouray means "Arrow" and is the name of a well-known Ute chief.

SIZE 55 x 78"/140 x 198 cm

TECHNIQUES Method A: Pu&k, sew
Method B: Pu&k, outside-in shapes on dpns

YARN Cascade 220 Superwash, worsted (100% superwash wool; 220 yds/200 m; 3.5 oz/100 g):

Pattern Color ID	Color Swatch	Color ID	Color Name	Color Description	# Skeins
A		815	Black	black	6
B		817	Ecru	white	3
C		252	Celestial	dark teal	5
D		907	Tangerine Heather	rust	3
E		849	Dark Aqua	aqua	3
F		289	Cream Puff	light peach	1

NEEDLES US Size 7/4.5 mm 40"/100 cm circular needles, US Size 7/4.5 mm dpns (Method B only), or size needed to obtain gauge

NOTIONS Stitch markers, tapestry needle, stitch holders or scrap yarn

GAUGE 19 sts x 38 rows = 4"/10 cm in garter st

NOTES

- There are two methods for working the blanket, as shown in Figure 1. Both begin with Corners, Internal Blocks, and Edges.
- In Method A, Blocks are sewn together.
- In Method B, Blocks are worked in sections and joined by squares worked in the round.
- Borders are picked up from the edges of the completed blanket.

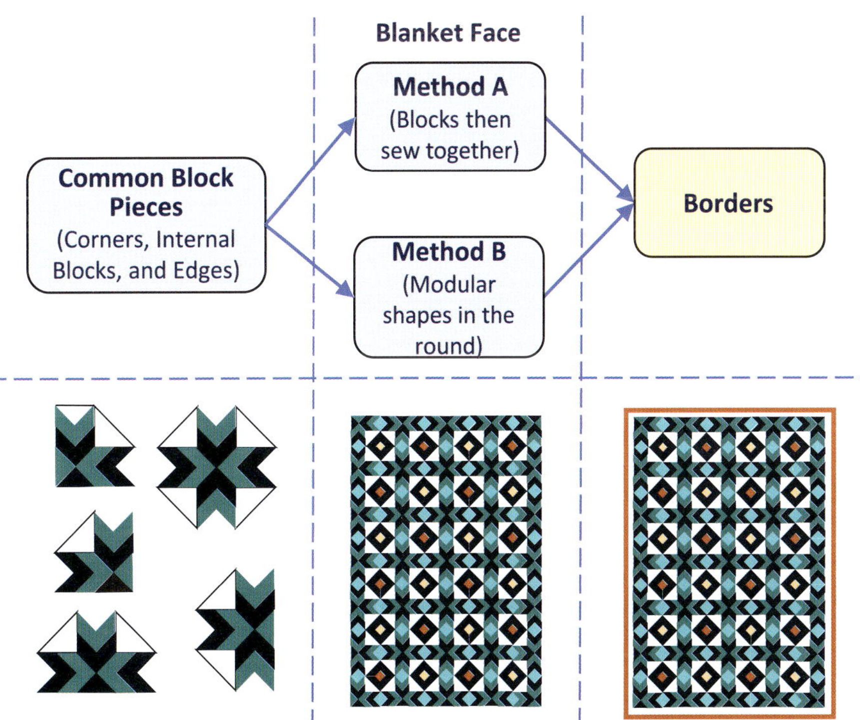

Figure 1: Overview of Construction Options

BLANKET INSTRUCTIONS

Common Block Pieces – Both Methods

Common Pieces, worked for both methods, include Interior Blocks, Edges, and Corners.

Interior Block (IB) – Make 15

See Figure 2 for construction, in which letters after shape names are the colors in order of their use [C1][C2]. Use a knitted CO throughout.

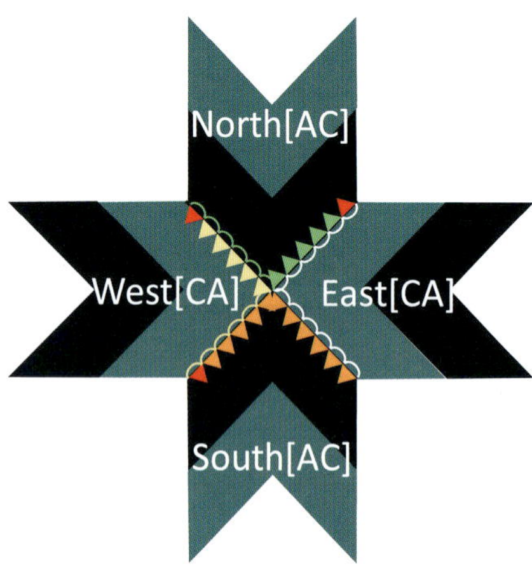

Step 1: Arms (East, North, West, and South)

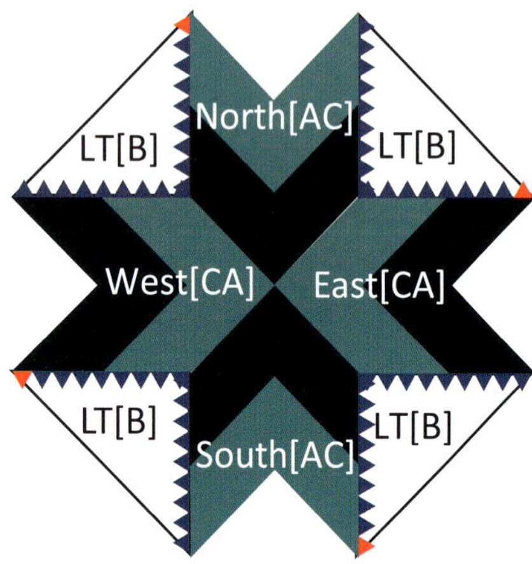

Step 2: Large Triangles

Figure 2: Both Methods: Construction of Interior Block (IB)

Step 1: Arms

East Arm

With C1, CO 14 sts, pm, CO 13 sts – 27 sts. Work [Arm].

Arm – 27 sts

Row 2 (WS): Knit.
Row 3 (RS): Kf&b, knit to 2 sts bef m, rm, cdd, pm, knit to last st, kf&b.
Row 4: Knit.
Rows 5-14: Rep [Rows 3 & 4] 5 times.
Cut C1. Attach C2.
Rows 15-26: Rep [Rows 3 & 4] 6 times.
Place 27 sts on holder. Do not remove m.

North Arm

On RS, with C1, and starting at red triangle on corner of East, pu&k 13 sts to next corner, 1 st in corner, pm, and then turn to WS and CO 13 sts – 27 sts. Work [Arm].

West Arm

Work as for North, starting at red triangle in lower left corner of North.

South Arm

On RS, with C1, and starting at red triangle in lower right corner of West, pu&k 13 sts to next corner, 1 st in corner, pm, and then pu&k 13 sts to next corner. Work [Arm].

Step 2: Large Triangles (LT)

On RS, in each space labeled "LT," attach B at red triangle on corner of each Arm, pu&k 18 sts to corner, 1 st in corner, pm, and 18 sts to next corner – 37 sts.

Work [MT]. Cut yarn and fasten off, leaving 12"/30 cm tail.

Mitered Triangle (MT) – odd # of sts dec'ing to 1 st

Row 2 (WS): Knit.
Row 3 (RS): K2tog, knit to 2 sts bef m, rm, cdd, pm, knit to last 2 sts, ssk – 4 sts dec'd.
Row 4: Knit.
Rep Rows 3 & 4 until 3 or 5 sts rem, ending after a RS row.
Last row (WS) when 3 sts rem: Cdd – 2 sts dec'd; 1 st.
Last row (WS) when 5 sts rem: Cdd2 – 4 sts dec'd; 1 st.
Cut yarn and fasten off.

Edge Blocks (EB)

See Figure 3 for construction.

Edge Block 1 (EB1) – Make 10

Work as for Internal Block (IB), omitting East and working North first, generating sts as for East Arm of IB (using pu&k).

In space labeled "Tr," attach C at red triangle in upper right corner of South. Pu&k 13 sts to corner, 1 st in corner, pm, and then 13 sts to next corner – 27 sts. Work [MT].

Edge Block 2 (EB2) – Make 6

Work as for Internal Block (IB), omitting South.

In space labeled "Tr," attach A at red triangle in lower right corner of West. Pu&k 13 sts to corner, 1 st in corner, pm, and 13 sts to next corner – 27 sts. Work [MT].

Corner Blocks (CB)

***Corner Block 1 (CB1)* – Make 2**

See Figure 4 for construction.

Work East, North, and LT of IB.

Tr1

In space labeled "Tr1," attach C at the red triangle in lower left corner of North. Pu&k 13 sts to corner, 1 st in corner, pm, CO 13 sts – 27 sts. Work [MT].

Tr2

In space labeled "Tr2," attach A at the red triangle in lower right corner of Tr1. Pu&k 13 sts to corner, 1 st in corner, pm, and 13 sts to next corner – 27 sts. Work [MT].

***Corner Block 2 (CB2)* – Make 2**

Work North, West, and LT of IB. Generate stitches for North as for IB East.

Tr1

In space labeled "Tr1," attach A at the red triangle in lower right corner of West. Pu&k 13 sts to corner, 1 st in corner, pm, CO 13 sts – 27 sts. Work [MT].

Tr2

In space labeled "Tr2," attach C at the red triangle in lower right corner of Tr1. Pu&k 13 sts to corner, 1 st in corner, pm, and 13 sts to next corner – 27 sts. Work [MT].

Continue at either "Method A – Construction" or "Method B – Construction."

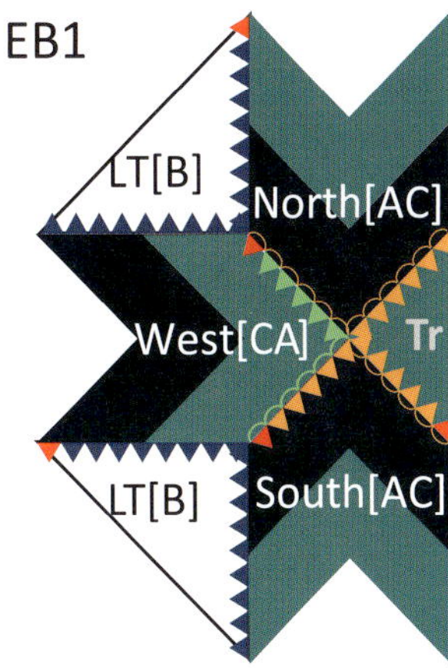

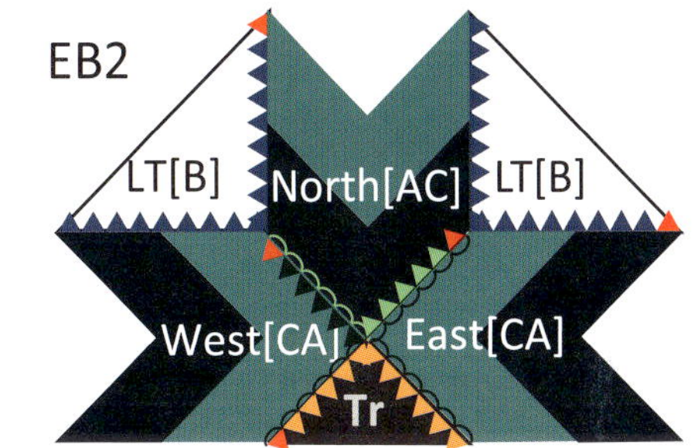

Figure 3: Both Methods: Construction of Edge Block 1 (EB1) and Edge Block 2 (EB2)

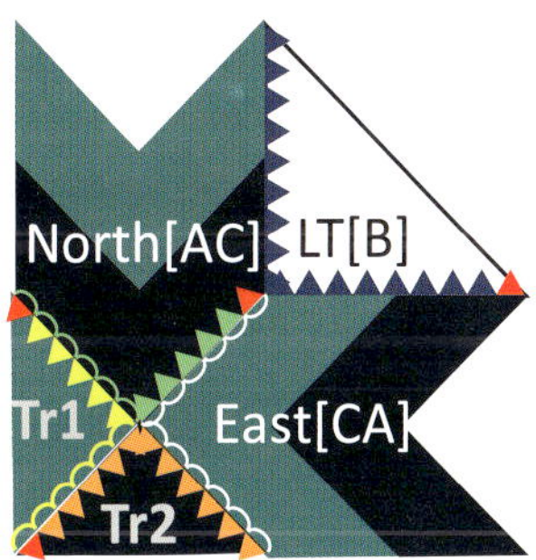

Corner Block 1 (CB1)

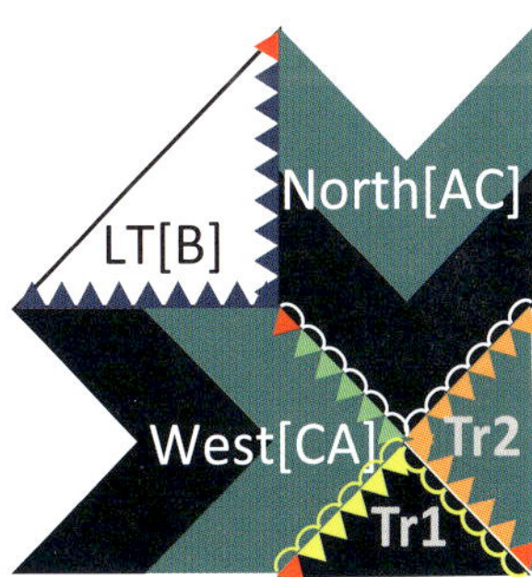

Corner Block 2 (CB2)

Figure 4: Both Methods: Construction of Corner Block 1 (CB1) and Corner Block 2 (CB2)

Method A - Construction

Block Extensions

Block Extensions may be added as soon as the Block they extend is complete.

Triangles (Tr)

See Figure 5 for construction.

At the end of each arm of each IB, EB, and CB in spaces labeled "Tr," on RS, transfer 27 sts and m from holder to needle. Starting on RS, with F, knit 1 row, and then work [MT].

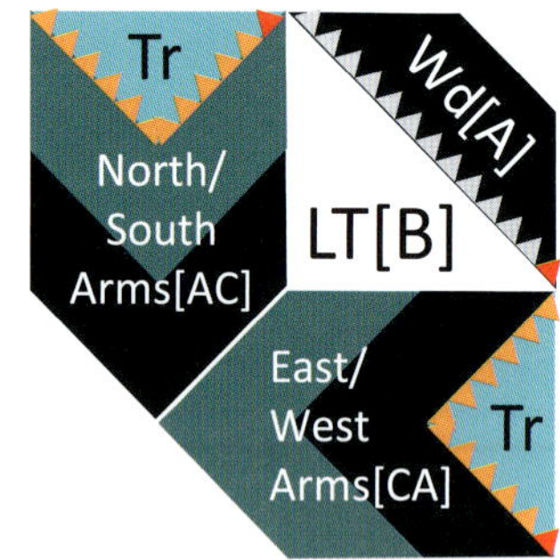

Figure 5: Method A: Construction of Triangles (Tr) and Wedge (Wd)

Wedges (Wd)

See Figure 5 for construction.

Between each pair of Arms on each IB, EB, and CB in spaces labeled "Wd," with A, and starting at red triangle at corner of LT. Pu&k 26 sts to corner. Work [Wd].

For all EBs, CBs, and 9 of the IBs, BO loosely after completing each Wedge. Cut yarn, leaving 12"/30 cm tail.

Wedge (Wd) – 26 sts dec'ing to 14 sts

Row 2 (WS): Knit.
Row 3 (RS): K2tog, knit to last 2 sts, ssk – 2 sts dec'd; 24 sts.
Rows 4-13: Rep [Rows 2 & 3] 5 times – 10 sts dec'd; 14 sts.

Squared IBs (SIB)

See Figure 6 for construction.

For rem 6 IB's, do not BO sts after completing a Wedge, and instead cut yarn, leaving 12"/30 cm tail, and work a Small Square (SS) on each corner in the colors specified in Figure 6. At each corner of the Block at location labeled "SS," on RS, attach color for SS at green triangle, leaving a 15"/44 cm tail.

Knit 28 rows. BO loosely. Cut yarn and fasten off.

Assembly

Layout

Arrange completed IBs, SIBs, EBs, and CBs as shown in Figure 7, orienting each Block with the North Arm in the direction of the arrows.

Sewing

See Figure 8. Using matching long tails and mattress st, sew Blocks into 5 vertical strips along the magenta dashed lines, matching corners and shape edges, and then sew vertical strips tog along green dashed lines.

Continue at "Borders."

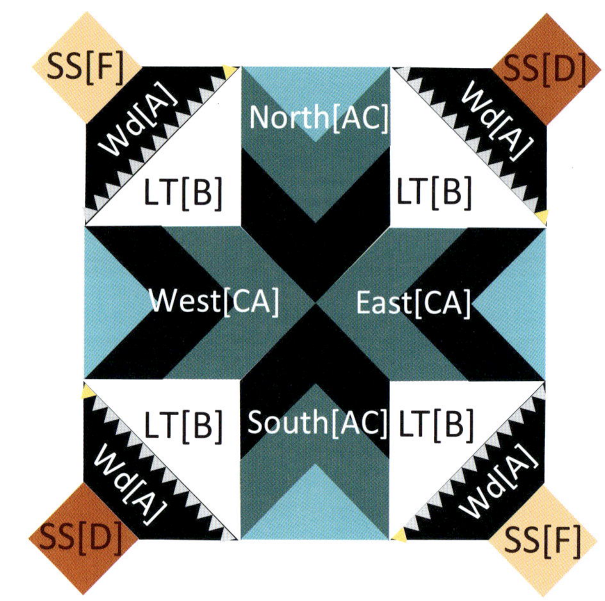

Figure 6: Method A: Construction of Wedges (Wd) and Small Squares (SS) for Squared Internal Blocks (SIB)

Figure 7: Method A: Layout

Figure 8: Method A: Sewing

Method B - Construction

Previously completed shapes are joined using Outside-In worked squares to create three sections (Upper, Middle, and Lower) shown in Figure 9. Then additional Outside-In squares are worked to join the sections together as shown in Figure 10.

Assemble Three Sections

Small Outside-In Squares (OS)

In spaces labeled "OS" in Figure 9, with E, knit 27 sts off holder for one arm as follows: Using a dpn, knit to 2 sts bef m, k2tog, rm, knit rem sts of Arm onto 2nd dpn – 26 sts. Rep across 27 sts of opposite Arm – 52 sts.

Work [OS] until 12 sts rem ending after an odd-numbered (purl) rnd. Rm's.

Next rnd: Sl1, cdd 4 times – 8 sts dec'd; 4 sts.

Note: The 4th cdd will cross the BOR.

Cut yarn, leaving 10"/25 cm tail. Thread tail onto tapestry needle and insert through all sts on dpns. Pull to tighten and fasten off securely.

> **Outside-In Square (OS)**
>
> Worked in the round.
> **Rnd 1:** Purl.
> **Rnd 2:** *K2tog, knit to last 2 sts on dpn, ssk; rep from * 3 times – 8 sts dec'd.
> **Rnd 3:** Purl.
> Rep Rnds 2 & 3 as indicated.

Large Outside-In Squares (OL)

Arrange shapes as shown in Figure 9 with the North Arm of each shape oriented according to arrows. In spaces labeled "OL," attach A at red triangle; *pu&k 26 sts to corner and place on dpn; rep from * 3 more times – 104 sts.

Work [OS] until 56 sts rem (14 sts per dpn), ending after an odd-numbered (purl) rnd. Cut A; attach yarn for center of diamond. Work [OS] until 8 st rem (2 per dpn). Cut yarn, leaving 10"/25 cm tail. Thread tail onto tapestry needle and insert through all sts on dpns. Pull to tighten and fasten off securely.

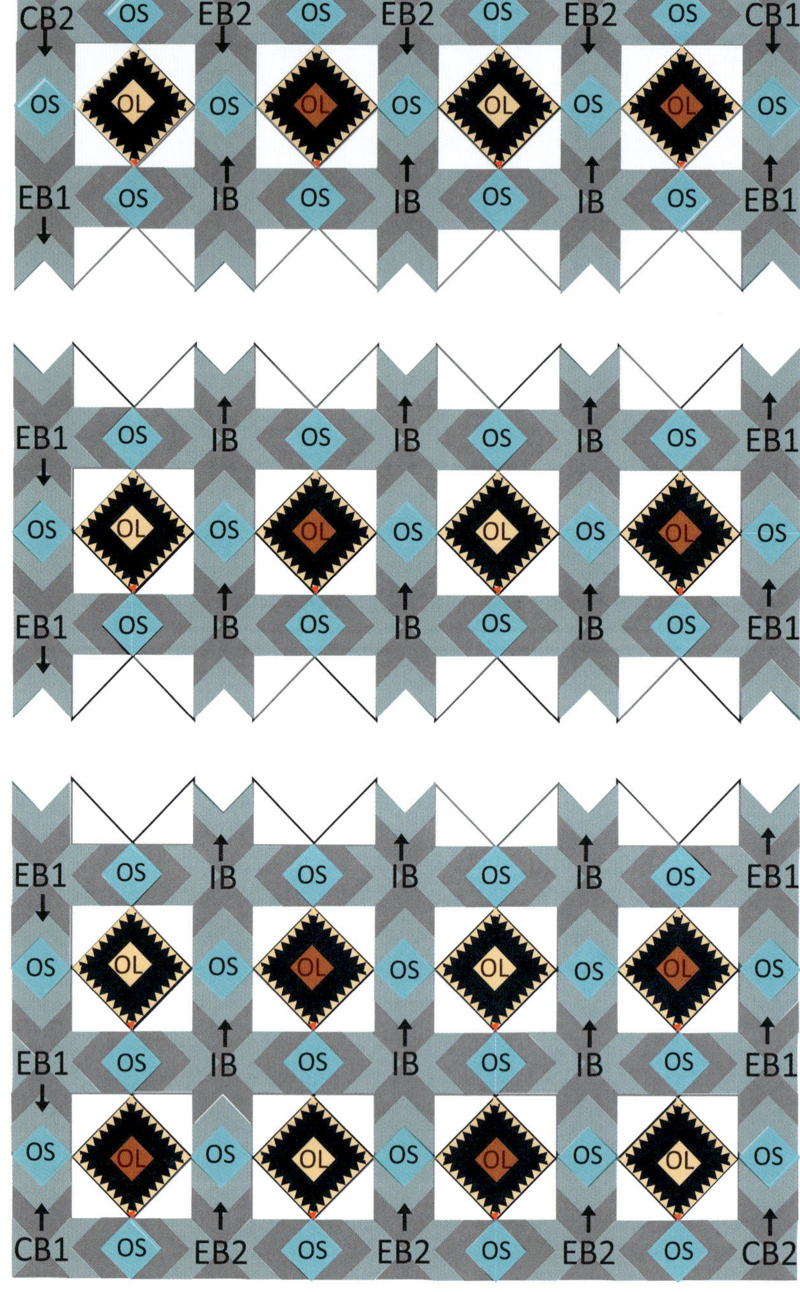

Colors for OL and OS shapes 

Figure 9: Method B: Assembly, OL and OS

Join Three Sections Together

Arrange the 3 sections (Upper, Middle, and Lower) as shown in Figure 10.

In spaces labeled "OL" in Figure 10, work as for OL.

In spaces labeled "OS" in Figure 10, work as for OS.

Continue at "Borders."

Figure 10: Method B: Joining Sections with OL and OS

BORDERS

Right Border

On RS, attach B at bottom right corner of blanket. Pu&k 342 sts (18 sts per Tr or Arm shape) on right edge of blanket. Work [Border].

Top Border

Starting at top right corner, pu&k 234 sts along top edge. Work [Border].

Left Border

Work as for Right Border, attaching B at top left corner.

Bottom Border

Work as for Top Border, attaching B at bottom left corner.

Border

Row 2 (WS): Knit.
Row 3 (RS): Kf&b, knit to last st, kf&b – 2 sts inc'd.
Row 4: Knit.
Rows 5-16: Rep [Rows 3 & 4] 6 times – 12 sts inc'd.
Cut B, leaving 15"/40 cm tail.
Attach D.
Rows 17-30: Rep [Rows 3 & 4] 7 times – 14 sts inc'd.
BO loosely. Cut D, leaving 15"/40 cm tail.

FINISHING

Using long tails of B and D from Borders and mattress st, sew corner seams. Weave in ends.

PINWHEELS

Whirling pinwheels are a wonder of childhood. Here they are worked in a rainbow of colors dramatically showcased by a black background.

SIZE 48 x 68"/122 x 173 cm

TECHNIQUES Intarsia (Method A only), pu&k, sewing

YARN Cascade Yarns Cherub Aran, heavy worsted (55% nylon, 45% acrylic; 240 yds/220 m; 3.5 oz/100 g):

Pattern Color ID	Color Swatch	Color ID	Color Name	Color Description	# Skeins
A		9	Ecru	off-white	4
B		40	Black	black	9
C		27	Navy	navy blue	1
D		28	Boy Blue	light blue	1
E		103	Prism Violet	medium purple	1
F		106	Lavender Mist	light purple	1
G		104	Strawberry	hot pink	1
H		105	Cherry Blossom	light pink	1
I		99	Harvest Pumpkin	medium orange	1
J		83	Orange Chiffon	light orange	1
K		101	Old Gold	medium yellow	1
L		38	Yellow	light yellow	1
M		98	Vibrant Green	medium green	1
N		56	Lime Chiffon	light green	1
O		33	Peacock	medium teal	1
P		12	Turquoise	light teal	1

NEEDLES US Size 7/4.5 mm 40"/100 cm circular needles or size needed to obtain gauge

NOTIONS Tapestry needle, stitch markers, stitch holders

GAUGE 21 sts x 42 rows = 4"/10 cm in garter st

NOTES

- The blanket is worked in Blocks that are sewn together. The border is picked up and knit (pu&k) from the blanket edges.
- A Block consists of a center square surrounded by 4 corners. There are two methods for working corners, as shown in Figure 1. Method A uses 2-color intarsia (charted), and Method B uses pu&k with shaping with only one color in use at a time. After corners are complete, the first and last corners are seamed together.

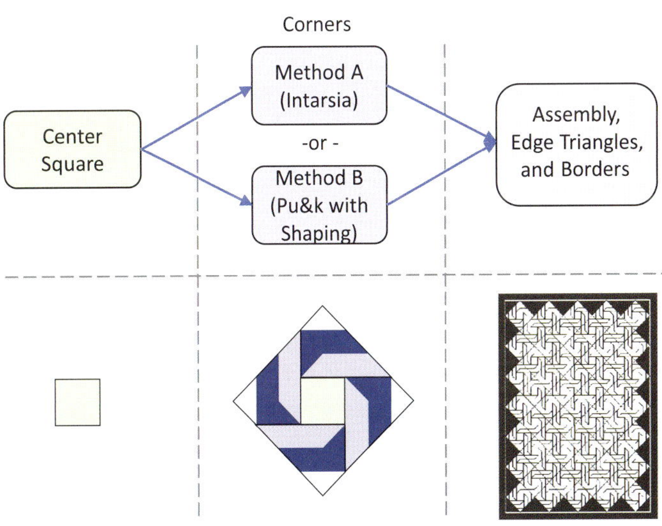

Figure 1: Overview of Construction Options

BLANKET INSTRUCTIONS

Blocks

Make 59 Blocks in these colors:

Main Color (MC)	Color 1 (C1)	Color 2 (C2)	# of Blocks to Make in these Colors
A	D	C	4
A	F	E	4
A	H	G	4
A	J	I	3
A	L	K	3
A	N	M	3
A	P	O	3
B	C	D	5
B	E	F	5
B	G	H	5
B	I	J	5
B	K	I	5
B	M	N	5
B	O	P	5

The placement of colors MC, C1, and C2 is illustrated in Figure 2.

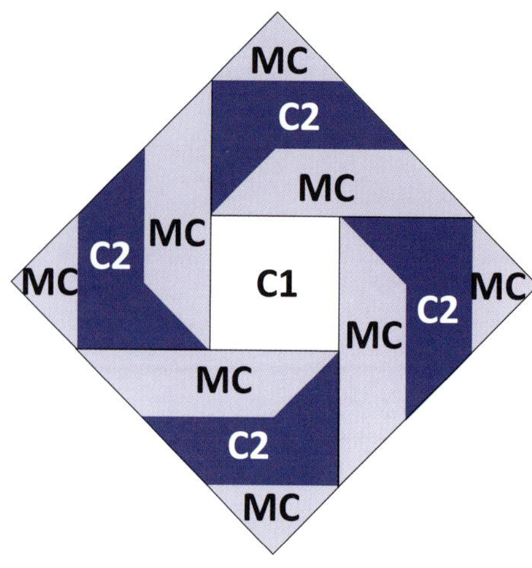

Figure 2: Color Schemes for Blocks

Center Square (Sq)

With C1 for Block, CO 12 sts. Knit 23 rows. Cut C1.

Four Corners

Use either Method A or Method B.

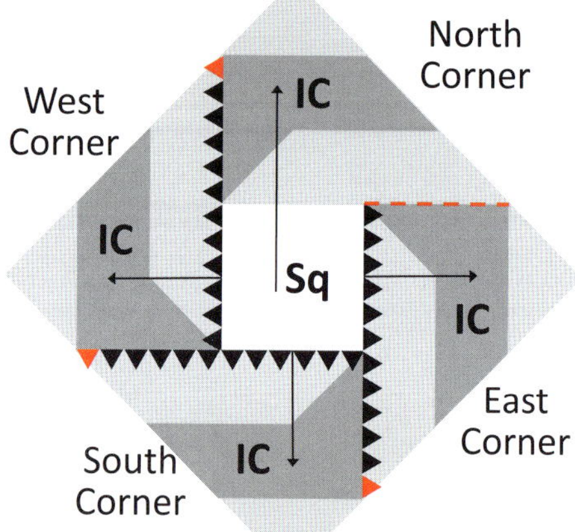

Figure 3: Method A: Construction

Method A

See Figure 3. Read about intarsia on page 204.

North Corner

With RS facing, and MC, CO 12 additional sts – 24 sts.

Note: Leave a 12"/30 cm tail of MC for sewing seam.

Work Corner Chart at right. Cut yarns and fasten off, leaving 12"/30 cm tails of C2 and MC. With a locking stitch marker or safety pin, mark the North Corner.

West, South, and East Corners

With MC, on RS, pu&k 12 sts from the red triangle on prev completed Corner, to Sq, and 12 sts on edge of Sq – 24 sts. Work Corner Chart.

Continue at "Seam" on next page.

Corner Chart

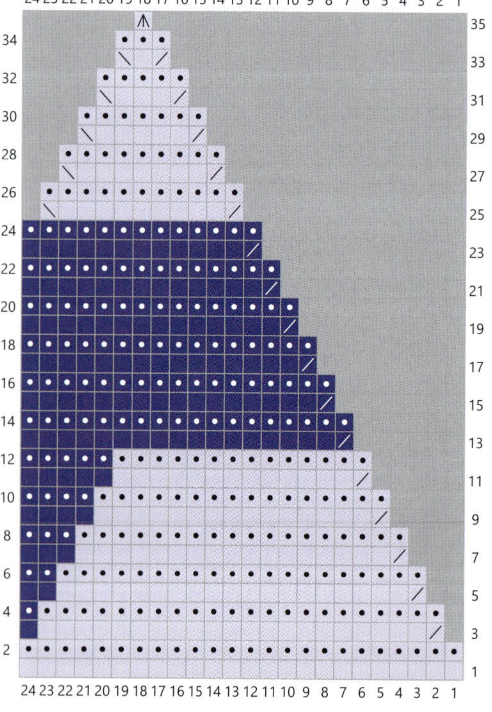

RS: knit · WS: knit · RS: cdd · RS: k2tog
RS: ssk · no stitch · Main Color (MC) · Color 2 (C2)

Method B

See Figure 4.

North Corner

Tr1

With RS facing and MC, CO 12 additional sts – 24 sts.

Continuing with MC, knit one row, *work [Tr], changing to C2 after 11 rows (when 14 sts rem after completing WS row).

Do not cut C2. Leave last st on needle.

Tr2

Triangle (Tr)

Row 2 (WS): Knit.
Row 3 (RS): K2tog, knit to last 2 sts, ssk – 2 sts dec'd.
Rep [Rows 2 & 3] until 2 or 3 sts rem.
Next row (if 2 sts rem): K2tog – 1 st dec'd; 1 st.
Next row (if 3 sts rem): Knit. (**Final row:** Cdd – 2 sts dec'd; 1 st.)

Continuing with C2, pu&k 16 sts from yellow triangle to next corner of Tr1 – 17 sts. Work [Tr]. Cut yarn and fasten off.

Note: For an even distribution of pu&k sts, pu&k as follows in ridges and valleys (i.e., between ridges): 1 st in each of first 4 ridges, (1 st in next valley, then 1 st in each of next 2 ridges) 4 times.

Tr3

With MC, pu&k 12 sts from green triangle to next corner of Tr2. Work [Tr]. Cut yarn and fasten off. *

Attach a safety pin or locking stitch marker to identify the North Corner.

West, South, and East Corners

With MC, on RS, pu&k 24 sts from red triangle on edge of previous Corner to end of Sq. Rep bet * and * of North Corner.

Continue at "Seam" (right).

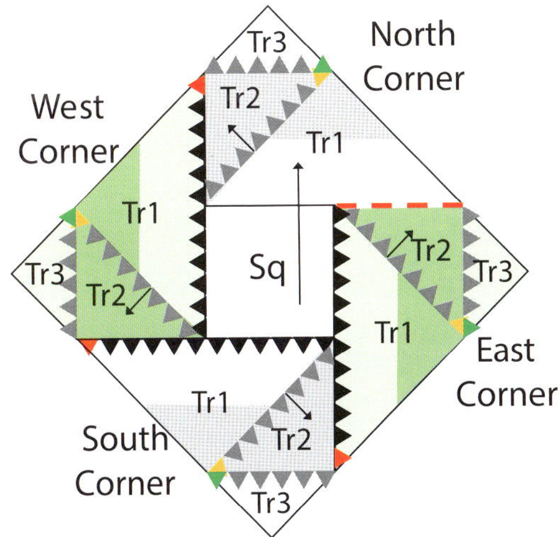

Figure 4: Method B: Construction

Seam (See Figure 4)

With long CO tail of MC (from North Corner) and mattress st, sew seam bet North Corner and East Corner, shown by red-dashed line.

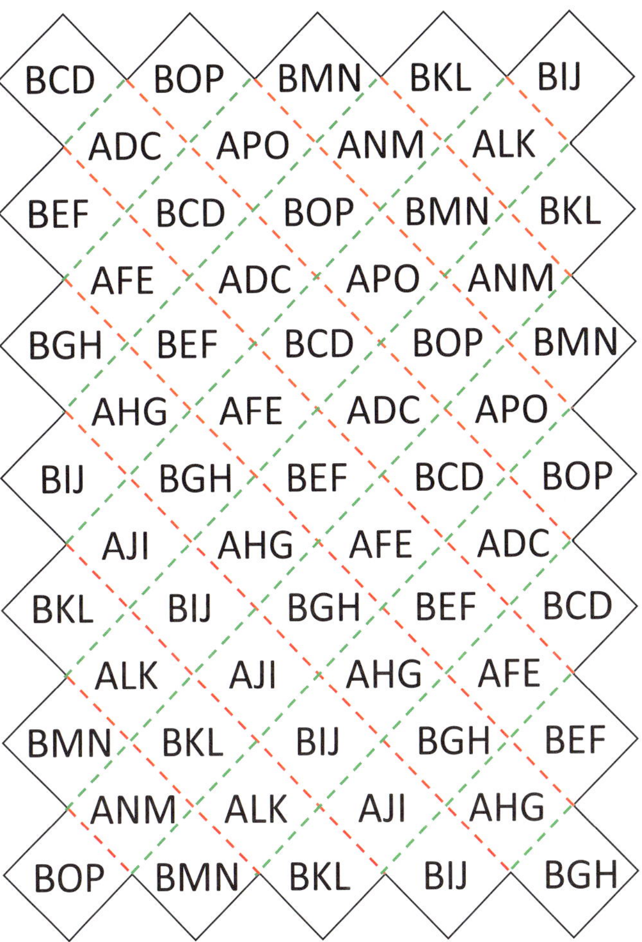

Figure 5: Arrangement of Blocks

Assembly of Blocks (See Figure 5, page 99)

Arrange 59 Blocks as shown, with North Corner of Block oriented to the top. Blocks are named by their colors: [MC][C1][C2]. Using long tails of matching color and mattress st, sew Blocks tog into diagonal strips along red dashed lines, and then sew strips tog along green dashed lines, matching corners and color transitions.

Edge Triangles (ET) (See Figure 6)

In each of the 20 spaces labeled "ET," attach B, pu&k 33 sts from red triangle to corner, 1 st in corner, pm, and 33 sts to next corner – 67 sts. Work [MT]. Cut yarn and fasten off.

Mitered Triangle (MT) – 67 sts dec'ing to 1 st

Row 2 (WS): Knit.
Row 3: K2tog, knit to 2 sts bef m, rm, cdd, pm, knit to last 2 sts, ssk – 4 sts dec'd; 63 sts.
Rows 4-33: Rep [Rows 2 & 3] 15 times – 60 sts dec'd; 3 sts.
Row 34: Rm. Cdd – 2 sts dec'd; 1 st.

Corner Triangles (CT) (See Figure 6)

In each of the 4 spaces labeled "CT," attach B and pu&k 33 sts from red triangle to next corner. Work [Tr]. Cut yarn and fasten off.

Figure 6: Edge Triangles and Corner Triangles

BORDERS

Right Border

Attach B at the bottom right corner of blanket, pu&k 336 sts (48 sts per ET and 24 sts per CT edge). Knit 11 rows. BO loosely, leaving last st on needle.

Top Border

Pu&k 6 sts on top edge of Right Border and 240 sts on top edge of blanket – 247 sts. Knit 11 rows. BO loosely, leaving last st on needle.

Left Border

Pu&k 6 sts on left edge of Top Border and 336 sts on left edge of the blanket – 343 sts. Knit 11 rows. BO loosely, leaving last st on needle.

Bottom Border

Pu&k 6 sts on bottom edge of Left Border, 240 sts on bottom edge of blanket, and 7 sts on bottom edge of the Right Border – 254 sts. Knit 11 rows. BO loosely. Cut yarn and fasten off.

FINISHING

Weave in ends.

PIROUETTE

Twirling color wheels dance across this blanket in subtle shades of greens and blues.

SIZE 50 x 62"/127 x 157 cm

TECHNIQUES All methods: Short rows, 3-needle BO, pu&k
Methods A & C: Sewing
Methods B & D: Shapes worked in the round

YARN REQUIREMENTS Jagger Spun Heather, worsted (100% wool; 160 yds/146 m; 3.5 oz/100 g):

Pattern Color ID	Color Swatch	Color Name	Color Description	# Skeins
A		Lava	black	12
B		Teal	teal	3
C		Bayberry	light green-blue	3
D		Cobalt	bright blue	3
E		Blue Mist	light gray-blue	3
F		Smoke	light gray	2
G		Slate	medium gray	2
H		Edelweiss	off-white	3

NEEDLES [2] US size 7/4.5 mm 40"/100 cm or longer circular knitting needles and dpns or size needed to obtain gauge, 1 larger needle for 3-needle BO
Methods B & D: 24"/60 cm US 7 circular needle

NOTIONS Tapestry needle, locking stitch markers, stitch holders or scrap yarn

GAUGE 20 sts and 40 rows = 4"/10 cm in garter st

NOTES

- The blanket is composed of Squares, beginning with Arcs that are worked using wrapped sts and color changes.
- There are multiple methods for constructing and assembling (see Figure 1 on page 104). Both begin by working Arcs and Half Arcs. Method A adds corners to Arcs and then sews sets of four squared-Arcs into a Square. Method B joins 4 Arcs into a Square by working a 4-point star from their edges. Squares are joined either by working mitered triangles between them and sewing (Method C) or by working a square outside-in (Method D). For a blanket worked in portable pieces, choose A and C. For a blanket worked all in one piece, choose B and D.
- If a pattern stitch does not specify that it is for a particular Method, then it is used in multiple Methods.
- For Arc, Half Arc 1, and Half Arc 2, do not cut C1 or A until specified. Carry non-working yarn along edge between uses, draping slightly loosely. Tack the draped yarn during subsequent pu&k along that edge. See "Tacking Draped Yarn" on page 210 for more information.

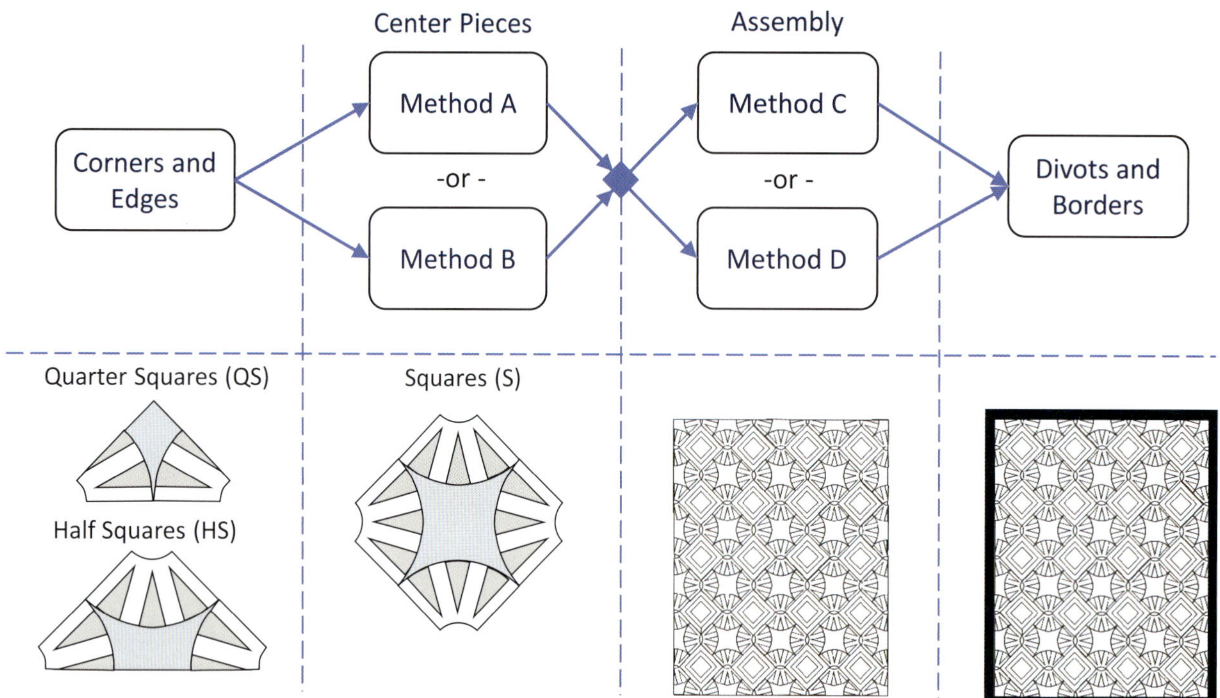

Figure 1: Overview of Construction Options

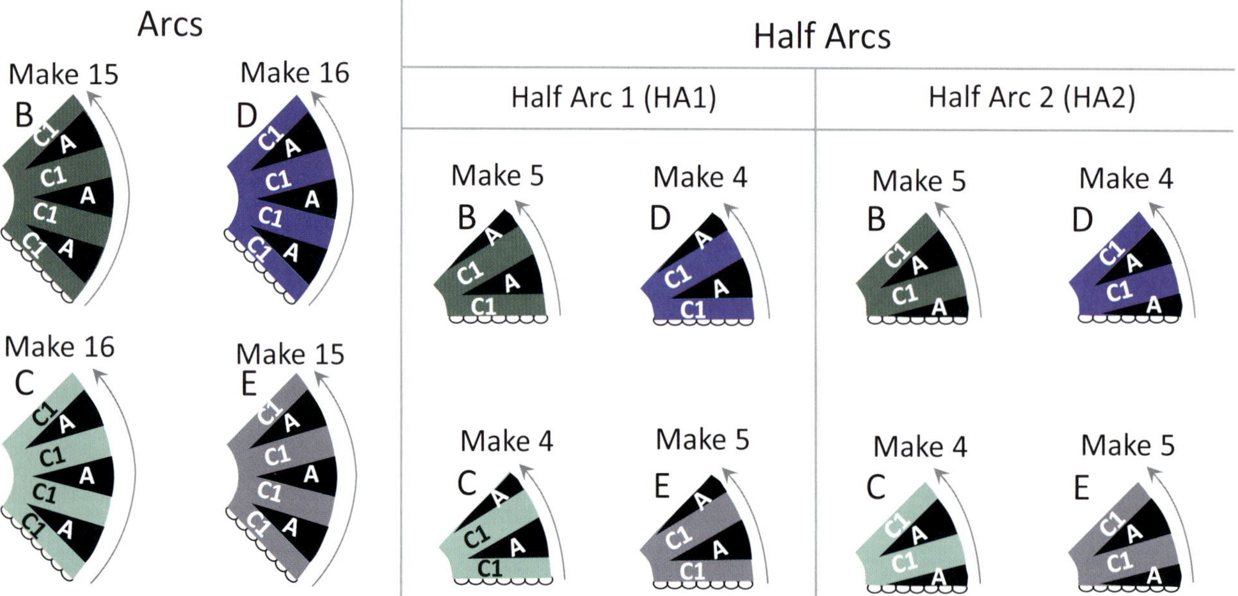

Figure 2: Arc and Half Arc (HA) Color Schemes (CS) and Quantities

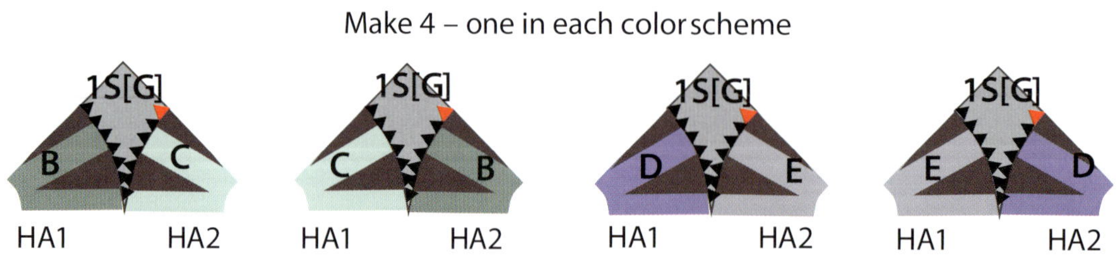

Make 4 – one in each color scheme

1S[G] B C HA1 HA2

1S[G] C B HA1 HA2

1S[G] D E HA1 HA2

1S[G] E D HA1 HA2

Figure 3: Quarter Squares Color Schemes and Quantities

BLANKET INSTRUCTIONS

Arcs and Half Arcs 1 & 2 (HA1 & HA2) - All Methods

Work Arcs, Half Arc 1's (HA1), and Half Arc 2's (HA2) in color schemes and quantities specified in Figure 2. Color Schemes (CS) are named after the color used for C1 of the shape.

For instance, CS "B" means that yarn color B is used for C1.

Quarter Squares (QS) - All Methods

Arrange pairs of Half Arcs in quantities and CSs shown in Figure 3.

Attach G at the top-right corner of right HA at red triangle, pu&k 20 sts to end of edge, pm, pu&k 20 sts on edge of left HA – 40 sts. Work [1S].

1 [2] point Star (1S [2S]) – 40 [80] sts dec'ing to 2 [4] sts

Number of reps and st counts are given as 1S [2S].

Row 2 (WS): (Knit to m, rm, 3-needle BO 5 times (9 sts dec'd), sl rem 1 st from 3rd needle to R needle, pm) 1 [2] times, knit to end – 9 [18] sts dec'd; 31 [62] sts.
Row 3 (RS): (Knit to m, k2tog tbl) 1 [2] times, knit to end – 1 [2] sts dec'd; 30 [60] sts.
Row 4: (Knit to m, rm, 3-needle BO 3 times (5 sts dec'd), sl rem 1 st from 3rd needle to R needle, pm) 1 [2] times, knit to end – 5 [10] sts dec'd; 25 [50] sts.
Row 5: Rep [Row 3] – 1 [2] sts dec'd; 24 [48] sts.
Row 6: (Knit to m, rm, 3-needle BO 2 times (3 sts dec'd), sl rem 1 st from 3rd needle to R needle, pm) 1 [2] times, knit to end – 3 [6] sts dec'd; 21 [42] sts.
Row 7: Rep [Row 3] – 1 [2] sts dec'd; 20 [40] sts.
Rows 8-11: Rep [Rows 6 & 7] twice – 8 [16] sts dec'd; 12 [24] sts.
Rows 12, 14, 16, 18, & 20: (Knit to 2 sts bef m, rm, cdd, pm) 1 [2] times, knit to end – 10 [20] sts dec'd; 2 [4] sts.
Rows: 13, 15, 17, 19, & 21: Knit.
Cut yarn, leaving 10"/25 cm tail. Thread tail onto tapestry needle and insert through rem 2 [4] sts, pull to tighten, and fasten off securely.

Arc – 18 sts (chart on page 114)

With C1, CO 18 sts.
Rows 2-4: Knit (3 rows).
Rows 5-8: Knit (4 more rows).
Row 9 (RS): With A, k2, w&t.
Row 10 and all even-numbered (WS) rows to 30: Knit in same color as prev RS row.
Row 11: K4, w&t.
Row 13: K5, w&t
Row 15: K7, w&t.
Row 17: K8, w&t.
Row 19: K10, w&t.
Row 21: K11, w&t.
Row 23: K13, w&t.
Row 25: Drop C1, cont with A. K14, w&t.
Row 27: Knit to 2 sts from end, w&t next st.
Row 29: Knit to last st, w&t next st.
Rows 31-82: Rep [Rows 5-30] 2 more times. Cut A and fasten off after Row 24 of 2nd rep (i.e., after Row 76).
Rows 83-84: Knit. BO loosely. Cut C1 and fasten off.

Half Arc 1 (HA1) – 18 sts (chart on page 114)

With C1, CO 18 sts.
Rows 2-30: Work [Arc, Rows 2-30] once.
Rows 31-34: Knit (4 rows). Cut C1.
Row 35 (RS): With A, k1, w&t.
Row 36 and even-numbered (WS) rows to 42: Knit.
Row 37: K5, w&t.
Row 39: K9, w&t.
Row 41: K13, w&t.
After Row 42, BO loosely. Cut yarns and fasten off.

Half Arc 2 (HA2) – 18 sts (chart on page 115)

With A, CO 18 sts.
Setup row (RS): K1, w&t.
Row 2 and all even-numbered (WS) rows to 8: Knit in same color as prev RS row.
Row 3 (RS): K5, w&t.
Row 5: K9, w&t.
Row 7: K13, w&t.
Rows 9-11: With C1, knit (3 rows).
Rows 12-40: Work [Arc, Rows 2-30] once.
A may be cut after Row 34 (which is after Row 24 of Arc).
Rows 41-42: Knit (2 rows). BO loosely. Cut C1 and fasten off.

Half Squares (HS) – All Methods

Arrange 28 rem HAs and 14 Arcs in quantities and CSs shown in Figure 4.

Attach color for 2S at red triangle, pu&k 20 sts to corner, pm, pu&k 40 sts to corner, pm, pu&k 20 sts to corner – 80 sts. Work [2S] on page 105.

Continue at "Squares – Method A" or "Squares – Method B."

Make 4 – 2 with 2S worked in G and 2 with 2S worked in F

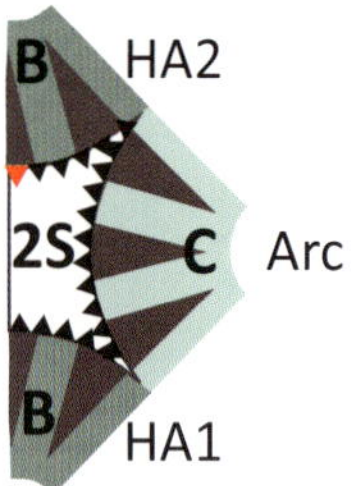

Make 4 – 2 with 2S worked in G and 2 with 2S worked in F

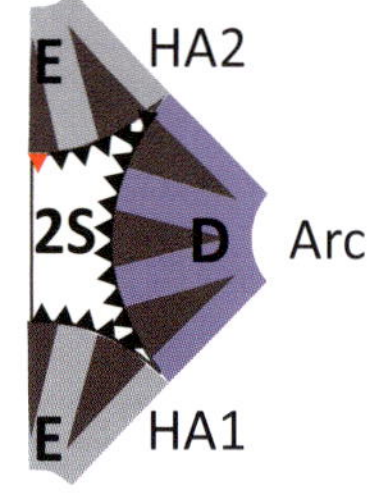

Make 3 – 2 with 2S worked in G, and 1 with 2S worked in F

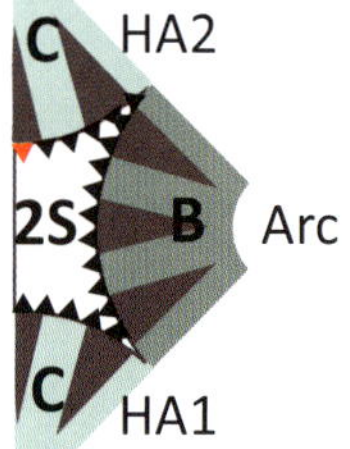

Make 3 – 2 with 2S worked in G, and 1 with 2S worked in F

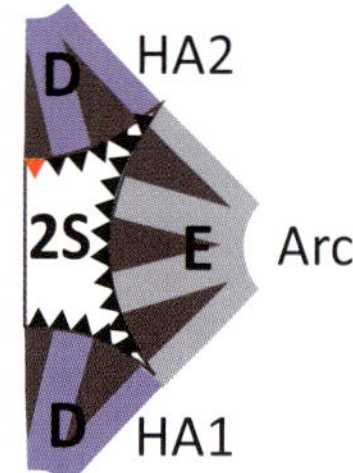

Figure 4: All Methods: Half Squares Color Schemes and Quantities

Squares – Method A

Adding Corners to Arcs

For each of the 48 rem Arcs (there are 12 in each of CSs B, C, D, and E), with the Corner (Cr) yarn color specified in Table 1, and starting at the red triangle in Figure 5, pu&k 40 along edge of Arc. Work [Cr].

Corner (Cr) – Method A – 40 sts dec'ing to 1 st

Row 2 (WS): BO 5, knit to end – 5 sts dec'd; 35 sts.
Row 3 (RS): Rep [Row 2] – 5 sts dec'd; 30 sts.
Rows 4 & 5: BO 3, knit to end – 6 sts dec'd; 24 sts.
Rows 6-11: BO 2, knit to end – 12 sts dec'd; 12 sts.
Rows 12-21: BO 1, knit to end – 10 sts dec'd; 2 sts.
Row 22: K2tog – 1 st dec'd; 1 st.
Cut yarn, leaving 18"/45cm tail, and fasten off.

Table 1: Color for Corners (Cr)

		Arc Color Scheme (CS)			
		B	**C**	**D**	**E**
Corner (Cr) yarn color	**F**	4	4	4	4
	H	8	8	8	8

Note: Table 1 specifies the Corner yarn colors. For instance, in the second column of the table, it specifies that the Corner should be worked in color F on 4 of the Arcs of CS B, and Corners should be worked in H on the remaining 8 Arcs of CS B.

Assembling Groups of 4 Arcs

Arrange groups of 4 completed squared-Arcs in CSs and quantities specified in Figure 6 into 12 Squares. Using long BO tails from Cr, sew tog along red lines using mattress st.

Continue at "Assembly – Method C" or "Assembly – Method D."

Figure 5: Method A: Squaring an Arc

Make 6 from pairs of B and C Arcs: 4 with H for Cr, and 2 with F for Cr.

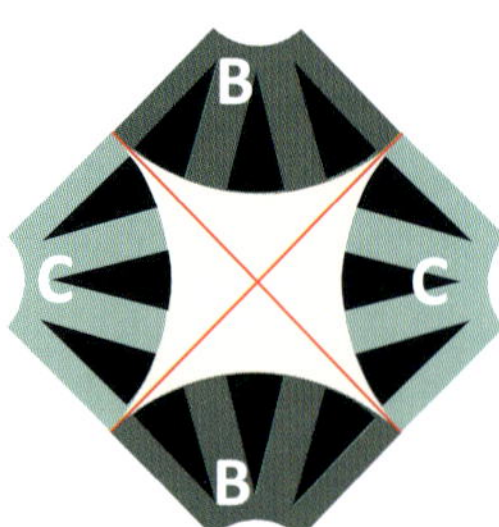

Make 6 from pairs of D and E Arcs: 4 with H for Cr, and 2 with F for Cr.

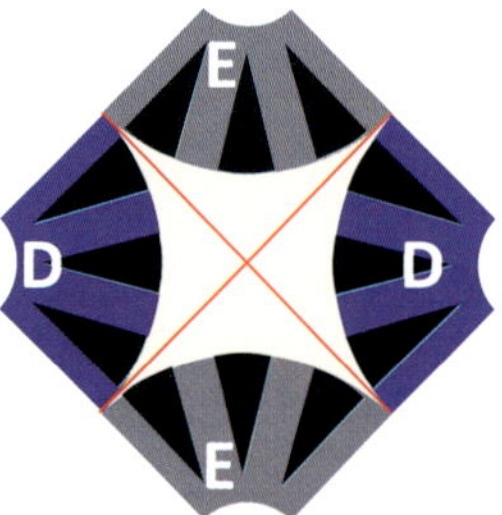

Figure 6: Method A: Quantities, Colors, and Construction of Squares

Squares – Method B

Make 12 Squares from 48 Arcs, in CSs and quantities specified in Figure 7.

With RS facing, arrange 4 Arcs as shown in Figure 7, with curved edges toward the center. Working with a 24"/60 cm circular needle, with yarn for 4S, beg pu&k at red triangle, and, working clockwise, *pu&k 40 sts along curved edge of Arc to corner, pm; rep from * 3 more times – 160 sts. Work [4S].

Continue at "Assembly – Method C" or "Assembly – Method D."

4-point Star (4S) – Method B – 160 sts dec'ing to 8 sts

Worked in the round. Switch to dpns when needed.

Note: When performing 3-needle BOs on odd-numbered Rnds 1-11, the BO crosses the BOR, using the last sts of the current rnd and the first sts of the next rnd. The last m is replaced at the new BOR.

Rnd 1: *Purl to m, rm, 3-needle BO 5 times (9 sts dec'd), sl rem 1 st from 3rd needle to R needle, pm; rep from * 3 more times – 36 sts dec'd; 124 sts.
Rnd 2: *Knit to 2 sts bef m, k2tog tbl, sm; rep from * 3 more times – 4 sts dec'd; 120 sts.
Rnd 3: *Purl to m, rm, 3-needle BO 3 times (5 sts dec'd), sl rem 1 st from 3rd needle to R needle, pm, rep from * 3 more times – 20 sts dec'd; 100 sts.
Rnd 4: Rep [Rnd 2] – 4 sts dec'd; 96 sts.
Rnd 5: *Purl to m, rm, 3-needle BO 2 times (3 sts dec'd), sl rem 1 st from 3rd needle to R needle, pm, rep from * 3 more times – 12 sts dec'd; 84 sts.
Rnd 6: Rep [Rnd 2] – 4 sts dec'd; 80 sts.
Rnds 7-10: Rep [Rnds 5 & 6] 2 times – 32 sts dec'd; 48 sts.
Rnd 11: *Purl to 2 sts bef m, rm, cddp, pm; rep from * 3 more times – 8 sts dec'd; 40 sts.
Rnd 12: Knit.
Rnds 13-20: Rep [Rnds 11 & 12] 4 times – 32 sts dec'd; 8 sts.
Rnd 21: Purl.
Thread tail through tapestry needle and insert through rem sts, pull to tighten, and fasten off securely.

Make 6 from pairs of B and C Arcs: 4 with H for 4S, 2 with F for 4S.

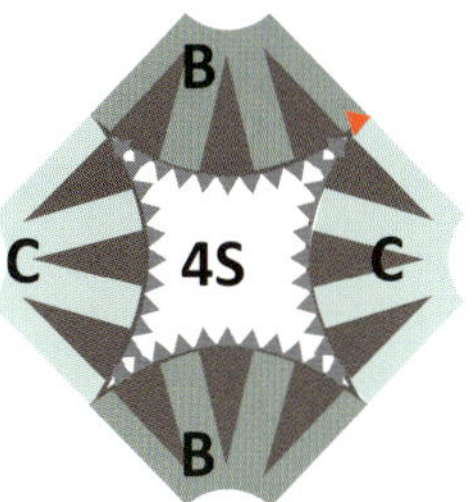

Make 6 from pairs of D and E Arcs: 4 with H for 4S, 2 with F for 4S.

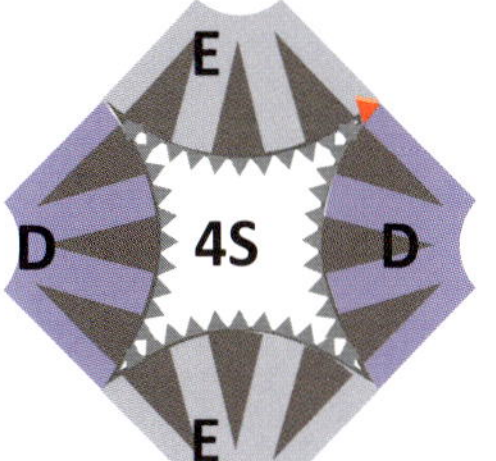

Figure 7: Method B: Quantities, Colors, and Construction of Squares

Assembly – Method C

Ovals

See Figure 8. Ovals are worked in each of the 28 curved sections labeled "O" in the color specified in brackets.

In each space labeled "O," attach the yarn color specified at the red triangle, leaving 25"/60 cm tail, and pu&k 10 sts to the next corner. Work [O].

Note: To manage long end, wind up and pin to edge.

Arrange Squares as shown. Using long pu&k tail of Ovals, sew upper edge of each oval to the adjacent Arc, aligning corners as shown by pairs of arrows, to make 5 vertical Strips.

Note: In Figure 8, Squares (S), Half Squares (HS), and Quarter Squares (QS) are labeled with CSs in brackets following the shape abbreviation for the two C1 colors of the Arcs/HAs followed by the color for the 1/2/4S. For instance, S[DEF] is a Square with Arcs worked in colors D and E (the two blues), with a center 4S worked in color F.

Oval (O) – Method C – 10 sts (chart on page 115)

Row 2 (WS): Knit to last st, w&t.
Row 3 (RS): Rep Row 2.
Row 4: K5, w&t.
Row 5: K3, w&t.
Row 6: Knit to last st, w&t.
Row 7: Knit to last 2 sts, w&t.
Row 8: K5, w&t.
Row 9: K4, w&t.
Row 10: K3, turn and drop yarn to WS and cut. Slip rem 4 sts to L needle. With long pu&k tail, BO all sts.

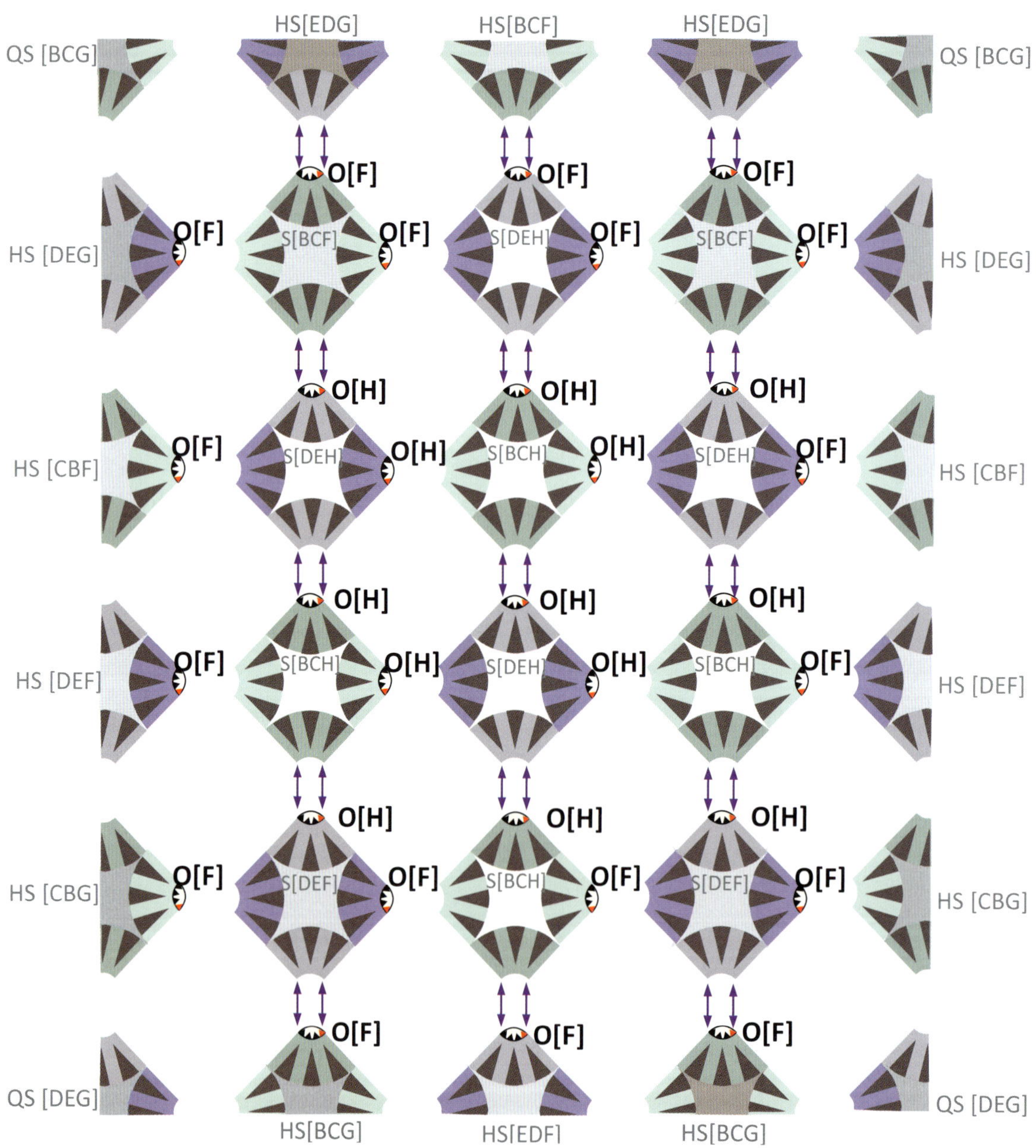

Figure 8: Method C: Ovals and Assembly

Triangular Inserts

In each of the 40 triangular spaces on edges of Strips, attach A at red triangle and pu&k 36 sts to corner, pm, and 36 sts to next corner – 72 sts.

Work [MT] using yarn color specified in Figure 9 for C1.

Sew Strips together using long tails of matching color and aligning stripes of the MT's, as shown in Figure 10 on page 110.

Continue at "Divots."

Mitered Triangle (MT) – Method C – 72 sts dec'ing to 4 sts

Row 2 (WS): Knit.
Row 3 (RS): K2tog, knit to 2 sts bef m, ssk, sm, k2tog, knit to last 2 sts, ssk – 4 sts dec'd; 68 sts.
Row 4 (WS): Knit.
Rows 5-10: Rep [Rows 3 & 4] 3 times – 12 sts dec'd; 56 sts. Cut A, leaving 10"/25 cm tail. Attach H.
Rows 11-18: Rep [Rows 3 & 4] 4 times – 16 sts dec'd; 40 sts. Cut H and attach C1.
Rows 19-36: Rep [Rows 3 & 4] 9 times – 36 sts dec'd; 4 sts.
Cut yarn, leaving 10"/25 cm tail. Thread tail onto tapestry needle, insert through rem sts, pull tightly, and fasten off securely.

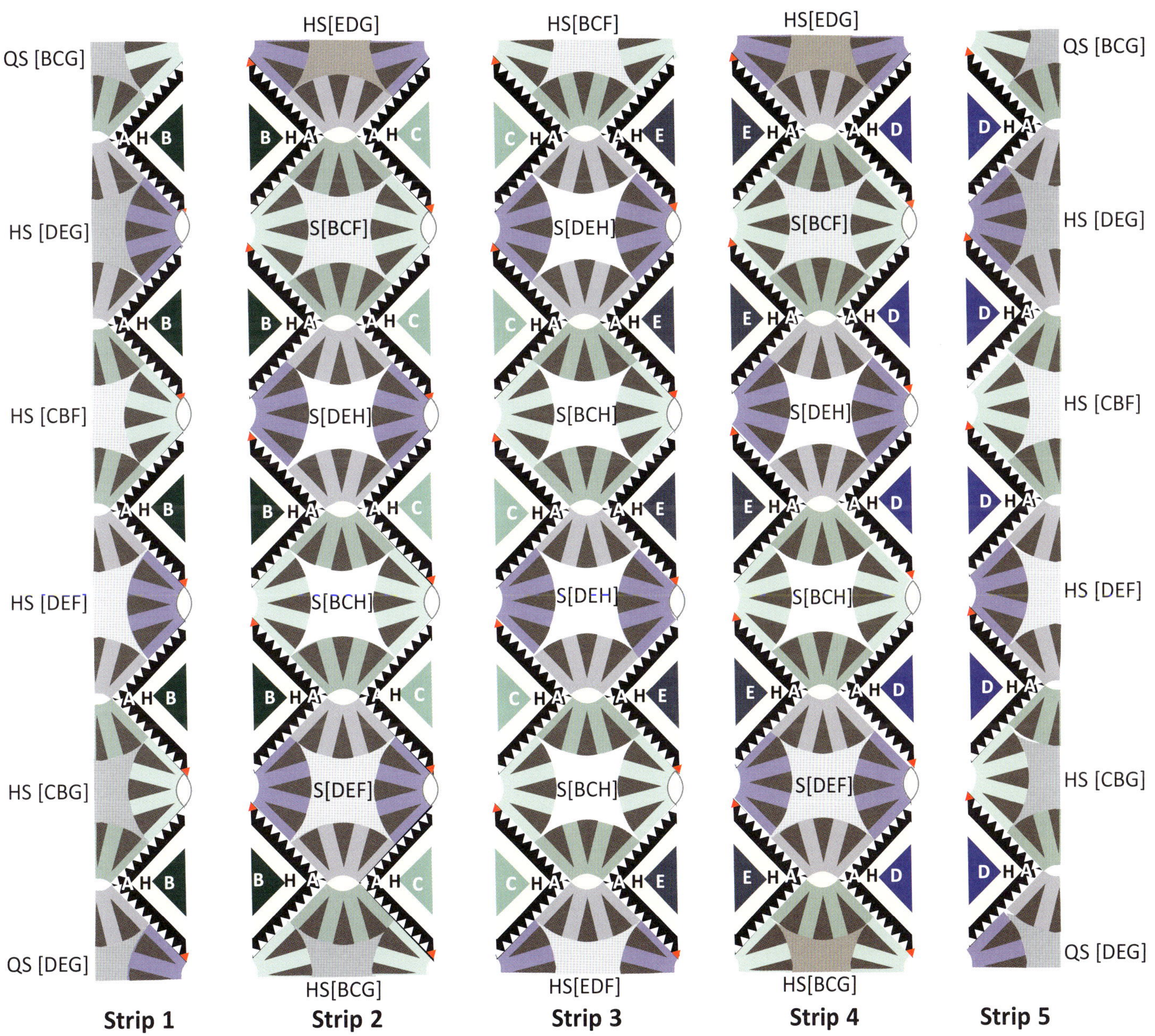

Figure 9: Method C: Triangular Inserts

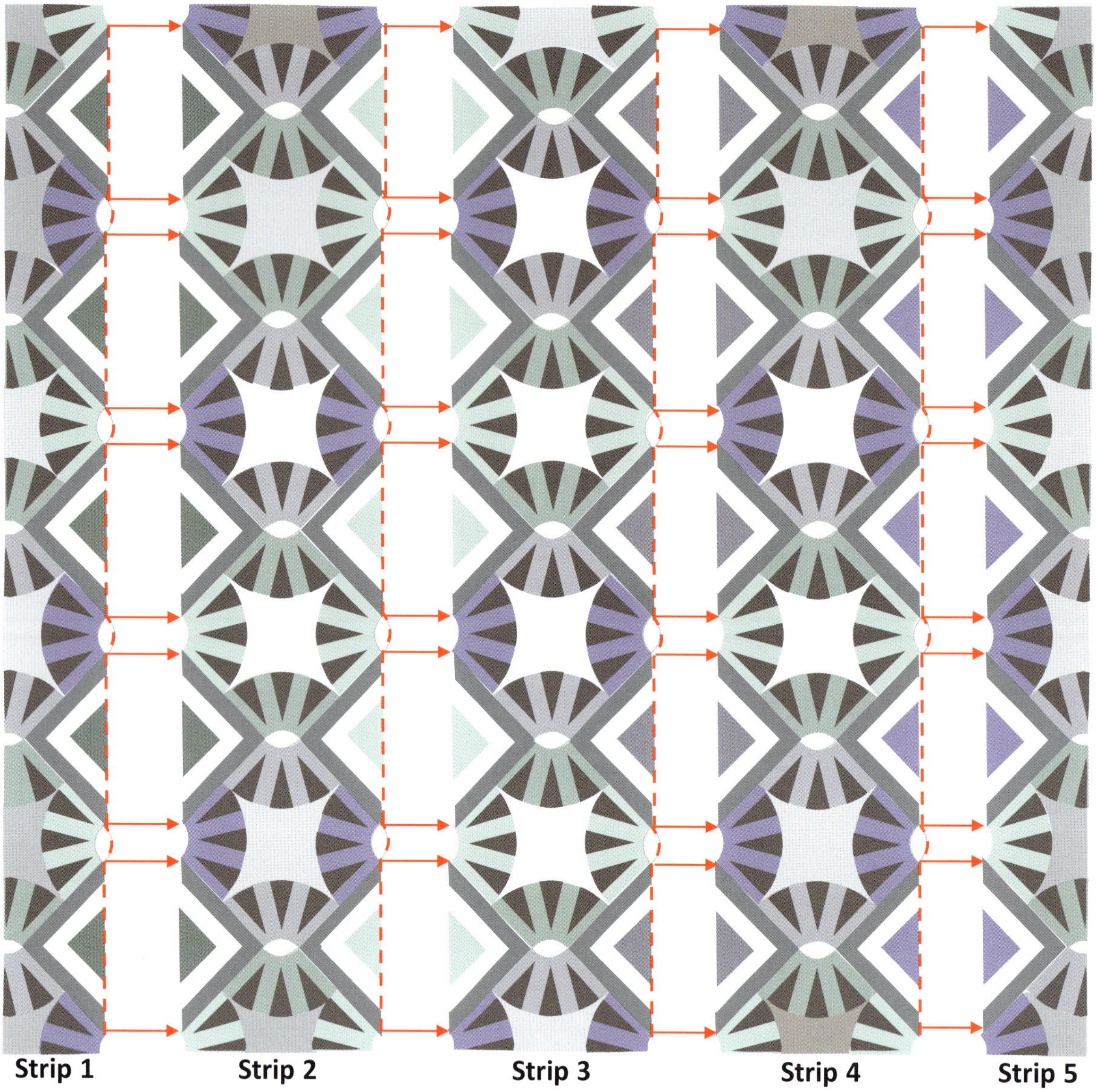

Strip 1 **Strip 2** **Strip 3** **Strip 4** **Strip 5**

Figure 10: Method C: Sew Strips Together

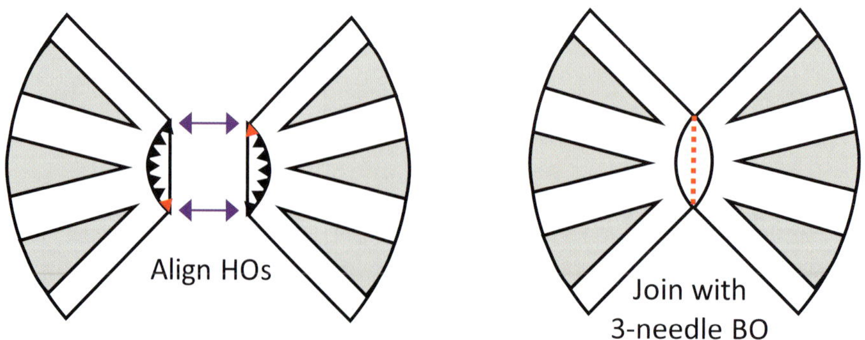

Figure 11: Method D: Assembly using HOs and 3-needle BO

Assembly – Method D

Arrange Squares, Half Squares, and Quarter Squares as shown in Figure 12.

Half Ovals

On the inner curve of first Arc, with yarn color specified at red triangle in Figure 11, pu&k 10 sts to next corner. Work [HO] and transfer sts to dpn. Cut yarn. Work [HO] in the same way on adjacent Arc, leaving sts on needle and leaving 10″/25 cm tail. Turn RSs together and join by performing 3-needle BO of sts on holder and sts on needle as shown in Figure 11. Cut yarn and fasten off.

Half Oval (HO) – Method D – 10 sts

See chart for Oval on page 115.

Rows 2-5: Work [Oval, Rows 2-5].

Row 6: Knit to last st, slip last st knitwise.

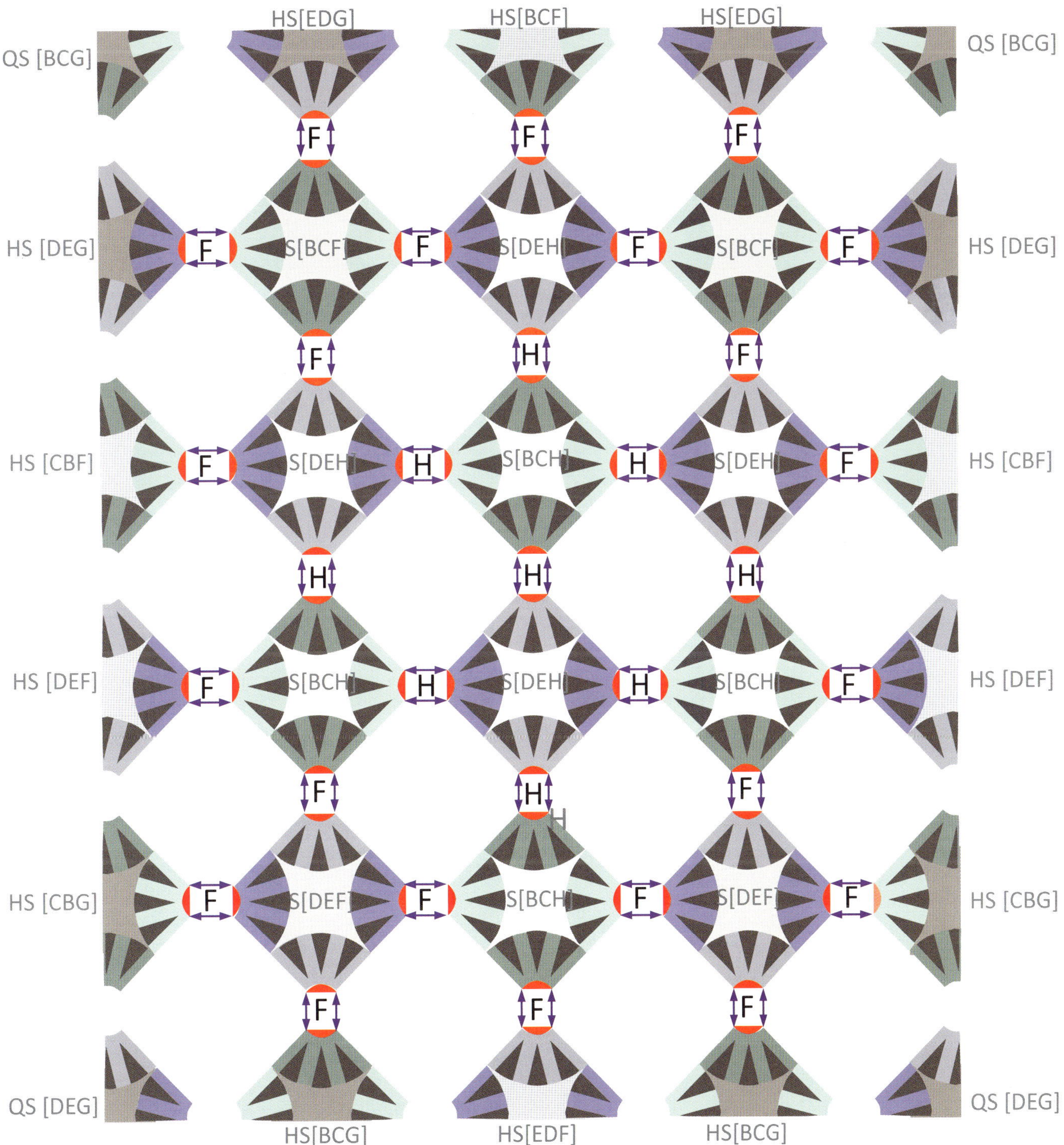

Figure 12: Method D: Half Ovals and Joining

Outside-In Squares

In each of the square spaces labeled [OS] in Figure 13, using a 24"/60 cm circular needle, starting at the red triangle, with A, *pu&k 36 sts to next corner, pm; rep from * 3 more times – 144 sts.

Work [OS] using yarn color specified in brackets in Figure 13 for C1.

Continue at "Divots."

Outside-In Square (OS) – Method D – 144 sts dec'ing to 8 sts

Worked in the round. Switch to dpns when needed.

Setup rnd: Purl.

Rnd 1: K2tog, (knit to 2 sts bef next m, ssk, sm, k2tog) 3 times, knit to last 2 sts, ssk – 8 sts dec'd; 136 sts.

Rnd 2: Purl.

Rnds 3-8: Rep [Rnds 1 & 2] 3 times – 24 sts dec'd; 112 sts. Cut A. Attach H.

Rnds 9-16: Rep [Rnds 1 & 2] 4 times – 32 sts dec'd; 80 sts. Cut H. Attach C1.

Rnds 17-34: Rep [Rnds 1 & 2] 9 times – 72 sts dec'd; 8 sts. Cut yarn, thread onto tapestry needle, insert into rem sts, tighten, and fasten off securely.

Figure 13: Method D: Outside-In Squares

Divots – All Methods

In each of the 18 gaps along edges of the blanket shown in Figure 14, attach yarn color specified; pu&k 6 sts to corner (yellow dot), pm, and 6 sts to end of inner curve. Work [Dv].

Divot (Dv) – 12 sts dec'ing to 1 st

Rows 2 & 3: Knit.
Row 4 (WS): Knit to m, rm, with RS of work together, 3-needle BO 3 times, pm. Sl rem st on 3rd needle to R needle, knit to end – 5 sts dec'd; 7 sts.
Row 5: Knit to 2 sts bef m, k2tog, knit to end – 1 st dec'd; 6 sts.
Row 6: Knit to m, rm, with RS of work together, 3-needle BO 3 times – 5 sts dec'd; 1 st.
Cut yarn and fasten off.

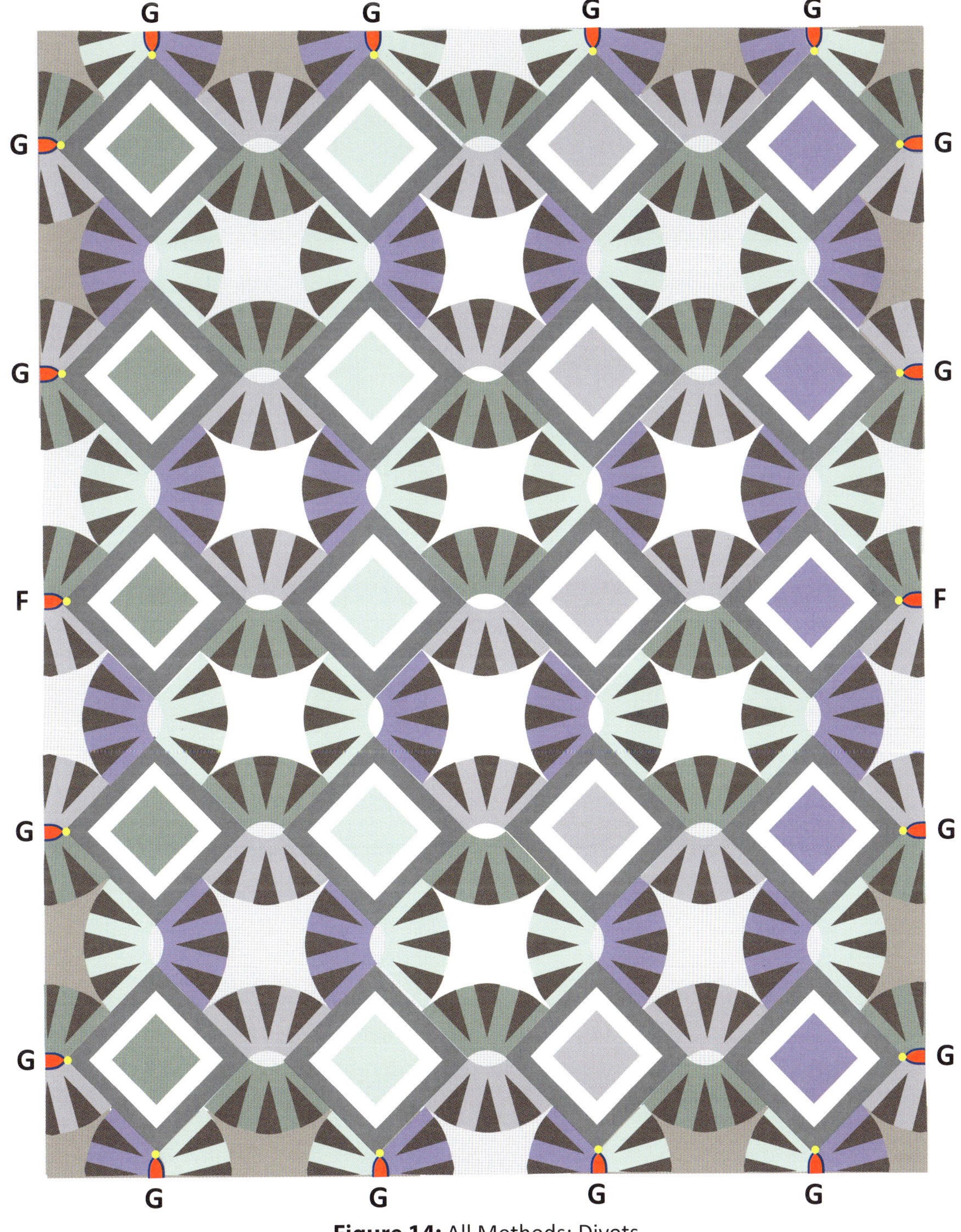

Figure 14: All Methods: Divots

BORDERS

Refer to Table 2 for number of sts to pu&k on the edge of each shape.

Table 2: Number of Stitches to Pu&k on Shape Edges for Border

	1 Point Square (1S)	2 Point Square (2S)	Half Arc (HA)	Divot
Number of Sts to pu&k	9	18	18	4

Right Border

On RS, attach A at bottom right corner of blanket. Pu&k 290 sts, distributed over shapes as in Table 2. Knit 17 rows. BO loosely.

Left Border

Work as for Right Border, attaching A at top left corner of blanket.

Top Border

On RS, attach A at top right corner of Right Border. Pu&k 10 sts on edge of Right Border, 232 sts on top blanket edge distributed over shapes as in Table 2, and 10 sts on edge of Left Border – 252 sts. Knit 17 rows. BO loosely.

Bottom Border

Work as for Top Border, attaching A at bottom left corner of Left Border.

FINISHING

Weave in ends.

CHARTS

Chart Symbols

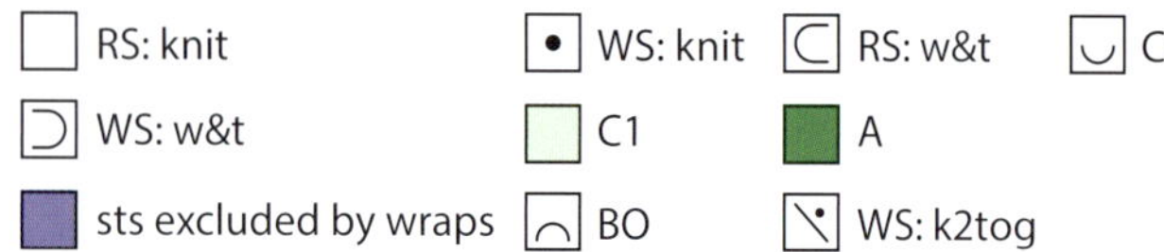

Arc

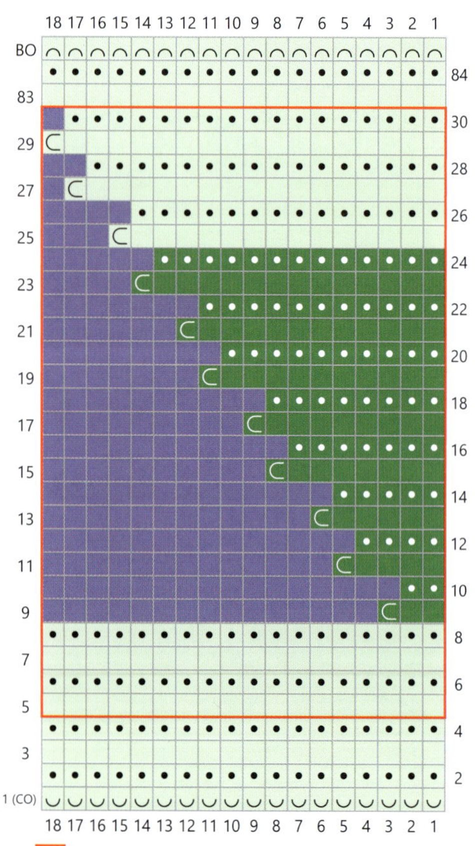

Rows 5–30 are repeated 2 more times

Half Arc 1 (HA1)

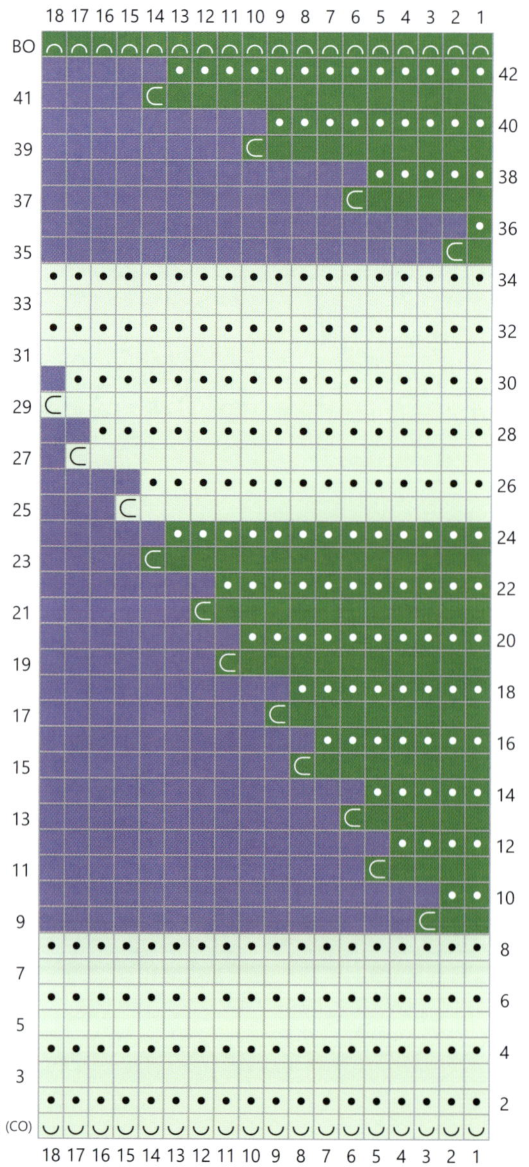

Half Arc 2 (HA2)

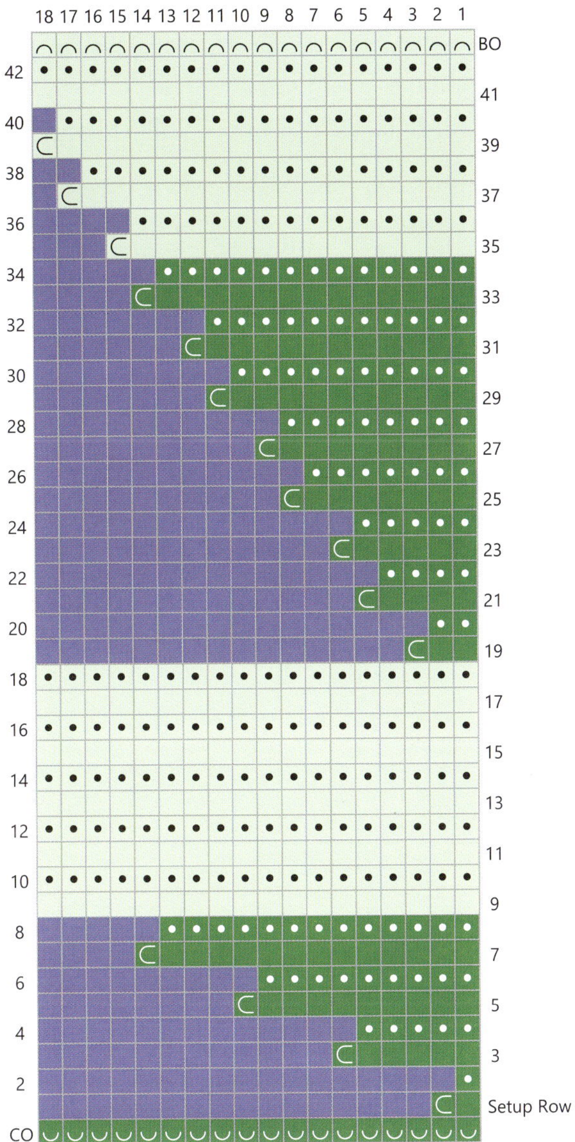

Oval (O)

For Oval, work all rows.
For Half Oval, work Rows 2-6.

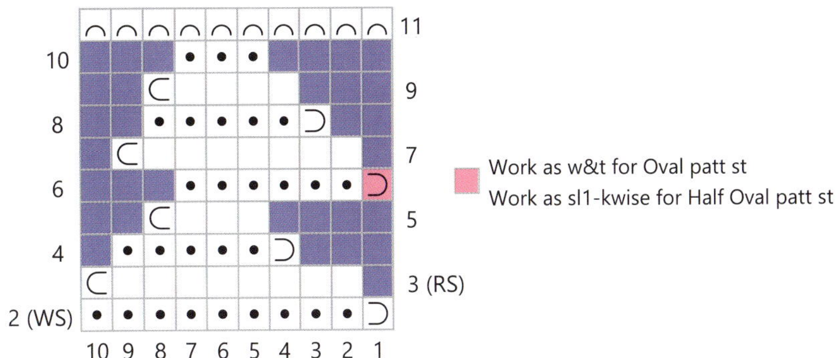

Work as w&t for Oval patt st
Work as sl1-kwise for Half Oval patt st

Corner (Cr)

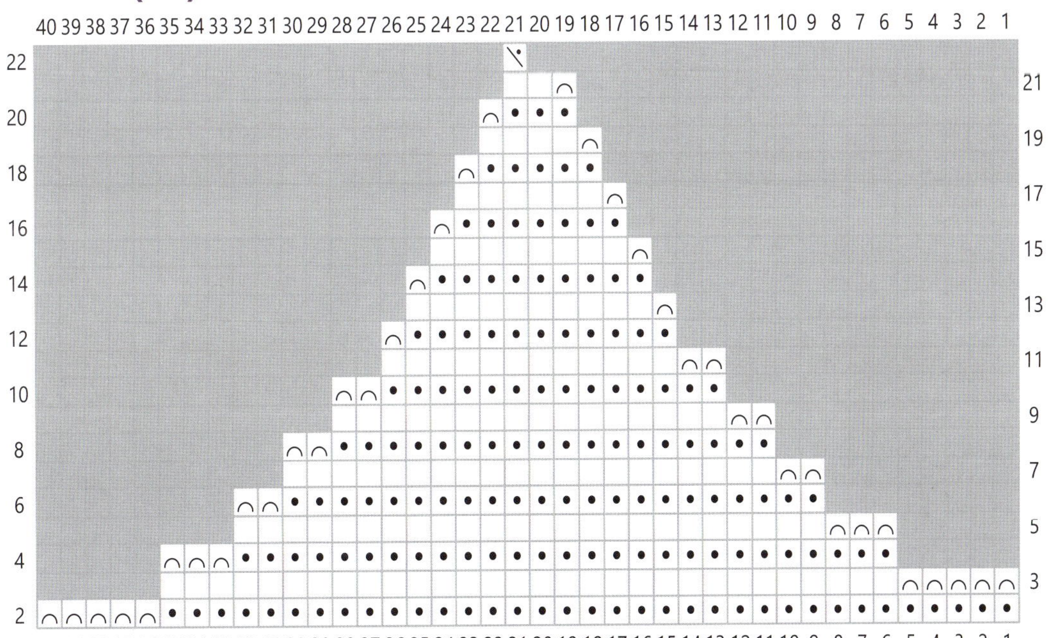

PISCES

Overlapping plates resembling fish scales are colored in shades of blue and teal with a contrast of copper gold.

SIZE 51.5 x 53.5"/131 x 136 cm

TECHNIQUES Pu&k, w&t

YARN Lion Brand Yarn Jeans, worsted (100% acrylic; 246 yds/225 m; 3.5 oz/100 g)
Lion Brand Yarn Vanna's Choice, worsted (100% acrylic; 170 yds/156 m; 3.5 oz/100 g):

Pattern Color ID	Color Swatch	Lion Brand Yarn Line	Color ID	Color Name	Color Description	# Skeins
A		Jeans	505-153AB	Stovepipe	blue-black	3
B		Jeans	505-105V	Faded	light blue	3
C		Jeans	505-109W	Stonewash	medium blue	2
D		Jeans	505-150Y	Vintage	gray-blue	4
E		Jeans	505-110AF	Classic	navy blue	2
F		Vanna's Choice	860-099H	Linen	off-white	2
G		Vanna's Choice	860-405G	Silver Heather	light gray	3
H		Jeans	505-121E	Top Stitch	gold-rust	2

NEEDLES US Size 7/4.5 mm 40"/100 cm circular needles or size needed to obtain gauge

NOTIONS Tapestry needle, stitch markers

GAUGE 17 sts and 34 rows = 4"/10 cm in garter st

NOTES

- The blanket is worked in one piece as horizontal Strips of scales. Additional Strips are picked up on the top of the previous completed Strip. The scale shapes are created using decreases and short rows. Optional charts, on pages 122 and 123, are provided for all shapes.
- Several live stitches are still on the needle after working the Scale shapes (Scale, Scale Right, Scale Left). Cut yarn, leaving 10"/25 cm tail, pull through remaining stitches, and fasten off.
- Instructions say to cut A after generating sts and working the setup row of each Strip. However, A may be draped slightly loosely along the right edge of the blanket between uses and tacked during the pu&k of the Right Border.
- The Borders are picked up on the edges of the completed blanket.

BLANKET INSTRUCTIONS

Yarn colors for shapes are provided in Figure 3 on page 121.

STRIP 1

See Figure 1 for construction.

Setup (RS)

With A, *CO 30 sts, pm;* rep bet * and * 7 more times, CO 30 sts – 270 sts.

Note: Markers (m) on needle identify beg and end of shapes.

Setup row (WS): Knit. Place m in the yarn strand between the 15th and 16th st of each group of 30 sts.

Cut A.

Scale 1 (SC1)

On RS, attach yarn color for SC1, work [SC] over 30 sts bet beg and m. Cut yarn and fasten off. Rm.

Scales 2-9 (SC2-SC9)

Work as for SC1 over next 30 sts.

Scale (SC) – 30 sts dec'ing to 2 sts

Row 1 (RS): K3, k2tog, k5, k2tog, k6, k2tog, k5, k2tog, k3 – 4 sts dec'd; 26 sts.
Rows 2-4: Knit.
Row 5: K2, (k2tog, k3) 4 times, k2tog, k2 – 5 sts dec'd; 21 sts.
Rows 6-8: Knit.
Row 9: K1, (k2tog, k2) 5 times – 5 sts dec'd; 16 sts.
Row 10: Knit.
Row 11: K11, w&t.
Row 12: K6, w&t.
Row 13: K7, w&t.
Row 14: K8, w&t.
Rows 15 & 16: Knit.
Row 17: K2, k2tog, k2, k2tog twice, k2, k2tog, k2 – 4 sts dec'd; 12 sts.
Rows 18-20: Knit.
Row 21: K1, k2tog, k1, k2tog twice, k1, k2tog, k1 – 4 sts dec'd; 8 sts.
Row 22: Knit.
Row 23: K1, k2tog, k2, k2tog, k1 – 2 sts dec'd; 6 sts.
Rows 24-26: Knit.
Row 27: K1, k2tog twice, k1 – 2 sts dec'd; 4 sts.
Row 28: Knit.
Row 29: K2tog twice – 2 sts dec'd; 2 sts.
Rows 30-32: Knit.
Cut yarn, leaving 10"/25 cm tail, pull through rem sts, and fasten off.

STRIP 2 AND ALL EVEN-NUMBERED STRIPS THROUGH 24

See Figure 1 for construction.

Setup (RS)

On RS, attach A on right corner of SC in Strip below at red triangle, pu&k 15 sts to center point of SC, pu&k 2 sts in center point, pm bet these sts, *pu&k 28 sts to next center point, pu&k 2 sts in center point, pm bet last 2 sts;* rep bet * and * 7 more times, pu&k 15 sts to end of Strip – 272 sts. Check that work is not twisted before proceeding.

Setup row (WS): Knit.

Cut A.

Scale Right (SR)

Attach yarn color for SR at red triangle. Work [SR] on first 16 sts bet beg of Strip and 1st m. Rm.

Scales 10-17 (SC10-SC17)

Working on RS, attach yarn color for SC and work [SC] over next 30 sts. Rm.

Scale Left (SL)

Attach yarn color for SL. Work [SL] over last 16 sts bet last m and end of Strip. Rm.

STRIP 3 AND ALL ODD-NUMBERED STRIPS THROUGH 23

See Figure 1 for construction.

Setup (RS)

At top point of SR on Strip below, attach A at red triangle, pu&k 29 sts to center point of next SC, pu&k 2 sts in point, pm bet last 2 sts, *pu&k 28 sts to center point of next SC, 2 sts in point, pm bet last 2 sts;* rep bet * and * 6 more times, pu&k 29 sts to end of Strip – 270 sts.

Setup row (WS): Knit.

Cut A.

Scale 18 (SC18)

Attach yarn color for S at red triangle. Work [SC] over first 30 sts. Cut yarn and fasten off. Rm.

Scales 19-26 (SC19-SC26)

Work as for S18 over next 30 sts.

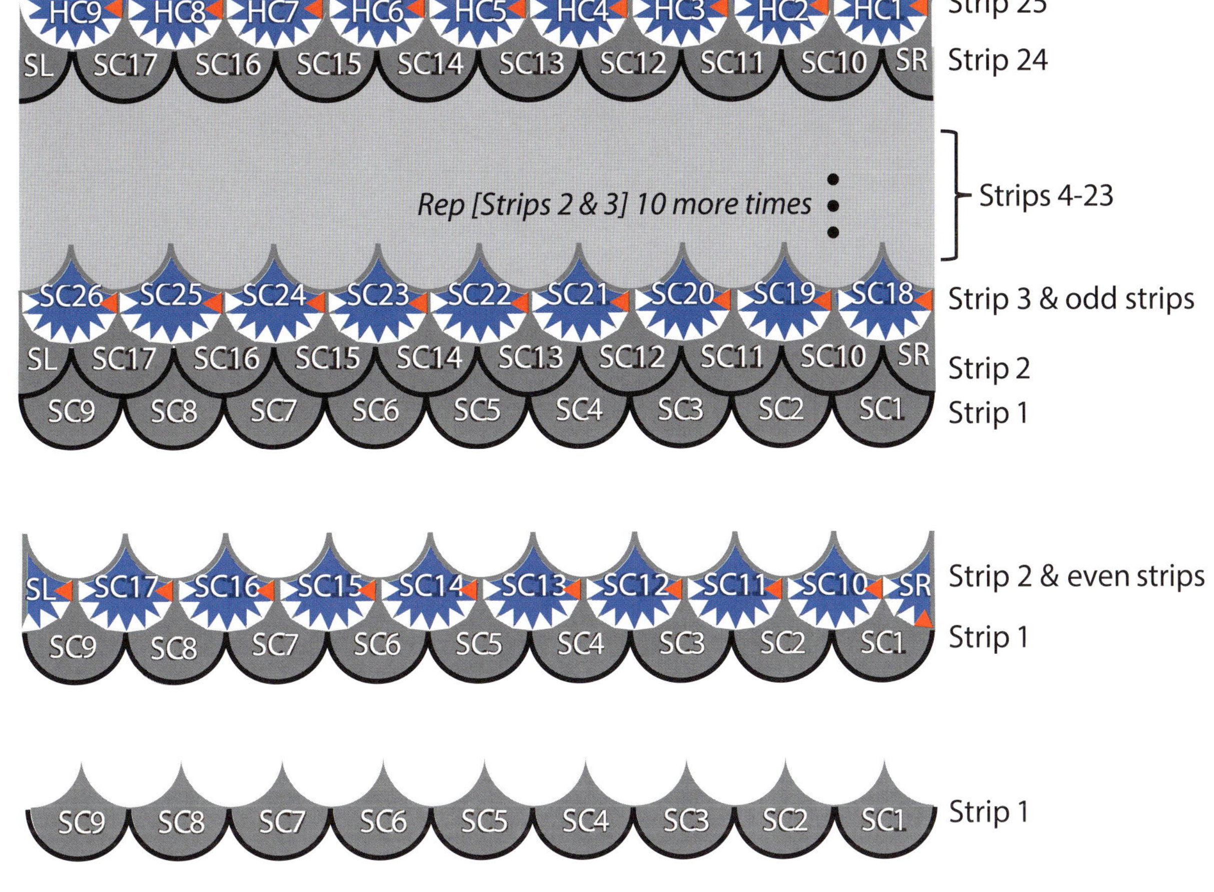

Figure 1: Construction of Strips 1-25

Scale Right (SR) – 16 sts dec'ing to 2 sts

Row 1 (RS): K4, k2tog, k5, k2tog, k3 – 2 sts dec'd; 14 sts.
Rows 2-4: Knit.
Row 5: K1, (k2tog, k3) twice, k2tog, k1 – 3 sts dec'd; 11 sts.
Rows 6-8: Knit.
Row 9: K3, (k2tog, k2) twice – 2 sts dec'd; 9 sts.
Row 10: Knit.
Row 11: K4, w&t.
Row 12: Knit.
Row 13: K5, w&t.
Rows 14-16: Knit.
Row 17: K1, (k2tog, k2) twice – 2 sts dec'd; 7 sts.
Rows 18-20: Knit.
Row 21: (K1, k2tog) twice, k1 – 2 sts dec'd; 5 sts.
Row 22: Knit.
Row 23: K2, k2tog, k1 – 1 st dec'd; 4 sts.
Rows 24-26: Knit.
Row 27: K1, k2tog, k1 – 1 st dec'd; 3 sts.
Row 28: Knit.
Row 29: K1, k2tog – 1 st dec'd; 2 sts.
Rows 30-32: Knit.
Cut yarn, leaving 10"/25 cm tail, pull through rem sts, and fasten off.

Scale Left (SL) – 16 sts dec'ing to 2 sts

Row 1 (RS): K3, k2tog, k5, k2tog, k4 – 2 sts dec'd; 14 sts.
Rows 2-4: Knit.
Row 5: K1, (k2tog, k3) 2 times, k2tog, k1 – 3 sts dec'd; 11 sts.
Rows 6-8: Knit.
Row 9: (K2, k2tog) twice, k3 – 2 sts dec'd; 9 sts.
Row 10: K4, w&t.
Row 11: Knit.
Row 12: K5 w&t.
Rows 13-16: Knit.
Row 17: (K2, k2tog) twice, k1 – 2 sts dec'd; 7 sts.
Rows 18-20: Knit.
Row 21: (K1, k2tog) twice, k1 – 2 sts dec'd; 5 sts.
Row 22: Knit.
Row 23: K1, k2tog, k2 – 1 st dec'd; 4 sts.
Rows 24-26: Knit.
Row 27: K1, k2tog, k1 – 1 st dec'd; 3 sts.
Row 28: Knit.
Row 29: K2tog, k1 – 1 st dec'd; 2 sts.
Rows 30-32: Knit.
Cut yarn, leaving 10"/25 cm tail, pull through rem sts, and fasten off.

Strip 25

See Figure 1 for construction.

Work setup rows of Strip 3.

Half-Circle 1 (HC1)

Attach yarn color for HC at first red triangle. Work [HC] over first 30 sts. Cut yarn and fasten off. Rm.

Half-Circle (HC) – 30 sts dec'ing to 6 sts

Row 1 (RS): K2, (k2tog, k3) 5 times, k2tog, k1 – 6 sts dec'd; 24 sts.
Rows 2-4: Knit.
Row 5: K1, (k2tog, k2) 5 times, k2tog, k1 – 6 sts dec'd; 18 sts.
Rows 6-8: Knit.
Row 9: (K2tog, k1) 6 times – 6 sts dec'd; 12 sts.
Rows 10-12: Knit.
Row 13: K2tog 6 times – 6 sts dec'd; 6 sts.
Rows 14-15: Knit.
Cut yarn, leaving 10"/25 cm tail, pull through rem sts, and fasten off.

Half-Circles 2-9 (HC2-HC9)

Work as for HC1 over the next 30 sts.

Bottom Wedges

See Figure 2 for construction.

Right Wedge (RW)

With yarn for RW, and starting at red triangle next to marked st, pu&k 16 sts to end of curve. Work [RW].

Right Wedge (RW) – 16 sts dec'ing to 1 st

Row 2 (WS): BO 4, knit to end – 4 sts dec'd; 12 sts.
Row 3 (RS): K3tog, knit to end – 2 sts dec'd; 10 sts.
Row 4: BO 2, knit to end – 2 sts dec'd; 8 sts.
Row 5: K2tog, knit to end – 1 st dec'd; 7 sts.
Row 6: BO 1, knit to end – 1 st dec'd; 6 sts.
Row 7: K2tog, knit to end – 1 st dec'd; 5 sts.
Row 8: Rep Row 6 – 1 st dec'd; 4 sts.
Row 9: Rep Row 6 – 1 st dec'd; 3 sts.
Row 10: Knit.
Row 11: K3tog – 2 sts dec'd; 1 st.
Cut yarn and fasten off.

Bottom Wedges 1-8 (BW1-BW8)

On the next Scale, with yarn for Wedge, starting at the red triangle next to the marked st, pu&k 15 sts to end of curve, 1 st bet SCs, pm, and 15 sts to center of next curve, at marked st.

Bottom Wedge (BW) – 31 sts dec'ing to 1 st

Row 2 (WS): Knit.
Row 3 (RS): BO 4, knit to 3 sts bef m, rm, cdd2, pm, knit to end – 8 sts dec'd; 23 sts.
Row 4: BO 4, knit to end – 4 sts dec'd; 19 sts.
Row 5: BO 2, knit to 2 sts bef m, rm, cdd, pm, knit to end – 4 sts dec'd; 15 sts.
Row 6: BO 2, knit to end – 2 sts dec'd; 13 sts.
Row 7: BO 1, knit to 2 sts bef m, rm, cdd, pm, knit to end – 3 sts dec'd; 10 sts.
Row 8: BO 1, knit to end – 1 st dec'd; 9 sts.
Row 9: Rep Row 7 – 3 sts dec'd; 6 sts.
Row 10: Rep Row 8 – 1 st dec'd; 5 sts.
Row 11: Cdd2 – 4 sts dec'd; 1 st.
Cut yarn and fasten off.

Left Wedge (LW)

With yarn for LW, starting at red triangle on left corner of SC9, pu&k 16 sts to m at bottom of SC9. Work [LW]. Rm's.

Left Wedge (LW) – 16 sts dec'ing to 1 st

Row 2 (WS): Knit.
Row 3 (RS): BO 4, knit to last 3 sts, sssk – 6 sts dec'd; 10 sts.
Row 4: Knit.
Row 5: BO 2, knit to last 2 sts, ssk – 3 sts dec'd; 7 sts.
Row 6: Knit.
Row 7: BO 1, knit to last 2 sts, ssk – 2 sts dec'd; 5 sts.
Row 8: Knit.
Row 9: Rep Row 7 – 2 sts dec'd; 3 sts.
Row 10: Knit.
Row 11: Sssk – 2 sts dec'd; 1 st.
Cut yarn and fasten off.

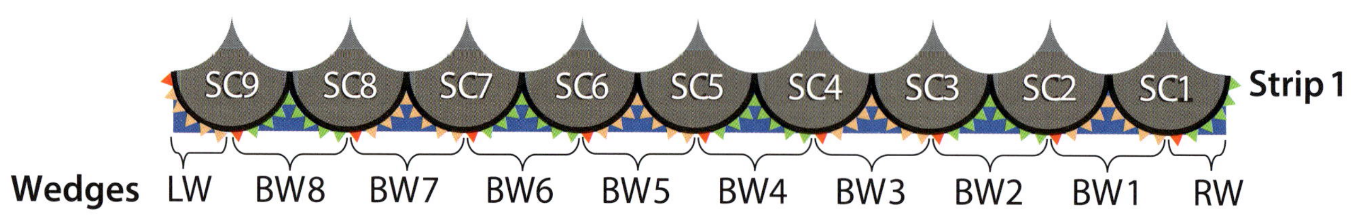

Figure 2: Construction of Wedges

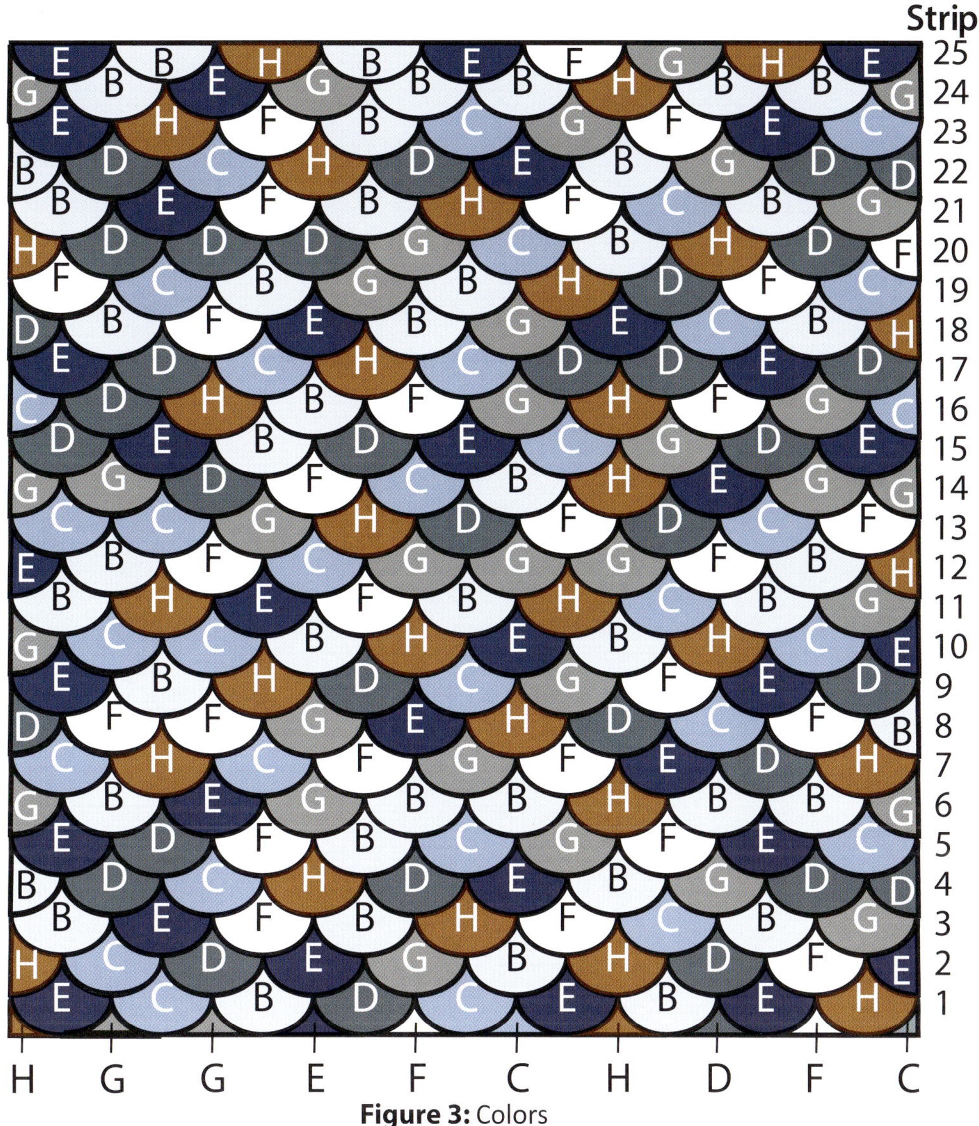

Figure 3: Colors

BORDERS

Right Border

On RS, with A, and starting at bottom right corner of blanket, pu&k 8 sts on edge of RW, and 17 sts on the edge of each SR – 212 sts.

Row 2 (WS): Knit.
Row 3 (RS): Kf&b, knit to last st, kf&b – 2 sts inc'd; 214 sts.
Row 4: Knit.
Cut A. Attach D.
Rows 5-18: Rep [Rows 3 & 4] 7 times – 14 sts inc'd; 228 sts.
BO loosely. Cut yarn, leaving 15"/38 cm tail.

Left Border

Rep as for Right Border, with A, starting at top left corner of blanket, and pu&k 17 sts per SL and 8 sts on LW.

Top Border

On RS, with A, and starting at top right corner of blanket, *pu&k 22 sts on edge of next HC, 23 sts on edge of next HC; rep from * 4 more times, and pu&k 22 sts on edge of last HC – 202 sts.

Work [Rows 2-18] of Right Border, ending with 218 sts.

BO loosely.

Bottom Border

On RS, with A, and starting at bottom left corner of blanket, pu&k 11 sts on edge of LW, *23 sts on next BW, 22 sts on next BW; work from * 3 more times, pu&k 11 sts on RW – 202 sts.

Work [Rows 2-18] of Right Border, ending with 218 sts.

BO loosely.

Using long tails and mattress st, sew border corners.

FINISHING

Weave in ends. Block if desired.

CHARTS

Scale (SC)

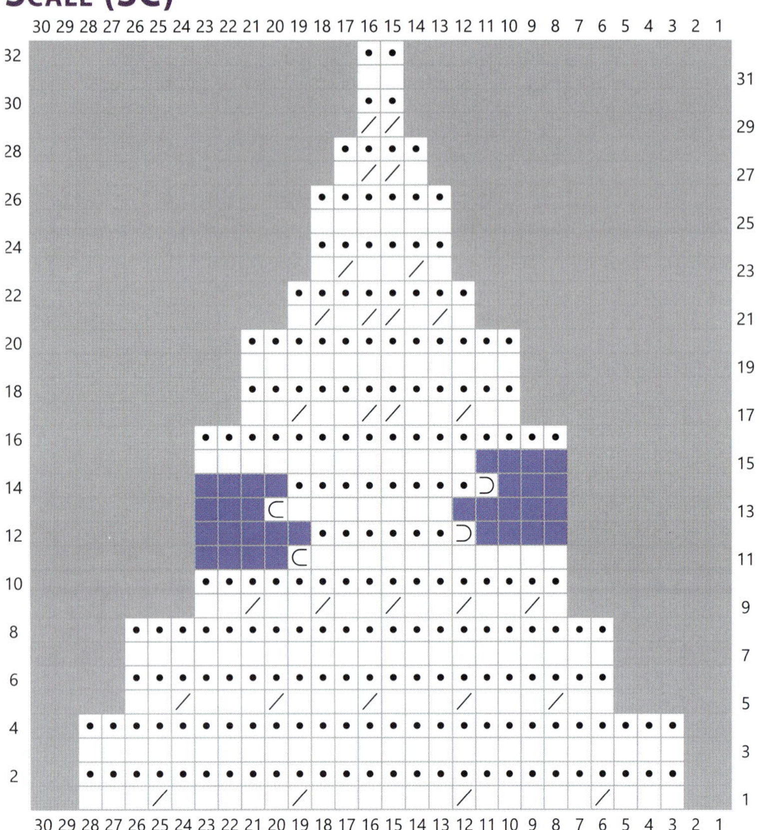

Chart Symbols

RS: Knit
RS: K2tog
RS: Cdd
RS: Cdd2
RS: W&t
RS: Sssk
unworked stitches
WS: Knit
RS: Ssk
BO
WS: W&t
RS: K3tog
no stitch

Scale Left (SL)

Scale Right (SR)

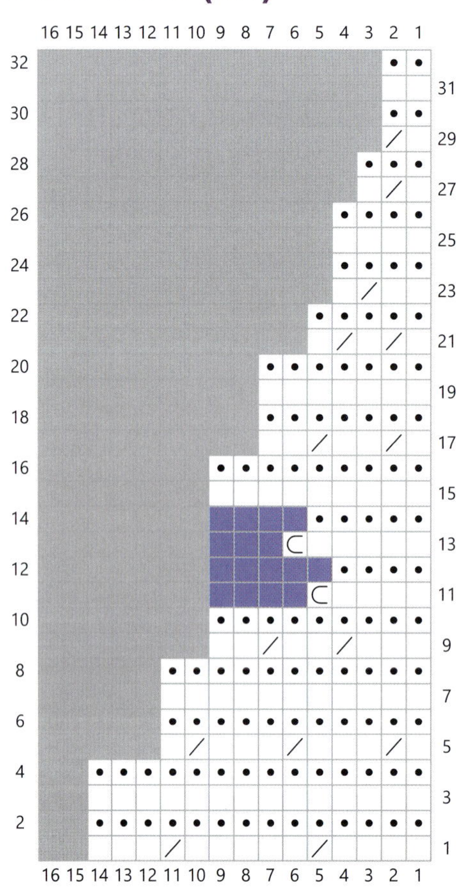

Half-Circle (HC)

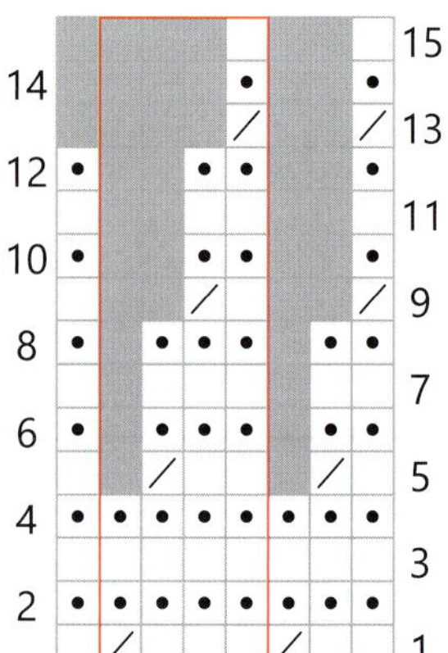

Bottom Wedge (BW)

marker (m)

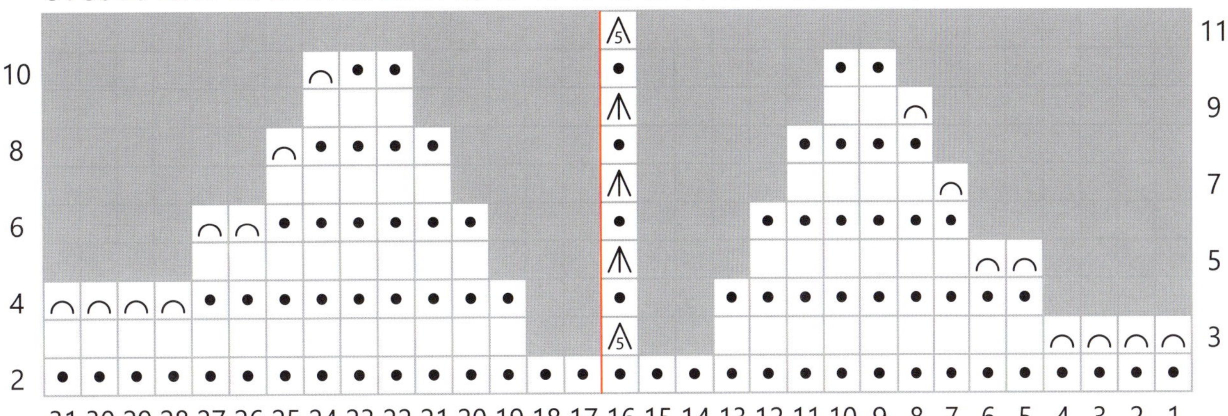

Left Wedge (LW)

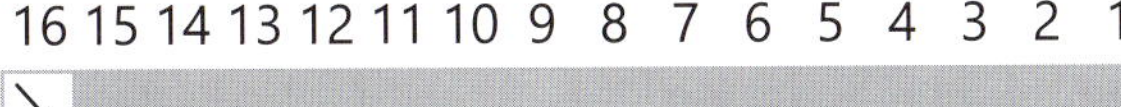

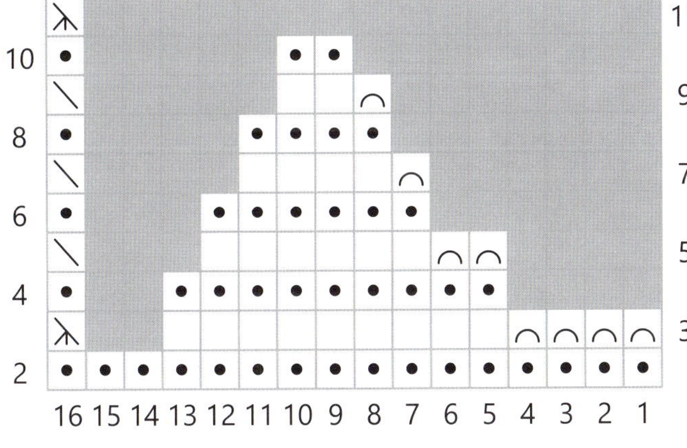

Right Wedge (RW)

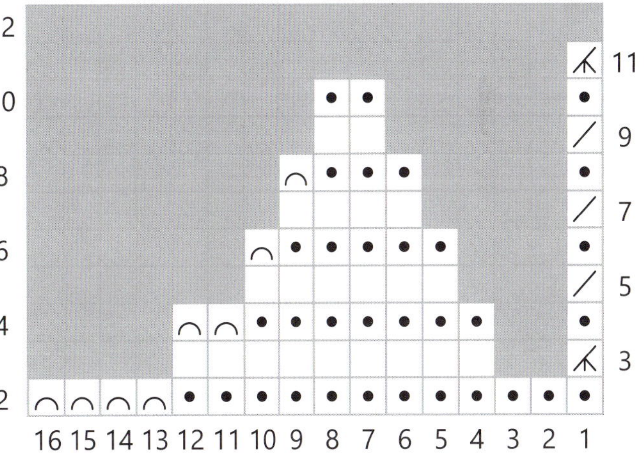

PLAZA

Open, beautiful spaces where people come together and enjoy outdoor cafes and conversation are the inspiration for this blanket.

SIZE 54.5 x 75"/138 x 191 cm

TECHNIQUES Pu&k, sewing and working in the round

YARN Rowan Felted Tweed, DK (50% wool, 25% alpaca, 25% viscose; 191 yds/175 m; 1.75 oz/50 g):

Pattern Color ID	Color Swatch	Color ID	Color Name	Color Description	# Skeins
A		197	Alabaster	off-white (with blue tones)	6
B		157	Camel	taupe	1
C		198	Zinnia	bright red-orange	1
D		154	Ginger	rust-orange	2
E		170	Seafarer	dark navy blue	8
F		178	Seasalter	medium blue	3
G		165	Scree	lightest blue	3

NEEDLES US Size 5/3.75 mm 40"/100 cm circular needles and dpns or size needed to obtain gauge

NOTIONS Tapestry needle, stitch markers, safety pins (optional)

GAUGE 20 sts and 40 rows = 4"/10 cm in garter st

NOTES

- The blanket is worked in Blocks that are sewn together. Four striped arms of each Block are worked first, and then the center two-tone square is worked in the round. The triangular openings on the sides of the Blocks are worked by picking up and knitting (pu&k) stitches on the edges of arms and working mitered triangles. The Borders are picked up and knit on the edges of the completed blanket.
- When adding a new yarn color, always leave a 10"/25 cm tail to use later for seaming Blocks.

BLANKET INSTRUCTIONS

Blocks

See Figure 1 for construction and Figure 2 for Block color schemes (CS).

Make 18 Blocks in CS1 and 17 Blocks in CS2. Directions are for CS1 with changes for CS2 in parentheses.

Cut yarn only when instructed. Drape yarn slightly loosely along edge to next use. Do not cut the E yarn until 4th Arm is complete.

Step 1: Arms 1-4

With E, CO 16 sts.

*Work [Arm] – 1 st rem.

Turn and CO 15 sts – 16 sts.

Knit 1 row.*

Rep between * and * 2 more times, and then work [Arm] once more.

After Arm 4 is complete, cut yarns and fasten off. Thread BO tail onto needle. Take a stitch in the corner of Arm 1 to attach Arm 4 to Arm 1.

Arm – 16 sts, inc'ing to 26 sts, dec'ing to 16 sts

Row 2 (WS): Knit.
Row 3 (RS): Kf&b, knit to end – 1 st inc'd; 17 sts.
Row 4: Knit.
Rows 5-10: Rep [Rows 3 & 4] 3 times – 3 sts inc'd; 20 sts.
Attach F (G) and drop E.
Rows 11-18: Rep [Rows 3-10] – 4 sts inc'd; 24 sts.
Drop F (G) and continue with E.
Rows 19-22: Rep [Rows 3 & 4] twice – 2 sts inc'd; 26 sts.
Row 23: K2tog, knit to end – 1 st dec'd; 25 sts.
Row 24: Knit.
Rows 25-26: Rep [Rows 23 & 24] – 1 st dec'd; 24 sts.
Drop E and continue with F (G).
Rows 27-34: Rep [Rows 23 & 24] 4 times – 4 sts dec'd; 20 sts.
Cut F (G) and continue with E.
Rows 35-42: Rep [Rows 23 & 24] 4 times – 4 sts dec'd; 16 sts.
With E, BO loosely, leaving last st on needle.

Step 1) Arms

Step 2) Outside-In Square (OS)

Step 3) Mitered Triangles (MT)

Figure 1: Block Construction

Color Scheme 1 (CS1)

Color Scheme 2 (CS2)

Figure 2: Block Color Schemes

Step 2: Outside-In Square

On RS, in space labeled "OS" in Figure 1, Step 2, with E, and starting at red triangle, *with dpn, pu&k 18 sts to next corner, while simultaneously inserting needle over and under draped yarn, and then pu&k 1 st in corner; rep from * 3 times – 76 sts.

Note: There are 20 garter st "bumps" per edge, so skip 2 bumps when performing pu&k.

Setup rnd: Purl.
Rnds 1-6: Rep [OS Rnds 1 & 2] 3 times – 24 sts dec'd; 52 sts.
Cut E and attach C (B).
Rnds 7-16: Rep [OS Rnds 1 & 2] 5 times – 40 sts dec'd; 12 sts.
Rnd 17: Cdd 4 times – 8 sts dec'd; 4 sts.
Cut yarn, leaving 10"/25 cm tail. Thread tail onto tapestry needle and insert through rem 4 sts on needle. Pull to tighten and fasten off securely.

Outside-In Square (OS)

Worked in the round.
Note: The cdd's use the last 2 sts of 1 dpn and the 1st st of the next dpn. The last cdd crosses the BOR.
Rnd 1: *Knit to last 2 sts bef end of dpn, cdd; rep from * 3 times – 8 sts dec'd.
Rnd 2: Purl.

Step 3: Mitered Triangles

On RS, in each space labeled "MT" in Figure 1, Step 3, attach A at red triangle and pu&k 16 sts to corner, 1 st in corner, pm, pu&k 16 sts to next corner – 33 sts.

Setup row (WS): Knit.
Rows 1-6: Rep [MT Rows 1 & 2] 3 times – 12 sts dec'd; 21 sts.
Cut A, leaving 10"/25 cm tail; attach D.
Rows 7-12: Rep [MT Rows 1 & 2] 3 times – 12 sts dec'd; 9 sts.
Row 13: Rep [MT, Row 1] – 4 sts dec'd; 5 sts.
Row 14: Cdd2 – 4 sts dec'd; 1 st.
Cut D and fasten of (MT) f, leaving 10"/25 cm tail.

Mitered Triangle (MT)

Row 1 (RS): K2tog, knit to 2 sts bef m, rm, cdd, pm, knit to last 2 sts, ssk – 4 sts dec'd.
Row 2 (WS): Knit.

Figure 3: Assembly

ASSEMBLY

Arrange Blocks as shown in Figure 3. Using long tails of matching color, sew seams at yellow lines, matching stripes and shape corners to form strips, and then sew strips together matching corners of Blocks, stripes, and corners of shapes.

BORDERS

Right Border

On RS, starting at bottom right corner of blanket, pu&k 51 sts per Block on right edge of blanket – 357 sts.

Knit 15 rows. BO loosely, leaving last st on needle for Top Border.

Top Border

On RS, pu&k 8 sts on edge of Right Border, and 51 sts per Block – 264 sts.

Knit 15 rows. BO loosely, leaving last st on needle.

Left Border

Pu&k 8 sts on left edge of Top border, and 51 sts per Block on left edge – 366 sts.

Knit 15 rows. BO loosely, leaving last st on needle.

Bottom Border

Pu&k 8 sts on bottom edge of Left border, 51 sts per Block on bottom edge, and 9 sts on bottom edge of Right Border – 273 sts.

Knit 15 rows. BO loosely. Cut yarn and fasten off.

FINISHING

Weave in ends.

PORTALS

The doors and windows of the Portals blanket remind us that every new experience begins with a step out into the unknown.

SIZE 55 x 73"/140 x 185 cm

TECHNIQUES Pu&k, sewing, and 3-needle BO

YARN Rowan Felted Tweed, DK (50% wool, 25% alpaca, 25% viscose; 191 yds/175 m; 1.75 oz/50 g):

Pattern Color ID	Color Swatch	Color ID	Color Name	Color Description	# Balls
A		177	Clay	very light gray	4
B		170	Seafarer	dark navy blue	4
C		181	Mineral	yellow	5
D		161	Avocado	yellow-green	3
E		205	Lotus Leaf	dark green	2
F		204	Vaseline Green	muted mint green	3
G		184	Celadon	light olive green	4
H		218	Fjord	light teal	3
I		202	Turquoise	turquoise	3
J		212	Peach	dusty pink	3
K		154	Ginger	brick red	3
L		198	Zinnia	bright pink	3
M		196	Barn Red	dark red	3

NEEDLES US Size 10/6 mm 40"/100 cm circular needles or size needed to obtain gauge, 1 straight or circular US Size 11 needle for 3-needle BO

NOTIONS Tapestry needle, stitch markers

GAUGE 14 sts x 28 rows = 4"/10 cm in garter st

NOTES

- Yarn is held double throughout.
- The blanket is worked in 5 sections as shown in Figure 1 and named for their position in the blanket as follows: Northwest (NW), Southwest (SW), North East (NE), Central East (CE), and South East (SE).
- Each Section is composed of multiple Squares and Rectangles that are worked modularly by picking up and knitting stitches on previously completed shapes. Squares and Rectangles are worked flat, and the open seam is sewn with long tails.
- There are two pattern stitches, one for the Square and one for a Rectangle. When cutting yarns after completing a color, leave a long tail 4 times the length of the seam to be sewn with that yarn color.

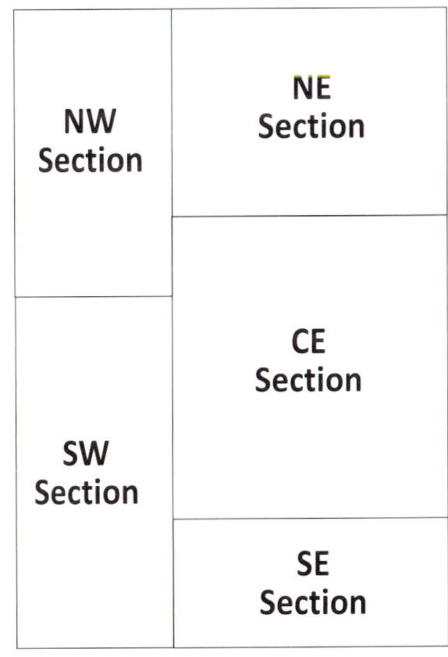

Figure 1: Blanket Sections

BLANKET INSTRUCTIONS

SW Section

Refer to left side of Figure 2 for construction and the right side for colors. This section contains 11 Blocks, named: <Shape abbreviation><Block #> (shown in purple font). For example, S1 is Square 1, and R2 is Rectangle 2. Blocks are worked in increasing Block # order. S1 is worked followed by R2, R3, R4, etc. The label for the first Block to work is highlighted in bright yellow. Five sets of stitches are generated to begin each Block. The 1st set of stitches starts at the midpoint of an edge for the Block at the location of the red half-circle and is always generated using CO. Using the outermost color for the Block indicated in Figure 2 (right), generate the number of stitches in italics using the method indicated by the symbols on that edge of the Block (either CO or pu&k) in Figure 2 (left), and place a marker between each set of stitches, working clockwise around the Block. There will be four placed markers, named m1 to m4 (see illustration of marker positions in Figure 3) after generating stitches. After the stitches have been generated for the Block, work the pattern stitch indicated by the Block's Shape abbreviation: If the Shape abbreviation is S, work the Square (S) pattern stitch, and if the Shape abbreviation is R, work the Rectangle (R) pattern stitch. For example, for Block R2, do as follows:

> With L, CO 10 sts, pm, CO 22 sts, pm, pu&k 20 sts on the right edge of S1 as shown in Figure 2 (left), pm, CO 22 sts, pm, CO 10 sts. The shape symbol for "R2" is "R" so the Rectangle pattern stitch is worked.

Blocks have color striping. New colors are always added at the beginning of RS (decrease) rows. When cutting yarns, leave a long tail for sewing the seam. The tail should be 4 times the length of the seam to be sewn in that color. The number of rows to work in each color is specified in Figure 2 (right) in italics at the upper left corner of the Block, and the color abbreviation is at the lower left corner of the Block. The number of rows to work in the first color is always odd because the stitch generation (Cast-ons and pu&k's) counts as the first RS row. The number of rows for the final color is not noted, as the pattern stitches (Square and Rectangle) provide instructions for finishing the Blocks.

After completing a Block, sew the open edge of the Block using mattress st and matching color yarn tails. See the technique video for tips on perfectly aligning the stripes during sewing (access code is on page 214).

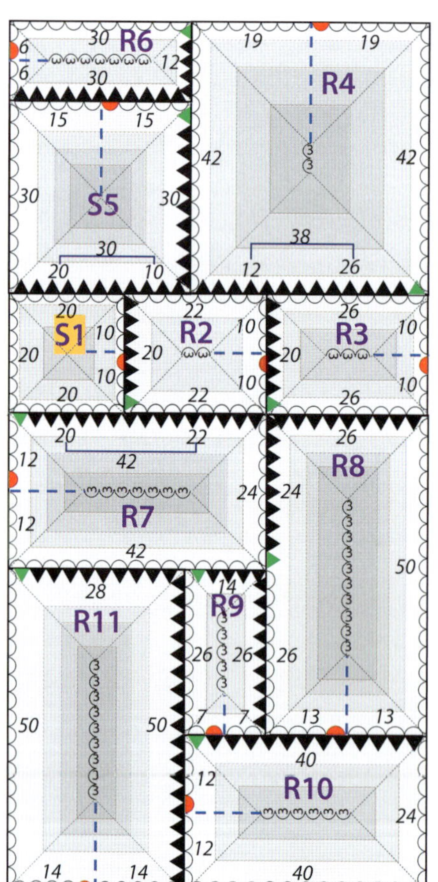

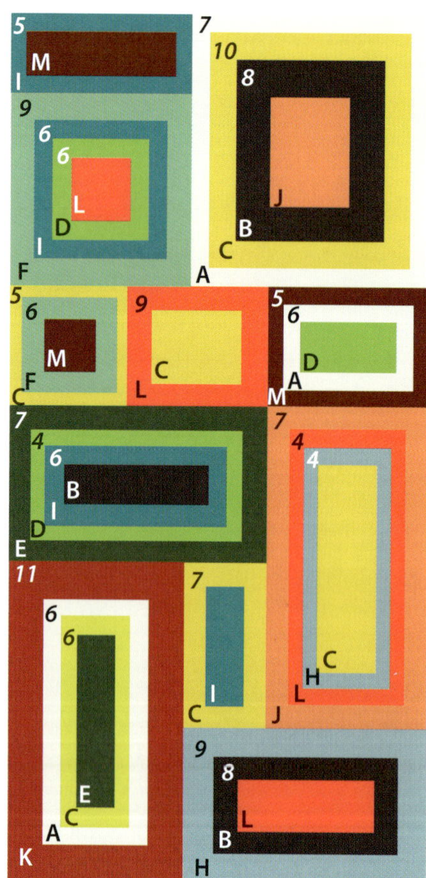

Figure 2: Construction (left), Colors (right), and Numbers of Rows to Work (in italics on right) for *SW Section*

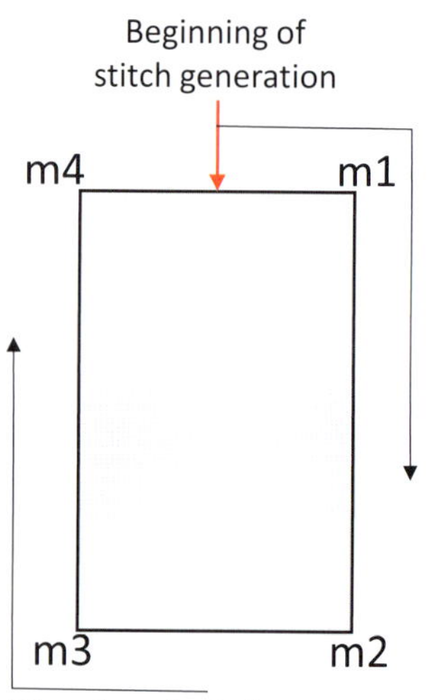

Figure 3: Locations of Markers and Direction of Stitch Generation

Square (S)

Row 1 and all odd-numbered (WS) rows: Knit.
Row 2 and all even-numbered (RS) rows: *Knit to 2 sts bef m, k2tog, ssk; rep from * 3 more times, knit to end – 8 sts dec'd.
Rep [Rows 1 & 2] until 8 sts rem, making color changes at beg of RS rows as directed.
Cut yarn. Thread yarn onto tapestry needle and insert needle through all sts rem on needle. Pull taut and fasten off securely.

Tip: When fastening off Squares, for an extra-secure center, insert tapestry needle through rem 8 stitches twice, and then weave in end on WS as described in "Weaving in Ends" on page 212.

Rectangle (R)

Row 1 and all odd-numbered (WS) rows: Knit.
Row 2 and all even-numbered (RS) rows: *Knit to 2 sts bef m, k2tog, ssk; rep from * 3 more times, knit to end – 8 sts dec'd.
Rep [Rows 1 & 2] until 2 sts rem bet m2 and m3, making color changes at beg of RS rows as directed.
Next row (WS): Knit. Rm1 and m4.
Next row (RS): Cdd, knit to 2 sts bef m2, rm3 and m2, cdd 2 times, pm (m5) between the two cdd's, knit to last 3 sts, cdd – 8 sts dec'd.
Next row (WS): Knit to m5, rm. Turn needles parallel with tips together and RS of work together. With 3rd (larger) needle, use 3-needle BO to BO all sts.
Cut yarn and fasten off. Insert yarn end through remaining loop on needle and tighten. Pull taut and fasten off securely.

NW Section

Refer to left side of Figure 4 for construction and the right side for colors. This section contains 9 Blocks numbered 12 through 20. Work as for SW Section.

Tips on Correct Stitch Counts

- St counts bet m1 and m2 (abbreviated as m1-m2) and m3-m4 should match.
- m2-m3 is equal to the sum of m4-end and beg-m1.
- For Squares, m2-m3 equals m1-m2 and m3-m4.
- For Rectangles, m1-m2 minus m2-m3 should always match what it was at st generation.
- Count often to catch errors early, using a k2tog to decrease on the next WS row or a kf&b to increase to adjust and avoid unpicking.

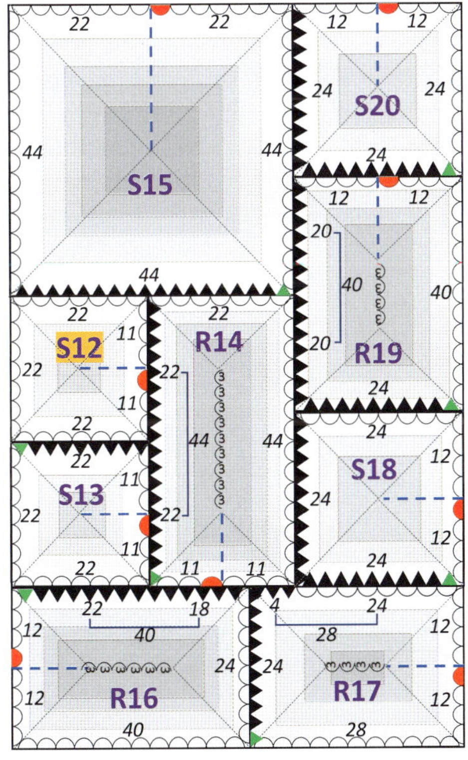

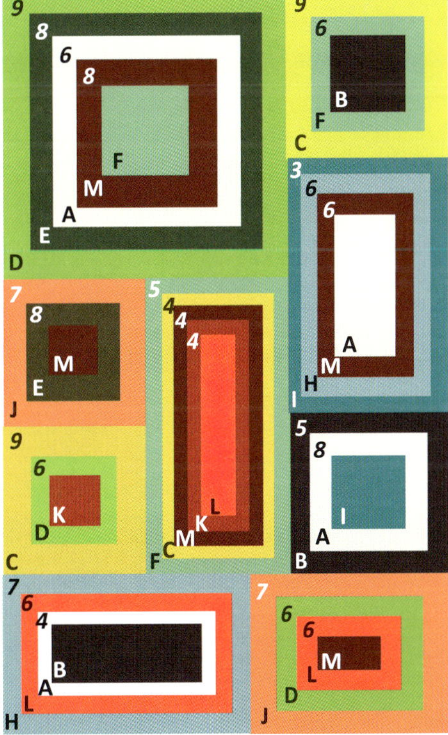

Figure 4: Construction (left), Colors (right), and Numbers of Rows to Work (in italics on right) for ***NW Section***

SE Section

Refer to top of Figure 5 for construction and bottom for colors. This section contains 7 Blocks numbered 21 through 27. Work as for SW Section.

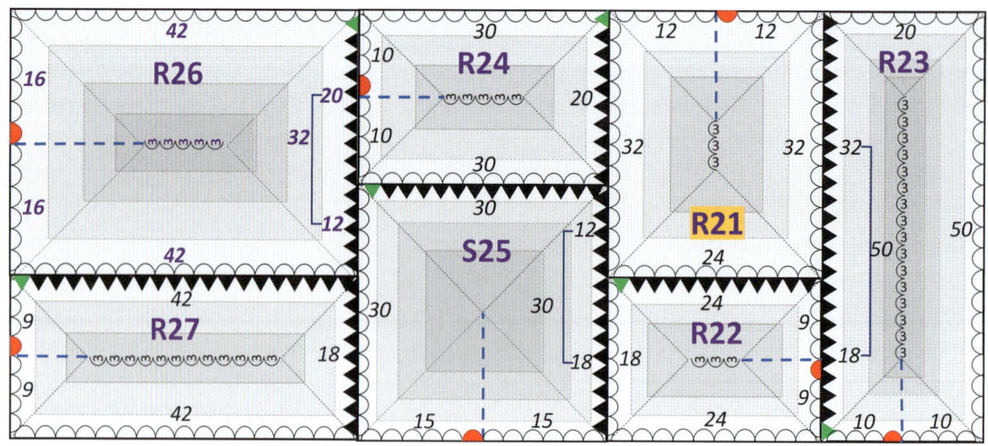

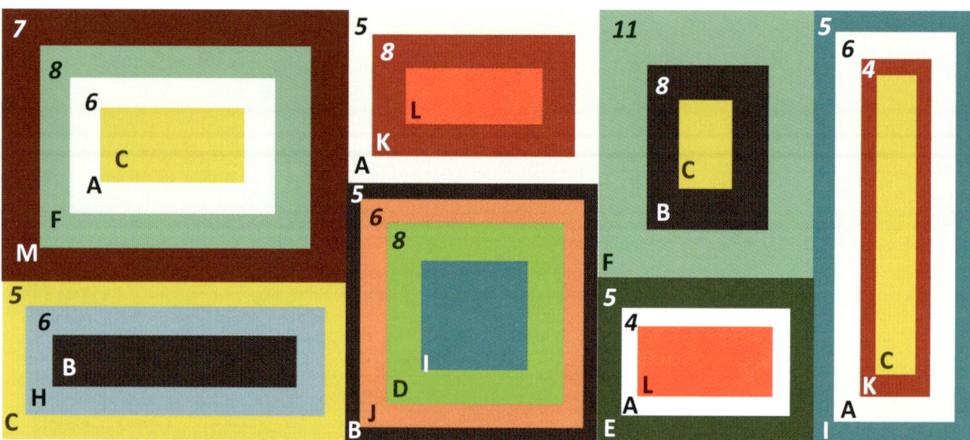

Figure 5: Construction (top), Colors (bottom), and Numbers of Rows to Work (in italics at bottom) for ***SE Section***

CE Section

Refer to top of Figure 6 for construction and bottom for colors. This section contains 18 Blocks numbered 28 through 45. Work as for SW Section.

Note: S35 does not have pu&k edges. S35 and R36 are worked and joined to the other, completed Blocks when R37 is worked.

**Note:* If desired, this section may be worked in 3 independent subsections: 28 through 34, then 35 through 41, and 42 through 45. The subsections would then be sewn together using mattress st.

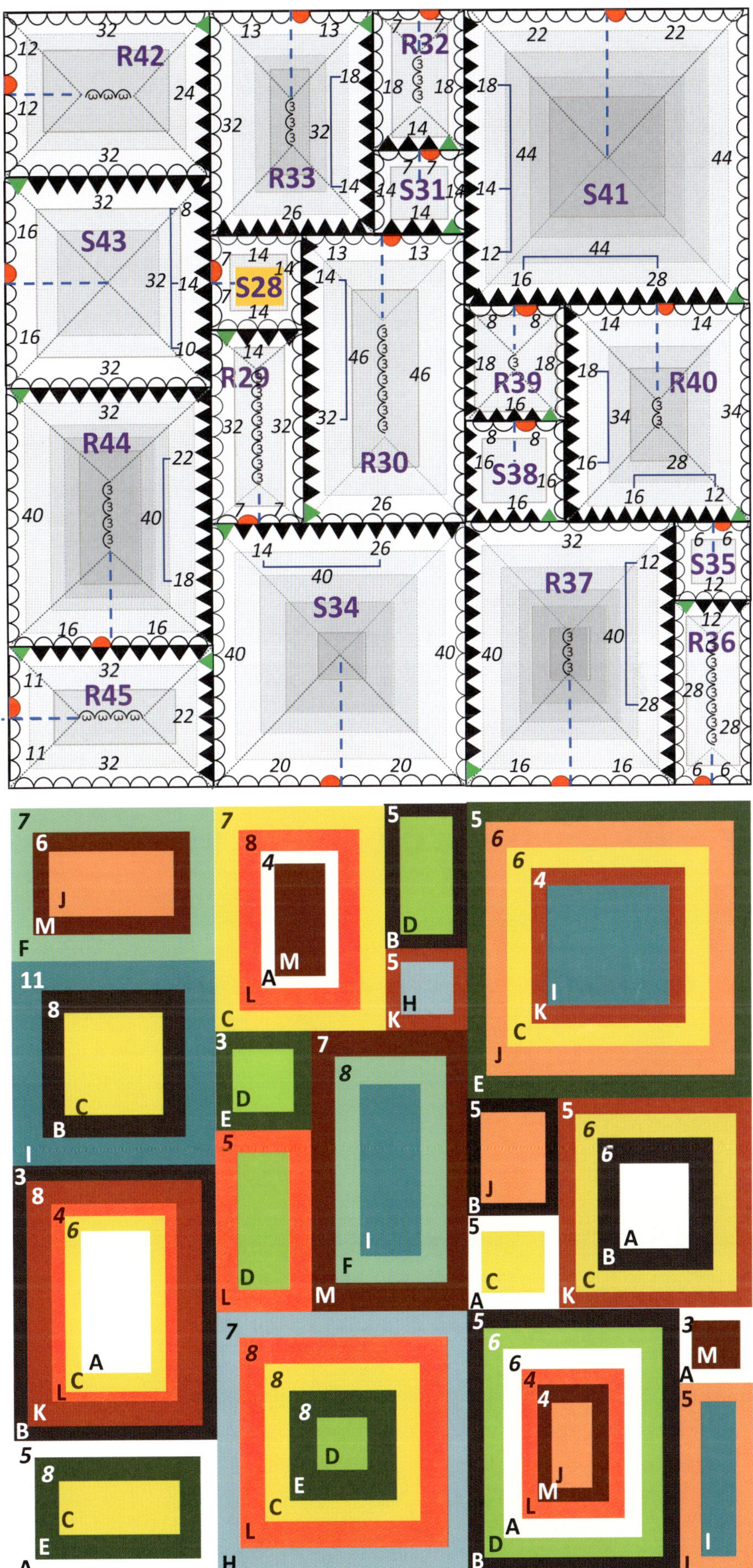

Figure 6: Construction (top), Colors (bottom), and Number of Rows to work (in italics at bottom) for ***CE Section***

NE Section

Refer to top of Figure 7 for construction and bottom for colors. This section contains 12 Blocks numbered 46 to 57. Work as for SW Section.

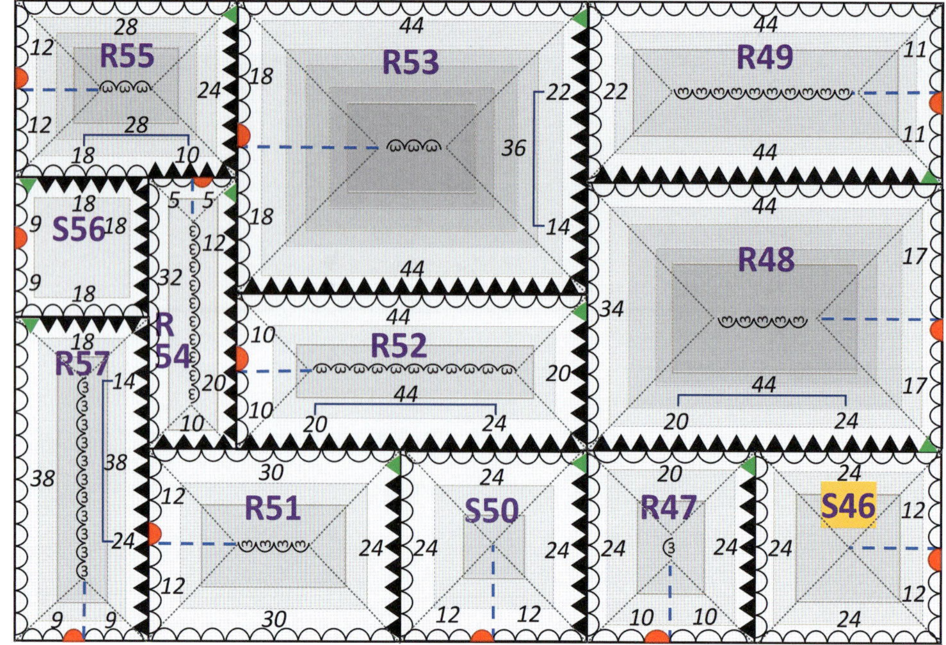

Figure 7: Construction (top), Colors (bottom), and Number of Rows to work (in italics at bottom) for ***NE Section***

ASSEMBLY

Arrange the 5 completed Sections—SW, NW, SE, CE, and NE—as shown in Figure 8. Using yarn color matching the outer edge of the Block on the right of the seam and of length 4 times the length of the seam to be sewn, sew red-dashed seams using mattress st, and then sew blue-dashed seams. For additional assistance in aligning Sections for sewing, see Figure 9 on page 138, where the colored numbers represent the number of stitches overlapping between shapes in adjacent Sections.

BORDERS

See Figure 8 for the number of stitches to pu&k on each Block. The stitch left on the needle at the end of each Border is used as the first stitch of the next Border.

Right Border

Attach G at lower right corner of blanket, pu&k 248 sts. Knit 7 rows. BO loosely, leaving last st on needle.

Top Border

Pu&k 4 sts on top edge of Right Border, 184 sts on top edge of blanket – 189 sts. Knit 7 rows. BO loosely, leaving last st on needle.

Left Border

Pu&k 4 sts on left edge of Top Border, 248 sts on left edge of blanket – 253 sts. Knit 7 rows. BO loosely, leaving last st on needle.

Bottom Border

Pu&k 4 sts on bottom edge of Left Border, 184 sts on bottom edge of blanket, and 4 sts on the bottom edge of the Right Border – 193 sts. Knit 7 rows. BO loosely. Cut yarn, and fasten off.

FINISHING

Weave in ends.

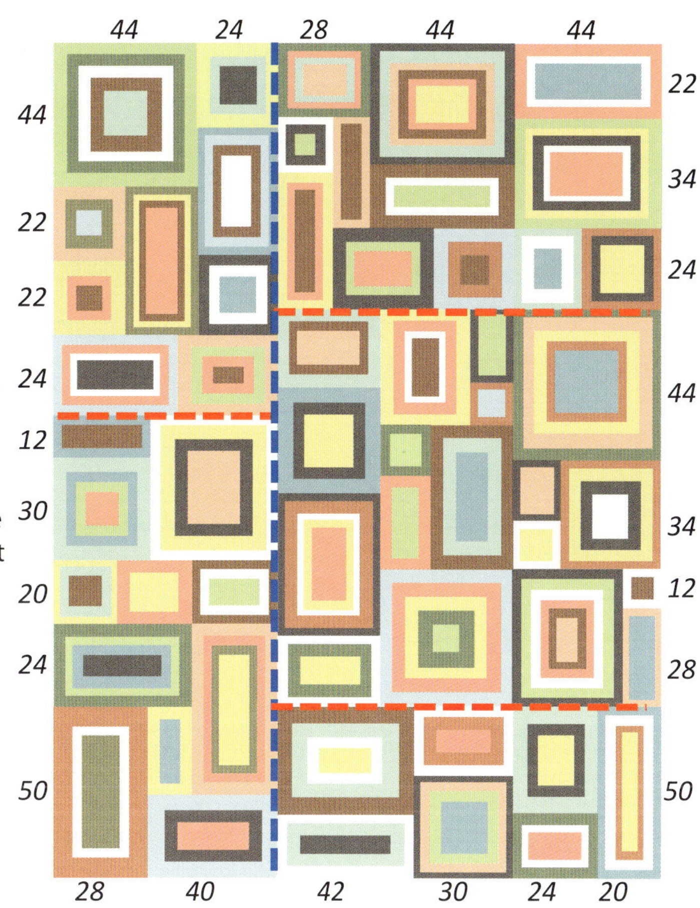

Figure 8: Assembly and Borders

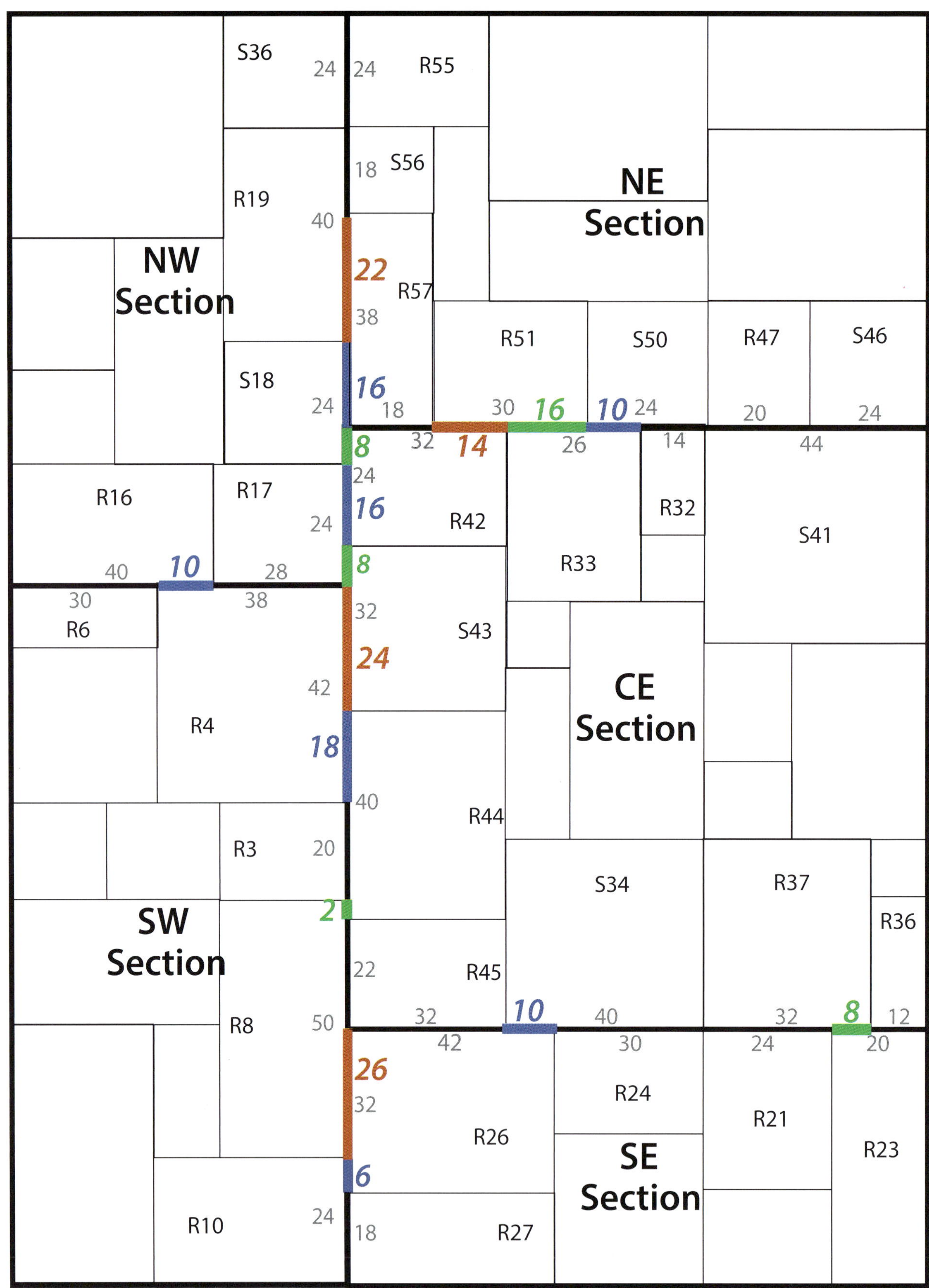

Figure 9: Sewing Aid: Colored Numbers Represent the Number of Overlapping Sts between Shapes in Adjacent Sections. Gray Numbers are the Edge St Counts for the Shape.

REEL DEAL

Grab some popcorn and a drink, and snuggle up under this colorful and warm blanket to watch your favorite flick.

SIZE 66.5 x 77.5"/169 x 195.5 cm

TECHNIQUES Pu&k and 3-needle BO

YARN Berroco Yarns Vintage Chunky, bulky (52% acrylic, 40% wool, 8% nylon; 136 yds/124 m; 3.5 oz/100 g):

Pattern Color ID	Color Swatch	Color ID	Color Name	Color Description	# Hanks
A		6101	Mochi	off-white	18
B		6189	Charcoal	off-black	4
C		6104	Mushroom	light tan	2
D		6167	Dewberry	magenta	1
E		6140	Orange	red-orange	1
F		61194	Rhubarb	medium pink	1
G		61170	Rose Quartz	light dusty pink	2
H		6121	Sunny	strong yellow-gold	1
I		6122	Banane	light yellow	1
J		6142	Jade	jade green	1
K		6125	Aquae	aqua	1
L		61174	Spruce	medium green-gray	2
M		6199	Sage	light gray-green	3
N		61195	Okra	light green-gray	2
O		61184	Twilight	muted navy	1
P		6194	Breezeway	muted teal	1

NEEDLES (2) US Size 10.5/6.5 mm 40"/100 cm circular needles or size needed to obtain gauge, 1 straight or circular US Size 11 or 13 needle (8 or 9 mm) for 3-needle BO

NOTIONS Tapestry needle, stitch markers

GAUGE 15 sts x 30 rows = 4"/10 cm in garter st

NOTES

- The blanket is worked in Strips that are joined using a 3-needle BO.
- Borders are picked up and knit from the edge of the completed blanket.

BLANKET INSTRUCTIONS

Strips

There are 6 Strips in the blanket. Odd-numbered Strips are worked differently from even-numbered Strips.

Instructions are for making all shapes and then joining. However, adjacent shapes can be joined as soon as they are complete.

Strip 1

Figure 1 shows the shapes used in Strip 1, their color abbreviations, quantities to make, and direction of growth (blue arrows).

Odd End **- Make 2**

Work [OE] using colors for OEs in Figure 2, Strip 1.

Odd End (OE) – 1 st inc'ing to 21 sts dec'ing to 1 st

With C1, CO 1 st.
Row 2 (WS): Knit.
Row 3 (RS): Kf&b, knit to end – 1 st inc'd; 2 sts.
Row 4: Knit.
Rows 5-42: Rep [Rows 3 & 4] 19 times – 19 sts inc'd; 21 sts. Drop C1 but do not cut.
Rows 43 & 44: With C2, knit.
Row 45: K2tog, knit to end – 1 st dec'd; 20 sts.
Row 46: Knit.
Rows 47-64: Rep [Rows 45 & 46] 9 more times – 9 sts dec'd; 11 sts (11 ridges worked in C2). Cut C2. Drape C1 from Row 42 to beg of Row 65, leaving a little slack yarn.
Row 65: Cont with C1, k2tog, knit to end – 1 sts dec'd; 10 sts.
Row 66: Knit.
Row 67: K2tog, knit to last 2 sts, ssk – 2 sts dec'd; 8 sts.
Row 68: Knit.
Rows 69-72: Rep [Rows 67 & 68] 2 times – 4 sts dec'd; 4 sts.
Row 73: Rep [Row 67] – 2 sts dec'd; 2 sts.
Row 74: K2tog – 1 st dec'd; 1 st. Cut C1 and fasten off.

Odd Kite **- Make 4**

Work [OK] using colors for OKs in Figure 2, Strip 1.

Odd Kite (OK) – 1 st inc'ing to 21 sts dec'ing to 1 st

With C1, CO 1 st.
Row 2 (WS): Knit.
Row 3 (RS): Kf&b, knit to end – 1 st inc'd; 2 sts.
Row 4: Knit.
Rows 5-42: Rep [Rows 3 & 4] 19 times – 19 sts inc'd; 21 sts. Drop C1, and add C2. Do not cut C1.
Rows 43-64: Cont with C2, knit (11 ridges worked in C2). Cut C2. Drape C1 from Row 42 to beg of Row 65, leaving a little slack yarn.
Rows 65 & 66: Cont with C1, knit.
Row 67: Knit to last st, ssk – 1 st dec'd; 20 sts.
Row 68: Knit.
Rows 69-104: Rep [Rows 67 & 68] 18 times – 18 sts dec'd; 2 sts.
Row 105: Ssk – 1 st dec'd; 1 st.
Cut C1 and fasten off.

Odd Clip **- Make 5**

Work [OC] using colors for OCs in Figure 2, Strip 1.

Notes:

- The short gray arrows in Figure 2 indicate the direction of work and growth.
- Clips have 5 contrast colors—C3, C4, C5, C6, and C7—used in that order, and a "separator" color that is always B and should not be cut until after its last use, after Row 48. Drape it slightly loosely along R edge to its next use.

Odd Clip (OC) – 1 st inc'ing to 7 sts dec'ing to 1 st

With C3 for the Odd Clip, CO 1 st.
Row 2 (WS): Knit.
Row 3: Kf&b – 1 st inc'd; 2 sts.
Row 4: Knit.
Row 5: Kf&b, knit to end – 1 st inc'd; 3 sts.
Row 6: Knit.
Rows 7-14: Rep [Rows 5 & 6] 4 times – 4 sts inc'd; 7 sts. Cut C3.
Rows 15 & 16: Cont with B, knit.
Rows 17-30: With C4, knit. Cut C4. (7 ridges)
Rows 31 & 32: Cont with B, knit.
Rows 33-46: With C5, knit. Cut C5. (7 ridges)
Rows 47 & 48: Cont with B, knit.
Rows 49-62: With C6, knit. Cut C6. (7 ridges)
Rows 63 & 64: Cont with B, knit. Cut B.
Rows 65 & 66: With C7, knit.
Row 67: Knit to last 2 sts, ssk – 1 st dec'd; 6 sts.
Row 68: Knit.
Rows 69-76: Rep [Rows 67 & 68] 4 times – 4 sts dec'd; 2 sts.
Row 77: Ssk – 1 st dec'd; 1 st. Cut C7 and fasten off.

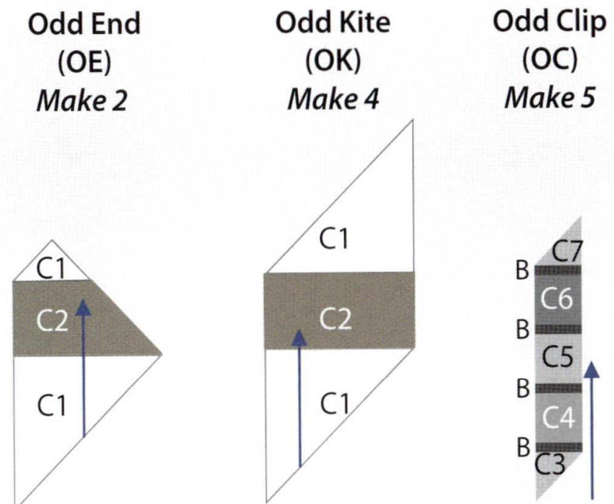

Figure 1: Shapes for Odd-Numbered Strips

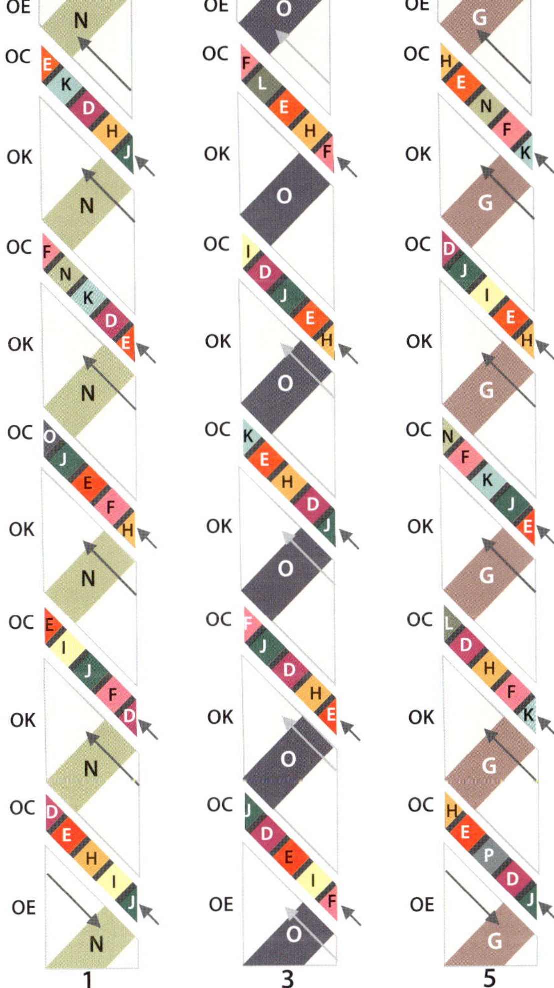

Figure 2: Odd-Numbered Strip Layout and Colors

Join Shapes Together to Form an Odd Strip

Strip 1

Arrange the completed shapes for Strip 1 as shown in Figure 2, Strip 1, orienting shapes using the gray arrows. Joins of adjacent shapes are labeled "a" through "j" on Figure 3, to indicate the order of joining. Join each pair of adjacent shapes using 3 steps: 1) Prep *lower* shape, 2) Prep *upper* shape, 3) Join prepped shapes.

1. Prep lower shape

With B, and circular needle, starting at red triangle on the *lower* shape, pu&k 32 sts to corner (11 sts on area worked in C2 and 21 sts on area worked in C1).

Next row (WS): Kf&b, knit to last 2 sts, ssk. Cut yarn. Set piece aside.

2. Prep upper shape

With the second circular needle, starting at the green triangle on the bottom left corner of the *upper* shape, pu&k 32 sts to corner (7 per each of the areas worked in C3, C4, C5, and C6; 1 on each B-colored separator).

Next row (WS): Kf&b, knit to last 2 sts, ssk. Do not cut yarn.

3. Join prepped shapes

Orient *lower* and *upper* shapes so that RS are together, needles are parallel, and tips are aligned. The *upper* shape, with the ball of B still attached, should be farther away, and the *lower* shape should be closest.

With a third, larger needle, 3-needle BO all pairs of stitches until 1 st rems on R needle. Cut B and insert end through rem loop and tighten.

Strips 3 and 5

Work as for Strip 1, referring to Figure 2, Strip 3 and Figure 2, Strip 5, respectively, for layout and orientation of shapes.

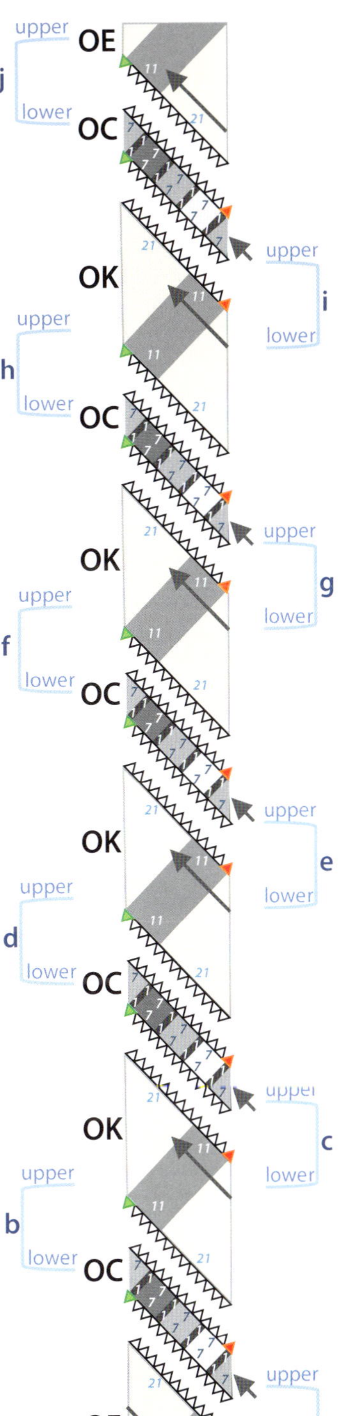

Figure 3: Assembly of Shapes into Strip for Odd-Numbered Strips

Strip 2

Figure 4 shows the shapes used in Strip 2, their color abbreviations, quantities, and direction of growth (blue arrows).

Even End - Make 2

Work [EE] using colors for EEs in Figure 5, Strip 2.

Even End (EE) – 1 st inc'ing to 21 sts dec'ing to 1 st

With C1, CO 1 st.
Row 2 (WS): Knit.
Row 3 (RS): Knit to last st, kf&b – 1 st inc'd; 2 sts.
Row 4: Knit.
Rows 5-42: Rep [Rows 3 & 4] 19 times – 19 sts inc'd; 21 sts. Drop C1 but do not cut.
Rows 43 & 44: With C2, knit.
Row 45: Knit to last 2 sts, ssk – 1 st dec'd; 20 sts.
Row 46: Knit.
Rows 47-64: Rep [Rows 45 & 46] 9 more times – 9 sts dec'd; 11 sts (11 ridges worked in C2). Cut C2. Drape C1 from Row 42 to beg of Row 65, leaving a little slack yarn.
Row 65: Cont with C1, knit to last 2 sts, ssk – 1 st dec'd; 10 sts.
Row 66: Knit.
Row 67: K2tog, knit to last 2 sts, ssk – 2 sts dec'd; 8 sts.
Row 68: Knit.
Rows 69-72: Rep [Rows 67 & 68] 2 times – 4 sts dec'd; 4 sts.
Row 73: Rep [Row 67] – 2 sts dec'd; 2 sts.
Row 74: Ssk – 1 st dec'd; 1 st. Cut C1, fasten off.

Even Kite - Make 4

Work [EK] using colors for EKs in Figure 5, Strip 2.

Even Kite (EK) – 1 st inc'ing to 21 sts dec'ing to 1 st

With C1, CO 1 st.
Row 2 (WS): Knit.
Row 3 (RS): Knit to last st, kf&b – 1 st inc'd; 2 sts.
Row 4: Knit.
Rows 5-42: Rep [Rows 3 & 4] 19 times – 19 sts inc'd; 21 sts. Drop C1, and add C2. Do not cut C1.
Rows 43-64: Cont with C2, knit (11 ridges worked in C2). Cut C2. Drape C1 from Row 42 to beg of Row 65, leaving a little slack yarn.
Rows 65 & 66: Cont with C1, knit.
Row 67: K2tog, knit to end – 1 st dec'd; 20 sts.
Row 68: Knit.
Rows 69-104: Rep [Rows 67 & 68] 18 times – 18 sts dec'd; 2 sts.
Row 105: K2tog – 1 st dec'd; 1 st. Cut C1 and fasten off.

Even Clip - Make 5

See *Notes* for Odd Clips, page 142.

Work [EC] using colors for ECs in Figure 5, Strip 2.

Even Clip (EC) – 1 st inc'ing to 7 sts dec'ing to 1 st

With C3 for the Even Clip, CO 1 st.
Row 2 (WS): Knit.
Row 3: Kf&b – 1 st inc'd; 2 sts.
Row 4: Knit.
Row 5: Knit to last st, kf&b – 1 st inc'd; 3 sts.
Row 6: Knit.
Rows 7-14: Rep [Rows 5 & 6] 4 times – 4 sts inc'd; 7 sts. Cut C3. Attach B.
Rows 15 & 16: Knit. Do not cut B.
Rows 17-30: With C4, knit. (7 ridges) Cut C4. Drape B slightly loosely along R edge.
Rows 31 & 32: Cont with B, knit. Do not cut B.
Rows 33-46: With C5, knit. (7 ridges) Cut C5. Drape B slightly loosely along R edge.
Rows 47 & 48: Cont with B, knit. Do not cut B.
Rows 49-62: With C6, knit. (7 ridges) Cut C6. Drape B slightly loosely along R edge.
Rows 63 & 64: Cont with B, knit. Cut B.
Rows 65 & 66: With C7, knit.
Row 67: K2tog, knit to end – 1 st dec'd; 6 sts.
Row 68: Knit.
Rows 69-76: Rep [Rows 67 & 68] 4 times – 4 sts dec'd; 2 sts.
Row 77: K2tog – 1 st dec'd; 1 st. Cut C7, fasten off.

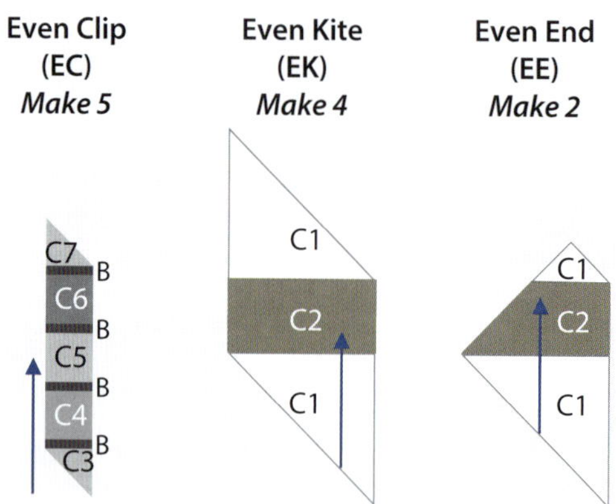

Figure 4: Shapes for Even-Numbered Strips

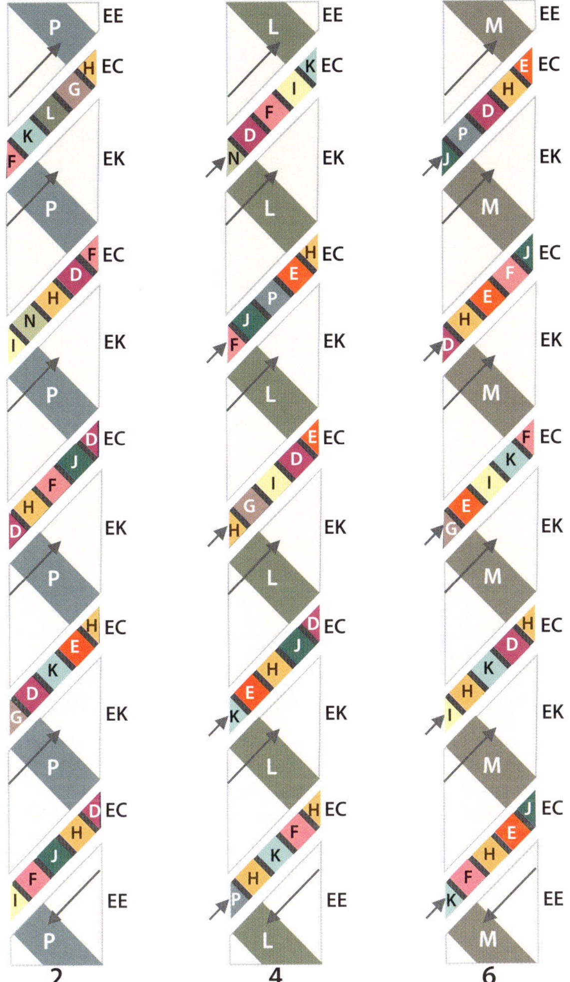

Figure 5: Even-Numbered Strip Layout and Colors

Join Shapes Together to Form an Even Strip

Strip 2

Arrange the completed shapes for Strip 2 as shown in Figure 5, Strip 2, orienting shapes using the small gray arrows. Joins of adjacent shapes are labeled "m" through "v" on Figure 6, to indicate the order of joining. Join each pair of adjacent shapes using 3 steps: 1) Prep *lower* shape, 2) Prep *upper* shape, 3) Join prepped shapes.

1. Prep lower shape

With B and circular needle, starting at red triangle on the *lower* shape), pu&k 32 sts to corner (11 sts on area worked in C2 and 21 sts on area worked in C1).

Next row (WS): K2tog, knit to last 2 st, kf&b. Cut yarn. Set piece aside.

2. Prep upper shape

With the second circular needle, starting at the green triangle on *upper* shape, pu&k 32 sts to corner (7 per each of the areas worked in C3, C4, C5, and C6; 1 on each B-colored separator).

Next row (WS): K2tog, knit to last st, kf&b. Do not cut yarn.

3. Join prepped shapes

Orient *lower* and *upper* shapes so RS are together, needles are parallel, and tips are aligned. The *upper* shape, with the ball of B still attached, should be farther away and the *lower* shape should be closest.

With a third, larger needle, 3-needle BO until 1 st rems on R needle. Cut B and insert end through rem loop and tighten.

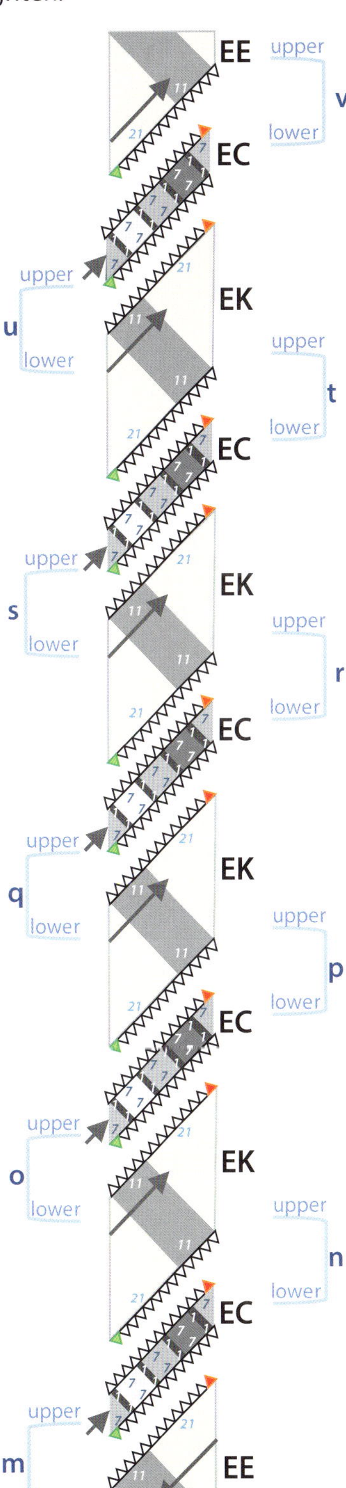

Figure 6: Assembly of Pieces into Strip for Even-Numbered Strips

Strips 4 and 6

Work as for Strip 2, referring to Figure 5, Strip 4 and Figure 5, Strip 6, respectively, for layout and orientation of shapes.

Join Strips

Lay out completed Strips in order 1-6 from left to right.

Join of Strips 1 and 2

See the left side of Figure 7 for layout of Strips and stitch counts for pu&k. Join Strips using 3 steps: 1) Prep left Strip, 2) Prep right Strip, and 3) Join prepped Strips.

1. Prep left Strip on first circular needle

With A, and starting at red triangle at bottom right corner of Strip on left, pu&k 232 sts (see Table 1 and Figure 7 for stitch counts per shape). Knit 9 rows. Cut yarn.

2. Prep right Strip on second circular needle

With A, and starting at green triangle at top left corner of Strip on right, pu&k 232 sts (see Table 1 and Figure 7 for stitch counts per shape). Knit 9 rows. Do not cut yarn.

3. Join prepped Strips

Orient prepped Strips so that RS are tog, needles are parallel, and tips are aligned. The Strip on right, with ball of A still attached, should be at the back. With third, larger needle, 3-needle BO until 1 st rems on R needle. Cut A and insert through rem loop and tighten.

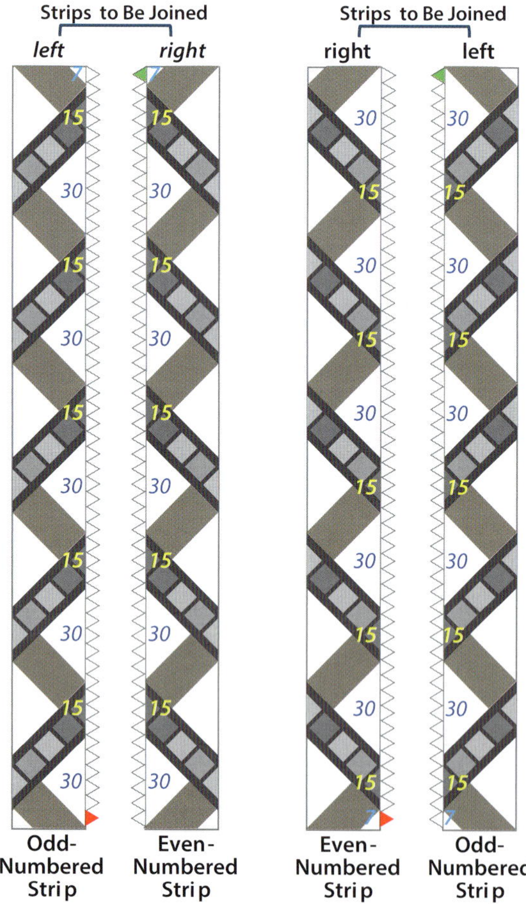

Figure 7: Pu&k Stitch Counts and Locations for Strip Pair Joining: Odd to Even Strips (left), Even to Odd Strips (right)

Join of Strips 3 & 4 and Strips 5 & 6

Work as for Join of Strips 1 and 2.

Join of Strips 2 & 3 and Strips 4 & 5

Work as for Join of Strips 1 and 2, using the right side of Figure 7 and Table 1 for stitch counts per shape.

Table 1: Number of Stitches to Pu&k per Shape for:

1) Joining Strip pairs
2) Right & Left Extensions and Borders

	Kite	Clip	OE or EE
# Stitches	30	15	7

Table 2: Number of Stitches to Pu&k for Top & Bottom Borders

	Strip	Strip Join	Right/Left Extension
# Stitches	23	10	5

Right Extension Strip and Border

On the bottom right corner of Strip 6, with A, and using a circular needle, pu&k 232 sts to the top right corner of Strip 6, using the stitch counts per shape in Table 2. Knit 9 rows. Cut A. Attach C. Knit 1 row. Work [MB].

Left Extension Strip and Border

Work as for Right Extension Strip and Right Border, starting pu&k at top left corner of Strip 1.

Top Border (See Table 2 for st counts per shape)

With C, starting at the top right corner of Strip 6, pu&k 198 sts. Work [MB].

Mitered Border (MB)

Row 2 (WS): Knit.
Row 3 (RS): Kf&b, knit to last st, kf&b – 2 sts inc'd.
Row 4: Knit.
Rows 5 & 6: Rep [Rows 3 & 4] once – 2 sts inc'd.
Cut C, leaving 10"/25 cm tail.
Rows 7-12: Cont with M, rep [Rows 3 & 4] 3 more times – 6 sts inc'd (3 ridges in M). BO loosely. Cut yarn and fasten off, leaving 10"/25 cm tail.

Bottom Border

Work as for Top Border, starting pu&k on bottom left corner of Strip 1.

FINISHING

Using long tails of matching color and mattress st, sew tog open corners of the Border, aligning color changes. Weave in ends.

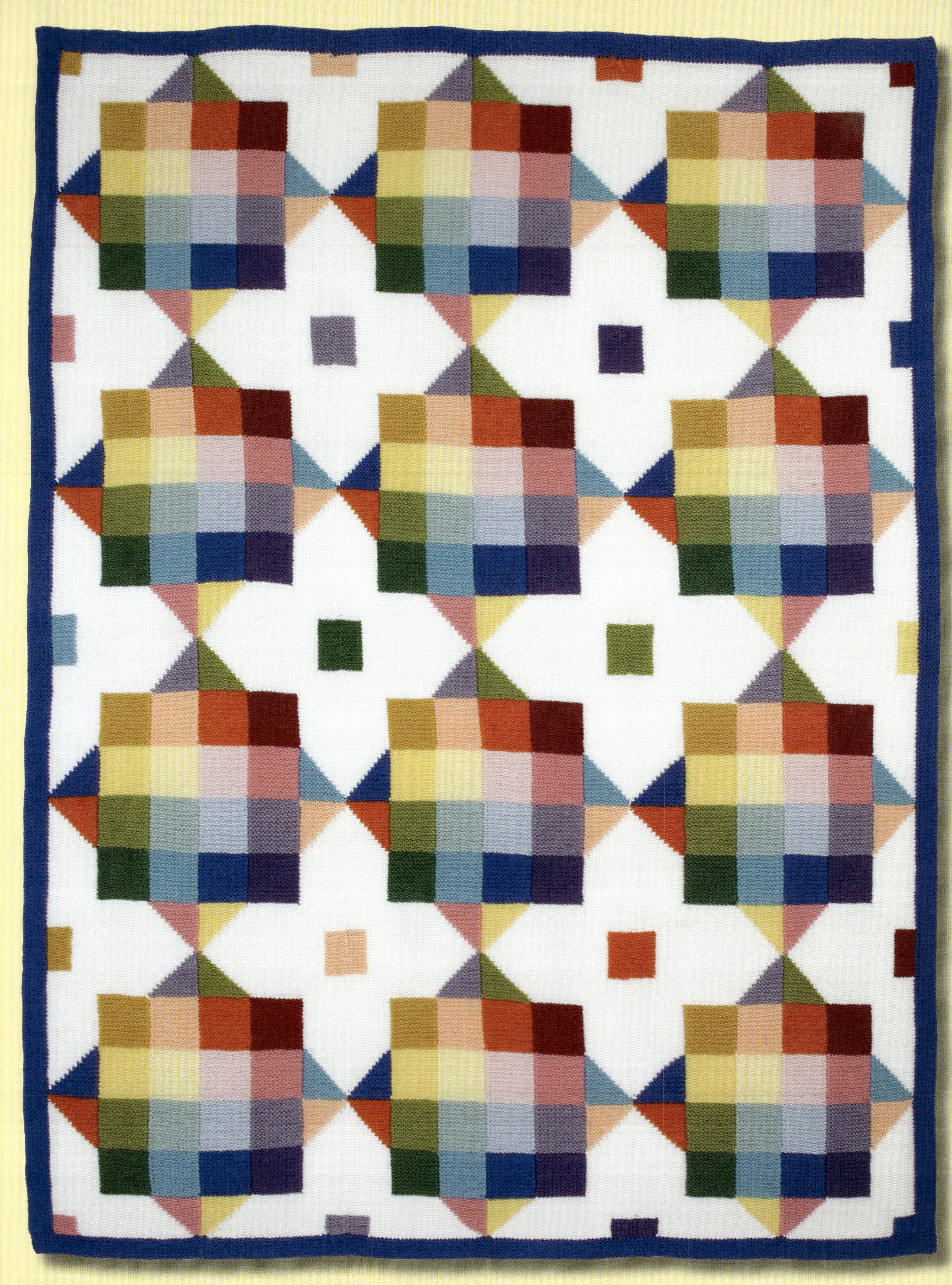

REFRACTION

Light refracting through water or a crystal separates by wavelengths in this colorful blanket.

SIZE 51 x 67"/130 x 170 cm

TECHNIQUES

Method A: Intarsia
Method B: Pu&k, 3-needle BO
Both: Sewing

YARN Paintbox Simply Aran, heavy worsted (100% acrylic; 201 yds/184 m; 3.5 oz/100 g):

Pattern Color ID	Color Swatch	Color ID	Color Name	Color Description	# Skeins
A		200	Paper White	white	7
B		223	Mustard Yellow	gold	1
C		254	Peach Orange	peach	1
D		220	Banana Cream	pale yellow	1
E		221	Daffodil Yellow	bright yellow	1
F		215	Red Wine	burgundy	1
G		250	Bubblegum Pink	bright pink	1
H		249	Candyfloss Pink	pale pink	1
I		219	Blood Orange	red-orange	1
J		247	Pansy Purple	purple	1
K		239	Sailor Blue	blue	3
L		235	Duck Egg Blue	pale blue	1
M		246	Dusty Lilac	pale purple	1
N		229	Grass Green	dark green	1
O		228	Lime Green	grass green	1
P		232	Washed Teal	pale aqua	1
Q		233	Marine Blue	aqua	1

NEEDLES US Size 8/5.0 mm (or size needed to obtain gauge) 40"/100 cm circular needles, US Size 8/5.0 mm dpns (Method B), 1 US Size 10/6 mm straight needle for 3-needle BO

NOTIONS Stitch markers, tapestry needle, 6 bobbins

GAUGE 18 sts x 36 rows = 4"/10 cm in garter st

NOTES

- There are two methods for making the blanket, intarsia and Mitered Shapes, as depicted in Figure 1. The intarsia method (Method A) is to work vertical Strips using intarsia for colored shapes and then sew the Strips together. The Modular with Mitered Shapes method is to work the colored stars using mitered squares and triangles, work the spaces between stars as mitered shapes, and then fill in remaining small squares by working squares in the round. There is no intarsia or sewing for Method B.
- Use a knitted CO whenever CO is required.

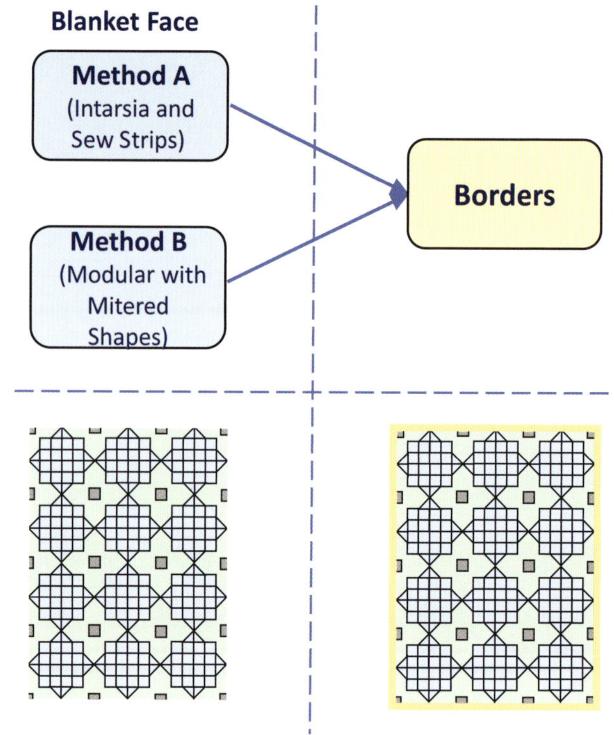

Figure 1: Overview of Construction Options

BLANKET INSTRUCTIONS

Method A (Intarsia and Sew Strips)

Read about "Intarsia" on page 204.

Strip 1

With smaller needles and yarn color for small square at bottom left of Strip (see Figure 2 for colors), CO 6 sts, with A, CO 29 sts, with G, CO 1, with E, CO 1, with a separate strand of A, CO 29 sts, with yarn color for small square at bottom right of Strip, CO 6 sts – 72 sts.

Knit 576 rows while working [Star Color Chart] 4 times substituting in colors specified in Figure 2 for the small gray colored squares in the corners of the chart.

Note: Star Color Chart shows RS rows only. For all WS rows, work sts in same color as previous RS row. New colors are introduced on RS rows 25, 49, 73, 97, and 121. Cut old colors when introducing new colors.

Strips 2 & 3

Work as for Strip 1.

Assembly

Using mattress st and matching color yarn (lengths of A or matching yarn tails from small corner squares), sew Strips 1 & 2 together, aligning adjacent small corner squares; then sew Strips 2 and 3 together in the same manner.

Continue at "Borders" on page 155.

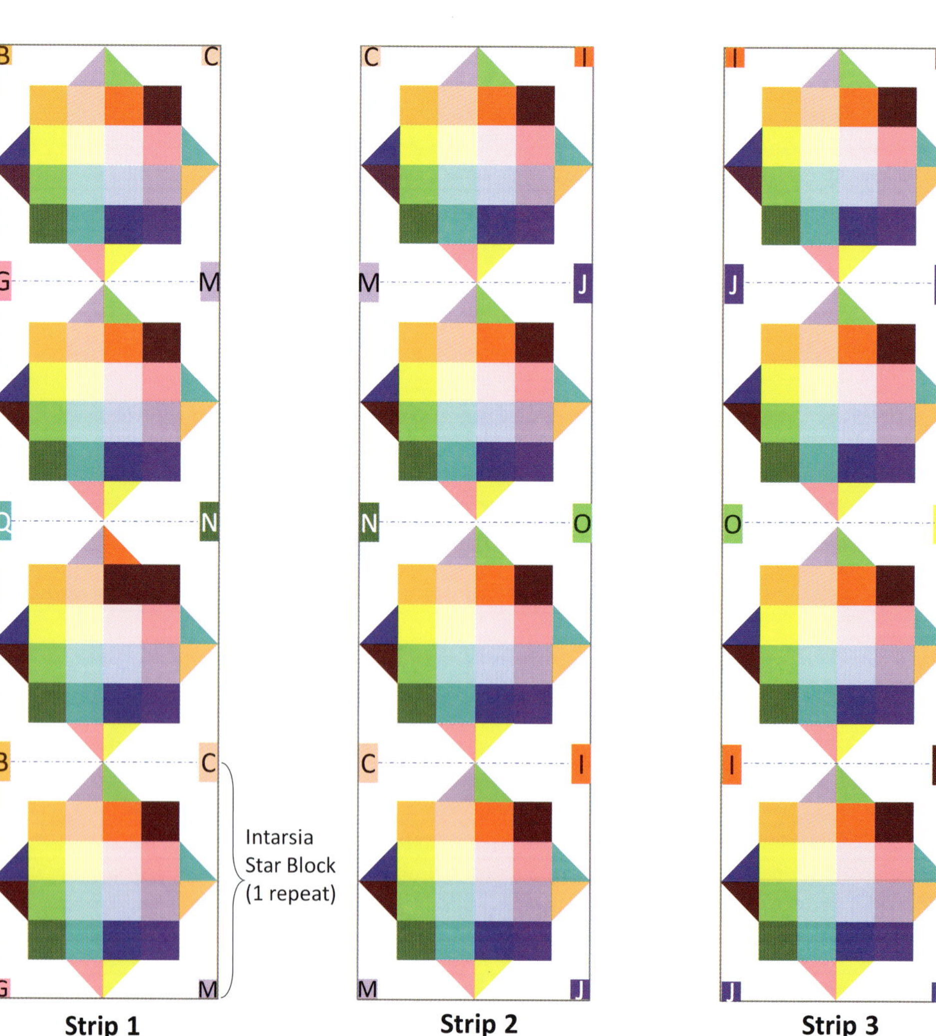

Figure 2: Method A: Construction and Colors for Small Corner Squares

This blanket was worked using Method A.

Star Color Chart, Method A (Intarsia and Sew Strips)

Pre-cut yarn and wind onto bobbins to avoid tangling yarns. For triangles, cut 5 yds/4.75 m; for square, cut 8.5 yds/ 7.75 m.

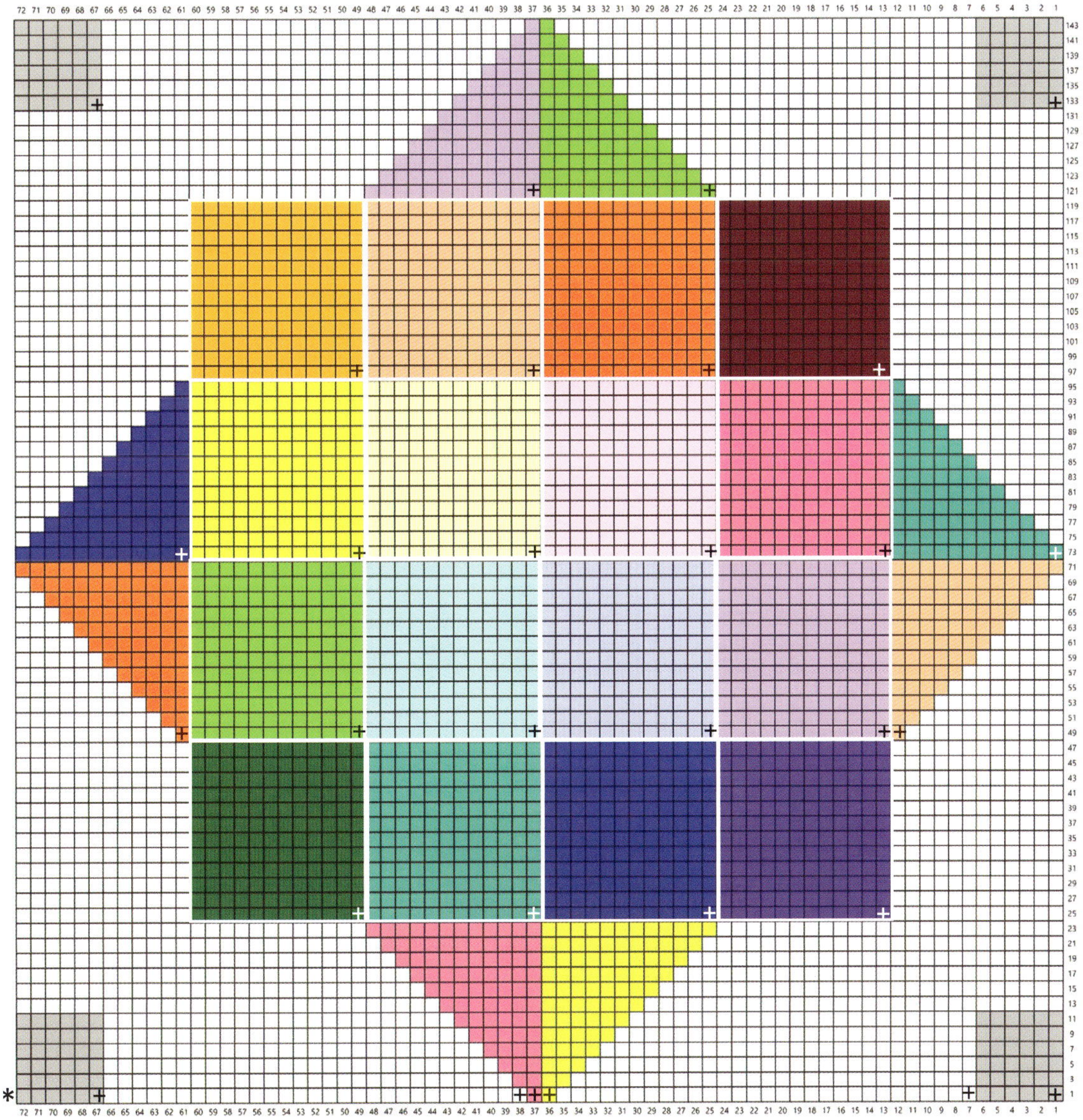

- RS: knit
  WS: knit (not shown)
- white (A)
- gold (B)
- peach (C)
- pale yellow (D)
- bright yellow (E)
- burgundy (F)
- bright pink (G)
- pale pink (H)
- red-orange (I)
- purple (J)
- blue (K)
- pale blue (L)
- pale purple (M)
- dark green (N)
- grass green (O)
- pale aqua (P)
- aqua (Q)
- See Figure 2 for color to work small corner squares
- + Add new color

*Note: For 2nd, 3rd, and 4th reps of Block Chart within a Strip, continue with color for corner square as shown in Figure 2.

Method B – Modular with Mitered Shapes

See Figure 3 for construction steps, color schemes, and how to generate the 24 sts needed for each Mitered Square (MS) and Triangle (MT). Work shapes in ascending numerical order.

Squares 1-16 (Steps 1 through 4 in Figure 3)

MS1

With smaller needles and yarn color for MS, CO 12, pm, CO 12 sts – 24 sts. Work [MS].

MS2-MS16

With yarn color for MS, CO or pu&k 12 (as indicated by symbols in Figure 3), pm, CO or pu&k 12 – 24 sts. Work [MS].

Mitered Square (MS) – 24 sts dec'ing to 1 st, Method B

Row 2 (WS): Knit.
Row 3 (RS): Knit to 2 sts bef m, ssk, k2tog, knit to end – 2 sts dec'd; 22 sts.
Row 4: Knit.
Rows 5-24: Rep [Rows 3 & 4] 10 times – 20 sts dec'd; 2 sts.
Row 25: K2tog – 1 st dec'd; 1 st.
Cut yarn and fasten off.

Triangles 1-8 (Step 5 in Figure 3)

MT1

With smaller needles and yarn color for MT, pu&k 12 on top edge of MS, pm, CO 12 sts – 24 sts. Work [MT].

MT2

Attach yarn for MT, pu&k 12 on left edge of MT, pm, pu&k 12 on top edge of MS. Work [MT].

MT3 & 4, MT5 & 6, MT7 & 8

Work as for MT1 & 2.

Mitered Triangle (MT) – 24 sts dec'ing to 1 st, Method B

Row 2 (WS): Knit.
Row 3 (RS): K2tog, knit to 2 sts bef m, ssk, k2tog, knit to 2 sts bef end, ssk – 4 sts dec'd; 20 sts.
Row 4: Knit.
Rows 5-12: Rep [Rows 3 & 4] 4 times – 16 sts dec'd; 4 sts.
Row 13: K2tog, ssk – 2 sts dec'd; 2 sts.
Row 14: K2tog – 1 st dec'd; 1 st.
Cut yarn and fasten off.

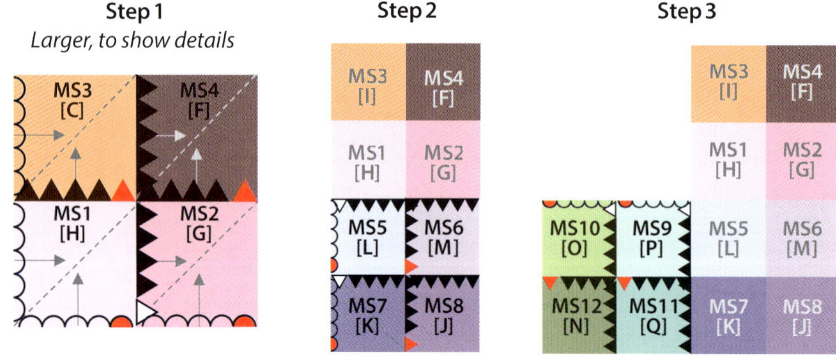

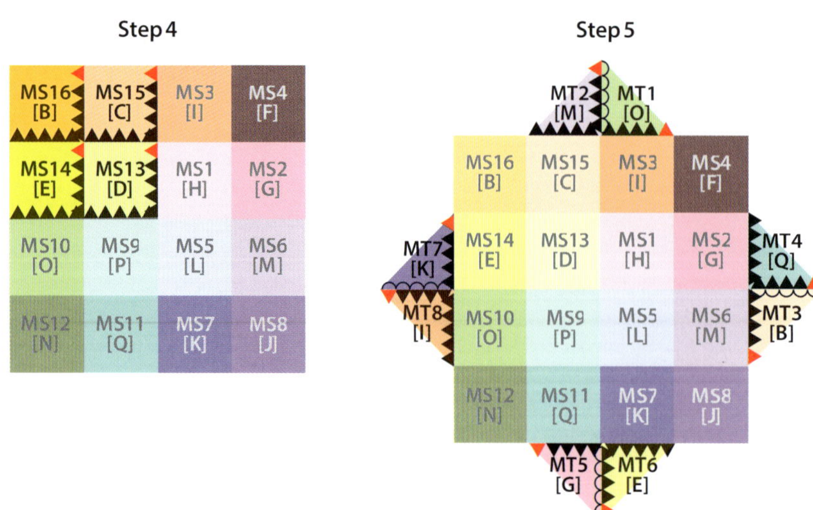

Figure 3: Method B: Star Construction and Colors

Interpreting Figure 3

An MS or MT begins with 2 edges for which sts are generated in a clockwise direction: 12 sts for each edge, with a marker placed in the middle. Triangles indicate pu&k, and semi-circles indicate CO. The red triangle or semi-circle at a corner indicates this is where st generation begins. Some MS have CO for the first edge and pu&k for the second edge. If so, the attachment point for the first st to be pu&k is shown by a white triangle with a black outline. These written-out examples are for the MS created in Step 1:

MS1: CO 12, pm, CO 12. Work [MS].

MS2: CO 12, pm, pu&k 12 starting at white-filled triangle on bottom left of MS1. Work [MS].

MS3: Pu&k 12 sts, starting at red triangle on top-right corner of MS1, pm, turn and CO 12. Work [MS].

MS4: Pu&k 12 sts starting at top-right corner of MS2, pm, pu&k 12 on right edge of MS3. Work [MS].

Arms, Half Arms, Outside-In Squares, and Assembly

See Figure 4 for construction and colors. Arrange completed Stars as shown in Figure 4.

Arms

In spaces labeled "Arm," attach A at red triangle, and pu&k 12 sts to next corner, pm, pu&k 17 sts to next corner, pm, pu&k 17 sts to next corner, pm, pu&k 12 sts to next corner – 58 sts. Work [Arm].

Arm – 58 sts dec'ing to 1 st, Method B

Numbers in parentheses are: (# sts bet beg of row & m1 – # sts bet m1 & m2 – # sts bet m2 & m3 – # sts bet m3 & end of row).

Row 2 (WS): Knit.
Row 3 (RS): Knit to 2 sts bef m2, ssk, k2tog, knit to end – 2 sts dec'd; 56 sts (12-16-16-12).
Row 4: Knit.
Row 5: *Knit to 2 sts bef next m, ssk, k2tog; rep from * 2 times, knit to end – 6 sts dec'd; 50 sts (11-14-14-11).
Row 6: Knit.
Rows 7-22: Rep [Rows 3-6] 4 times– 32 sts dec'd; 18 sts (7-2-2-7).
Row 23: Rm's. K6, cdd twice, knit to end – 4 sts dec'd; 14 sts.
Row 24: Knit 7. Turn needles so RS are tog. With larger needle, 3-needle BO off rem sts.
BO loosely. Cut yarn and fasten off.

Outside-In Squares (OS)

In each space labeled "OS," starting at the green triangle, and using a circular needle, pu&k 24 sts to next corner; rep from * 3 times – 96 sts. Work [OS].

Outside-In Square (OS)– 96 sts dec'ing to 8 sts, Method B

Change to dpns when needed to accommodate sts.
Rnd 1: Purl.
Rnd 2: *Ssk, knit to 2 sts bef m, k2tog; rep from * 3 times – 8 sts dec'd; 88 sts.
Rnd 3: Purl.
Rnds 4-11: Rep [Rnds 2 & 3] 4 times – 32 sts dec'd; 56 sts.
Cut A.
Rnds 12-23: With C1, rep [Rnds 2 & 3] 6 times – 48 sts dec'd; 8 sts.
Cut C1, leaving 10"/25cm tail. Thread tail onto needle and insert through all loops. Pull tightly and fasten off securely.

Half Arm 1 (H1)

In spaces labeled "H1," attach A at red triangle, pu&k 17 sts to corner, pm, pu&k 12 sts to next corner – 29 sts. Work [H1].

Half Arm 1 (H1)– 29 sts dec'ing to 7 sts, Method B

Row 2 (WS): Knit.
Row 3 (RS): K2tog, knit to end – 1 st dec'd; 28 sts.
Row 4: Knit.
Row 5: K2tog, knit to 2 sts bef m, ssk, k2tog, knit to end – 3 sts dec'd; 25 sts.
Row 6: Knit.
Rows 7-22: Rep [Rows 3-6] 4 times – 16 sts dec'd; 9 sts.
Row 23: Rm. Cdd, knit to end – 2 sts dec'd; 7 sts.
BO loosely. Cut yarn and fasten off.

Half Arm 2 (H2)

In each space labeled "H2," attach A at red triangle, pu&k 12 sts to corner, pm, pu&k 17 sts to next corner – 29 sts. Work [H2].

Half Arm 2 (H2)– 29 sts dec'ing to 7 sts, Method B

Row 2 (WS): Knit.
Row 3 (RS): Knit to last 2 sts, ssk – 1 st dec'd; 28 sts.
Row 4: Knit.
Row 5: Knit to 2 sts bef m, ssk, k2tog, knit to last 2 sts, ssk – 3 sts dec'd; 25 sts.
Row 6: Knit.
Rows 7-22: Rep [Rows 3-6] 4 times – 16 sts dec'd; 9 sts.
Row 23: Knit to last 3 sts, cdd – 2 sts dec'd; 7 sts.
BO loosely. Cut yarn and fasten off.

Mitered Rectangles (MR)

Mitered edge shapes start with color A and change to the alternate color, C1, specified in Figure 4.

In each space labeled "MR," with A, and starting at green triangle, pu&k 12 sts to corner, pm, pu&k 24 sts to next corner, pm, pu&k 12 sts to next corner – 48 sts. Work [MR].

Mitered Rectangle (MR) – 48 sts dec'ing to 1 st, Method B

Row 2 (WS): Knit.
Row 3 (RS): *Knit to 2 sts bef m, ssk, k2tog; rep from * once more, knit to end – 4 sts dec'd; 44 sts.
Row 4: Knit.
Rows 5-12: Rep [Rows 3 & 4] 4 times – 16 sts dec'd; 28 sts. Cut A.
Rows 13-24: With C1, rep [Rows 3 & 4] 6 times – 24 sts dec'd; 4 sts.
Row 25: Sl 2 sts to R needle, k2tog, psso – 3 sts dec'd; 1 st.
Cut yarn and fasten off.

Mitered Squares (MS)

In each space labeled "MS," with A, and starting at green triangle, pu&k 12 sts to corner, pm, pu&k 12 sts to next corner – 24 sts. Work [MS, on page 152], cutting A after Row 12, and continuing with Color C1 specified in Figure 4.

Continue at "Borders" on page 155.

Figure 4: Method B: Arms, Half Arms (H1 and H2), and Outside-In Squares (OS)

BORDERS

If Method A was used, pu&k 1 st per garter stitch ridge or CO/BO stitch. If Method B was used, use Table to determine the number of stitches to pu&k per shape.

Table: Number of Stitches to Pu&k on Edge of Each Shape

Shape	# Sts to Pu&k per Shape
Mitered Square (MS)	12
Mitered Rectangle (MR)	24
Half Arms (H1 & H2)	24

Right Border

On RS, attach K at lower right corner of blanket, and with circular needle, pu&k 288 sts along right edge of blanket.

Knit 11 rows. BO loosely, do not cut yarn and leave last st on needle.

Top Border

Pu&k 6 sts on top edge of Right Border, 216 sts across top of blanket – 223 sts. Knit 11 rows. BO loosely, do not cut yarn and leave last st on needle.

Left Border

Pu&k 6 sts on left edge of Top Border, 288 sts on left edge of blanket – 295 sts. Knit 11 rows. BO loosely, do not cut yarn and leave last st on needle.

Bottom Border

Pu&k 6 sts on edge of Left Border, 216 sts across bottom of blanket and 7 sts on edge of Right Border – 230 sts. Knit 11 rows. BO loosely. Cut yarn and fasten off.

FINISHING

Weave in ends.

REGATTA

Sail away with a nautical themed blanket worked in just a few dramatic colors.

Size 60.5 x 60.5"/154 x 154 cm

Techniques Pu&k, sewing, intarsia

Yarn Red Heart Soft, worsted (100% acrylic; 513 yds/469 m; 10 oz/283 g):

Pattern Color ID	Swatch	Red Heart ID	Color Name	Color Description	# Skeins
A		E855.4600	White	white	4
B		E855.9770	Rose Blush	light pink	3
C		E855.4608	Wine	red	3
D		E855.4604	Navy	navy blue	3

Needles US Size 7 (4.5 mm) 40"/100 cm circular needle and 10"/25 cm straights or size needed to obtain gauge

Notions Stitch markers, tapestry needle

Gauge 18 sts and 36 rows = 4"/10 cm in garter st

Notes

The blanket is worked in Blocks that are sewn together. Each Block consists of 4 mitered squares that are worked in intarsia with 2 active strands. Borders are picked up and knit from the edges of the blanket.

BLANKET INSTRUCTIONS

BLOCKS – Make 25

Each Block consists of 4 Mitered Squares worked modularly. See Figure 1 for color abbreviations and Figure 2 for Color Schemes. Read about "Intarsia" on page 204.

Mitered Squares in Color Scheme 1 – Make 50 (2 per Block)

With B (C1), CO 32 sts. With D (C2), CO 32 sts – 64 sts.

Work [MS] in Color Scheme 1 (CS1).

Mitered Squares in Color Scheme 2 – Make 50 (2 per Block)

Arrange 2 completed MS's in CS1 as shown in Figure 3. In each of the 2 spaces labeled "CS2" in Figure 3, attach D (C1) at green triangle and then pu&k 32 sts to end of edge of one of the MS's, then attach B (C2) pu&k 32 sts along edge of the other MS – 64 sts. Sts should be pu&k at rate of 1 st per garter stitch ridge.

Work [MS] in Color Scheme 2 (CS2).

Mitered Square (MS) – 64 sts dec'ing to 1 st

When switching colors in the center of the row, twist yarns on WS of work. When working WS rows, yarns must be moved forward to the WS for twisting then back to the RS to complete the row. Leave 15"/40 cm long tails when cutting yarn.

Row 2 (WS): With C2, knit to end of C2 sts, with C1 knit to end.
Row 3 (RS): With C1, knit to 2 sts bef end of C1 sts, ssk, with C2, k2tog, knit to end – 2 sts dec'd; 62 sts.
Row 4: Rep Row 2.
Rows 5-16: Rep [Rows 3 & 4] 6 times – 12 sts dec'd; 50 sts.
Cut C1 & C2. Attach C3 at beg and C4 in center of row.
Rows 17-32: With C3 and C4, rep [Rows 3 & 4] 8 times – 16 sts dec'd; 34 sts.
Cut C3 and C4. Attach C4 at beg and C3 at center of row.
Rows 33-48: With C4 and C3, rep [Rows 3 & 4] 8 times – 16 sts dec'd; 18 sts.
Cut C4 and C3. Attach C2 at beg and C1 at center of row.
Rows 49-64: With C2 and C1, rep [Rows 3 & 4] 8 times – 16 sts dec'd; 2 sts. Cut yarns, insert yarn ends of matching color through last two stitches, and tie yarns together to fasten off.

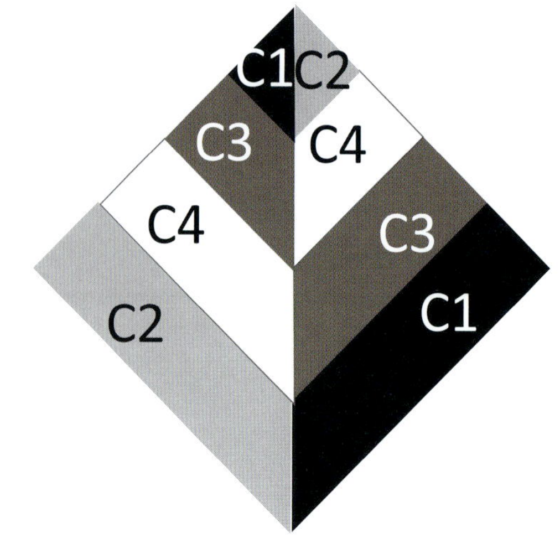

Figure 1: Color Abbreviations

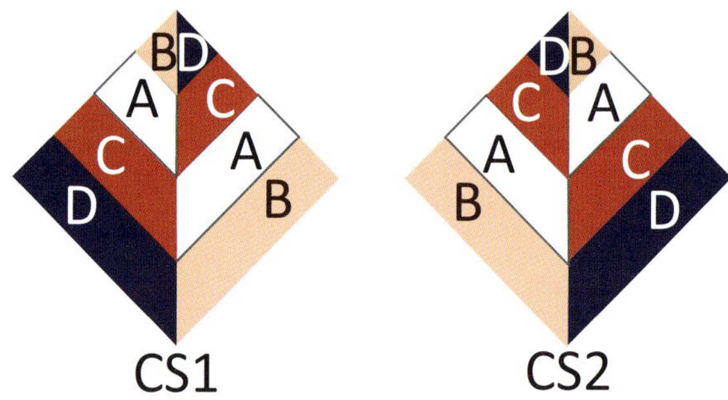

Figure 2: Color Schemes

ASSEMBLY

Arrange 25 Blocks as shown in Figure 4 so that orientation arrows in Figure 3 are pointing up and aligning corners of MS's. Using mattress st and matching long tails, sew adjacent Blocks together along yellow dashed lines to form vertical strips, and then sew strips together, sewing each CO st to the adjacent garter bump.

Figure 3: Assemble Pieces into Blocks

Figure 4: Assemble Blocks into Strips

BORDERS

Right Border

On RS, attach A to bottom right corner of blanket face. Pu&k 320 sts (32 per MS/1 st per garter st ridge or CO st).

Knit 15 rows. BO loosely, leaving last st on needle. Do not cut yarn.

Top Border

Pu&k 7 sts on edge of Right Border, then 320 sts along top edge of blanket – 328 sts.

Knit 15 rows. BO loosely, leaving last st on needle. Do not cut yarn.

Left Border

Work as for Top Border, on left edge of Top Border and left edge of blanket.

Bottom Border

Pu&k 7 sts on edge of Left Border, 320 sts along bottom edge of blanket, and 8 sts on edge of Right Border – 336 sts.

Knit 15 rows. BO loosely. Cut yarn and fasten off.

FINISHING

Weave in ends.

Photographed sample uses Methods A and D.

SANGUINE

This blanket reminds us to stay optimistic and work toward a brighter future.

SIZE 58 x 71.5"/147 x 182 cm

TECHNIQUES Method A: Intarsia
Method B: Smaller amount of intarsia and pu&k
Method C: Pu&k and sewing
Method D: Sewing
Method E: Working in the round

YARN Plymouth Worsted Merino Superwash, worsted (100% superwash fine merino; 218 yds/199 m; 3.5 oz/100 g):

Pattern Color ID	Color Swatch	Color ID	Color Name	Color Description	# Hanks
A		0001	Natural	off-white	13
B		0091	Peach Beach	peach	3
C		0040	Pumpkin	orange-rust	3
D		0087	Lime Heather	lime green	3
E		0088	Spruce Heather	muted teal	3

NEEDLES US Size 7/4.5 mm (or size needed to obtain gauge) 40"/100 cm circular needles and 8"/20 cm dpns or a 16" circular needle (Method E)

NOTIONS Tapestry needle, stitch markers, and stitch holders (Method B)

GAUGE 18 sts x 36 rows = 4"/10 cm in garter st

NOTES

There are multiple methods for this blanket, as shown in Figure 1. Method A works 4 intarsia strips, using 5-9 simultaneous strands. Method B makes Crosses using pick up and knit (pu&k) on previously completed shapes and some intarsia. Method C adds Triangles to Crosses using pu&k on previously completed shapes and sews Blocks into strips. Method E joins and fills in the spaces between Four-Point Stars with Squares worked outside-in. Method D joins Strips created with Method A or Method C with mattress stitch. Borders are picked up and knitted on the edge of the completed blanket. Color charts for intarsia are at the end of the pattern.

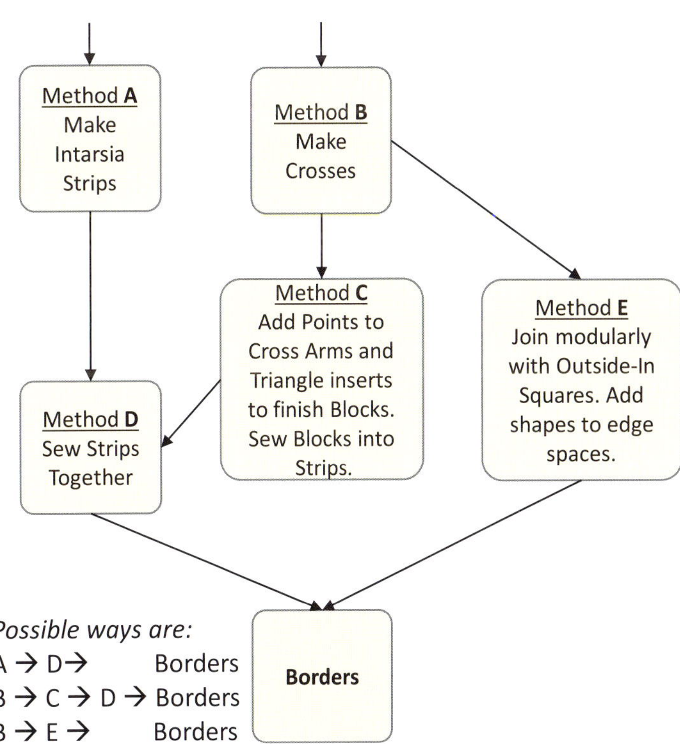

Figure 1: Overview of Construction Options

BLANKET INSTRUCTIONS

METHOD A – Make Strips Using Intarsia

Strip 1

With A, CO 60 sts. Work [Chart A, page 166] 5 times.

Cut yarns when each color section is complete, and if yarn being cut is on the right edge, leave a tail that is 4 times the length of the seam to be sewn with that color.

Strips 2-5

Work as for Strip 1.

Continue at "Method D."

METHOD B - Crosses – Make 25

See Figure 2 for construction.

A Cross consists of:

- A Central Square (CS)
- 4 Arms (Arm1-Arm4)

With A, CO 14 sts. *Note:* If desired, may use provisional CO.

Center Square (CS)

With A, knit 27 rows (14 ridges). Cut A, attach D.

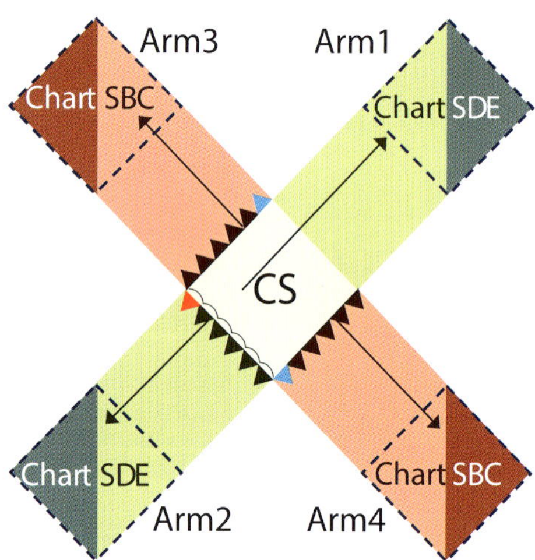

Figure 2: Method B: Construction of Center Square (CS) and Arms for Crosses

Arm1

With D, knit 28 rows (14 ridges in D). Do not cut D. Work [Chart SDE, page 166]. Cut D & E. Place sts on holder.

Arm2

With D, starting at red triangle, pu&k 14 sts (1 st per CO st) to next corner. Knit 27 rows (14 ridges in D). Do not cut D. Work [Chart SDE, page 166]. Cut D & E. Place sts on holder.

Arm3 & Arm4

With B, starting at blue triangle, pu&k 14 sts to next corner (1 st per garter st ridge). Knit 27 rows. Do not cut B. Work [Chart SBC, page 166]. Cut B & C. Place sts on holder.

Continue at "Method C" or "Method E."

METHOD C – Make Blocks from Crosses

The addition of Large and Small Triangles converts a Cross into a square Block.

See Figure 3 for construction and colors.

Points for Arms

At the end of each Arm, transfer 14 sts on holder to needle, attach A, and starting on RS, work [TS].

Small Triangle (TS)– 14 sts dec'ing to 1 st, Method C

Row 1 (RS): K2tog, knit to last 2 sts, ssk – 2 sts dec'd; 12 sts.
Row 2 (WS): Knit.
Rows 3-12: Rep [Rows 1 & 2] 5 times – 10 sts dec'd; 2 sts.
Cut yarn, leaving 8"/20 cm tail. Thread tail onto tapestry needle, and insert through rem 2 sts on needle. Fasten off.

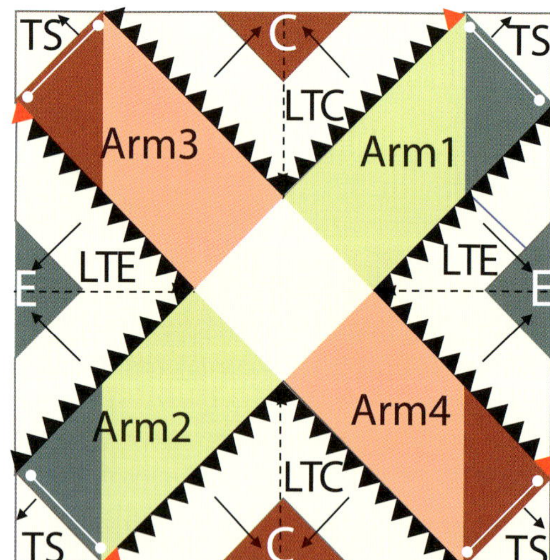

Figure 3: Method C: Block Construction of Large Triangles (LTE & LTC) and Small Triangle (TS)

Large Triangles

2 Large Triangles with E (LTE)

In each of the 2 spaces labeled "LTE" in Figure 3, with A, and starting at the red triangle, pu&k 27 to next corner, 1 st in the corner, pm, and 27 sts to next corner – 55 sts. Work [LT], changing to alternate color E after Row 15 (8 ridges in A).

Large Triangle (LT) – 55 sts dec'ing to 1 st, Method C

Row 2 (RS): Knit.
Row 3 (WS): K2tog, knit to 2 sts bef m, rm, cdd, pm, knit to last 2 sts, ssk – 4 sts dec'd; 51 sts.
Row 4: Knit.
Rows 5-16: Rep [Rows 3 & 4] 6 times – 24 sts dec'd; 27 sts.
Cut A, leaving 15"/40 cm tail.
Rows 17-28: With alternate color, rep [Rows 4 & 5] 6 times – 24 sts dec'd; 3 sts.
Row 29: Cdd – 2 sts dec'd; 1 st.
Cut yarn, leaving 10"/25 cm tail.

2 Large Triangles with C (LTC)

In each of the 2 spaces labeled "LTC," work as for LTE, changing to alternate color C after Row 15.

Strips from Blocks

Arrange 25 Blocks as shown in Figure 4 with LTC's oriented north-south as shown. With long tails of matching color, sew together Blocks along black dashed lines into horizontal strips, matching color transitions.

Continue at "Method D."

Figure 4: Method C: Sew Blocks into Strips

METHOD D – Sew Strips Together

Arrange 5 Strips as shown in Figure 5. With tails of matching color and mattress stitch, sew Strips together aligning corners and color transitions.

Continue at "Borders."

Figure 5: Method D: Sew Strips Together

METHOD E – Join Modularly with Outside-In Squares. Add Shapes to Edge Spaces.

Small Squares (SS)

In each space labeled "SS" in Figure 6, attach A at yellow triangle, and, using circular needle (for magic loop) or dpn, *pu&k 12 sts to next corner, 1 st in corner, pm if using circulars; rep from * 3 times; if using dpns, use a different dpn for each edge – 52 sts. Work [OS] until 4 sts rem, ending after a Rnd 3.

Cut yarn, leaving 10"/25 cm tail. Thread yarn onto tapestry needle and insert through all 4 sts rem on needle. Pull to tighten. Fasten off securely.

Outside-In Square (OS) – Multiple of 8 sts dec'ing to 8 sts, Method E

Worked in the round. The last cdd crosses the BOR. *Note:* When working on dpns, work to 2 sts bef end of dpn. The cdd uses the last 2 sts of 1 dpn and the 1st st of the next.

Rnd 1: Purl.

Rnd 2: *Knit to last 2 sts bef m, rm, cdd, pm; rep from * 3 times – 8 sts dec'd.

Rnd 3: Purl.

Rep Rnds [2 & 3] for pattern.

Figure 6: Method E: Add Edge Shapes and Outside-In Squares to Join Crosses

Large Squares (LS)

In each space labeled LS in Figure 6, attach A at pink triangle and *using circular needle (for magic loop), or dpn, pu&k 27 sts to next corner, then 1 st in corner, pm if using circulars; rep from * 3 times; if using dpns, use a different dpn for each edge – 112 sts. Work [OS] until 56 sts rem (8 ridges in A), ending after a Rnd 3. Cut A and attach alternate color for square (C or E as indicated in Figure 6). Work [OS] until 8 sts rem, ending after a Rnd 3. Cut yarn, leaving 10"/25 cm tail. Thread yarn onto tapestry needle and insert through all 8 sts rem on needle. Pull to tighten. Fasten off securely.

Edge Triangles-Large (ETL)

In each space labeled "ETL," attach A at blue triangle and pu&k 27 sts to next corner, 1 st in corner, pm, 27 sts to next corner – 55 sts. Work [LT, page 163], referring to Figure 6 for alternate color.

Edge Triangles-Small (ETS)

In each space labeled "ETS," with A and starting at green triangle, pu&k 14 sts, 1 st in corner, and 14 sts on next edge - 29 sts. Work [LT, Rows 5-16] - 28 sts dec'd; 1 st. Cut yarn and fasten off.

Corners

In each space labeled "TS," transfer sts on holder to needle, and starting at green triangle on the RS, with A, work [TS, page 162]. Cut yarn and fasten off.

Continue at "Borders."

BORDERS

For Borders, pu&k 60 sts per Block. For Method A, rate of pick up is 1 st per garter stitch ridge or CO/BO stitch. See Figure 7 for the number of stitches to pu&k per edge shape/color.

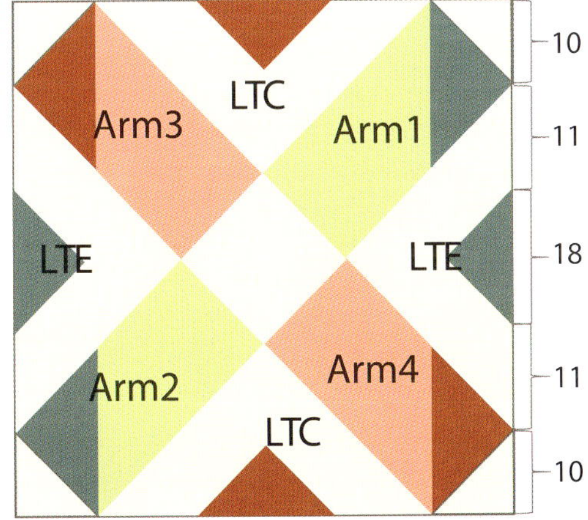

Figure 7: Number of Stitches to Pu&k per Edge Shape for Borders

Right Border

Attach A at lower right corner of blanket, pu&k 300 sts. Knit 19 rows. BO loosely, leaving last st on needle. Do not cut yarn.

Top Border

With A, pu&k 10 sts on edge of Right Border and 300 sts on top edge of blanket – 311 sts. Knit 19 rows. BO loosely, leaving last st on needle. Do not cut yarn.

Left Border

With A, pu&k 10 sts on left edge of Top Border and 300 sts on left edge of blanket – 311 sts. Knit 19 rows. BO loosely, leaving last st on needle. Do not cut yarn.

Bottom Border

With A, pu&k 10 sts on bottom edge of Left Border, 300 sts on bottom edge of blanket, and 11 sts on bottom edge of Right Border – 322 sts. Knit 19 rows. BO loosely. Cut yarn and fasten off.

FINISHING

Weave in ends.

CHARTS

A for Method A

SDE for Method B

SBC for Method B

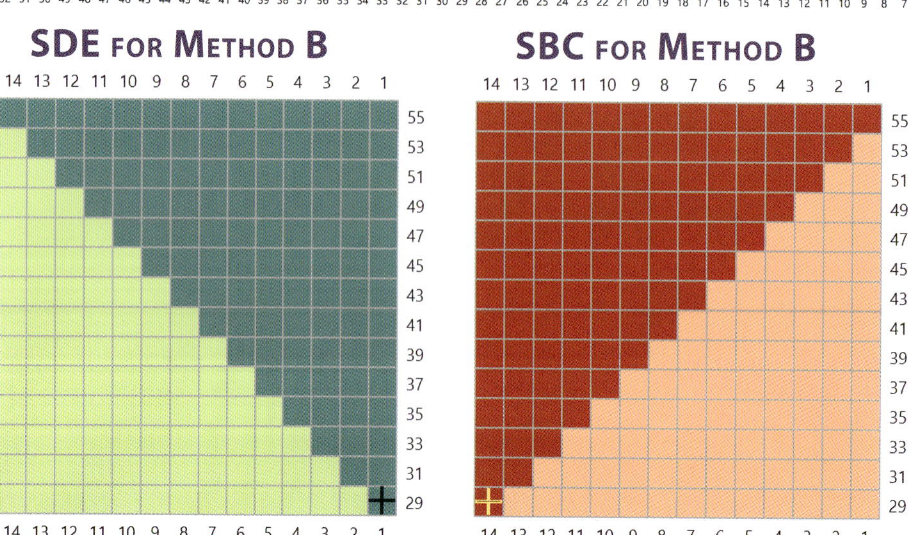

Chart Symbols

RS: knit in color indicated
Note: WS are not included in the chart but are knitted using the same color yarn as the prev RS Row.

A

B

C

D

E

Carry A to next section

Add new yarn color

Add new yarn color only when working first repeat of chart. On subsequent repeats continue with yarn already in use.

Separator between 2 sections worked in different strands of the same color yarn.

SHEAVES

As the days are getting shorter, bring in the harvest before the cold weather arrives with this blanket of fall colors.

SIZE 63 x 67"/160 x 170 cm

TECHNIQUES Both Methods: Pu&k, intarsia, sewing

YARN Lion Brand Yarn Heartland, worsted (100% acrylic; 251 yds/230 m; 5 oz/142 g):

Pattern Color ID	Color Swatch	Color ID	Color Name	Color Description	# Skeins
A		136-098	Acadia	cream	11
B		136-135	Yosemite	rust	2
C		136-131	Canyonlands	medium yellow	2
D		136-176	Saguaro	yellow-green	2
E		136-180	Kings Canyon	dark green	2
F		136-130	Bryce Canyon	dark gold	2
G		136-126	Sequoia	brown	1

NEEDLES US Size 7/4.5 mm 40"/100 cm circular needles or size needed to obtain gauge

NOTIONS Tapestry needle, 2 bobbins

GAUGE 16 sts x 32 rows = 4"/10 cm in garter st

NOTES

- The blanket is composed of 10 Strips that are sewn together.
- There are two methods for working Strips (see Figure 1). Method A (All Intarsia) utilizes intarsia on all rows with a maximum of 4 colors in play at a time and is charted only. Method B (Some Intarsia) also uses intarsia on half the rows with a maximum of 2 colors in play at a time and is both charted and written.
- Borders are picked up on edges of assembled blanket.
- When instructions say to cut a yarn and attach a new yarn color, do so after completing the next WS (even-numbered) row.
- Charts begin on page 172.
- Before beginning, read about intarsia on page 204.

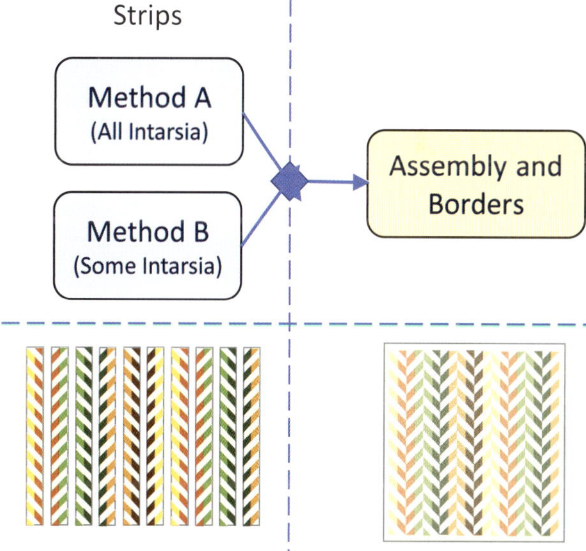

Figure 1: Overview of Construction Options

BLANKET INSTRUCTIONS

See Figure 2 (a) for Color Labels, and 2 (b) for Strip Color Schemes.

Method A (All Intarsia) Use charts

Strips 1, 3, 5, 7, and 9

With C3 for Strip, CO 12 sts, with C1 for Strip, CO 12 sts – 24 sts. Work chart for Sheave Left - Method A (page 172), 10 times, and then work Rows 1-24 of chart once more.

Strips 2, 4, 6, 8, and 10

With C3 for Strip, CO 12 sts, with C1 for Strip, CO 12 sts – 24 sts. Work chart for Sheave Right - Method A (page 172), 12 times, and then work Rows 1-24 of chart once more.

Continue at "Assembly."

Method B (Some Intarsia)

Work from written instructions or from charts on page 174 and page 175.

Strips 1, 3, 5, 7, and 9

With C3 for Strip, CO 2 sts. Work [Sheave Left - Method B] or work from chart for Sheave Left - Method B.

Strips 2, 4, 6, 8, and 10

With C1 for Strip, CO 2 sts. Work [Sheave Right - Method B] or work from chart for Sheave Right - Method B.

Continue at "Assembly."

ASSEMBLY

Arrange Strips 1-10 as shown in Figure 2 (b) with CO at bottom. Using long tails of matching color and mattress st, sew Strips together, matching color transitions.

BORDERS

Right Border

On RS, attach A at lower right corner of blanket. Pu&k 252 sts along right edge of blanket (12 sts per color Strip edge) – 252 sts. Knit 11 rows. BO loosely, do not cut yarn, and leave last st on needle.

Top Border

Pu&k 5 sts on top edge of Right Border, 1 st in join bet border and blanket, 240 sts across top of blanket (12 sts per color Strip edge) – 246 sts. Knit 11 rows. BO loosely, do not cut yarn, and leave last st on needle.

Left Border

Pu&k 5 sts on left edge of Top Border, 1 st in join, 252 sts on left edge of blanket (12 sts per color Strip edge) – 258 sts. Knit 11 rows. BO loosely, do not cut yarn, and leave last st on needle.

Bottom Border

Pu&k 5 sts on edge of Left Border, 1 st in join, 240 sts across bottom of blanket, 1 st in join, 6 sts on Right Border – 252 sts. Knit 11 rows. BO loosely. Cut yarn and fasten off. Weave in ends.

a) Color Labels

b) Color Schemes for Strips 1 - 10

Figure 2: (a) Color Labels, (b) Strip Color Schemes

Sheave Right – 2 sts inc'ing to 38 sts dec'ing to 1 st – Method B

Yarns are cut after completing a WS (even-numbered) row. Leave a long tail of 15"/40 cm tail for seaming when cutting C1 and C2 on Strips 1-9.

For those preferring to work from a chart, see Chart for Sheave Right, Method B, page 175.

Rows 1 & 2: Knit.
Row 3 (RS): Kf&b twice – 2 sts inc'd; 4 sts.
Row 4 and all even-numbered (WS) rows to 412: Knit, working stitches in same color as prev RS row.
Row 5: Kf&b, knit to last st, kf&b – 2 sts inc'd; 6 sts.
RS Rows 7-17: Rep [Row 5] 6 times – 12 sts inc'd; 18 sts.
Cut C1. Attach C2.
Row 19: With C2, kf&b, k16; attach C3, kf&b – 2 sts inc'd; 20 sts.
Row 21: With C2, kf&b, k17. With C3, knit to last st, kf&b – 2 sts inc'd; 22 sts.
RS Rows 23-35: Rep [Row 21] 7 times – 14 sts inc'd; 36 sts.
Cut C2 and C3 after Row 36.
Row 37: With C1, kf&b, knit to last 2, kf&b – 2 sts inc'd; 38 sts.
Row 39: Kf&b, knit to last 2 sts, ssk.
RS Rows 41-53: Rep [Row 39] 7 times.
Cut C1.
Row 55: With C2, kf&b, k17; with C3, knit to last 2 sts, ssk.
RS Rows 57-71: Rep [Row 55] 8 times.
Cut C2 and C3.
Row 73: With C1, rep Row 39.
RS Rows 75-361: Rep [Rows 39-73] 8 times.
RS Rows 363-377: Rep [Rows 39-53] once.
Cut C1.
Row 379: With C2, k2tog, k16; attach C3, knit to last 2 sts, ssk – 2 sts dec'd; 36 sts.
Row 381: With C2, k2tog, k14, with C3, knit to last 2 sts, ssk – 2 sts dec'd; 34 sts.
Row 383: With C2, k2tog, k12, with C3, knit to last 2 sts, ssk – 2 sts dec'd; 32 sts.
Row 385: With C2, k2tog, k10, with C3, knit to last 2 sts, ssk – 2 sts dec'd; 30 sts.
Row 387: With C2, k2tog, k8, with C3, knit to last 2 sts, ssk – 2 sts dec'd; 28 sts.
Row 389: With C2, k2tog, k6, with C3, knit to last 2 sts, ssk – 2 sts dec'd; 26 sts.
Row 391: With C2, k2tog, k4, with C3, knit to last 2 sts, ssk – 2 sts dec'd; 24 sts.
Row 393: With C2, k2tog, k2, with C3, knit to last 2 sts, ssk – 2 sts dec'd; 22 sts.
Row 395: With C2, k2tog, with C3, knit to last 2 sts, ssk – 2 sts dec'd; 20 sts.
Cut C2 and C3.
Row 397: With C1, k2tog, knit to last 2 sts, ssk – 2 sts dec'd; 18 sts.
RS Rows 399-411: Rep [Row 397] 7 times – 14 sts dec'd; 4 sts.
Row 413 (RS): K2tog, ssk – 2 sts dec'd; 2 sts.
Row 414 (WS): K2tog – 1 st dec'd; 1 st.
Cut C1 and fasten off.

Sheave Left – 2 sts inc'ing to 38 sts dec'ing to 1 st – Method B

For those preferring to work from a chart, see Chart for Sheave Left, Method B, page 174.
Rows 1 & 2: Knit.
Row 3 (RS): Kf&b twice – 2 sts inc'd; 4 sts.
Row 4 and all even-numbered (WS) rows to 412: Knit, working stitches in same color as prev RS row.
Row 5: Kf&b, knit to last st, kf&b – 2 sts inc'd; 6 sts.
RS Rows 7-17: Rep [Row 5] 6 times – 12 sts inc'd; 18 sts.
Cut C3.
RS Rows 19-35: With C1, rep [Row 5] 9 times – 18 sts inc'd; 36 sts.
Cut C1.
Row 37: With C2, kf&b, k17, with C3, knit to last st, kf&b – 2 sts inc'd; 38 sts.
Row 39: With C2, k2tog, k18, with C3, knit to last st, kf&b.
RS Rows 41-53: Rep [Row 39] 7 times.
Cut C2 and C3.
Row 55: With C1, k2tog, knit to last st, kf&b.
RS Rows 57-71: Rep [Row 55] 8 times.
*Cut C1.
RS Rows 73-89: With C2, rep [Row 39] 9 times.
Cut C2 and C3.
RS Rows 91-107: With C1, rep [Row 55] 9 times.*
RS Rows 109-359: Rep bet * and * 7 more times.
Cut C1.
RS Rows 361-377: With C2, rep [Row 39] 9 times.
Cut C2 and C3.
Row 379: With C1, k2tog, knit to last 2 sts, ssk – 2 sts dec'd; 36 sts.
RS Rows 381-395: Rep [Row 379] 8 times – 16 sts dec'd; 20 sts.
Cut C1.
RS Rows 397-411: With C2, rep [Row 379] 8 times – 16 sts dec'd; 4 sts.
Row 413 (RS): K2tog, ssk – 2 sts dec'd; 2 sts.
Row 414 (WS): K2tog – 1 st dec'd; 1 st.
Cut C2 and fasten off.

CHARTS

Chart Symbols

knit

RS: knit into fb

RS: k2tog

RS: ssk

C1

C2

C3

no stitch

+ Add new yarn color

+ Add new yarn color on 1st repeat only

Repeat

Note: Charts show RS rows only. Work WS rows in the same color(s) are previous RS row.

Sheave Left - Method A

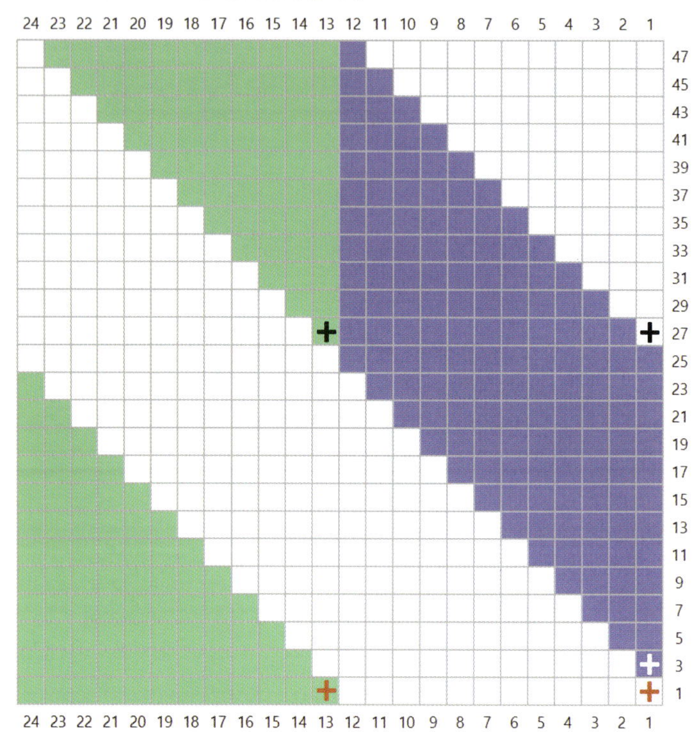

Work Rows 1–48, 10 times,

then work Rows 1–24 once.

Sheave Left

Sheave Right

Sheave Right - Method A

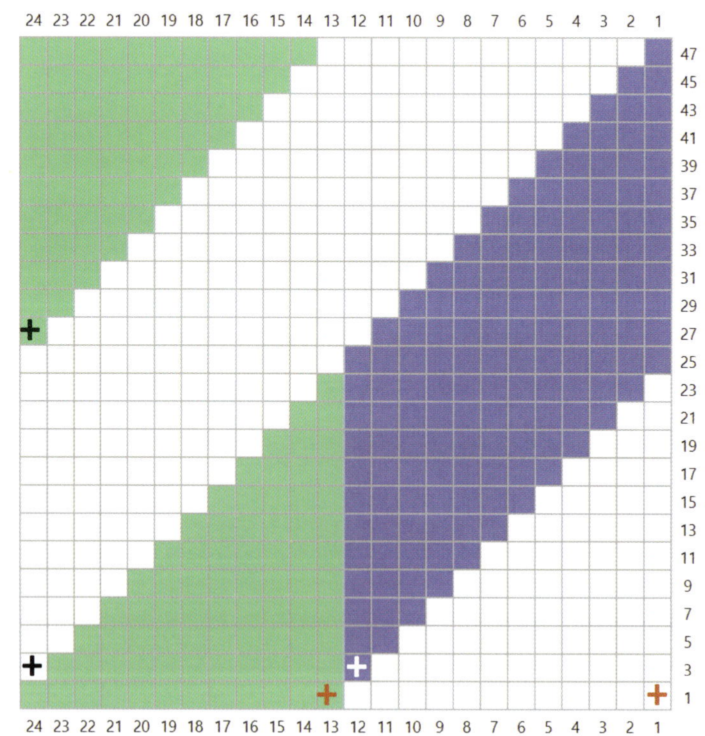

Work Rows 1–48, 10 times,

then work Rows 1–24 once.

Sheave Left - Method B. See Chart Symbols on page 172

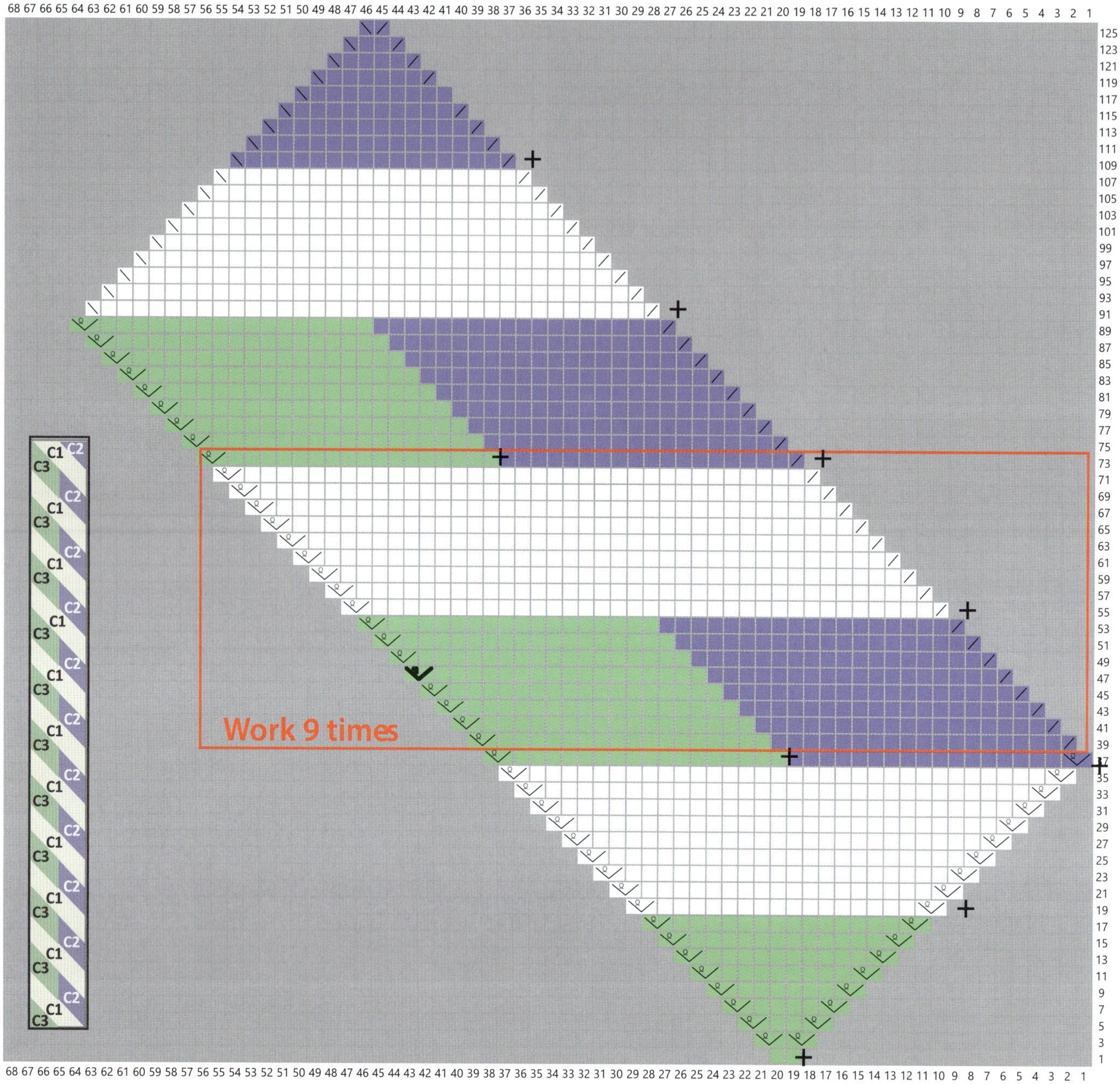

68 67 66 65 64 63 62 61 60 59 58 57 56 55 54 53 52 51 50 49 48 47 46 45 44 43 42 41 40 39 38 37 36 35 34 33 32 31 30 29 28 27 26 25 24 23 22 21 20 19 18 17 16 15 14 13 12 11 10 9 8 7 6 5 4 3 2 1

125 123 121 119 117 115 113 111 109 107 105 103 101 99 97 95 93 91 89 87 85 83 81 79 77 75 73 71 69 67 65 63 61 59 57 55 53 51 49 47 45 43 41 39 37 35 33 31 29 27 25 23 21 19 17 15 13 11 9 7 5 3 1

Work 9 times

C1 C2 C3

Sheave Right - Method B. See Chart Symbols on page 172

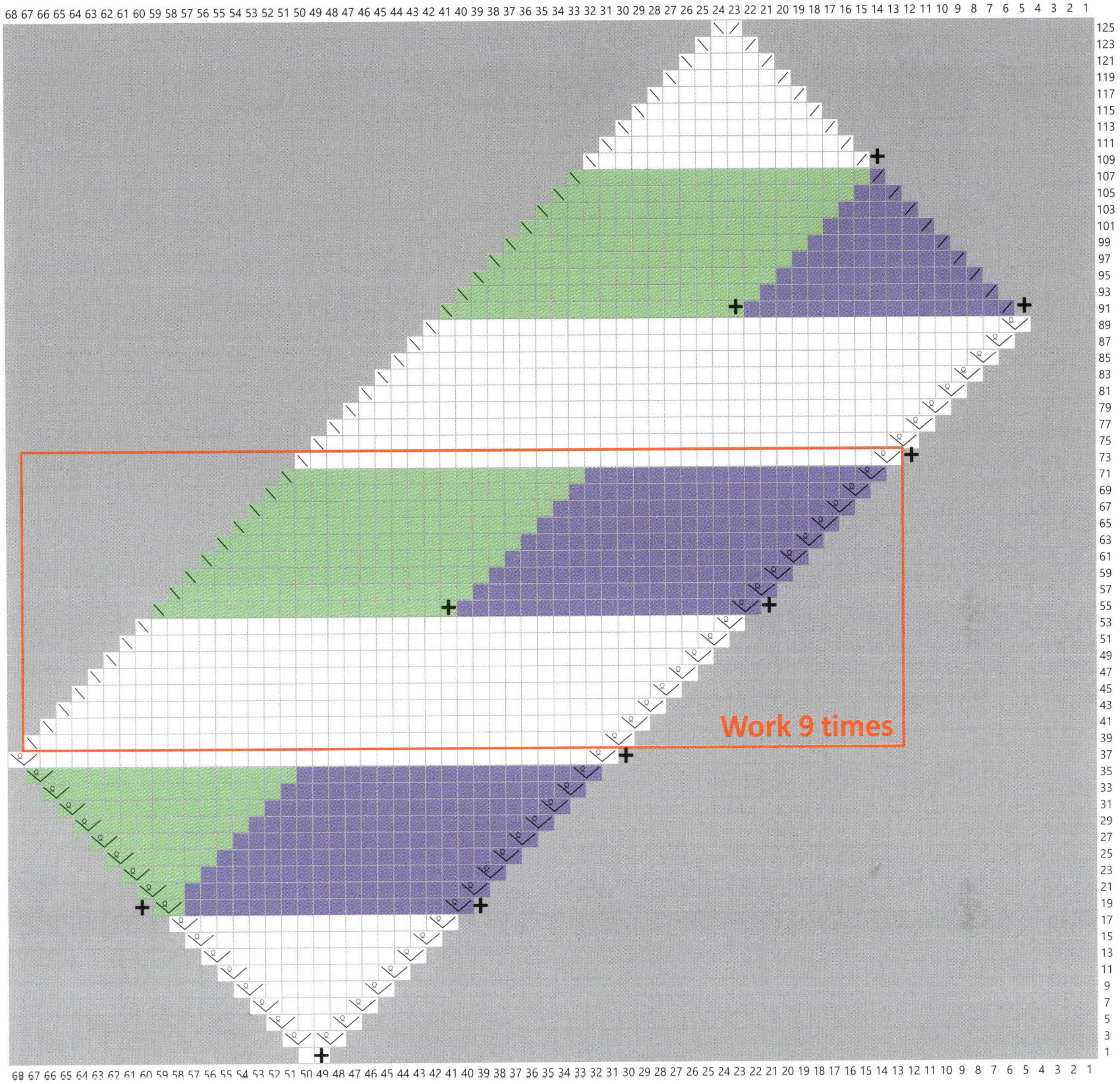

68 67 66 65 64 63 62 61 60 59 58 57 56 55 54 53 52 51 50 49 48 47 46 45 44 43 42 41 40 39 38 37 36 35 34 33 32 31 30 29 28 27 26 25 24 23 22 21 20 19 18 17 16 15 14 13 12 11 10 9 8 7 6 5 4 3 2 1

125 123 121 119 117 115 113 111 109 107 105 103 101 99 97 95 93 91 89 87 85 83 81 79 77 75 73 71 69 67 65 63 61 59 57 55 53 51 49 47 45 43 41 39 37 35 33 31 29 27 25 23 21 19 17 15 13 11 9 7 5 3 1

Work 9 times

68 67 66 65 64 63 62 61 60 59 58 57 56 55 54 53 52 51 50 49 48 47 46 45 44 43 42 41 40 39 38 37 36 35 34 33 32 31 30 29 28 27 26 25 24 23 22 21 20 19 18 17 16 15 14 13 12 11 10 9 8 7 6 5 4 3 2 1

STITCHES IN TIME

The subtle hourglass shapes in this blanket remind us that time is precious.

SIZE 62.5 x 78.5"/159 x 199 cm

TECHNIQUES 3-needle BO, pu&k

YARN Cascade Pacific, worsted (60% acrylic, 40% superwash merino wool; 213 yds/195 m; 3.5 oz/100 g):

Pattern Color ID	Color Swatch	Color ID	Color Name	Color Description	# Skeins
A		09	Sand	light beige	2
B		15	Taupe	taupe	5
C		06	Baby Pink	light pink	1
D		161	Salmon Rose	medium pink/peach	2
E		98	Deep Sea Coral	dark coral	2
F		113	Bordeaux	burgundy	2
G		65	Denim Heather	dusty blue	3
H		47	Navy	dark navy	2
I		12	Yellow	yellow	2
J		164	Grasshopper	medium green	2
K		156	Cedar Green	dark green	2

NEEDLES (2) US Size 8/5 mm 40"/100 cm circular needles or size needed to obtain gauge, 1 US Size 9/5.5 mm straight or circular needle for 3-needle BO

NOTIONS Tapestry needle, stitch markers

GAUGE 16 sts x 32 rows = 4"/10 cm in garter st

NOTES

- The blanket is worked in vertical Strips that are joined using pu&k and 3-needle bind-off.
- Strips are worked from left to right. Each Strip has a Main Color (MC), which is used for casting on, and two alternate colors (referred to as C1 in pattern stitches).
- Borders are picked up and knit on the edges of the completed blanket.

BLANKET INSTRUCTIONS

STRIPS

Instructions for 17 Strips are in Tables starting on page 179, one table per Strip. Work the rows top-to-bottom, twice. CO, and then work the Table from top to bottom, twice. For example, "LEG, G, E, 13" is interpreted as follows: Work the LEG pattern stitch, with color G for MC, E for C1 – 13 sts.

Add C1 when it is called for in the pattern stitches. Cut C1 when changing to the alternate C1 for the Strip, but do not cut MC until the Strip is finished. Drape C1 and MC between uses ("Tacking Draped Yarn" on page 210). After completing the second repeat of the Table, BO loosely.

Draped yarn should be tacked during pu&k of Join pieces.

Figures 2 and 3 on page 182 provide the same information as the Tables but as an illustration.

The cast on for Strips is not counted as Row 1 in this pattern.

Left Edge Grow (LEG) – inc'ing by 5 sts

Rows 1-6: With MC, knit.
Row 7 (RS): Kf&b, knit to end – 1 st inc'd.
Row 8 (WS): Knit.
Rows 9-16: With C1, rep [Rows 1-8] – 1 st inc'd.
Rows 17-32: Rep [Rows 1-16] – 2 sts inc'd.
Rows 33-40: Rep [Rows 1-8] – 1 st inc'd.

Left Edge Shrink (LES) – dec'ing by 5 sts

Rows 1-6: With MC, knit.
Row 7 (RS): K2tog, knit to end – 1 st dec'd.
Row 8 (WS): Knit.
Rows 9-16: With C1, rep [Rows 1-8] – 1 st dec'd.
Rows 17-32: Rep [Rows 1-16] – 2 sts dec'd.
Rows 33-40: Rep [Rows 1-8] – 1 st dec'd.

Lean Right (LR)

Rows 1-6: With MC, knit.
Row 7 (RS): Kf&b, knit to last 2 sts, ssk.
Row 8 (WS): Knit.
Rows 9-16: With C1, rep [Rows 1-8].
Rows 17-32: Rep [Rows 1-16].
Rows 33-40: Rep [Rows 1-8].

Lean Left (LL)

Rows 1-6: With MC, knit.
Row 7 (RS): K2tog, knit to last st, kf&b.
Row 8 (WS): Knit.
Rows 9-16: With C1, and rep [Rows 1-8].
Rows 17-32: Rep [Rows 1-16].
Rows 33-40: Rep [Rows 1-8].

Hourglass Shrink (HS) – dec'ing by 10 sts

Rows 1-6: With MC, knit.
Row 7 (RS): K2tog, knit to last 2 sts, ssk – 2 sts dec'd.
Row 8 (WS): Knit.
Rows 9-16: With C1, rep [Rows 1-8] – 2 sts dec'd.
Rows 17-32: Rep [Rows 1-16] – 4 sts dec'd.
Rows 33-40: Rep [Rows 1-8] – 2 sts dec'd.

Hourglass Grow (HG) – inc'ing by 10 sts

Rows 1-6: With MC, knit.
Row 7 (RS): Kf&b, knit to last st, kf&b – 2 sts inc'd.
Row 8 (WS): Knit.
Rows 9-16: With C1, rep [Rows 1-8] – 2 sts inc'd.
Rows 17-32: Rep [Rows 1-16] – 4 sts inc'd.
Rows 33-40: Rep [Rows 1-8] – 2 sts inc'd.

Right Edge Grow (REG) – inc'ing by 5 sts

Rows 1-6: With MC, knit.
Row 7 (RS): Knit to last st, kf&b – 1 st inc'd.
Row 8 (WS): Knit.
Rows 9-16: With C1, rep [Rows 1-8] – 1 st inc'd.
Rows 17-32: Rep [Rows 1-16] – 2 sts inc'd.
Rows 33-40: Rep [Rows 1-8] – 1 st inc'd.

Right Edge Shrink (RES) – dec'ing by 5 sts

Rows 1-6: With MC, knit.
Row 7 (RS): Knit to last 2 sts, ssk – 1 st dec'd.
Row 8 (WS): Knit.
Rows 9-16: With C1, rep [Rows 1-8] – 1 st dec'd.
Rows 17-32: Rep [Rows 1-16] – 2 sts dec'd.
Rows 33-40: Rep [Rows 1-8] – 1 st dec'd.

Tables for Working Strips

On each Strip, work table twice. "Sts" is the stitch count at completion of the shape.

Left Edge
With G, CO 8 sts

patt st	MC	C1	Sts
LEG	G	E	13
LEG	E	G	18
LES	G	E	13
LES	E	G	8
LEG	G	I	13
LEG	I	G	18
LES	G	I	13
LES	I	G	8

Strip 1
With A, CO 8 sts

patt st	MC	C1	Sts
LR	A	J	8
LR	J	A	8
LL	A	G	8
LL	G	A	8
LR	A	G	8
LR	G	A	8
LL	A	J	8
LL	A	A	8

Strip 2
With H, CO 28 sts

patt st	MC	C1	Sts
HS	H	K	18
HS	K	H	8
HG	H	K	18
HG	K	H	28
HS	H	G	18
HS	G	H	8
HG	H	G	18
HG	H	G	28

Strip 3
With I, CO 8 sts

patt st	MC	C1	Sts
LL	I	G	8
LL	G	I	8
LR	I	G	8
LR	G	I	8
LL	I	D	8
LL	D	I	8
LR	I	D	8
LR	D	I	8

Strip 4
With F, CO 8 sts

patt st	MC	C1	Sts
HG	F	E	18
LL	E	F	18
HS	F	E	8
LR	E	F	8
HG	F	D	18
LL	D	F	18
HS	F	D	8
LR	D	F	8

Strip 5
With G, CO 8 sts

patt st	MC	C1	Sts
LR	K	J	8
LL	J	K	8
LL	K	A	8
LR	A	K	8
LR	K	A	8
LL	A	K	8
LL	K	J	8
LR	J	K	8

Strip 6
With A, CO 18 sts

patt st	MC	C1	Sts
HS	D	I	8
HG	I	D	18
HG	D	I	28
HS	I	D	18
HS	D	C	8
HG	C	D	18
HG	D	C	28
HS	C	D	18

Strip 7
With H, CO 18 sts

patt st	MC	C1	Sts
HG	G	E	28
HS	E	G	18
HS	G	F	8
HG	F	G	18
HG	G	F	28
HS	F	G	18
HS	G	E	8
HG	E	G	18

Strip 8
With I, CO 8 sts

patt st	MC	C1	Sts
LR	D	F	8
LL	F	D	8
LL	D	F	8
LR	F	D	8
LR	D	I	8
LL	I	D	8
LL	D	I	8
LR	I	D	8

Strip 9
With F, CO 8 sts

patt st	MC	C1	Sts
LR	A	H	8
HG	H	A	18
LL	A	G	18
HS	G	A	8
LR	A	G	8
HG	G	A	18
LL	A	H	18
HS	H	A	8

Strip 10
With G, CO 8 sts

patt st	MC	C1	Sts
LR	E	C	8
LR	C	E	8
LL	E	C	8
LL	C	E	8
LR	E	D	8
LR	D	E	8
LL	E	D	8
LL	D	E	8

Strip 11
With A, CO 28 sts

patt st	MC	C1	Sts
HS	J	G	18
HS	G	J	8
HG	J	H	18
HG	H	J	28
HS	J	H	18
HS	H	J	8
HG	J	G	18
HG	G	J	28

Tables continue on the next page.

Strip 12
With H, CO 8 sts

patt st	MC	C1	Sts
HG	I	E	18
HG	E	I	28
HS	I	F	18
HS	F	I	8
HG	I	F	18
HG	F	I	28
HS	I	E	18
HS	E	I	8

Strip 13
With H, CO 8 sts

patt st	MC	C1	Sts
LR	H	A	8
LR	A	H	8
LL	H	A	8
LL	A	H	8
LR	H	G	8
LR	G	H	8
LL	H	G	8
LL	G	H	8

Strip 14
With F, CO 18 sts

patt st	MC	C1	Sts
HS	F	D	8
LR	D	F	8
HG	F	E	18
LL	E	F	18
HS	F	E	8
LR	E	F	8
HG	F	D	18
LL	D	F	18

Strip 15
With G, CO 8 sts

patt st	MC	C1	Sts
LL	K	I	8
LR	I	K	8
LR	K	I	8
LL	I	K	8
LL	K	J	8
LR	J	K	8
LR	K	J	8
LL	J	K	8

Right Edge
With A, CO 13 sts

patt st	MC	C1	Sts
REG	C	G	18
RES	G	C	13
RES	C	E	8
REG	E	C	13
REG	C	E	18
RES	E	C	13
RES	C	G	8
REG	G	C	13

Join Strips

Arrange Left Edge, Strips 1-15, and Right Edge as shown in Figure 1 on page 181.

Join pairs of Strips starting with the Left Edge and Strip 1, then Strip 1 and Strip 2, then Strip 2 and Strip 3, etc., ending with the join of Strip 15 to the Right Edge, in that order. For each pair to be joined, the Strip to the Left is referred to as "Left Strip," and the Strip to the right is referred to as "Right Strip."

For each Join of a pair of Strips, work the 3 steps below: 1) Left Preparation, 2) Right Preparation, 3) 3-needle BO to Join Left and Right Strips.

Left Preparation

With B, and circular needle, pu&k 336 sts from lower right corner of Left Strip to end of Strip. Pm's every 21 sts – 15 markers. (See Tips below.) Knit 1 row. Cut yarn.

Right Preparation

Repeat bet * and * on Right Strip, attaching yarn to top left corner of Strip at yellow triangle.

Tips for pu&k of sts for Left and Right Preparation

21 stitches need to be pu&k over 20 ridges of knitting; therefore there are not enough ridges. So some stitches must be pu&k on the "valleys" that are between ridges.

Use this cadence: Pu&k 1 st per ridge for 10 ridges, pu&k 1 st in the leg or valley before the next ridge, and then pu&k 1 stitch per ridge for 10 more ridges.

It is very useful to place the m's during pu&k to help with counting.

See also "Pick Up and Knit (Pu&k)" on page 208.

3-needle BO to Join Left and Right Strips

Turn Left Strip and Right Strip with RS together and needle tips parallel. Rotate work so that Strip with working yarn attached is farther away. With 3rd (larger) needle and working yarn, perform 3-needle BO loosely over all 336 sts, using m's to check that stitch pairs are matched properly and rm m's after use – 1 st rem. Cut yarn and fasten off.

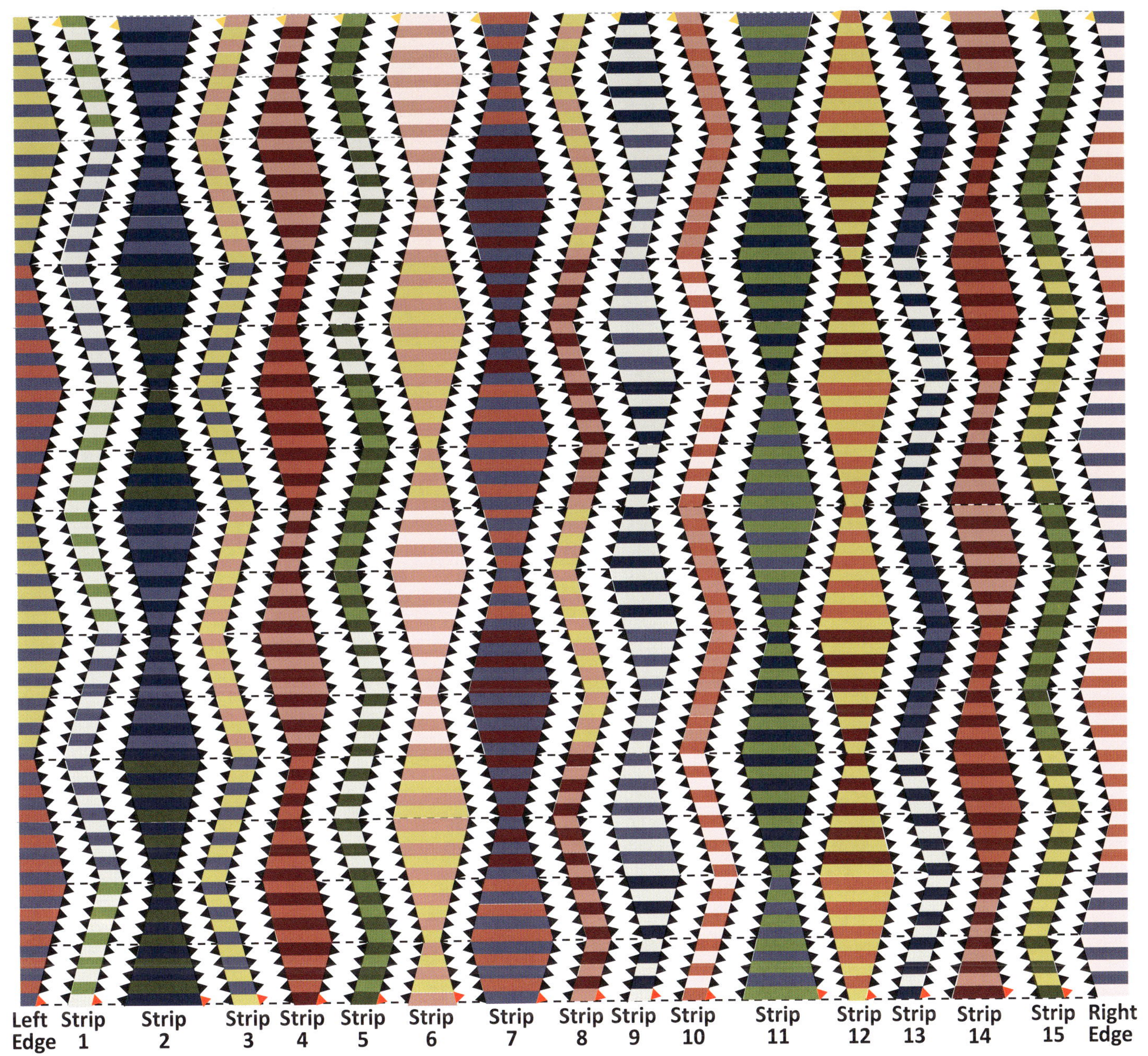

Figure 1: Preparation Steps for Joins

LES: I, G
LES: G, I
LEG: I, G
LEG: G, I
LES: E, G
LES: G, E
LEG: E, G
LEG: G, E
Left Edge
LL: J, A
LL: A, J
LR: G, A
LR: A, G
LL: G, A
LL: A, G
LR: J, A
LR: A, J
Strip 1
HG: G, J
HG: H, G
HS: G, H
HS: H, G
HG: K, H
HG: H, K
HS: K, H
HS: H, K
Strip 2
LR: D, I
LR: I, D
LL: D, I
LL: I, D
LR: G, I
LR: I, G
LL: G, I
LL: I, G
Strip 3
LR: D, F
HS: F, D
LL: D, F
HG: F, D
LR: E, F
HS: F, E
LL: E, F
HG: F, E
Strip 4
LR: J, K
LL: K, J
LL: A, K
LR: K, A
LR: A, K
LL: K, A
LL: J, K
LR: K, J
Strip 5
HS: C, D
HG: D, C
HG: C, D
HS: D, C
HS: I, D
HG: D, I
HG: I, D
HS: D, I
Strip 6
HG: E, G
HS: G, E
HS: F, G
HG: G, F
HG: F, G
HS: G, F
HS: E, G
HG: G, E
Strip 7

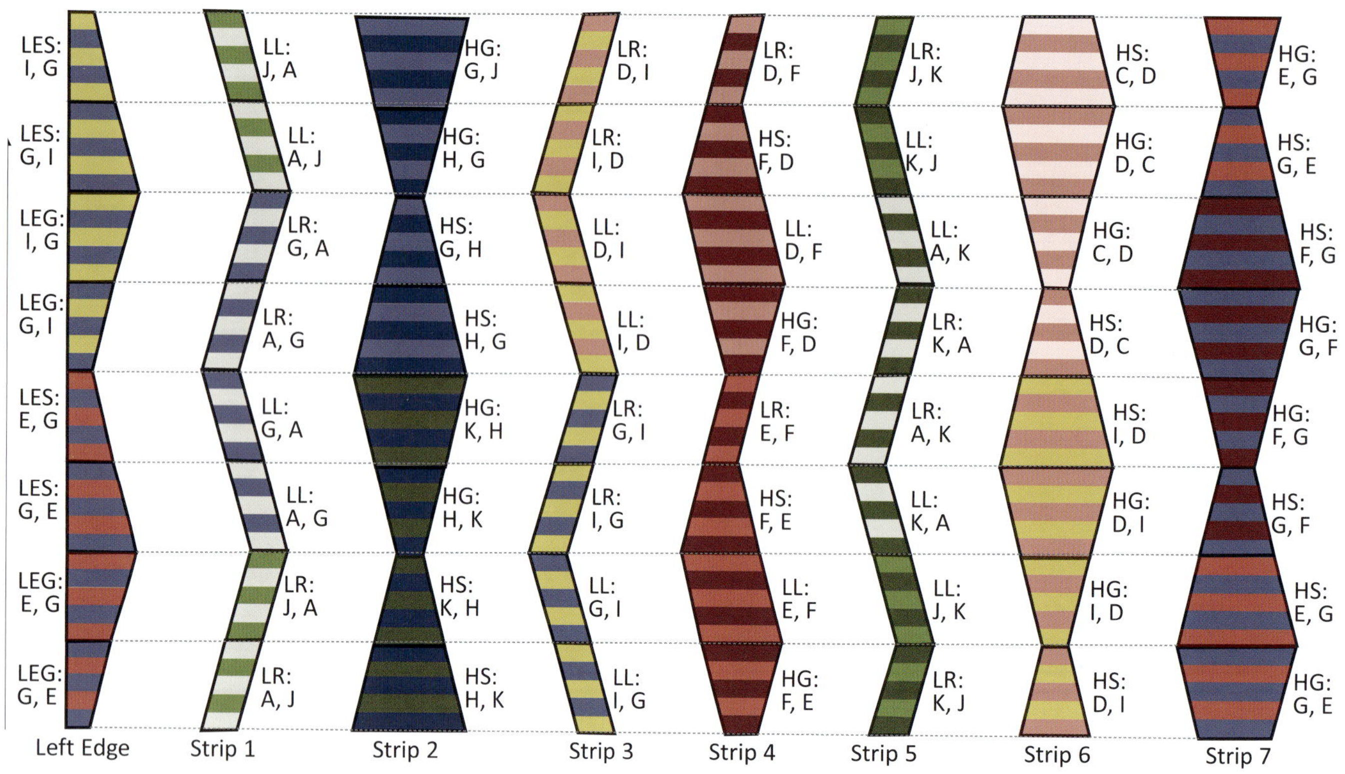

Figure 2: Construction and Colors for Left Edge (LE), and Strips 1-7

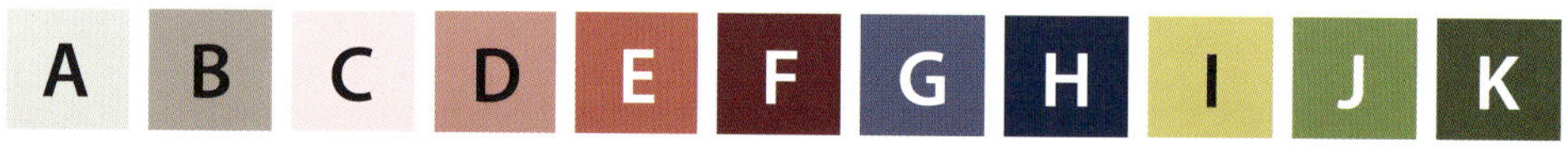

A
B
C
D
E
F
G
H
I
J
K

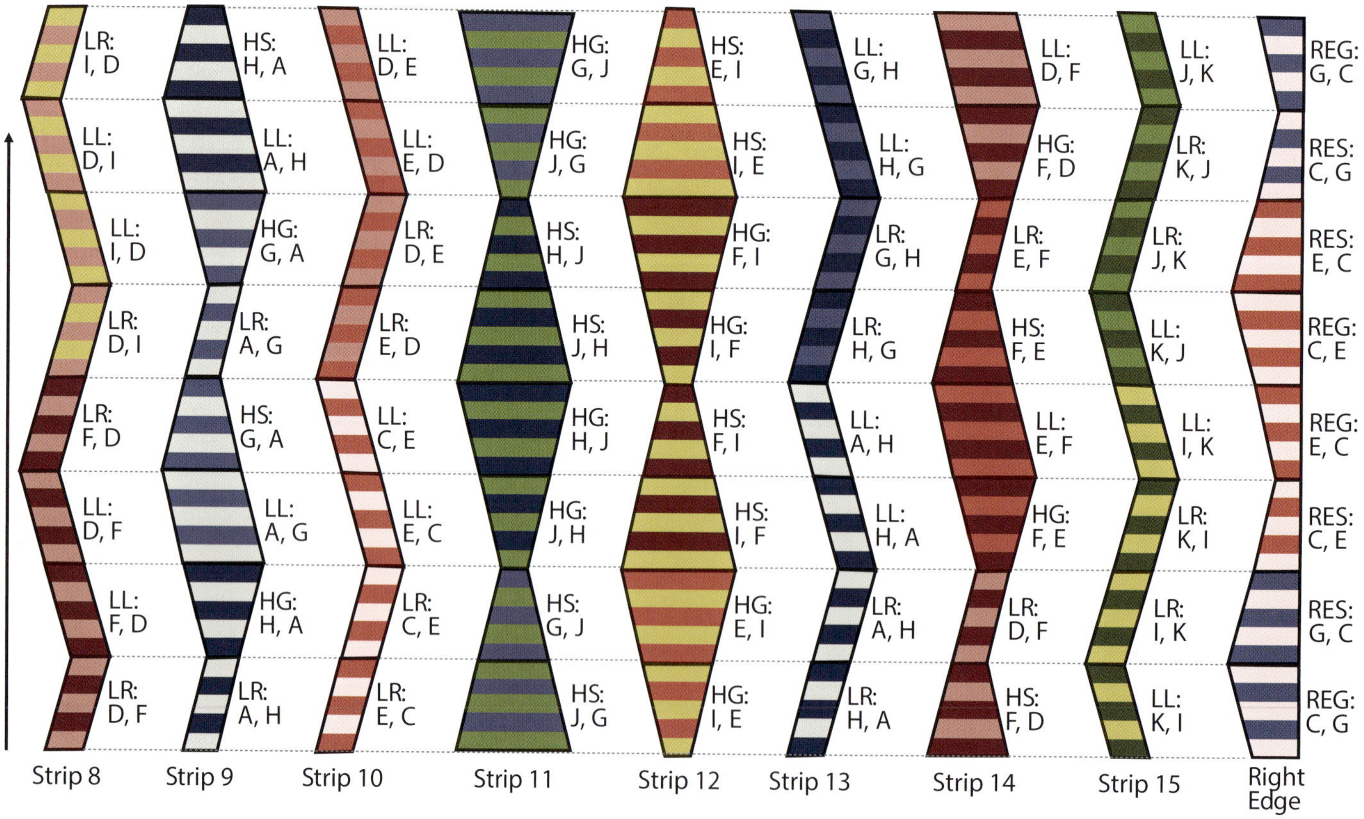

LR: I, D
LL: D, I
LL: I, D
LR: D, I
LR: F, D
LL: D, F
LL: F, D
LR: D, F
Strip 8
HS: H, A
LL: A, H
HG: G, A
LR: A, G
HS: G, A
LL: A, G
HG: H, A
LR: A, H
Strip 9
LL: D, E
LL: E, D
LR: D, E
LR: E, D
LL: C, E
LL: E, C
LR: C, E
LR: E, C
Strip 10
HG: G, J
HG: J, G
HS: H, J
HS: J, H
HG: H, J
HG: J, H
HS: G, J
HS: J, G
Strip 11
HS: E, I
HS: I, E
HG: F, I
HG: I, F
HS: F, I
HS: I, F
HG: E, I
HG: I, E
Strip 12
LL: G, H
LL: H, G
LR: G, H
LR: H, G
LL: A, H
LL: H, A
LR: A, H
LR: H, A
Strip 13
LL: D, F
HG: F, D
LR: E, F
HS: F, E
LL: E, F
HG: F, E
LR: D, F
HS: F, D
Strip 14
LL: J, K
LR: K, J
LR: J, K
LL: K, J
LL: I, K
LR: K, I
LR: I, K
LL: K, I
Strip 15
REG: G, C
RES: C, G
RES: E, C
REG: C, E
REG: E, C
RES: C, E
RES: G, C
REG: C, G
Right Edge

Figure 3: Construction and Colors for Strips 8-15, and Right Edge (RE)

Figure 4: Stitch Counts for Borders

BORDERS

Right Border

Attach B at bottom right corner of Blanket. Pu&k 320 sts to top right corner (1 st per garter st ridge/5 sts per color stripe). Knit 11 rows. BO loosely, do not cut yarn, and leave last st on needle.

Top Border

Pu&k 5 sts along left edge of Right Border, and 238 sts to the top left corner – 244 sts. Refer to stitch counts in Figure 4 for the number of stitches to pick up at the end of each Strip (in black) and Join (in blue). Knit 11 rows. BO loosely, do not cut yarn, and leave last st on needle.

Left Border

Pu&k 5 sts along left edge of Top Border and 320 sts to bottom left corner (1 st per garter st ridge/5 sts per color stripe). Knit 11 rows. BO loosely, do not cut yarn, and leave last st on needle.

Bottom Border

Pu&k 5 sts along left edge of Left Border, 238 sts to right bottom of Blanket, and 6 sts on right edge of Right Border. Refer to st counts in Figure 4 for the number of sts to pu&k at bottom of each Strip and Join. Knit 11 rows. BO loosely. Cut yarn and fasten off.

FINISHING

Weave in ends.

TWIST

Alternating light and dark yarns creates the illusion of twisting ropes.

SIZE 56 x 61.5"/142 x 156 cm

TECHNIQUES 3-needle BO, pu&k, short rows

YARN Tahki Yarns Donegal Tweed, worsted (100% wool; 183 yds/167 m; 3.5 oz/100 g):

Pattern Color ID	Color Swatch	Color ID	Color Name	Color Description	# Hanks
A		890	Black	black	5
B		806	Amber	golden-brown	3
C		859	Green	dark olive green	2
D		851	Bright Olive	light olive green	2
E		802	Light Teal	light teal	2
F		848	Cream	cream	9

NEEDLES US Size 7/4.5 mm 40"/100 cm circular needles and dpns or size needed to obtain gauge

NOTIONS Tapestry needle, stitch markers

GAUGE 18 sts x 36 rows = 4"/10 cm in garter st

NOTES

- The blanket is worked in diagonal strips from the lower left corner to the upper right corner. In each Strip, the Twist pieces—Twist (Tw) and Half Twists 1 & 2 (HT1 & HT2)—are worked and then connected by working the Squares (S) between them.
- One of the Triangle types is worked on each end of a Strip: T1 on bottom edges, T2 on left edges, T3 on right and top edges, and C2 in corners.
- The Borders are picked up and knit from blanket edges.

BLANKET INSTRUCTIONS

See Figure 1 for stitch counts used in stitch generation (blue lines) for shapes. See Figure 2 on page 190 for blanket construction, yarn color for each shape, and the method to use (pu&k or CO) to generate stitches for each edge of each shape.

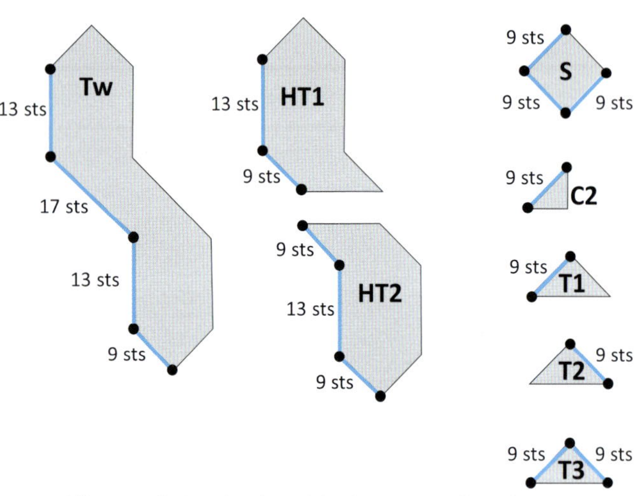

Figure 1: Beginning Stitch Counts for Shapes

Corner 1 (C1)

With A, CO 1 st. Work [C1].

Strip 1 (S1)

Working on RS, with F, knit 9 sts from C1, turn and CO 13 sts – 22 sts. Work [HT1]. With A, and starting at red triangle at tip of HT1, pu&k 9 sts to end of edge. Work [T2].

Even Strips S2-S26

Twists

Note: For bottom Tw of Strip, start pu&k at bottom right corner of HT1 of prev Strip. For rem Tw's of Strip, start pu&k at marked st on Tw of prev Strip.

**Note:* For top Tw of Strip, the last 13 sts are generated by casting on. See symbols on edges of Figure 2 for stitch generation methods.

For each space labeled "Tw" in Strip, on RS, and starting at the red triangle, pu&k: 9 sts to next corner, pm, 13 sts to next corner, pm, 17 sts to next corner, pm, and then pu&k/CO 13 sts – 52 sts. Work [Tw].

Squares

Between each pair of Tw's, attach D at red triangle at top of lower Tw, *pu&k 9 sts to next corner, pm; rep from * once, pu&k 9 sts to next corner – 27 sts. Work [S].

Strip End Shapes

Add the shape specified in Figure 2 (C2, T1, T2, or T3) to each end of the Strip as follows:

C2, T1, and T2 Attach A at red triangle on Tw at end of Strip, and pu&k 9 sts and work [Shape] where Shape is one of C2, T1, or T2.

T3 Attach A at red triangle on Tw at end of Strip, pu&k 9 sts to corner, pm, pu&k 9 more sts on prev Strip's HT2 edge (see Figure 2 for location of pu&k). Work [T3].

Odd Strips S3-S27

HT1 (S3-S17)

At bottom of prev Strip on RS, attach yarn color for HT1 at red triangle, pu&k: 9 sts to next corner, pm, 13 sts to next corner – 22 sts. Work [HT1].

Twists (S3-S25)

Work as for Even Strip Twists, beginning pu&k at st after m on Tw of prev Strip.

HT2 (S11-S27)

Attach yarn for HT2 at red triangle at st after m in last Tw of prev Strip, pu&k: 9 sts to next m, pm, 13 sts to next m, and 9 sts – 31 sts. Work [HT2].

Squares

Work as for Even Strip Squares.

End Triangles

Work as for Even Strip Triangles.

Corner 2 (C2)

Attach A at red triangle on HT2 of S27, and pu&k 9 sts. Work [C2].

BORDERS

Right Border

Attach A at lower right corner of blanket, pu&k 6 sts on first corner, 13 sts on edge of each Tw and triangle (T1/T2/T3), and 6 sts on last corner – 259 sts. Knit 17 rows. BO loosely.

Left Border

Work as for Right Border, attaching A at top left corner of blanket.

Top Border

Attach A at top right corner of Right Border, pu&k 10 sts on right border, 6 sts on first corner, 13 sts on edge of each HT and edge triangle (T1/T2/T3), 6 sts on last corner, and 10 sts on edge of left border – 253 sts. Knit 17 rows. BO loosely.

Bottom Border

Work as for Top Border, attaching A at lower left corner of Left Border.

FINISHING

Weave in ends.

Corner 1 (C1) – 1 st inc'ing to 9 sts

Row 1 (RS): (K1 tbl, p1 tbl, k1 tbl) in 1 st – 2 sts inc'd; 3 sts.
Row 2 and all even-numbered (WS) rows to 8: Knit.
Rows 3, 5, and 7: Kf&b, knit to last st, kf&b – 6 sts inc'd; 9 sts.
Cut yarn and fasten off.

Corner 2 (C2) – 9 sts dec'ing to 1 st

Row 2 and all even-numbered (WS) rows to 8: Knit.
Rows 3, 5, and 7 (RS): K2tog, knit to last 2 sts, ssk – 6 sts dec'd; 3 sts.
Row 9: Cdd – 2 sts dec'd; 1 st.
Cut yarn and fasten off.

Half Twist 1 (HT1) – 22 sts inc'ing 28, dec'ing to 22 sts

On RS, pm after st 9.
Row 2 and all even-numbered (WS) rows to 28: Knit.
Rows 3, 5, 7, 9, 11, and 13 (RS): Kf&b, knit to 2 sts bef m, ssk, knit to last st, kf&b – 6 sts inc'd; 28 sts.
Row 15: Kf&b, knit to 2 sts bef m, ssk, knit to end.
Rows 17, 19, 21, 23, 25, and 27: Kf&b, knit to 2 sts bef m, ssk, knit to last 2 sts, ssk – 6 sts dec'd; 22 sts. Rm. BO loosely. Cut yarn and fasten off.

Half Twist 2 (HT2) – 31 sts dec'ing to 22 sts

On RS, pm after st 10 (mA) and 22 (mB).
Row 2 (WS): Knit.
Row 3 (RS): Knit to 2 sts bef mA, ssk, knit to mB, kf&b, knit to last 2 sts, ssk – 1 st dec'd; 30 sts.
Rows 4 & 5: Rep [Rows 2 & 3] – 1 st dec'd; 29 sts.
Row 6: Knit to mA, w&t.
Row 7: Knit to mB, kf&b, knit to last 2 sts, ssk.
Rows 8-25: Rep [Rows 2-7] 3 times – 6 sts dec'd; 23 sts.
Rows 26 & 27: Rep [Rows 2 & 3] – 1 st dec'd; 22 sts.
Rm. BO loosely. Cut yarn and fasten off.

Square (S) – 27 sts dec'ing to 1 st

Row 2 (WS): Knit.
Row 3 (RS): *Knit to 2 sts bef m, ssk, sm, k2tog; rep from * once, knit to end – 4 sts dec'd; 23 sts.
Rows 4-7: Rep [Rows 2 & 3] 2 times – 8 sts dec'd; 15 sts.
Row 8: Knit.
Row 9: Knit to 2 sts bef m, ssk, cdd, k2tog, knit to end – 4 sts dec'd; 11 sts.
Row 10: Rm's. K4, k2tog – 10 sts. Turn RSs tog, 3-needle BO of rem 10 sts – 9 sts dec'd; 1 st.
Cut yarn and fasten off.

Triangle (T1) – 9 sts dec'ing to 1 st

Row 2 (WS): Knit.
Row 3 (RS): K2tog, knit to end – 1 st dec'd; 8 sts.
Rows 4-17: Rep [Rows 2 & 3] 7 times – 7 sts dec'd; 1 st.
Cut yarn and fasten off.

Triangle 2 (T2) – 9 sts dec'ing to 1 st

Row 2 (WS): Knit.
Row 3 (RS): Knit to last 2 sts, ssk – 1 st dec'd; 8 sts.
Rows 4-17: Rep [Rows 2 & 3] 7 times – 7 sts dec'd; 1 st.
Row 18: Knit. Cut yarn and fasten off.

Triangle 3 (T3) – 18 sts dec'ing to 1 st

On RS, pm after st 9.
Row 2 (WS): Knit.
Row 3 (RS): K2tog, knit to 2 sts bef m, ssk, sm, k2tog, knit to last 2 sts, ssk – 4 sts dec'd; 14 sts.
Rows 4-7: Rep [Rows 2 & 3] 2 times – 8 sts dec'd; 6 sts.
Row 8: Knit.
Row 9: Cdd, twice – 4 sts dec'd; 2 sts. Cut yarn, leaving 10"/25 cm tail. Thread yarn onto tapestry needle and insert through rem 2 sts, pull to tighten, and fasten off.

Twist (Tw) – 52 sts inc'ing to 54, dec'ing to 43 sts

On RS, pm after st 10 (mA), 22 (mB), and 39 (mC).
Row 2 (WS): Knit.
Row 3 (RS): Knit, to 2 sts bef mA, ssk, knit to mB, kf&b, knit to 2 sts bef mC, ssk, knit to last st, kf&b.
Rows 4 & 5: Rep [Rows 2 & 3].
Row 6: Knit to mA, w&t next st.
Row 7: Knit to mB, kf&b, knit to 2 sts bef mC, ssk, knit to last st, kf&b – 1 st inc'd; 53 sts.
Rows 8-13: Rep [Rows 2-7] – 1 st inc'd; 54 sts.
Row 14: Knit.
Row 15: Knit to 2 sts bef mA, ssk, knit to mB, kf&b, knit to 2 sts bef mC, ssk, knit to end – 1 st dec'd; 53 sts.
Row 16: Knit.
Row 17: Knit to 2 sts bef mA, ssk, knit to mB, kf&b, knit to 2 sts bef mC, ssk, knit to 2 sts bef end, ssk – 2 sts dec'd; 51 sts.
Row 18: Knit to mA, w&t.
Row 19: Knit to mB, kf&b, knit to 2 sts bef mC, ssk, knit to last 2 sts, ssk – 1 st dec'd; 50 sts.
Row 20: Knit.
Row 21: Rep [Row 17] – 2 sts dec'd; 48 sts.
Rows 22-27: Rep [Rows 16-21] – 5 sts dec'd; 43 sts.
Rms. On RS, pm 8 sts after mB (before 9th st).
Note: This marks the boundary bet the Square and the Tw in the next Strip.
Row 28: Knit.
BO loosely.
Cut yarn and fasten off.

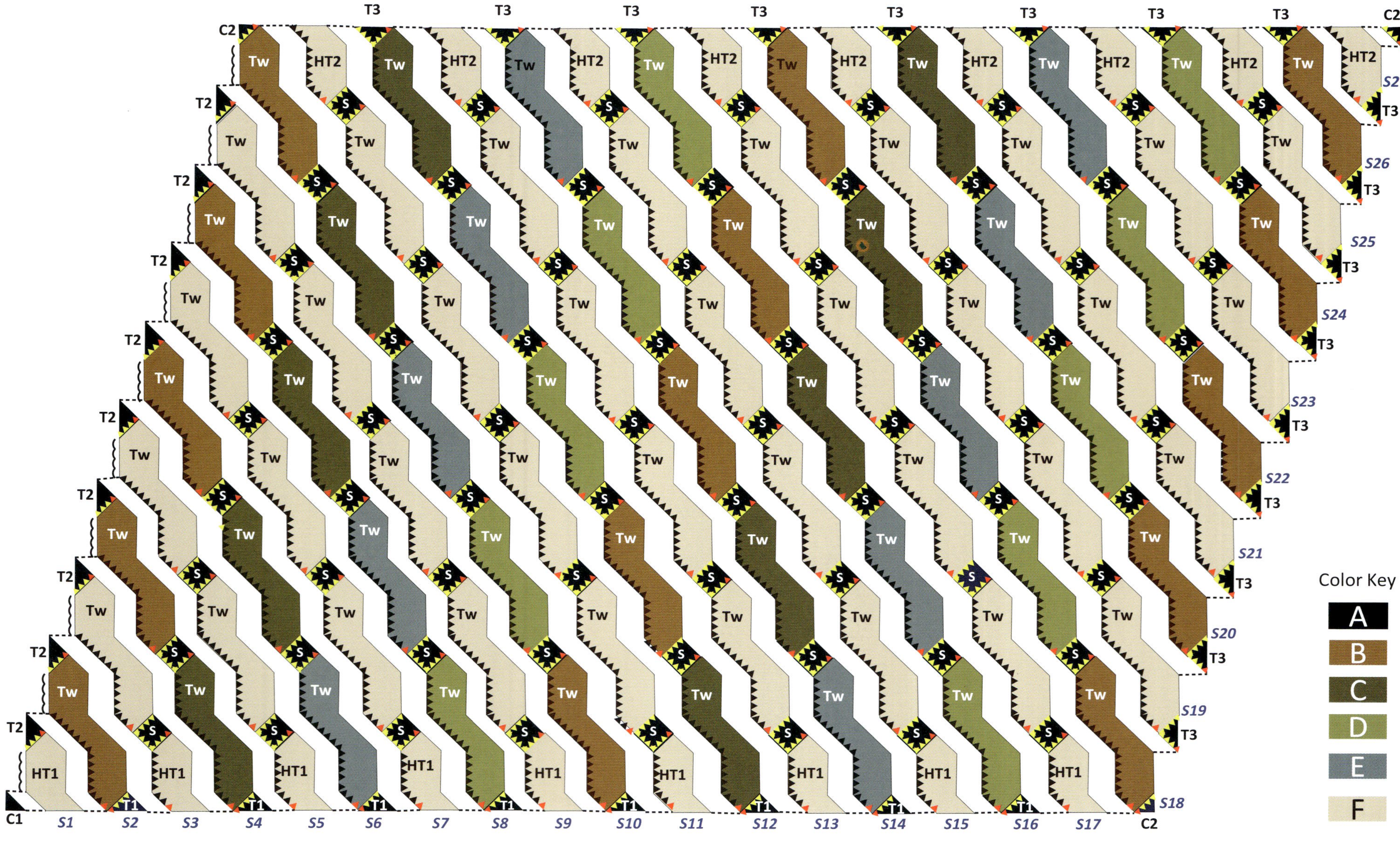

Figure 2: Complete Construction Diagram

WONKY WALKING

Take a meandering walk just for the joy of it with this blanket of whimsical pathways and colors.

SIZE 54.5 x 80.5"/138 x 204 cm

TECHNIQUES 3-needle BO, pu&k, short rows

YARN Cascade 220 Superwash, worsted (100% superwash wool; 220 yds/200 m; 3.5 oz/100 g):

Pattern Color ID	Color Swatch	Color ID	Color Name	Color Description	# Skeins
A		817	Ecru	off-white	6
B		815	Black	black	3
C		1923	Red Wine Heather	burgundy	2
D		314	Garnet	bright red	2
E		877	Golden	bright yellow-orange	2
F		820	Lemon	yellow	1
G		1950	Hunter Green	deep green	1
H		1985	Duck Egg Blue	medium green-blue	2
I		1942	Mint	light green-blue	1
J		885	In the Navy	navy blue	3
K		814	Hyacinth	medium blue	2
L		873	Extra Creme Cafe	beige	1

NEEDLES 2 US Size 7/4.5 mm 40"/100 cm circular needles or size needed to obtain gauge, 3rd needle Size US 9/5.5 mm for 3-needle BO

NOTIONS Tapestry needle, stitch markers

GAUGE 17 sts x 34 rows = 4"/10 cm in garter st

NOTES

- The blanket is worked in Blocks composed of mitered shapes. Within a Block, a black-and-white path is worked first; then stitches for mitered shapes are picked up and knitted (pu&k) off of the edges of the path or of mitered shapes. A joining border is picked up and knit on edges of all Blocks, and then the joining borders are connected with a 3-needle BO.
- Do not cut yarns until instructed. Drape yarns bet uses. See "Tacking Draped Yarn" on page 210.
- Use a larger 3rd needle for the 3-needle BOs to avoid puckering of Joins.

BLANKET INSTRUCTIONS

Blocks

Make 24 Blocks in colors and quantities shown in Figure 1. Construction of a Block begins with Path and then shapes: NW, SW, SE, and NE. All shapes have striping. The number of rows to work in each color is specified in each stripe. Colors for stripes are in parentheses after the shape's name. Directions are for Color Scheme 1 with changes for Color Scheme 2 in parentheses. Color changes are made at beg of RS rows.

Path

With B, CO 8 sts.

(With B, knit 10 rows, with A, knit 6 rows) twice, with B, knit 10 rows.

With A, work [RTS] following written instructions below or chart on page 197.

Work bet * and * once. Cut A and B. BO loosely.

Right Turning Square (RTS) – 8 sts

Row 1 and all odd-numbered (RS) rows to 29: Knit.
Row 2 (WS): Knit to last st, w&t last st.
Row 4: Knit to 1 st bef prev wrap, w&t.
Rows 6, 8, 10, & 12: Rep Row 4.
Rows 14 & 16: K1, w&t (on Row 16, same st is wrapped as in Row 14).
Rows 18, 20, 22, 24, 26, & 28: Knit to and including prev wrapped st, w&t next st.
Row 30 (WS): Knit.
Rm. BO loosely. Cut yarn and fasten off.

NW

With E (F), pu&k 21 sts from pink triangle to corner, 1 st in corner (through front bumps of 2 corner sts), pm, and 21 sts to next corner – 43 sts.

Work [MS], alternating bet E (F) and C (D) working the number of rows indicated in the stripes of the NW shape in Figure 1.

Mitered Shape (MS) – odd number of sts dec'ing to 1 st

Row 1 (WS): Knit.
Row 2 (RS): Knit to 2 sts bef m, rm, cdd, pm, knit to end – 2 sts dec'd.
Row 3: Knit.
Rep [Rows 2 & 3], making yarn changes as specified, until 3 sts rem, ending after WS row.
Next row (RS): Rm. Cdd – 2 sts dec'd; 1 st. Rm. Cut yarn and fasten off.

SW

With C (D), pu&k 28 sts from blue triangle to corner, pm, turn needle, and CO 21 sts – 49 sts. Work [MS], alternating bet C (D) and L (H) working the number of rows indicated in the stripes of the SW shape in Figure 1, until 9 sts rem, ending after a WS row.

Next row (RS): Knit to 2 sts bef m, rm, cdd – 2 sts dec'd; 7 sts.

Next row (WS): K2tog, BO rem 5 sts loosely. Cut yarn and fasten off.

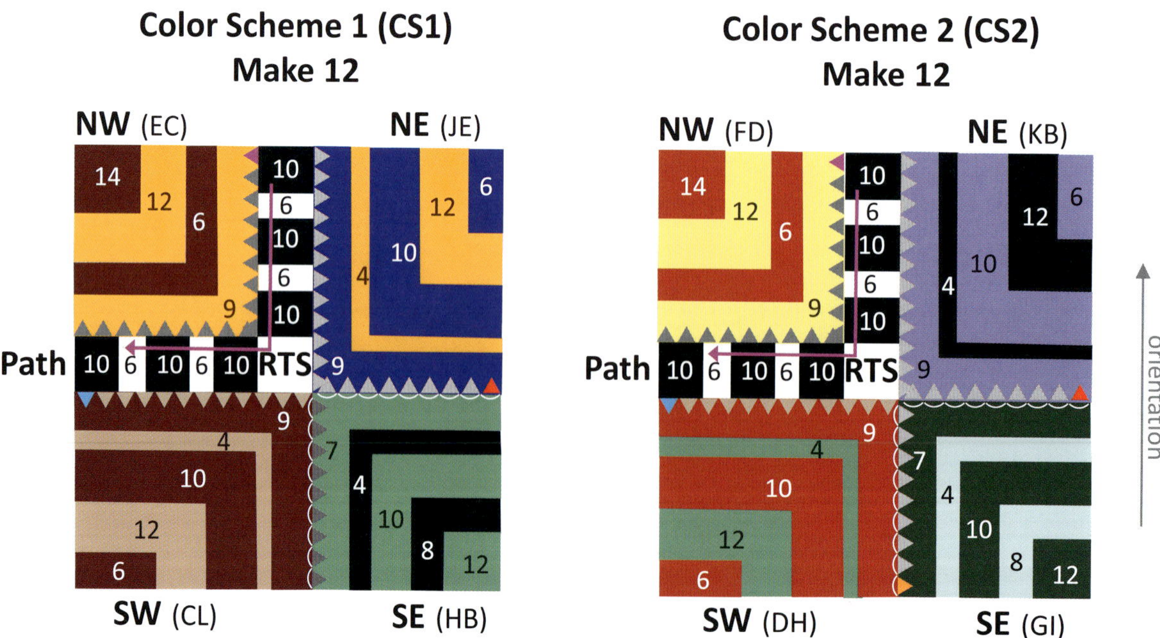

Figure 1: Color Schemes, Quantities, and Number of Rows to Work for Each Stripe

SE

With H (G), pu&k 21 sts bet yellow triangle and next corner, 1 st in corner of RTS of the NW shape, pm, turn needle, and CO 21 sts – 43 sts.

Work [MS], alternating bet H (G) and B (I) working the number of rows indicated in the stripes of the SE shape in Figure 1.

NE

With J (K), pu&k 21 sts bet red triangle and corner, pm, and 28 sts to next corner – 49 sts.

Work [MS], alternating bet J (K) and E (B) working the number of rows indicated in the stripes of the NE shape in Figure 1, until 9 sts rem, ending after a WS row.

Next row (RS): Rm. Cdd – 2 sts dec'd; 7 sts. BO sts loosely.

ASSEMBLY

Arrange 24 completed Blocks as shown in Figure 2, turning Blocks according to the orientation arrow in Figure 1.

Blocks are organized into groups of 4, named Strip 1 through Strip 6 in Figure 2.

Figure 2: Layout for Assembly

Strips 1-6

Join Blocks Together for Strip 1

See Figure 3 for construction.

Between Blocks 1 & 2, 2 & 3, and 3 & 4, work [Join 1].

Join Blocks Together to make Strips 2-6

Rep as for Joins for Strip 1.

Join Strips Together

See Figure 4 for construction.

Work [Join 2] bet Strips 1 & 2, 2 & 3, 3 & 4, 4 & 5, and 5 & 6.

Figure 3: Block Joining into Horizontal Strips

Join 1

See Figure 3.

With A and circular needle, on RS of the left Block, *pu&k 49 sts from red triangle to next corner, at a rate of 1 st per garter stitch ridge or 1 st per CO/BO st on Path pieces. (See Figure 3 for number of sts to pu&k on the edge of each stripe.) Knit 5 rows. Leave sts on needle.* Cut yarn.

With a 2nd circular needle, attach A at green triangle on the right Block to next corner. Rep bet * and *.

Bring RS of work tog, and needle tips parallel. With 3rd needle, 3-needle BO all sts loosely. Cut yarn, insert end through loop of rem st on 3rd needle, and fasten off.

Join 2

See Figure 3.

With A and circular needle, on RS, *pu&k 210 sts from red triangle across the top edge of lower Strip (49 sts per Block and 6 sts on each Join 1). Knit 5 rows. Leave sts on circular needle.* Cut yarn.

With second circular needle, on RS, attach A at green triangle. Rep bet * and *.

Turn Strips 1 & 2 with RS together and needle tips parallel. 3-needle BO all sts loosely. Cut yarn, insert end through loop of rem st on 3rd needle, and fasten off.

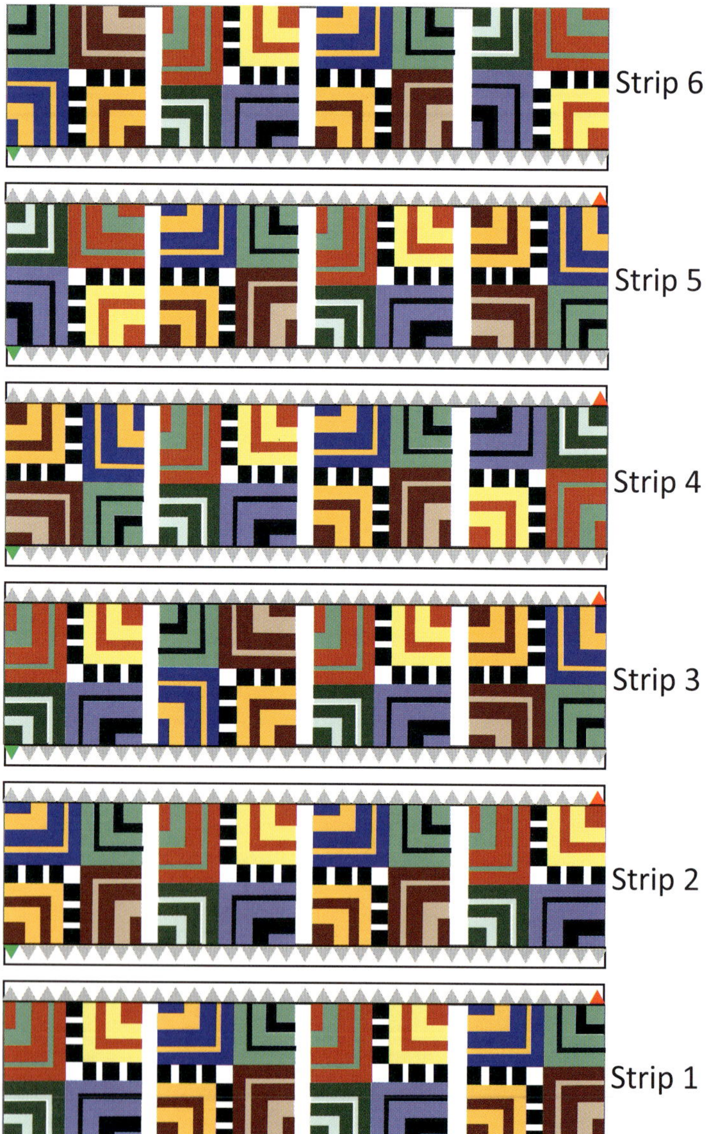

Figure 4: Joining Strips Together

BORDERS

Right Border

On RS, attach A at bottom right corner of blanket and pu&k 324 sts (49 sts per Block and 6 sts per Border) on right edge. Work [Border].

Border

Row 2 (WS): Knit.
Row 3 (RS): Kf&b, knit to last st, kf&b – 2 sts inc'd.
Row 4: Knit.
Rows 5-10: Rep [Rows 3 & 4] 3 times – 6 sts inc'd. Cut A, leaving 10"/25 cm tail.
Rows 11-20: With J, rep [Rows 3 & 4] 5 times – 10 sts inc'd. BO loosely. Cut yarn and fasten off, leaving 10"/25 cm tail.

Left Border

On RS, attach A at top left corner of blanket. Work as for Right Border on left edge.

Top Border

On RS, attach A at top right corner or blanket and pu&k 214 sts on top edge. Work [Border].

Bottom Border

On RS, attach A at bottom left corner of blanket. Work as for Top Border on bottom edge.

Seaming Corners

With long tails of matching color and mattress st, sew together corners of Borders.

FINISHING

Weave in ends.

CHART

Right Turning Square (RTS)

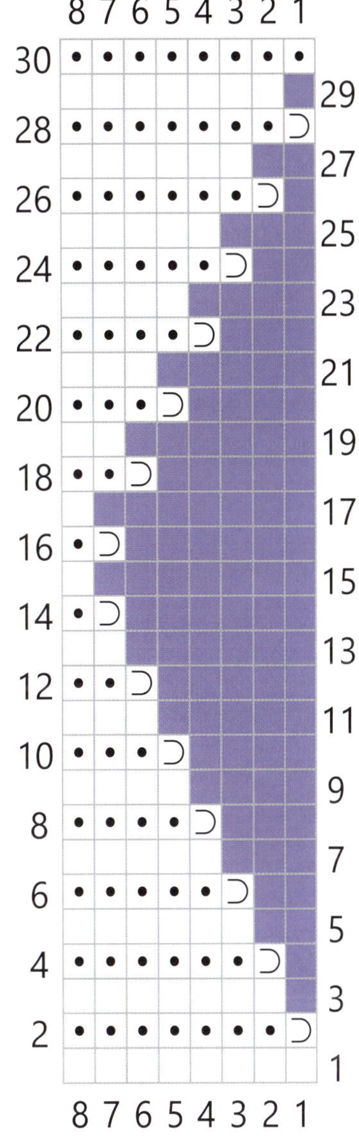

Chart Symbols

RS: knit

WS: knit

sts outside w&t

WS: w&t

RESOURCES

ABBREVIATIONS

bef	before
beg	begin(ning)
bet	between
bli	backward loop increase
BO	bind off
BOR	beginning of round
cdd	central double decrease: slip 2 sts as if to k2tog, k1, pass slipped sts over (2 sts dec'd)
cdd2	slip 3 sts as if to k3tog, k2tog, pass slipped sts over (4 sts dec'd)
cddp	slip 2 sts tog, p1, then pass slipped sts over
CO	cast on
cont	continu(e)(ing)
dec('d)(ing)	decrease(d)(ing)
dpns	double-pointed needles
inc('d)(ing)	increase(d)(ing)
k	knit
k2tog	knit 2 sts together (1 st dec'd)
kf&b	knit into the front leg of the next st, leaving it on the left needle, then knit into the back leg of the same st, then transfer the st to the right needle (1 st inc'd)
kyok	(k1, yo, k1) into 1 st (2 sts inc'd)
L	left, left hand
m	marker
p	purl
p2sso	pass 2 slipped stitches over
p2tog	purl 2 together (1 st dec'd)
pm	place marker
prev	previous
psso	pass 1 slipped stitch over
pu&k	pick up & knit
R	right hand
rem	remain(ing)
rep(s)	repeat(s) (ing)
rm	remove marker
rnd(s)	round(s)
RS	right side
sl	slip
sm	slip marker
ssk	slip 2 sts knitwise, knit these 2 sts together through back loops (1 st dec'd)
sssk	slip 3 sts knitwise and together to the right needle, knit the next 2 sts together, insert left needle, left-to-right, through all 3 slipped sts, and pass over the k2tog st
st(s)	stitch(es)
tbl	through back loop(s)
tog	together
w&t	wrap & turn
WS	wrong side
yo	yarn over

GLOSSARY

Common knitting techniques are on this page, and less common techniques are covered in more depth on the pages that follow.

Techniques with a camera icon have an instructional video. See page 214 for access to videos.

Backward Loop Increase (bli)

With yarn in back, wrap yarn around left index finger, back to front, once with yarn exiting to right. Insert R needle, right to left, under the front leg of the loop and slip loop off finger and onto R needle. Tighten yarn (1 st inc'd).

I-cord

Set up: Onto a dpn of same size used to work blanket, using provisional technique, CO 3 sts. Starting at the edge location specified in the pattern, *insert the working needle front to back through next a selvage st, yarn around working needle, and pull a loop through. Using the non-working dpn, pass 3rd (last) st on needle over new st.

Slide sts to the other tip of the working needle, k2, insert working needle through next selvage st and knit the 3rd st on the needle and the selvage st together. Rep bet * and * around the blanket, making 2 extra repeats in each corner by inserting the working needle into the same corner stitch 3 times. Graft ends together.

Knitted Cast-On

Six inches from end of yarn, make a slipknot and slide loop onto L needle. *Insert R needle left-to-right through front leg of last-made loop (i.e., knitwise), wind working end of yarn around R needle counterclockwise, and pull new loop through existing loop. Transfer new loop on R needle to the L needle. Pull yarn to adjust tension. Rep from * to add more sts. For a tighter BO, insert needle through both legs of the last-made loop.

Pinhole Cast-On

To begin, wrap yarn around index finger twice, making a circle from front to back with working yarn hanging to front.

1. Using a crochet hook, insert hook into circle, bet yarn circle and finger.

2. Draw working yarn through center of circle, and then draw another loop through the loop on the needle, as for crochet chain st. One st is now complete.

Rep steps [1 & 2] to add additional sts to the crochet hook. Circle may be slipped off finger and held once a few sts have been created. When desired number of sts have been created, transfer sts one-by-one to dpns as instructed by pattern. After several rounds are completed, pull tail to tighten center sts and fasten off securely.

Provisional Cast-On

Method 1: Traditional Crochet Chain: Using a crochet hook and contrasting yarn of the same weight as working yarn, make a chain with twice the number of sts as need to be CO plus 1. Using crochet hook and working yarn, insert hook into the back "bump" of the 2nd chain st, draw yarn through and transfer to needle. Rep in every 2nd back bump until the number of sts needed for the CO are on the needle. Begin knitting from these sts.

When provisionally CO sts need to become "live," undo the crochet chain from the end, one stitch at a time, and transfer sts to needle as they become free.

Method 2: Wrapping a Yarn: Use a piece of scrap yarn about 3 times the length of the edge to be cast on. With working yarn, make a slipknot on one end of the scrap yarn, and then lay scrap yarn parallel to the needle used for casting on, with the slip knotted end farthest from the needle tip. Wind the working yarn around both the needle and the scrap yarn snugly until there are the same number of winds on needle as needed for the cast-on. Tie ends of the scrap yarn tog. With working yarn, begin work. *Note:* It may be easier to use the cable of an interchangeable needle set or a stitch holder in place of the scrap yarn.

Single Crochet for Edging

*Insert hook through next edge st. Yarn over the hook and draw a yarn loop through the edge stitch. Yarn over the hook again and draw through rem loop(s) on hook. Rep from *.

TECHNIQUE TUTORIALS

3-NEEDLE BIND-OFF

The 3-needle bind-off is used to join 2 sets of live stitches and is a great modular method for making a geometric shape.

How to

A 3-needle BO used for joining and shaping is generally commenced after working part or all of a right side row, as follows:

1) On the next (a WS) row, knit half the stitches on the row only.

2) Rotate needles so that tips are parallel, RS are tog, WS facing out. Pull working yarn out from bet needles. The needle closer to you is the front needle, and the one behind is the back needle.

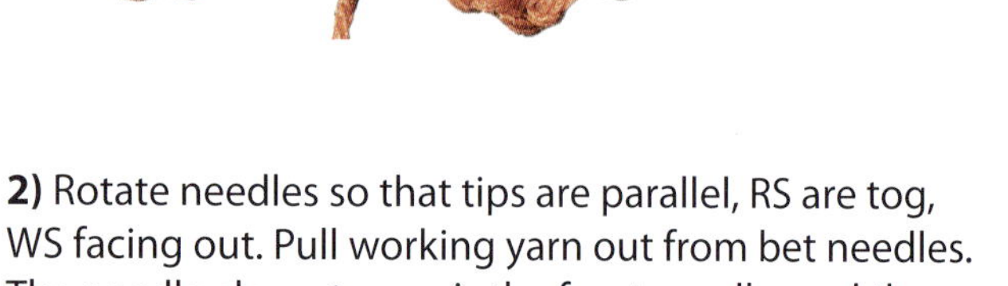

3) Insert third needle, as if to knit, through 1st st on front needle, then 1st st on back needle. Wrap yarn around third needle, as if to knit.

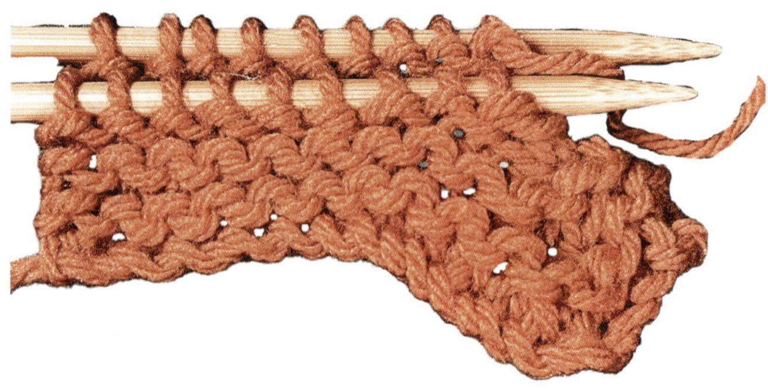

4) With third needle, draw yarn loop through the 1st loop on the back needle, then through 1st loop on the front needle.

5) Slip both stitches off the two needles. There is now one loop on the third needle.

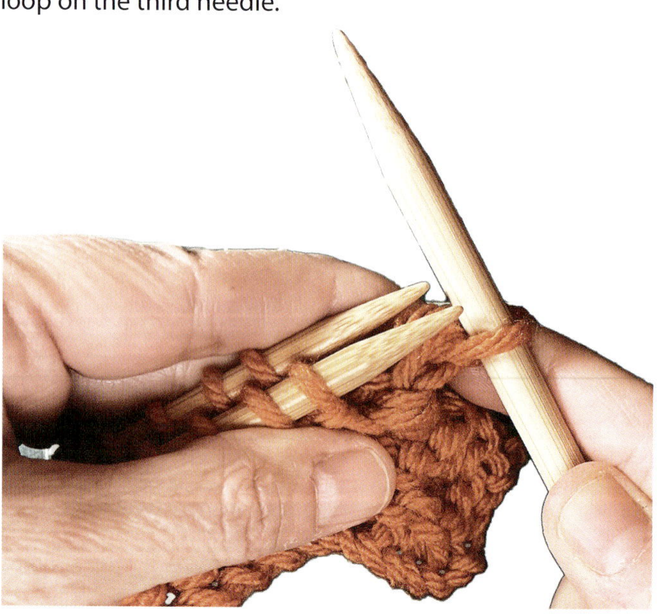

6) Repeat Steps 3 through 5 with the next pair of stitches on the front and back needles.

7) There are now 2 sts on the third needle. Insert the back needle into 2nd (right-most) st on third needle, and pull over the 1st stitch on the third needle, to bind off.

8) Now there is just 1 stitch remaining on the third needle. Repeat Steps 6 and 7 until there are no stitches remaining on the front and back needles and 1 st remaining on the third needle. Follow pattern instructions for handling the remaining stitch.

Hints for Success

- Avoid dropping stitches by keeping the front and back needle tips aligned, working near the needle tips, and using your left index finger to prevent stitches on the back needle from falling off.
- If there are too many stitches on the front needle, decrease during the BO by inserting the third needle through 2 stitches on the front needle, instead of through just 1 st. Likewise, if there are too many stitches on the back needle, insert the third needle through 2 sts on the back needle. Space out multiple decreases evenly over the BO.
- A BO that is too tight will distort the shape. If your BO tends to be tight, choose a larger size needle as your third needle.

BORDERS AND BACKINGS

BORDERS

Each blanket in this book has a border selected to complement the blanket. This section has ideas and how-to instructions for alternate border treatments.

A border provides a consistent and flat edging that doesn't curl or distort. It terminates the pattern by framing the design elements. Audition different colors for the border to see what the blanket needs to look complete. Using a dominant color from the blanket makes the border part of the design. A more muted version of a color in the blanket or a neutral color will frame the blanket without drawing attention or competing with the design.

Log Cabin (See Figure 1)

A Log Cabin border is used when the Border is worked in a single color. It is used in most of the blankets in this book. "Nr" is the number of complete ridges knitted in the Border. The number of stitches to pu&k on the short edge of a completed border is 1 + Nr.

Figure 1: Construction of a Log Cabin Border

Join-as-you-go Border (JAYG)

If you don't have a circular needle, a JAYG border can be worked counterclockwise around the blanket starting at the middle of an edge, using two dpns. CO 5 to 10 stitches (aka Border stitches). Knit all rows, making a join to the blanket edge at the end of every RS row by inserting the R needle through both the back loop of the last Border stitch and the edge of the blanket. Use the original instructions from the blanket's Border for the number of Joins to make per shape along the blanket's edge.

At corners, use the following pattern stitch to turn the corner (see "Wrap & Turn (w&t)" on page 211):

Row 1 (RS): Knit to last st, wrap & turn (w&t) last st.

Row 2 (WS): Knit.

Row 3: Knit to 1 st before prev wrap, w&t next stitch.

Row 4: Knit.

Rep [Rows 3 and 4] until the 2nd st from the beginning of the RS row is wrapped.

Next RS row: K1, w&t.

Note: In this phase, we are wrapping stitches for the second time.

Next WS row: Knit.

Row 5: Knit to end, including the stitch that was wrapped on the prev RS row, w&t next stitch.

Row 6: Knit.

Repeat [Rows 5 & 6] until the last st on a RS row is wrapped.

Next WS row: Knit.

Crochet Border

A scalloped crocheted edge is fast and attractive. With yarn and crochet hook, on RS, attach yarn to center of right edge of blanket face by pulling loop up from back of work. Ch1. *Skip 2 garter st ridges/CO/BO sts and make 7 double crochet (dc) in next ridge/st, skip 2 garter st ridges/CO/BO sts and make sl st in next ridge/CO/BO st.*

Rep between * and * to end of edge, making adjustments if needed to end the scallop exactly at the corner. Sl st in the blanket corner, ch3, sl st in same corner location, and continue scallops on the next border. When the starting point is reached, sl st in the initial chain stitch. Cut yarn, fasten off, and weave in ends. If there are diagonal pieces on the blanket edge, you may first work a single crochet around the entire blanket, making 1 single crochet for each st that would have otherwise been pu&k on the pieces.

BACKING A BLANKET

A fabric backing adds a nice finish to a knitted blanket, makes it warmer, reduces stretch, and allows you to skip the weaving in.

Select a fabric for the backing. For the lightest backing, use double gauze. A good option for a non-stretch backing is double-brushed flannel. It is warm, strong, affordable, and easy to work with. Double-brushed flannels are fuzzy on both sides, which helps the fabric stick to the knitted blanket, requiring less tacking in the middle of the blanket. Fleece, a synthetic, is thicker and stretchier than flannel. If the blanket is wool, or extra warmth is desired, use a woven wool fabric for the backing.

Prepare the blanket by blocking it, following the laundering instructions on the yarn label.

Mark the center of the blanket with a stitch marker by folding it into quarters with right sides together and corners aligned.

On a large surface, spread out and flatten the blanket, right side down, so it lays flat and is not skewed. Using masking or painter's tape, attach edges to the work surface so they don't move.

Measure the width of the blanket in several places, average, and record. Do the same for the length.

Determine the fabric requirements. If the width of the fabric, after selvages are removed, is smaller than the width of the blanket, the amount of fabric needed will be 2 times the blanket length.

If the width of the fabric is the same or more than the width of the blanket, then the amount of fabric needed is the same as the length of the blanket.

Prepare the fabric. Cotton fabric should be washed, dried, and pressed to remove wrinkles, following manufacturer's instructions. Before washing the fabric, cut off all the selvage edges (where the printing is), because they shrink at a faster rate than the fabric.

Construct the fabric backing. The backing will be the same size as the blanket.

Measure the fabric. If the blanket is wider than the fabric, sew two widths of fabric together to span the width. It will be easiest with a sewing machine but can be done by hand. With RS of the fabric together, sew a vertical seam, leaving a ½"/1.25 cm seam allowance. Press the seam out flat. When seaming together two lengths of fabric, it is more aesthetically pleasing to cut one in half along the vertical, and center the uncut piece between the two halves. For design interest, piece together a backing from smaller pieces of fabric. Using a bed sheet avoids seaming, but the high thread count of most sheets makes sewing by hand tiring.

Mark the center of the backing by folding it in half twice, matching corners exactly, and then inserting a safety pin through the corner of the folds.

Center the fabric, right side up, on top of the blanket using this approach:

> With the backing folded in quarters with right sides together, place it on the blanket, matching the marked center of the backing with the marked center of the blanket, and then unfold the backing carefully, maintaining alignment of the centers of the fabric and blanket.

Trim the backing almost even with the blanket edge, cutting ⅛"/.3 cm to ¼"/.6 cm outside the blanket edge. Be careful not to cut the blanket.

Proceed in one of the following ways:

1) With safety pins, lift the backing edge slightly and turn in a ½"/1.25 cm hem and finger press, and then insert a safety pin through the turned hem and the knitted blanket edge to secure. Continue around the blanket in this manner to pin the edge in place.

2) Separate the layers and with a hot iron, press a ½"/1.25 cm hem all around the edge of the backing. *Optional:* Using a 3 mm long straight stitch, sew the hem down ¼"/.6 cm from the edge around entire perimeter of the fabric piece. Reassemble and align the center of the backing and blanket, wrong sides together, as they were initially, and use safety pins to pin them together.

Sewing the layers must be done by hand. With the fabric side facing up, take a sewing needle and sewing thread that matches the border color, and, using whip stitch, sew the hem of the fabric to the back of the border making a stitch about every ¼"/.6 cm. The fabric hem will lie about ½"/1.25 cm in from the blanket edge. So that thread doesn't show on the knitted blanket side, take stitches into the bumps of the garter stitch ridges whenever possible.

Lay the blanket out flat again with the knitted side up. Take a few discrete stitches through both layers in about 8–10 different locations scattered around the blanket surface. Hide the thread ends between layers. This should be enough to keep the layers together during use and laundering.

INTARSIA

Intarsia is used when a large one-color motif is to be added. For example, the large pink heart on the left in Figure 2 should be worked in intarsia. If you imagine knitting across a row in the heart area of the top, you first knit with the background (peach) color and then the pink heart color, ending with the background color. That row slice only has 3 colors.

Rule for Intarsia: When the row has a small number of colors compared to the number of stitches on the needle, and there are large numbers of contiguous stitches worked in each color of yarn, use intarsia.

Contrast that top with one in the center of Figure 2. Imagine you are knitting across one of the rows in the heart section and are alternating frequently between the background and heart colors.

Rule for Stranded: When switching between the background color and contrast color often and predictably (in a repeating pattern), use stranded (aka "fair isle").

What about the design on the right in Figure 2 with the hearts staggered diagonally? This is a murky situation. It doesn't meet the requirements for stranded because the heart pattern doesn't repeat across the row, but the hearts are very small, so it doesn't meet the requirement for intarsia, in which the area of contrast color is large. For this area, you could work it either in intarsia or in duplicate stitch (or a combination of the two).

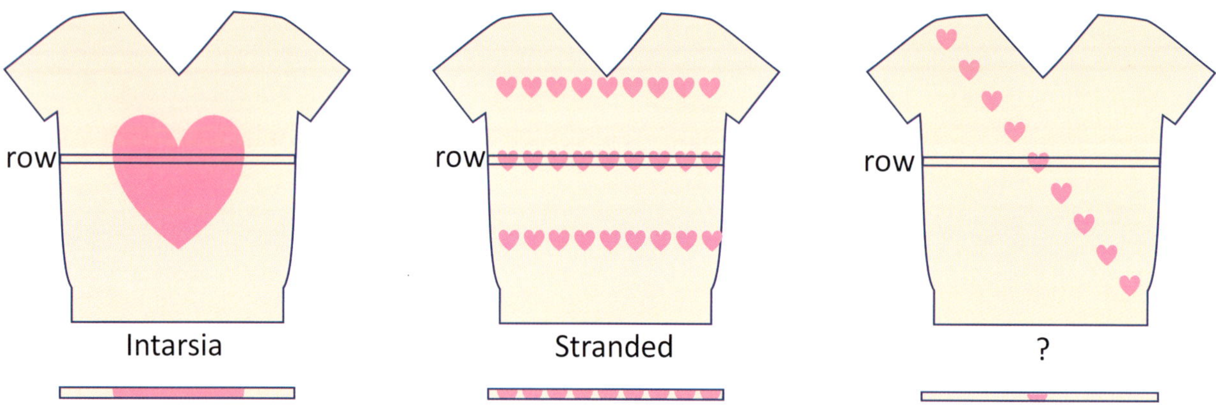

Figure 2: Selecting the Right Technique for Colorwork

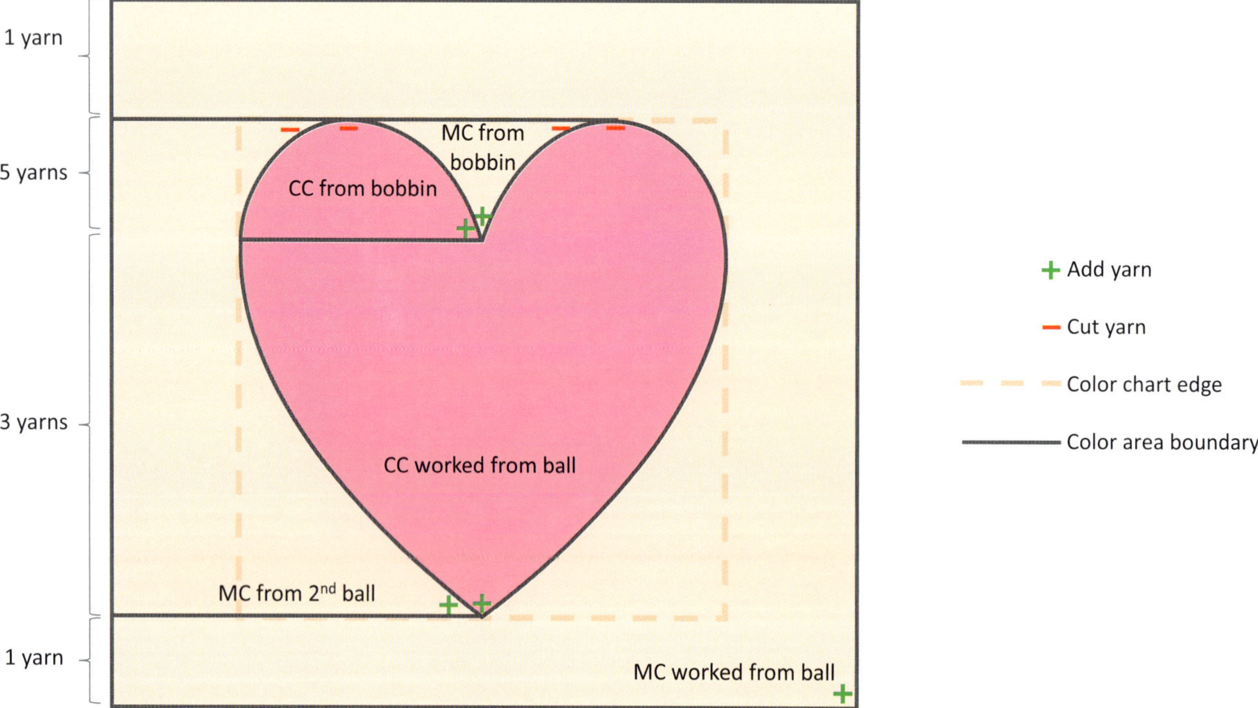

Figure 3: Adding and Cutting Yarn

How It works

With intarsia, a separate yarn strand (ball) is needed for each noncontiguous area of color, as shown in Figure 4. In most of this Heart design there are 3 balls of yarn active at a time, but when we get to the row where the lobes split, 5 balls are needed until the heart is complete. Once the heart is complete, all four "extra" yarns that were added are cut, and the work continues with the main ball.

When knitting a row, each yarn is positioned at the right edge of the area to be worked in that color. When working across the row, the yarn is dropped at the left edge of the color area, and the new color is picked up. Figure 4 shows the positions of the yarn balls at the beginning and end of a row. When the work is turned for starting the next row, the yarn ball positions are automatically at the right edge of each color area, just where they need to be to work the next row.

Intarsia designs are described via a color chart. The chart in Figure 5 contains 50 rows and is 25 stitches wide. For each row the chart specifies the stitch to use and the color to work the stitch. For instance, on Row 1, work sts 1–12 in MC, st 13 in CC, and sts 14–25 in MC.

This chart is for garter stitch, so it looks different from color charts you may have worked for stockinette stitch. A garter stitch chart will look elongated (stretched) when compared with the final knitted piece. On a chart, each stitch is represented by a square, but in garter stitch each ridge is 1 st wide and 2 sts tall. Every row is knitted, so on WS rows there is a dot symbol indicating to knit on the WS. In some patterns, simple edge shaping is combined with intarsia, so there will be k2tog or ssk symbols on some rows. Some of the intarsia charts in this book include only RS rows. It is assumed the WS rows are knitted in the same color as the prev RS row.

In some patterns, there will be estimated yarn amounts for areas that should be worked from bobbins. Use those amounts as estimates, and then adjust yardage to actual use after the chart is worked the first time. Another way to

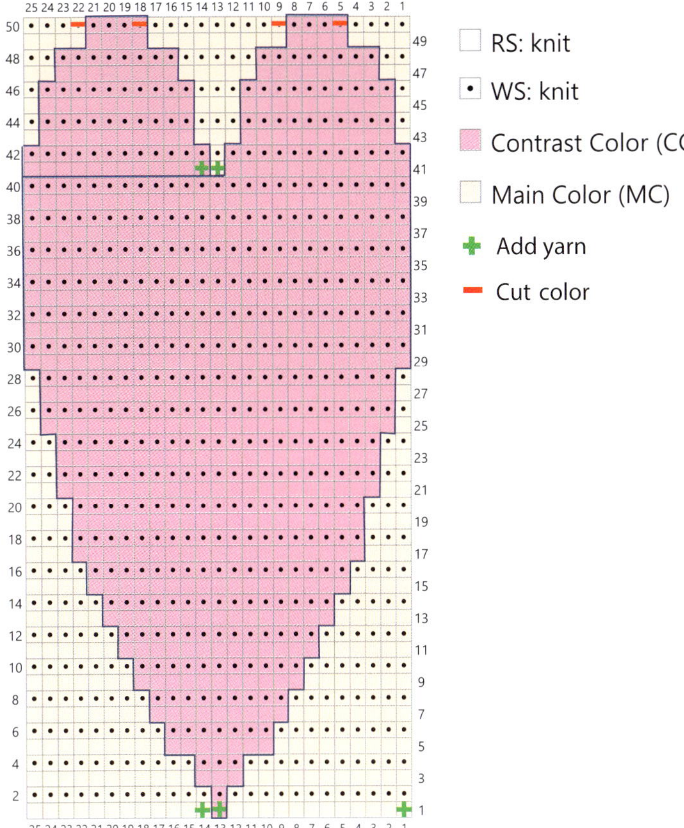

Figure 5: Heart Chart

Note: A separate yarn strand (ball) is required for each noncontiguous color section.

Figure 4: Yarn Ball Positions for Intarsia at Beginning and End of Rows

estimate the length of yarn needed is to work an area from the ball, undo those rows, and measure how much yarn was used.

Added to this chart (Figure 5) are some additional symbols and outlines that show when to add and cut yarn. The dark gray lines enclose areas where separate yarns are used. The green plus sign indicates where to add yarn, and the red minus sign is where yarn is cut. A suggestion is made as to whether to work the yarn directly from the ball or to wind yarn onto a bobbin. It is not practical to put very long lengths of yarn onto a bobbin, but smaller areas that require less yardage may be knit from bobbins to help with yarn management.

Yarns are not cut until a color area is complete.

Avoiding Holes

When making color changes (dropping Old Yarn and continuing with New Yarn), we need to do something special to connect the yarns; otherwise we will have independent columns of stitches at the color transitions and therefore holes in the knitting.

This *something* is to cross the yarns. How to cross depends on whether we're working a RS or WS row.

RS row yarn changes/crossing (see Figure 6): Yarns are already on the WS of the work because we are knitting. Take the Old Yarn (yarn that is about to be dropped) and cross it over and to the left of the New Yarn on the WS of the work, pick up the New Yarn color, draw up any extra slack yarn, and continue.

Old Yarn over New Yarn,
continue with New Yarn.

WS row yarn changes/crossing (see Figure 7): A WS row is always knitted, which means that the Old Yarn (yarn that is about to be dropped) is away from you, on the RS of the work. Yarn crossing must always occur with both the yarns on the WS of the work, so move the Old Yarn (the yarn that is about to be dropped) between the needles and toward you (to the WS) and move it to the left so that it crosses over the New Yarn. Move the New Yarn between the needles to the RS of the work (away from you), draw up extra yarn, and continue knitting with the New Yarn.

Old Yarn forward, Old Yarn left over New Yarn,
New Yarn to back,
continue with New Yarn.

Despite crossing yarns, there will still be small holes next to locations where yarn was added and cut. Thread the yarn end onto a tapestry needle and on the WS, insert needle through the bump of the stitch of different color next to the hole, then back through the first stitch. On the WS, weave in yarn.

Figure 6: Yarn "cross" shown above. Crossing yarns is always done on the WS. New Yarn always goes under Old Yarn.

Figure 7: Color change when working a WS Row: Initially, the Old Yarn is away from you on RS. Bring Old Yarn forward (to WS), then cross as shown in Figure 5, and then move only the New Yarn away from you (to the RS) and continue knitting with New Yarn.

MATTRESS STITCH

Sewing garter stitch pieces together with mattress stitch produces the neatest and most invisible seam.

When to Use Mattress Stitch

Mattress stitch can be used to sew together: Side edge to side edge, CO edge to CO edge, CO edge to BO edge, or side edge to CO/BO edge. We focus on side edge to side edge, which is the most common.

How to Seam with Mattress Stitch

1) Thread long CO/BO tail, or yarn the color of one of the pieces, onto tapestry needle.

Insert up through the first edge bump of the piece opposite where the yarn is emerging. In this example, the yarn is emerging from the left piece, so we insert first through the right edge and then through the first edge bump of the left edge.

Pull yarn to eliminate some but not all of the slack.

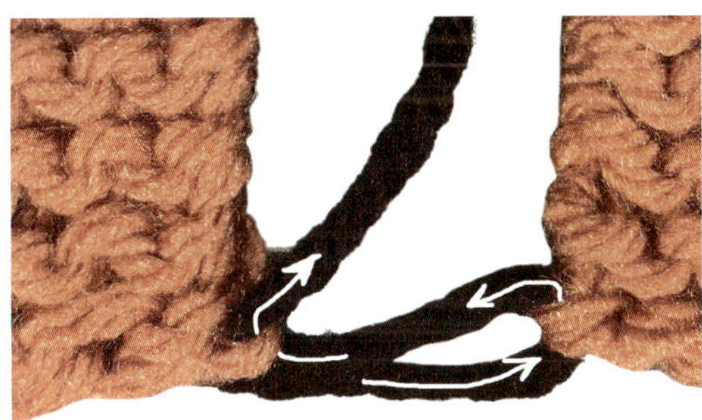

2) Insert needle upward through the next bump on the right edge, and pull to eliminate slack.

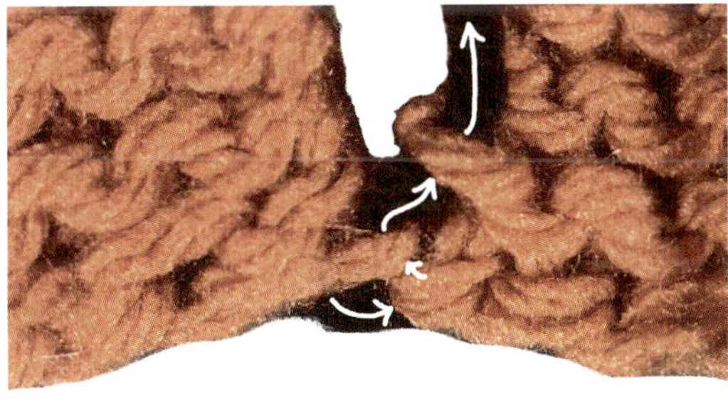

3) Continue inserting tapestry needle upward through alternating left and right edge bumps.

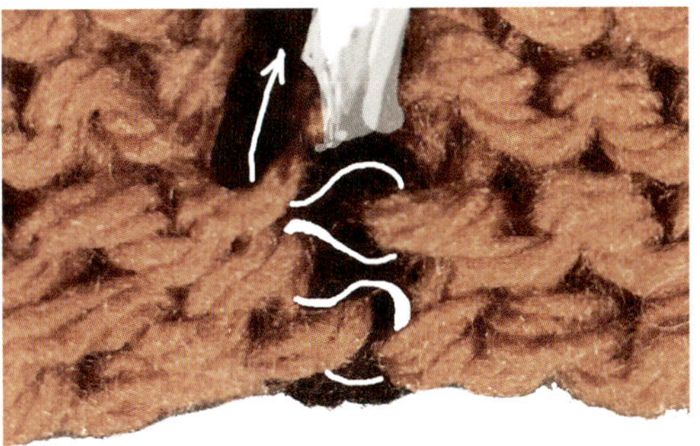

Aligning Color Stripes

Aligning color transitions presents a challenge because the ridges of one edge will nest in the valleys of the other edge, causing striping to appear slightly misaligned (aka "jogging") along the seam. To align stripes, we will need to do an "around the world" maneuver, as shown below.

1) Insert needle upward through the last edge bump of the old color on the left edge.

On the right edge, insert needle downward through the last edge bump of the old color.

2) Insert needle upward through the last bump on the left edge again. Draw up slack.

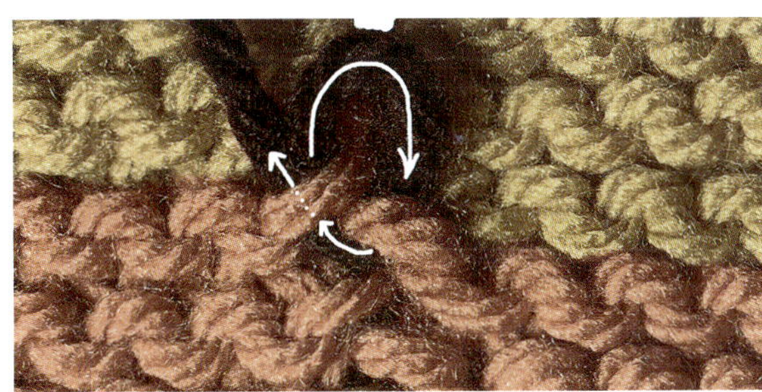

3) Un-thread and trim current sewing yarn. Thread new yarn color onto needle, and continue.

Note: Sts before the "around the world" are blue, "around the world" sts are white, and sts in the new yarn color are pink.

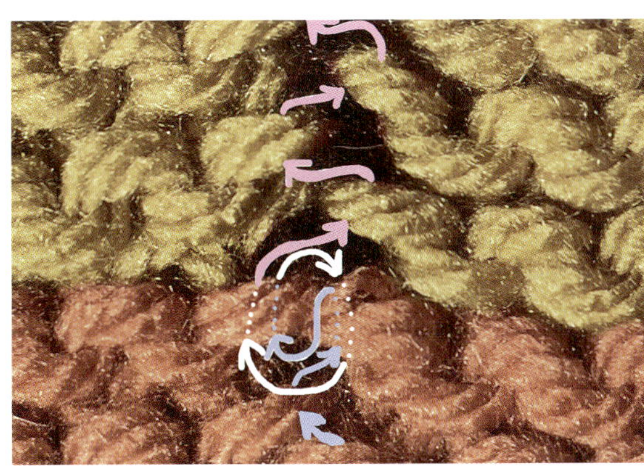

PICK UP AND KNIT (PU&K)

Pick up and knit (pu&k) is a technique used to generate live stitches on the edge of a previously completed piece (PCP) of knitting. It is used in modular knitting in place of sewing pieces together.

Pu&k differs from *picking up* stitches because a loop of working yarn is drawn through a small hole made by poking a knitting needle or crochet hook through the edge of the PCP. With *picking up,* the needle is loaded with loops of yarn that are *picked up* or *borrowed* from the PCP's edge.

When pu&k'ing on an edge perpendicular to (at right angles to) a CO/BO edge, as shown in Figure 8, 1 st is generated per every two rows of knitting. Two rows of knitting form an easily recognized surface feature on the knitting called a "ridge" as shown in Figure 9. The area between ridges is referred to as the "valley."

Start pu&k at location indicated in pattern. Hold the working yarn in your left hand and provide the proper tension by winding the yarn over and under your fingers.

For the neatest result, insert through bumps when available. A bump is the last st of a ridge. Working on the RS, and with a knitting needle, insert front to back through the next bump and draw a yarn loop to front of work. If working on the left or right edge that has no shaping, insert needle through each bump on the edge. If more sts are needed than there are bumps available, insert into the outside strand of the edge stitch bet ridges (aka, the "valley"). If working on a CO or BO edge, insert the needle through both strands of yarn.

Bind-off Edge

Perpendicular (w.r.t. BO/CO) Edge

Cast-on Edge

Figure 8: Identification of Edges

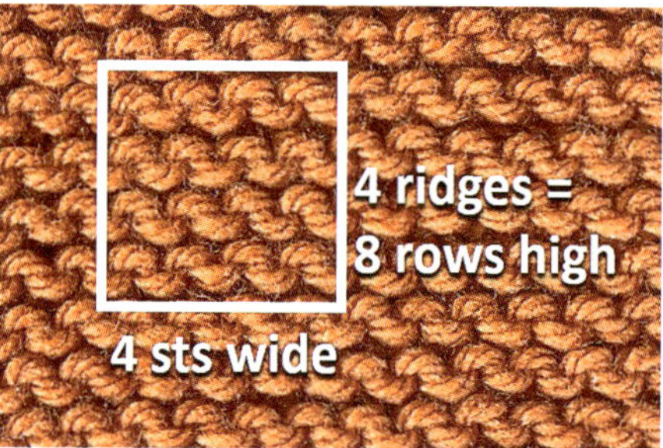

Figure 9: 4 Ridges High by 4 Stitches Wide

When picking up on a 45 degree diagonal edge, as shown in Figure 10, *pu&k in two consecutive ridges, then in the valley bef the next ridge; rep from * cont this cadence. When close to the ending point, count the sts generated and plan out the remaining pu&k locations. If the stitch count is incorrect by a few sts, make increases (bli) or decreases (k2tog) on the next WS row. Place markers as a reminder, where a marker through 2 sts indicates a planned decrease (k2tog) and a marker through 1 st indicates a planned increase (bli).

A crochet hook may be used instead of a knitting needle. If using a crochet hook, use the same size (in mm) as the working knitting needle or up to 0.5 mm smaller than needle size. If working with a crochet hook, sts may be accumulated on the crochet hook's shaft and then transferred off the non-hook end to needle. The crochet hook must have a thin shank.

ridge
valley
45 degrees w.r.t. CO/BO
valley
ridge
ridge
valley
ridge
ridge
valley
ridge
ridge

Figure 10: Pu&k on Diagonal Edge

SLIP STITCH TRAVELING

Slip stitch traveling is used to move the working yarn to a new location along an edge that will later be sewn to another piece. The purpose is to avoid cutting yarn, which generates more ends to weave in, and to produce a neat and regular edge to which other pieces may be sewn. The pattern's instructions will state how many stitches to work along an edge.

How to

1) In this example we want to move the working yarn from point A to B.

2) Using a crochet hook or knitting needle (latter shown here) and working on the RS, insert R needle front to back through the outer leg of the edge stitch of the first valley, yarn around counterclockwise, and pull a loop through. There are now 2 stitches on the needle.

3) Insert L needle, left to right, through the front leg of the rightmost stitch on the R needle and slip stitch over the leftmost stitch. 1 stitch remains on the R needle. Adjust tension so that edge does not pull in.

4) Repeat Steps 2 and 3 along the edge to B, inserting R needle into the next valley.

Note: If ridges are perpendicular to edge, insert in every valley. If ridges are diagonal to edge, insert needle in every valley and in every other ridge in order to generate enough stitches. Stop occasionally to count stitches and plan out the remainder of the locations for inserting needle.

The slipped stitches should look like chaining.

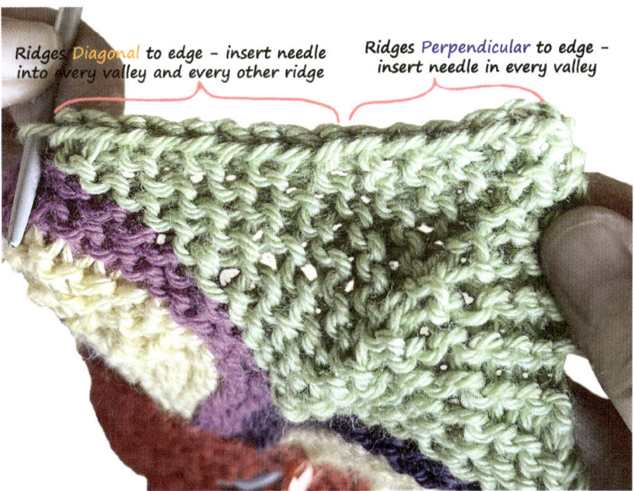

TACKING DRAPED YARN

When an edge of knitting will later have stitches picked up and knitted (pu&k) along it, pattern instructions may say to drape yarn between uses instead of cutting and reattaching. Later, during a pu&k on the same edge, the draped yarn will be tacked to the edge. This reduces the number of yarn ends to weave in during finishing and saves yarn.

How to

1) When draping, leave about ½"/1.25 cm extra for every 1"/2.5 cm that yarn must be carried. Another way to get the right amount of drape is to stretch the edge of the garter stitch, and leave enough draped yarn to span the stretched edge.

2) Later, when performing pu&k along an edge with a draped yarn, alternate inserting the R needle over and under the draped yarn. In the photo below, the needle is being inserted UNDER the draped yarn.

3) And on the next stitch, shown here, the needle is inserted OVER the draped yarn.

4) The WS of the completed pu&k shows that the mint green draped yarn is now neatly tacked to the edge of the orange stripe.

WRAP & TURN (W&T)

Wrap & turn, aka short rows, is used to work only some of the stitches in a row. In apparel knitting, it is used for shoulder shaping, sock heels, and bust darts. In geometric knitting, it is used to create curved shapes.

How to

When instructed to wrap & turn, you will be wrapping the next stitch on the L needle and turning the work, leaving the remaining stitches unworked.

Whether working a RS or WS row, to wrap the next stitch, do as follows:

1. Work to the indicated turning point, slip the next stitch purlwise to the R needle.
2. Bring yarn forward.
3. Turn work (the slipped stitch is now on the L needle, and the yarn is now at the back of the work), leaving rem sts of row unworked.
4. Insert R needle purlwise into the *slipped stitch* and slip it (again) back to the R needle.
5. Begin working the following row as instructed by the pattern.

Tensioning the Wrap

When wrapping the stitch, do not leave a lot of loose yarn. Wrap it snugly.

What's Different about Garter Stitch?

In w&t for stockinette stitch, the wrap and the wrapped stitch are knitted together on the following row to avoid the little hole that normally forms.

But in garter stitch, we don't do this. On the following row, the wrapped stitch is just knitted. Nothing special needs to be done with the wrap. And there will not be a noticeable hole in the fabric because garter stitch is denser and the surface ridges hide the wraps that are in the *valleys* between ridges.

How to Determine Which Side Is the RS

All the turning of the work can cause you to lose track of which side is the RS. In garter stitch knitting, the front and back of the work look the same until color changes begin. Therefore, mark the RS of your work with a locking stitch marker. To determine which is the RS, note the position of the CO tail, which is on the bottom right corner of the RS. If it is on the bottom left corner, you are looking at the WS. Recall that for the patterns in this book, you are always using a knitted CO, and the cast-on counts as Row 1 (see General Notes on page v).

Perfect Opportunity to Purl Backward

Also, so that you don't have to turn your work at all, you can purl backward on WS rows. In this case, you work Steps 1 and 2 of the w&t; with the current side still facing you, slip the slipped stitch back to the L needle, and then begin purling backward the stitches on the R needle. *Note:* By purling backward, you are working a WS row with the RS facing you, so if there is a wrap & turn instruction on the RS row, you will do this:

1. Slip the stitch to be wrapped from R to L needle.
2. Move yarn from front to back of work.
3. Slip *slipped stitch* from L to R needle.
4. Begin knitting RS stitches.

Note: A final piece of advice is that the German short rows technique should not be combined with garter stitch.

Figure 11: In the Pirouette blanket, short rows are used in black wedges of the Arc to create the rounded shape.

WEAVING IN ENDS

When the wrong, or "private," side of the work will be seen, the best but not the fastest way to weave in ends is to work duplicate stitch on the WS of the work. The advantages are: 1) it is less visible on the WS, 2) it is more secure because the yarn ends are buried and won't poke out later, 3) there is no need to fasten off because the friction of the yarn will keep it securely in place, 4) it saves yarn because only 6"/15 cm of yarn is needed *if* you use a Susan Bates Finishing needle (recommended).

How To

If using a tapestry needle, leave a yarn end of 8"/20 cm, and if using a Susan Bates Finishing Needle, leave 6"/15 cm. Don't fasten off unless the yarn is very slippery, like silk. Thread the yarn end onto the needle.

On the WS, near the place where the yarn emerges from the work, select a ridge of the same color yarn as the end to be woven in. Observe the smiley and frowny faces of the ridge. Now follow Steps 1–7.

1) Insert needle upward through nearest smiley face, and pull yarn through.

2) Following the yarn strand around the frowny face, insert needle downward through next smiley face and pull yarn through.

3) Follow the yarn strand down and insert needle right to left underneath the stitch below the current smiley face and pull yarn through.

4) Repeat Steps 1-3, following the strand until about 1"/2.5 cm of yarn remains (3"/7.5 cm if using tapestry needle).

5) Working from left to right, insert needle between the stitches being duplicated (orange) and the duplicate stitches (blue) and pull yarn through.

6) Stretch knitting along ridges to see if end will nest. If necessary, trim yarn end flush with edge.

Final Tip: Tension of the duplicate stitches should match the tension of the stitches being duplicated.

7) Turn work over and observe the slight shadow stitches on the RS. When worked in matching yarn color, these will not show.

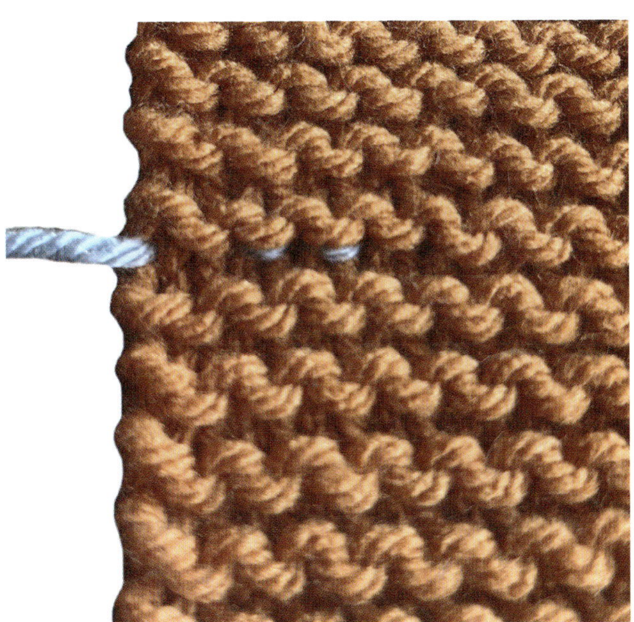

This is the WS of the Felicity blanket. This blanket has many yarn ends, which have been woven in using the technique I've just described. The duplicate stitches cannot be found even on close inspection, which brings me to my final point: Don't weave in using this method if there is any possibility that you will need to unravel your knitting!

SUPPLEMENTAL MATERIAL

Technique Videos, coloring pages for planning your own color schemes, and more can be found at:

http://www.theknitwit.org/dm3ffvpn8ovtnu49

Or point your smartphone's camera at the QR code for access.

YARN SUPPLIERS

The following yarn companies have generously provided yarn for the sample blankets in this book. Unless otherwise noted, each company provided yarn for one blanket. Thank you for supporting my design work.

Berroco (3 blankets)
Berroco.com
1 Tupperware Dr., Suite 4
N. Smithfield, RI 02896

Cascade Yarns (6 blankets)
Cascadeyarns.com

Jagger Spun Yarn
(Sadly, this company has gone out of business.)
Springvale, ME 04083

Knitpicks
Knitpicks.com

Lion Brand (2 blankets)
Lionbrand.com
135 Kero Rd
Carlstadt, NJ 07072

Noro
Knittingfever.com/brand/noro/yarns
Knitting Fever Inc.
315 Bayview Ave.
Amityville, NY 11701

Paintbox Yarns provided by Lovecrafts
Lovecrafts.com

Plymouth Yarn
Plymouthyarn.com
500 Lafayette St.
Bristol, PA 19007

Red Heart (2 blankets)
Yarnspirations.com

Rowan (5 blankets)
Knitrowan.com

Tahki Yarns (2 blankets)
Yarn.com
Webs
75 Service Center Rd.
Northhampton, MA 01060

Valley Yarns
Yarn.com
Webs
75 Service Center Rd.
Northhampton, MA 01060

PHOTOGRAPHY

The photos for this book were taken by my husband, Gerard Holzmann, aka: edsger-studio.com, at his studio in Monrovia, California.

TECHNICAL EDITING

Natalie Delbusso, Mary Rose, and Susan Hislop are gratefully acknowledged for their work to correct and improve these patterns.

SAMPLE KNITTING

Sample blankets were made by:

Julie Anderson (Magical, Pirouette)

Alan Berry (Regatta)

Jill Fauble (Plaza)

Marie Franzosa (Interlock, Modulate)

Linette Grayum (Coronado, Twist)

Rachel Herald (Chromatic, Ouray)

Margaret Holzmann (Ancestry, Carousel, Felicity, Heartstrings, High Rise, Portals, Wonky Walking)

Erika Loftin (Sheaves)

Sonia Savoulian (Currents, Pinwheels, Reel Deal, Refraction, Sanguine, Stitches in Time)

Amy Tat (Pisces)

Lori Veteto (Intwined)

Thank you to each sample knitter for sharing their talents and time. They tested and helped me improve the clarity of the patterns.

ADDITIONAL PATTERNS

Get Margaret's other books:

Geometric Knit Blankets – 30 Innovative and Fun-to-Knit Blankets

theknitwit.org/geometric-knit-blankets-book

At Home with Margaret Holzmann – 10 Beautiful Blanket Patterns to Knit for Every Season

theknitwit.org/at-home-with-margaret-holzmann-book

Margaret Holzmann's Iconic Knit Blankets and More – 30+ Graphic Patterns for Blankets, Pillows, Tops, and Table Runners

https://www.theknitwit.org/iconic-book

Buy individual digital/pdf patterns by Margaret:

ravelry.com/designers/margaret-holzmann

Or

theknitwit.org/store

YOUTUBE

Get all the help you need on Margaret's YouTube channel. Subscribe to be notified when she posts something new: **youtube.com/@knitwitme**

GROUP

Join Margaret's Facebook group. Post about your project and see what's been made from Margaret's patterns: **facebook.com/groups/geometricknitblankets**

CLASSES

Take a class with Margaret: **theknitwit.org/classes**

NEWSLETTER

Be the first to learn about Margaret's new knitting patterns, contests and give-aways, pattern discounts, and the latest news. Sign up for Margaret's newsletter at **theknitwit.org/contact**

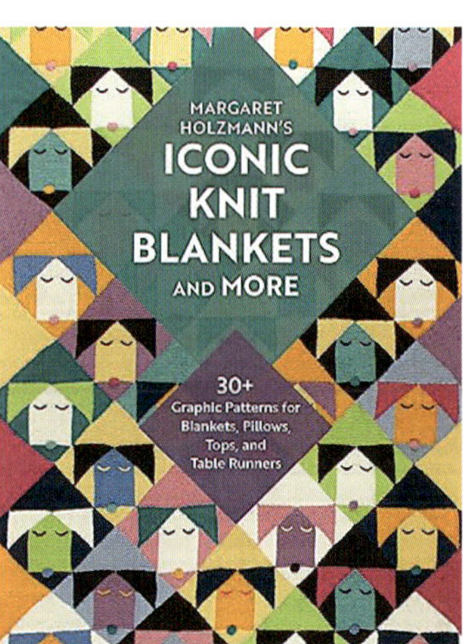